TABLE OF CONTENTS

W9-BNU-963

CONTENTS

NEWCOMER'S HANDBOOK®

FOR MOVING TO AND LIVING IN

Washington D.C.

Including Northern Virginia
and Suburban Maryland

4th Edition

6750 SW Franklin
Portland, OR 97223
503-968-6777
www.firstbooks.com

FIRST BOOKS®

4th Edition

Newcomer's Handbook® is a registered trademark of Firstbooks.com, Inc.

Firstbooks.com, Inc. is not legally responsible for any change in the value of any enterprises by reason of their inclusion in or exclusion from this work. Contents are based on information believed to be accurate at the time of publication.

Firstbooks.com, Inc. has not accepted payment from any firms or organizations for inclusion in this book.

Author: Mike Livingston
Series Editor: Linda Weinerman
Publisher: Jeremy Solomon
Cover and Interior Design: Erin Johnson Design
Maps: DesignMaps.com, Jim Miller/fennana design
Transit map courtesy of the Washington Metropolitan Area Transit Authority

ISBN-13: 978-0-912301-66-2
ISBN-10: 0-912301-66-X
ISSN: 1557-9913

Printed in the USA on recycled paper.

Published by Firstbooks.com, Inc., 6750 SW Franklin Street, Suite A, Portland, OR 97223-2542, 503-968-6777.

What readers are saying about Newcomer's Handbooks:

I recently got a copy of your Newcomer's Handbook for Chicago, and wanted to let you know how invaluable it was for my move. I must have consulted it a dozen times a day preparing for my move. It helped me find my way around town, find a place to live, and so many other things. Thanks.

—Mike L.
Chicago, Illinois

Excellent reading (Newcomer's Handbook for San Francisco and the Bay Area) ... balanced and trustworthy. One of the very best guides if you are considering moving/relocation. Way above the usual tourist crap.

—Gunnar E.
Stockholm, Sweden

I was very impressed with the latest edition of the Newcomer's Handbook for Los Angeles. It is well organized, concise and up-to-date. I would recommend this book to anyone considering a move to Los Angeles.

—Jannette L.
Attorney Recruiting Administrator for a large Los Angeles law firm

I recently moved to Atlanta from San Francisco, and LOVE the Newcomer's Handbook for Atlanta. It has been an invaluable resource — it's helped me find everything from a neighborhood in which to live to the local hardware store. I look something up in it everyday, and know I will continue to use it to find things long after I'm no longer a newcomer. And if I ever decide to move again, your book will be the first thing I buy for my next destination.

—Courtney R.
Atlanta, Georgia

In looking to move to the Boston area, a potential employer in that area gave me a copy of the Newcomer's Handbook for Boston. It's a great book that's very comprehensive, outlining good and bad points about each neighborhood in the Boston area. Very helpful in helping me decide where to move.
—no name given (online submit form)

CONTENTS

INTRODUCTION

WELCOME TO WASHINGTON! "AMERICA'S HOMETOWN" IS NOW your hometown. Perhaps you've moved "inside the Beltway" where, according to legend, everyone is a policy analyst or a bureaucrat. Not true. Yes, although many people come here to work on "The Hill" or in the real-life West Wing, Washington isn't just a government town. You'll find America's best and brightest coming here to work in academia, the information technology or biotech industries, national and international nonprofits, corporate law, and in the services and trades it takes to feed, shelter, transport, and entertain a city of three million people.

So, what's it like here? Northerners consider Washington a southern city and Southerners consider it northeastern. Both have a point. Hot and steamy summer days, tree-lined avenues, and 19th-century mansions converted into offices give Washington the physical feel of a southern city, but the frenetic "type A" culture makes it seem more northern. Newcomers from Maine or Georgia are equally likely to find people here to be self-absorbed, hurried, and seemingly rude. It is President Kennedy who is credited with the observation, now a cliché, that Washington combines northern charm with southern efficiency.

Washington isn't just one city. In addition to the District of Columbia, the Washington metropolitan area includes parts of two states, Virginia and Maryland. (In this book, "Washington" refers to the metropolitan area and "D.C." refers to the city itself.) Northern Virginia, suburban Maryland, and "the District" have some things in common—most notably, high levels of income and education, congested roads and long commutes, and a high cost of living.

Virginia is generally more conservative and southern than Maryland and the District. Suburban subdivisions with names like Fox Mill Estates and Hunter's Valley reflect Northern Virginia's not-too-distant past as horse country. The Potomac River is a striking cultural boundary—many Virginians seldom venture into Maryland, and many Marylanders only go to Virginia to work in Tysons Corner or to scour antique stores in the countryside. Suburban Maryland is more liberal and more closely tied to the city. In fact, many Marylanders are former city dwellers who have moved out of D.C. to get their kids into some of the best public schools in the country. These are "soccer mom" suburbs where many parents are active in the PTA and quite a few residents actually show up for zoning hearings about new roads or strip malls. The District generally attracts a younger crowd than the suburbs—many new residents are singles or young couples, some fresh out of college and eager to change the world. Many choose to put up with the city's high taxes and slow services in exchange for the ability to walk home from a neighborhood nightclub or a late night at the office.

In terms of local government, the District of Columbia, a federal colony governed by Congress, was granted limited "home rule" in 1973, allowing residents to choose their city council and school board. More than 90% of the District's registered voters are either Democrats or independents. In 1980, District residents voted to become the 51st state, a move blocked by Congress. Today, the words "Taxation Without Representation" emblazon D.C. license plates, to remind out-of-towners that they're visiting the only place in America without the right to self-government.

Most people arrive here with a lot of preconceptions. Let's try to sort out the myths from the reality:

- **Washington is not a revolving door.** Since administrations come and go every four to eight years, there's a tendency to assume that Washington's population is transient. Actually, more than half of the area's adult residents have been here for 20 years or more, and there are proud lifelong residents here as well. So yes, new people are always arriving, but many ultimately decide to stick around. This is not a government camp—it's a living city where people raise families, walk the dog, go to the movies, and get picked for jury duty.

- **Washington is not just government.** Tourism and hospitality are big business here, of course, but the late 1990s also saw a boom in startup high-tech and biotech businesses. Northern Virginia rivals Silicon Valley as the capital of cyberspace, and Montgomery County in Maryland is a hotbed of genetics research. In 2000, Black Entertainment Television and XM Satellite Radio opened their new headquarters in a once desolate industrial area just off Capitol Hill, near the offices of CNN and Amtrak. These industries provide a growing share of the region's jobs and a growing market for support services.

- **Washington is diverse.** People settle here from all over the world; roughly 800,000 area residents were born in other countries. There are some neighborhoods in D.C. with a large Latino population, such as

Mt. Pleasant and Columbia Heights, and there's an official Chinatown, but mostly Washington is a city where hyphenated Americans come to lose their hyphens. That's not to say Washington is a paradise of racial harmony, but social and political tension here has less to do with race than with economic class. It is often said that Washington is "a tale of two cities"—indeed, D.C. has a bigger income gap than any state, with the richest fifth of the population 27 times as wealthy as the poorest fifth. (Nationwide, the richest fifth is 10 times as wealthy as the poorest.) The District has some 20,000 residents earning more than $100,000 a year, and about twice as many residents living in homeless shelters or on the street. And the nation's capital leads the nation in rates of infant mortality, diabetes, and HIV/AIDS; one out of five D.C. residents lacks health insurance. On the other hand, the Washington area is also well above the national average in wages; according to figures reported by the *Washington Post* in 2005, average income in D.C. is more than $66,000, compared to about $40,000 nationally. Incomes and property values tend to be higher to the west of Rock Creek Park than to the east—the most affluent neighborhoods are concentrated in Northwest D.C. and the western suburbs, and almost all of the struggling neighborhoods are on the east side. There are plenty of exceptions, though—while some neighborhoods are exclusively rich and some poor, many are in fact economically diverse.

- **Washington is expensive.** And getting more expensive. From 2000 to 2005, average property tax assessments doubled in D.C. and rose even more in parts of the suburbs. Among the 20 largest metropolitan areas in the United States, your housing dollar will go further in any city except New York, San Francisco, Boston, or Chicago than in Washington. If you earned $50,000 a year in Seattle and you want to maintain the same standard of living in D.C., you'll need to earn $55,000 here; if you moved from Denver or Atlanta, the amount is roughly $65,000; from Pittsburgh or Houston, more than $75,000. (Commercial real estate is even more expensive—at an average of $356 per square foot, according to the *D.C. Examiner*, it's the most expensive in the country—and that naturally affects the price of consumer goods.)

- **Washington is indeed "inside the Beltway," but not completely.** The Capital Beltway is a highway that circles the District and the inner suburbs. The Beltway is also the symbol for a stereotype of Washingtonian thinking: politicians and pundits talk about the culture "inside the Beltway" as a delusional Never-Never Land where policy is made by people who are out of touch with the rest of us. There are certainly plenty of bureaucrats who could stand to "get a life," but their cubicles are not necessarily located inside the Beltway. With so many federal agencies located in the suburbs, including the Census Bureau, the National Institute of Standards & Technology (formerly the National Bureau of Standards), the National Institutes of Health, the CIA, and major facilities for NASA and the Department of Agriculture, thousands of federal employees live and work *outside* the Beltway, at least in the geographic sense. And not all policy wonks are sheltered in an ivory tower. According to studies by the market research firm Claritas, Washingtonians tend to read books, jog, play tennis, drink Scotch, travel, and take adult-education courses more than residents of other U.S. cities. This is also the place with the nation's highest percentage of women in the workforce and two-career couples.

- **Washington is brainy.** A majority of adults in the Washington area are college graduates and many have advanced degrees. Commuters on the Metro read thick books—biographies, essay collections, and political novels; in the evening or even at lunchtime, crowds jostle in bookstores for Q&A sessions with the latest hot author. Washingtonians raise brainy kids, too—according to a 2005 report in the *Washington Post*, 65% of local teens take at least one college-level Advanced Placement course in high school.

- **Washingtonians talk like lawyers and bureaucrats.** While not everyone in Washington is a "fed," practically everyone speaks the language. In a city where people actually watch "Meet the Press" and "Face the Nation," the latest policy jargon makes its way quickly into everyday conversation, as do acronyms and initials—GSA, GOA, EPA, NIH, SEC, OSHA, FOIA, and OMB, just for example. And everyone here knows that "GS-9" indicates a rank on the federal pay scale and "SES" indicates someone much more powerful than even a GS-15.

- **Washington is wired—and wireless.** By the end of the 20th century, the *Washington Business Journal* proclaimed Washington to be "the nation's most-wired metropolitan area"—that is, the area with the nation's highest percentage of households connected to the internet. More than 70% of the region's households have internet access; many Washingtonians have unplugged their phone lines and use a cell phone even at home, and wireless phones are quickly giving way to BlackBerry-type wireless handheld computers. In the summer of 2005, the suburban city of Alexandria became the first municipality in the country to provide outdoor wi-fi access to the internet from the downtown commons.

- **Washington is safer than you think.** While personal safety is not guaranteed anywhere, it seems Washington has a much worse reputation than it deserves. In any metropolitan area in the United States, there are some neighborhoods to avoid, and Washington is no exception. Most violent crime in D.C. is related to gang feuds, which are usually confined to a single block or intersection. While it makes for grisly stories on the evening news, most Washingtonians never encounter violent crime firsthand.

- **Washington is *nice*.** It's not just the monuments, museums, and halls of government, but a living city of green and charming neighborhoods. Many elegant homes and downtown buildings have stood for 150 years or more, and the city's historic preservation laws keep them close to their original appearance. Rock Creek Park is one of the largest urban parks in the world, and on its woodland trails you can easily forget you're in a city. Bald eagles live along the Anacostia River and white-tailed deer live all over the place. There are smaller parks and open spaces in every neighborhood. Even little wedges formed by traffic patterns are landscaped and tended by the National Park Service and the Casey Trees Endowment Fund. Many small parks feature statues of early American heroes—obscure as well as famous ones. And unique local building codes based on George Washington's own specifications limit the height of buildings in the capital city—so no matter where you are in Washington, you can always see the sky.

THE L'ENFANT PLAN FOR THE FEDERAL CITY

The District of Columbia is renowned as an eye-catching city with lots of trees and open space—and the lowest skyline of any East Coast city its size. None of that happened by accident. Long before any schools offered degrees in "urban planning," John Adams and Thomas Jefferson commissioned architects to design the capital city—at a site personally selected by former land surveyor George Washington—in unprecedented detail.

One of the nation's first government contractors was Pierre L'Enfant, hired to turn a 68-square-mile expanse of swamps and hills into a capital city of broad, tree-lined avenues and panoramic views. The principal government buildings would boast classical columns, domes, and friezes worthy of Greek and Roman temples, and nothing would block the view of the Capitol from anywhere in the city. To the west of the Capitol, there would be a "vast esplanade" lined with "the sort of places as may be attractive to the learned and afford diversion to the idle." And, in the spirit of federalism, the national capital would honor the states it served by naming an avenue after each one.

Track down a map drawn by L'Enfant—or his assistant, Benjamin Banneker, the son of two former slaves—and you would find it to be mostly applicable to D.C.'s current layout. Most of the principal streets would be recognizable, although the antique map would show a canal along the path of present-day Constitution Avenue; Tiber Creek had not yet been buried in a tunnel; and there was a J Street in those days. But the L'Enfant Plan is largely intact today—thanks to Banneker, who copied the maps

6

NEWCOMER'S HANDBOOK FOR MOVING TO AND LIVING IN WASHINGTON D.C.

from memory after President Jefferson fired L'Enfant and the hot-tempered architect took the originals with him.

In the planning stages the District of Columbia was divided into four jurisdictions: Washington City, the area south of Florida Avenue NW (which was then called Boundary Avenue); Washington County, the "uptown" part of the modern city, which was still mostly farmland; and the independent cities of Georgetown and Arlington, which had their own mayors. Georgetown remained independent until 1871, and Arlington was returned to Virginia in 1847 (a long story made short in the **Neighborhood Profile** for Arlington). L'Enfant was mainly concerned with Washington City, but the rules L'Enfant devised for the names of streets apply to the whole city, all the way to the four moss-covered stones marking the corners of the diamond-shaped District.

South of Florida Avenue, the land between the Potomac and Anacostia rivers was mostly swamp, now filled in and paved over. The Capitol and the White House are situated on dry ground, but the Washington Monument is slowly sinking at the rate of an inch per century.

THREE VISIONARIES: SHEPHERD, McMILLAN, AND OLMSTED

Despite the grand layout by L'Enfant, as the nation celebrated its centennial, the capital city was still lined with muddy dirt roads. Pigs and chickens ran around loose in the streets, and malaria-bearing mosquitoes bred in puddles in the carriage ruts. Ambassadors from northern Europe got high-risk pay for spending the summer in Washington. It remained in such a state until Alexander "Boss" Shepherd, the director of public works, decided to pave the city and get it ready for the 20th century—never mind the niceties of bookkeeping and bureaucracy. Skipping bureaucratic red tape, he gathered a bunch of laborers and had them lay sewers and asphalt faster than anyone could ask how the city was going to pay for it. For his efforts he was appointed governor of the District (a position that no longer exists); he then drained the city treasury to flatten hilly streets, bury obsolete canals, install streetlights, build parks, and plant some 60,000 trees. When the bills came due, he fled to Mexico and lived out his days making questionable investments in silver mines.

Sure, the Boss was corrupt and a bit of a maverick, but none deny that he made Washington a nicer and safer place to live. Today, in fitting tribute both to his important work and his unsavory methods, his statue stands at the entrance to the city's sewage treatment plant.

In 1901, Congress created the Park Improvement Commission of the District of Columbia, chaired by Sen. James McMillan. The McMillan Commission, as it came to be called, picked up where L'Enfant left off, outlining the growth of parks and greenspace in the expanding city. The commission created the Mall, fulfilling L'Enfant's vision of the nation's front lawn, and called on Congress to establish Rock Creek Park and to preserve the "Fort Circle"—the ring of forts that defended the city during the Civil War. Many of the small parks throughout the uptown residential neighborhoods are Civil War sites preserved at the initiative of the McMillan Commission.

One of the commissioners was Frederick Law Olmsted, the renowned landscape architect who designed New York's Central Park as well as the Capitol grounds and the National Zoo. Olmsted shares with L'Enfant much of the credit for the prominence of greenspace in the nation's capital.

THE 21ST CENTURY

The National Capital Planning Commission, the successor to the McMillan Commission, is a federal agency with three commissioners appointed by the President of the United States and two appointed by the Mayor of the District of Columbia. Certain public officials are also commissioners ex officio: the Interior and Defense secretaries, the head of the General Services Administration, the chairs of the House and Senate committees on government affairs, and the mayor and council chair. Their job is to provide the District and surrounding jurisdictions with a general framework for development decisions affecting federal land and buildings.

In 1996, the commission unveiled the third master plan for the District—the "Legacy Plan," short for Extending the Legacy: Planning America's Capital for the 21st Century. The Legacy Plan seeks to preserve the spirit and effect of the L'Enfant Plan while responding to the needs of a growing and changing city. In the commission's words, "The Legacy Plan preserves the historic character and open space of the Mall and its adjacent ceremonial corridors while accommodating growth and new development. The plan expands the reach of public transit and eliminates obsolete freeways, bridges, and railroad tracks that fragment the city. It reclaims Washington's historic waterfront for public enjoyment, and adds parks, plazas, and other amenities to the urban fabric. Using federal resources to generate local investment, the Legacy Plan will spur community renewal well into the twenty-first century." (For more information, visit www.ncpc.gov.) It is important to understand that the details of the Legacy Plan are offered as possibilities or guidelines illustrating the sort of development that may be considered in the new century; these are not actual projects that have been authorized or funded. That said, the Legacy Plan envisions these changes within the 21st century:

- Since the Mall is "full," with no room for new museums, a second Mall will be built along South Capitol Street from the Capitol to the Anacostia River. An important civic building will "anchor" the south

NEWCOMER'S HANDBOOK FOR MOVING TO AND LIVING IN WASHINGTON D.C.

8

end of the new Mall; as this book goes to press, the new stadium of the Washington Nationals is planned for this prestigious site.

- The Southeast-Southwest Freeway will be removed, since the Beltway will be able to carry more traffic between Prince George's County and Alexandria when the new, improved Woodrow Wilson Bridge is finished. The waterfront along the Anacostia and Potomac will be lined with parks and promenades, and a network of "water taxis" will provide public transportation to riverside offices and attractions.
- An entertainment complex at the site of aging RFK Stadium will serve as an eastern gateway to the heart of the city.
- Downtown D.C. will be served by a paratransit network or "circulator" providing cheap, frequent trips for people traveling a short distance within the city. The first circulator buses hit the streets in the summer of 2005, with more routes coming soon.
- As needed, new federal buildings will be built along 16th Street NW or North Capitol Street, and more museums and monuments will be located outside the Monumental Core, especially along the improved waterfront.

Whether or not these particular visions come to pass, it's a good bet that the District in 2100 will still fit the description set forth in the L'Enfant Plan of 1790.

FINDING YOUR WAY AROUND

Today the city is divided into four quadrants whose center is the Capitol and whose boundaries are North Capitol Street, East Capitol Street, South Capitol Street, and the Mall. In relation to the Capitol, the quadrants are known as Northwest, Northeast, Southeast, and Southwest, and every street name in the District includes a two-letter abbreviation indicating the quadrant. Downtown, east-west streets are named with letters of the alphabet, proceeding away from the Capitol; numbered streets run north-south and count away from the Capitol. So the corner of 7th & D streets NW is seven blocks west of North Capitol Street and four blocks north of the Mall; 7th Street NE is 14 blocks away, parallel to 7th Street NW.

After the alphabet streets (and actually there's no X, Y, or Z Street, and no J Street either), crosstown streets bear two-syllable names in alphabetical order: Adams, Belmont, Clifton, and so on; this is the "second alphabet." Beyond Webster, the "third alphabet" bears three-syllable names—Allison, Buchanan, Crittenden. Finally, near the northern tip of the District, there's a "fourth alphabet" named after plants and flowers—Aspen, Butternut, Cedar. Avenues run diagonally, and most are named after states—and yes, there is an avenue for every state. (Okay, California is represented by California Street NW and Ohio by Ohio Drive SW, but every other state has an avenue.)

Simple, right? Usually, but there are exceptions: Constitution and Independence avenues run east-west along the Mall, and East Executive Avenue and West Executive Avenue run north-south along the White House grounds. There's no J Street. And there are the notorious traffic circles ("rotaries" if you're from New England, "roundabouts" if you're from Old England, intimidating messes if you're from anywhere else), and square parks seemingly plunked in the middle of many major through streets. Some streets, such as Park Road NW and Military Road NW, simply violate the naming convention.

Perhaps the most confusing twist is that while many of the inner suburbs follow the same nomenclature as the District; streets with the same name may be separate short neighborhood streets, not continuous thoroughfares. For example, the Rittenhouse Street crossing 16th Street NW doesn't connect to the Rittenhouse Street crossing Wisconsin Avenue NW; likewise, the Hamilton Street you encounter on Georgia Avenue NW doesn't connect to the Hamilton Street in Hyattsville, Md. (But cross-streets of the same name are the same distance north of the Capitol.)

If you know the general rules and the major exceptions, you'll do fine, but if you invest in a good street atlas and study it, you will quickly find it time and money well spent. (See the section on **Maps** below.)

Cyclists and pedestrians should bear in mind that the city is hilly. Just north of Florida Avenue NW, lofty Meridian Hill stretches from Rock Creek east to Howard University, and it's a steep climb of three or four blocks. Neighborhoods that border Rock Creek Park can also exercise your leg muscles or your parking brakes. The city's most famous physical feature, Capitol Hill, isn't much of a hill, but it offers great views because L'Enfant wanted to provide great views from the Capitol.

TRAFFIC CIRCLES

The District has 18 traffic circles, most dating from the L'Enfant Plan or the Civil War. Some are attractive parks; others are little more than a bend in the road. A few are just D-shaped remnants of old circles. The five downtown circles—Dupont, Logan, Scott, Thomas, and Washington—are major landmarks and chronic traffic jams; others, such as Sherman and Pinehurst, are little known and seldom visited except by those who live nearby. Here are the principal streets intersecting at each circle:

- **Barney**: K Street SE, Kentucky Avenue, Pennsylvania Avenue
- **Chevy Chase**: Connecticut Avenue NW, Western Avenue
- **Columbus**: Massachusetts Avenue NE between 1st and 2nd streets

NEWCOMER'S HANDBOOK FOR MOVING TO AND LIVING IN WASHINGTON D.C.

10

- **Dupont**: 19th Street NW, P Street, Connecticut Avenue, Massachusetts Avenue, New Hampshire Avenue
- **Grant**: 5th Street NW, Illinois Avenue, New Hampshire Avenue
- **Kalorama**: Belmont Road NW, Kalorama Road
- **Logan**: 13th Street NW, P Street, Rhode Island Avenue, Vermont Avenue
- **Memorial**: encircles the Lincoln Memorial at the western end of the Mall—23rd Street NW, Henry Bacon Drive NW, Ohio Drive SW, Daniel French Drive SW
- **Observatory**: 34th Street NW, Massachusetts Avenue
- **Pinehurst**: 33rd Street NW, Western Avenue, Utah Avenue
- **Scott**: 16th Street NW, N Street, Massachusetts Avenue, Rhode Island Avenue
- **Sheridan**: Massachusetts Avenue NW between 22nd and R streets
- **Sherman**: 7th Street NW, Crittenden Street, Illinois Avenue, Kansas Avenue
- **Tenley**: Nebraska Avenue NW, Wisconsin Avenue
- **Thomas**: 14th Street NW, M Street, Massachusetts Avenue, Vermont Avenue
- **Ward**: Massachusetts Avenue NW, Nebraska Avenue, Loughboro Road
- **Washington**: 23rd Street NW, K Street, New Hampshire Avenue, Pennsylvania Avenue
- **Westmoreland**: Massachusetts Avenue NW, Western Avenue, Dalecarlia Parkway

Note that all traffic goes counterclockwise in traffic circles; in other words, you turn right to enter the circle and turn right again to leave it.

BRIDGES

Traffic reports on the radio assume the listener knows where these named bridges are. The towns and neighborhoods are identified in the **Neighborhood Profiles**.

POTOMAC RIVER
- **American Legion Bridge**: Capital Beltway between Bethesda and McLean, also known as Cabin John Bridge (it's near Cabin John Creek on the Maryland side). This is the northernmost Potomac River crossing in the metropolitan area except for White's Ferry, a small cable-guided auto ferry between Poolesville, Md., and Purcellville, Va.
- **Chain Bridge**: Connects Canal Road NW in Palisades to Chain Bridge Road (Route 123) in McLean.
- **Key Bridge**: Connects the Whitehurst Freeway in Georgetown to N. Lynn Street and Ft. Myer Drive in Rosslyn. Named after Francis Scott Key.

- **Arlington Memorial Bridge**: Connects Independence Avenue NW at the Lincoln Memorial to the George Washington Memorial Parkway at Arlington National Cemetery.
- **14th Street Bridge**: Actually three spans carrying I-395 between the Jefferson Memorial and the Pentagon. The George Mason Bridge westbound and the Rochambeau Bridge eastbound connect Shirley Highway in Virginia to the Southwest Freeway in D.C.; the Arland D. Williams Memorial Bridge connects Shirley Highway to 14th Street SW (U.S. Route 1).
- **Woodrow Wilson Bridge**: Capital Beltway between Alexandria and Oxon Hill. This is the southernmost Potomac River crossing in the metropolitan area.

ANACOSTIA RIVER

- **Benning Bridge**: Benning Road NE.
- **Whitney Young Bridge**: East Capitol Street near RFK Stadium.
- **John Philip Sousa Bridge**: Pennsylvania Avenue SE near Barney Circle. The composer lived in D.C.
- **11th Street Bridge**: Northbound, connects the Anacostia Freeway (I-295) to the Southeast Freeway (I-395).
- **Officer Kevin J. Welsh Memorial Bridge**: Southbound, connects the Southeast Freeway to the Anacostia Freeway.
- **Frederick Douglass Memorial Bridge**: South Capitol Street. The abolitionist leader lived nearby in Anacostia.

MAPS

- ***ADC Street Atlases***, available at most bookstores and large drugstores, are detailed, reliable, and indexed to show post offices, libraries, police stations, recreation centers, and other useful facilities. Atlases of the District and of each neighboring county are available for $13 each; the regional atlas, which covers the entire area profiled in this book, is a bargain at $40. ADC also publishes an excellent bicycle map of the District. For a complete catalog, visit www.adcmap.com.
- **Flashmaps**, a series of laminated city maps published by Fodor's, has a Washington edition that is easy to read and well indexed. Available from First Books, www.firstbooks.com, 503-968-6777 (no sales tax).
- See the **Washington Reading List** for special topical maps and walking tours. And if you're buying real estate and you need to look at a precise surveyor's map, visit the Washingtoniana Division at Martin Luther King Jr. Library, 901 G St. NW, 202-727-1213.
- On the web, **Google Maps**, http//maps.google.com, lets you superimpose a labeled street map over a satellite photo of the ground (not

necessarily an up-to-date photo), and **Mapquest.com** generates detailed, easy-to-read street maps.

LOCAL LINGO

ANC: Advisory Neighborhood Commission, an elected panel in D.C. that has a formal but nonbinding role in decisions about building permits, liquor licenses, and other neighborhood concerns

Beltway bandits: defense contractors with corporate headquarters in the suburbs (not as common a term as it was in the 1980s)

BID: Business Improvement District, a commercial zone in which businesses agree to pay higher taxes in exchange for extra street cleaning, security patrols, and other services

Black Broadway: nickname for the U Street NW theater scene during the 1940s and '50s

Blue Plains: the D.C. sewage treatment plant near the southern tip of the District

Boot: a device used by parking enforcement agents to immobilize cars with unpaid fines; also known as a wheel clamp

BWI: Thurgood Marshall Airport, formerly Baltimore-Washington International Airport

B-W Parkway: Baltimore-Washington Parkway

CFC: Combined Federal Campaign, charitable payroll deduction program for federal employees

D.C. Delegate: nonvoting elected observer in the House of Representatives

Diplomatic immunity: the doctrine of international law and protocol under which embassy officials and their families are generally not prosecuted for crimes they commit on U.S. soil; as a practical matter, in D.C., this means cars with diplomatic tags can park anywhere

District Building: name of the John A. Wilson Building (city hall) prior to 2001, still heard occasionally

Downtown: to suburbanites, the District; to District residents, the area between Florida Avenue NW and Constitution Avenue NW

East Front: side of the Capitol facing the Supreme Court; by tradition, the Capitol is not considered to have a "front" and "rear" entrance, but an East Front and West Front

East of the river: the section of D.C. between the Anacostia River and Maryland

The Ellipse: oval-shaped lawn between the White House and the Washington Monument grounds

Embassy Row: neighborhood where dozens of major embassies are concentrated along Massachusetts Avenue NW

Facadectomy: a construction project that incorporates the empty shell of an older building at the same site (an attempt to please historic preservationists and developers at the same time, often pleasing neither)

Federal Triangle: government office complex bounded by Pennsylvania Avenue, Constitution Avenue, and 15th Street NW

Fort Circle: ring of defensive earthworks built to protect the capital during the Civil War; now a series of neighborhood-based National Park Service sites

FOSE: annual technology trade show for government agencies; rhymes with "bossy" and originally stood for "Federal Office Solutions Expo"

Foundry: a mixed-use complex on the Georgetown waterfront in a converted 19th-century iron foundry

Height limit: statute restricting the height of buildings in D.C., generally to 20 feet more than the width of the street in front

Homestead exemption (homestead deduction): a tax break for D.C. homeowners in residence (see **Finding a Place to Live**)

HOT lane: high-occupancy/toll lane (on a major highway) reserved for carpools and cars bearing prepaid decals or electronic tags

HOV lane: high-occupancy vehicle (carpool) lane on major commuter highways such as I-66 and I-270

HR-57: nonprofit jazz club and conservatory named after the congressional resolution declaring jazz a national treasure (see **Cultural Life**)

ICC: Intercounty Connector, a planned superhighway from Gaithersburg to Laurel in the Maryland suburbs

Inner Loop: the clockwise lanes of the Capital Beltway

Juneteenth: June 19 holiday commemorating the announcement of the Emancipation Proclamation

K Street: nickname for the lobbying industry, a reference to the high concentration of lobbying firms along K Street NW between Georgetown and Penn Quarter

L'Enfant Plan: the 18th-century design for the capital city, still governing street names and many aspects of urban design in the District

Liberal leave: a severe weather plan in which federal employees may elect to stay home, taking personal leave without prior approval

Malcolm X Park: local name of the walled gardens and fields officially known as Meridian Hill Park

The Mall: ceremonial plaza stretching from the Capitol to the Lincoln Memorial

Metro: short for Washington Metropolitan Area Transit Authority, the agency in charge of the Metrorail subway system, Metrobus local buses, and MetroAccess transportation services for persons with disabilities; "the Metro" refers to Metrorail, as in, "I'll take the Metro to work."

NEWCOMER'S HANDBOOK FOR MOVING TO AND LIVING IN WASHINGTON D.C.

14

Metropolitan: slang for Metropolitan Police Department, the regular D.C. police (as opposed to any of the other 30-plus uniformed law enforcement agencies that have some jurisdiction in D.C.)

Mixing Bowl: the complicated and congested junction of I-95, I-395, and the Capital Beltway in Springfield, Va.

National: Reagan National Airport, formerly Washington National Airport; "National" is the only name locals have ever called it

One Judiciary Square: District government office building at 4th and D streets NW

Outer Loop: the counterclockwise lanes of the Capital Beltway

Reeves Center: D.C. government office building (officially the Frank D. Reeves Center of Municipal Affairs) at 14th and U streets NW

Retrocession: the 1846 deal to return to Virginia the part of the original District of Columbia west of the Potomac River (land which had been donated by Virginia to the federal government)

Shadow Representative, Shadow Senators: elected members of Congress from the hypothetical state of New Columbia, established by a constitutional convention after D.C. voters chose in 1980 to become a state; not recognized by the federal government, the shadow delegation serves as the District government's official lobbyists for statehood

Slug line: an unofficial gathering place for commuters to organize impromptu carpools in order to qualify for HOV lanes (see **Transportation**)

270 Spur: a branch of Interstate 270 north of the Capital Beltway that provides a shortcut to and from Northern Virginia

John A. Wilson Building: city hall (1350 Pennsylvania Avenue NW)

Wintry mix: snow, sleet, and freezing rain falling simultaneously, a hallmark of Washington winters

N EIGHBORHOODS IN THE WASHINGTON AREA ARE KNOWN LESS for distinctive housing styles or geography and more for the profile of their residents. You'll have about 4 million new neighbors—554,000 of them in the District and more than three million around the Beltway—and they tend to settle in clusters based on culture and lifestyle.

In workaholic Washington, a lot of accurate guesses can be made about a neighborhood by looking at the major employers nearby. Active and retired military officers gravitate toward Northern Virginia neighborhoods, near the Pentagon; congressional aides and lobbyists tend to be in Capitol Hill; diplomats cluster in Embassy Row; and nonprofit staffers trying to change the world are usually within biking distance of Dupont Circle. The inner suburbs, especially to the north of D.C., attract civil service workers in search of affordable homes and good public schools. In the outer suburbs, it's more complicated—in the land of sprawling subdivisions and office parks, employees of America Online in Dulles or the USDA in Beltsville might not find housing close to the office and therefore may have a long commute.

If you move here with a job lined up, it's a good idea to find a home near your job. It will save you a lot of time and frustration, not to mention money, and it's easier on the environment. In this city where many work 50 or 60 hours a week, where the unwritten rule at some firms is "if you don't come in on Sunday, don't come in on Monday," the most common complaint about the quality of life in the Washington area has to do with traffic congestion and long commutes. Mass transit is such an attractive alternative to clogged commuter thoroughfares that many Washingtonians rate Metrorail access among their main considerations when looking for housing—and a house within a quarter-mile of a Metro station can cost 30% to 40% more than an identical house a mile away.

NEWCOMER'S HANDBOOK FOR MOVING TO AND LIVING IN WASHINGTON D.C.

16

These neighborhood profiles are intended to help you get a feel for the character of each neighborhood. There is no substitute for meeting face-to-face with a local real estate agent or scouting out a neighborhood where you've seen an attractive listing in the classified ads, but these introductions will let you know what to expect. The median home prices for each jurisdiction are rounded from figures in a 2004 year-end report in the *Washington Times*. And the cost-of-living estimates are the annual income required to meet basic needs for one adult with an infant and preschooler, as reported by the *Washington Post* in 2005.

THE DISTRICT OF COLUMBIA

D.C. is home to 554,000 people, 360,000 of whom are registered voters—the only voters in the United States who are not represented in Congress. District residents pay federal taxes—more, per capita, than residents of most states—but have no voting voice in the branch of government that collects and spends those taxes. And D.C. is the only city in the nation where every law passed by the city council and signed by the mayor must be approved by Congress before it goes into effect.

The home of Duke Ellington and Howard University, the District was once nicknamed "Chocolate City," and the majority of the population has always been so-called minorities. The District still has a strong African-American heritage, but the Latino and Asian communities are large and growing. There are plenty of international residents, too—including diplomats, journalists, students, translators, and their families—adding to the cultural diversity of many D.C. neighborhoods.

In 1980, District residents voted to join the Union as the 51st state—and Congress laughed the matter off the floor. Some citizens continue to push for statehood; others advocate "retrocession"—returning the District to Maryland, which donated the land to the federal government in 1790—and still others would settle for voting seats in Congress, though Congress would retain the power to overturn local laws and micromanage local affairs. D.C. voters elect the "shadow" congressional delegation of the proposed state of New Columbia—two shadow Senators and a shadow U.S. Representative, who serve as elected lobbyists for D.C. statehood. There is also a nonvoting D.C. "delegate" to the House of Representatives—a position with some influence, perhaps, but no real power.

Meanwhile, the District government features an innovative layer of local representation: 37 elected **Advisory Neighborhood Commissions** have the power to hold hearings on zoning decisions, liquor licenses, building permits, and other neighborhood quality-of-life issues. Each commissioner represents about 2,000 households. The city council and regulatory agencies are required by law to give "great weight" to recommendations made by ANCs. In some neighborhoods, the local ANC is an active group of dedicated civic leaders; in others, few residents can even name their commissioner and seats may go vacant for years. Some people attend ANC meetings, or run for a seat on the commission, out of genuine concern for quality of life in the neighborhood; others, it seems, get involved just to debate or to fatten a political résumé.

Almost every neighborhood also has a neighborhood association, a nonprofit corporation working to improve living conditions (and, in mixed residential and commercial neighborhoods, the business atmosphere). Call the Mayor's Office of Community Outreach, 202-442-8150, to find a civic association in your community.

Some civic-minded residents gather in cyberspace in a twice-weekly e-mail forum called "Themail," hosted by the editors of the online magazine www.dcwatch.com. It's the digital equivalent of the cracker barrel at the general store—a place to chat with neighbors, share reviews of neighborhood businesses, swap advice about dealing with city bureaucrats, and debate current events in the community. In addition, many neighborhoods have their own e-mail forums or group weblogs.

As in any big city, residents have plenty of things to complain about. In Washington, potholes, traffic, and the humidity are perennial favorites, along with a few serious and contentious concerns: management of the public schools, federal/District relations, and displacement of low-income residents by gentrification of long-neglected neighborhoods. The city's aging electrical infrastructure occasionally causes an explosion in an underground electrical conduit, sending manhole covers flying. Traffic and parking downtown are such that it is often faster to walk a mile than to drive one. Still, Washingtonians are proud of their city, and take particular joy in showing off the non-tourist sites—the dark staircase from the film The Exorcist, the panoramic view from 13th and Euclid, the Japanese springhouse on the Capitol grounds, and their second-favorite restaurant (first is Ben's Chili Bowl).

The myth of Washington as a "revolving door" city where nobody settles down is largely due to the pattern of people relocating within the Washington area. Ambitious young graduates flock to the nation's capital and live downtown where the action is. As they get older and start families, city living loses its appeal, partly because of chronically unimpressive city services. Mayors and city council members come and go, but the District government never manages to get most things right most of the time. Why not? Mainly because the city is ultimately governed not by local officials,

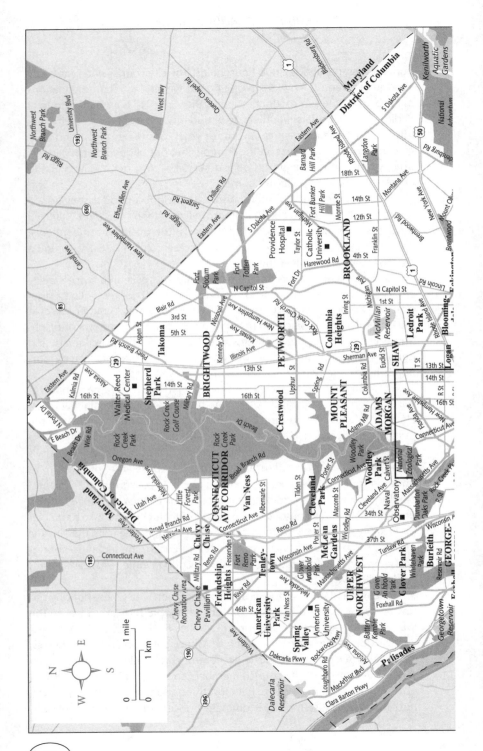

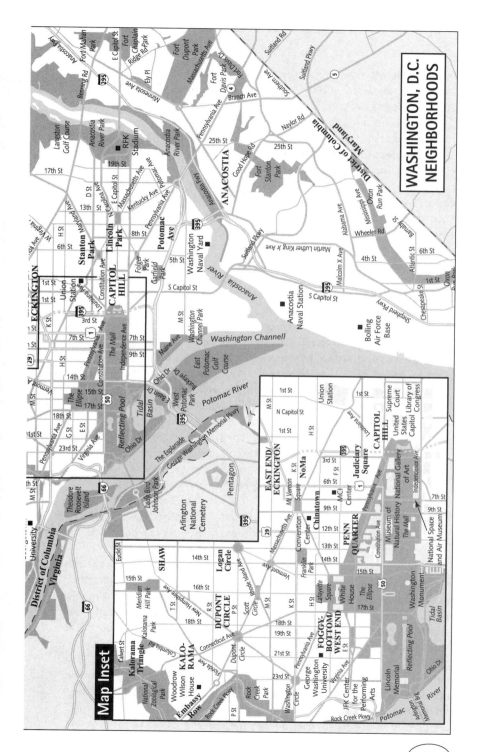

WASHINGTON, D.C. NEIGHBORHOODS

Map Inset

19

NEWCOMER'S HANDBOOK FOR MOVING TO AND LIVING IN WASHINGTON D.C.

20

but by Congress—whose members represent the interest of all Americans *except* D.C. residents, and therefore have no incentive to hold themselves accountable to District residents.

It's not just a matter of voting rights in Congress—even if D.C. were represented in the House and Senate, its local budget and local laws would still be subject to congressional approval; Congress would remain, in effect, the District's 535-member city council. Without the power to set its own budget priorities and tax codes—in particular, without the power to collect income tax from Maryland and Virginia residents who work in D.C.—the District government structurally has its hands tied. The 2004 annual report of the city's chief financial officer says it best, in an attempt to explain why taxes are so high here:

> *Unlike every state in the nation that has an income tax, Washington, D.C., does not have the authority to tax nonresident income earned within its borders. Nonresidents earn about 2/3 of all income in the District of Columbia.*
>
> *About 36 percent of all property value in the District is exempt from property taxation due to the federal and diplomatic presence (23 percent) as well as other tax-exempt properties (13 percent).*
>
> *An estimated 6 percent of sales are not subject to sales and use tax in the District due to military and diplomatic exemptions.*
>
> *The District has a relatively high percentage of low-income tax-payers, which further limits the District's revenue-raising capacity.*
>
> *Despite these limitations in the tax base, the District of Columbia funds most of the functions usually provided by state and local levels of government. The non-municipal functions include responsibility for welfare programs, physical and mental health care and maintenance of the public education system—including a "state" university. To provide an adequate level of funding for these state and local responsibilities given the limited tax base, the District's tax rates often are higher than those in the states.*

The economic burden of hosting the federal government—tax-exempt real estate, special police responsibilities, and homeland security infrastructure—is calculated by the office of the D.C. Delegate to be approximately $800 million per year. The federal government helps meet some of those expenses, but District taxpayers still pay millions of dollars to support the federal presence before they begin addressing their own urban needs.

Still, the city is trying, and by many accounts it is improving. The Office of Customer Service, a District agency created in 2001, employs undercover citizens to rate city agencies for prompt, courteous, and helpful responses to information requests. Agencies' ratings on a scale of 1 to 5 are posted quarterly on the mayor's page of the city's web site, www.washingtondc.gov.

If the District's lettered and numbered streets, grid quadrants, and traffic circles are making you dizzy, grab your trusty ADC Street Atlas and read the introductory section on the L'Enfant Plan to get your bearings. On the web, your first stop should be the District government's online Resident Resource Center, www.rrc.dc.gov, which includes a section on relocation.

Government: www.washingtondc.gov, 202-727-1000

Mayor: 202-727-2980, http://dc.gov/mayor

D.C. Council: 13-member legislature with eight members representing wards, four elected at large and one chairperson elected at large: 202-724-8000, www.dccouncil.washington.dc.us

Advisory Neighborhood Commissions: 202-727-2525, http://anc.washingtondc.gov

Public Schools: 202-724-4222, www.k12.dc.us; charter schools, 202-328-2660, www.dcpubliccharter.com

Libraries: 202-727-0321, http://dclibrary.org

Police: non-emergency 311, www.mpdc.org

Online Guides: www.rrc.dc.gov, www.washington.org, www.dclibrary.org/community, www.exploredc.org, www.dcpages.com, www.dcwatch.com, www.washdc.org

Area Code: 202

Median Home Price: $316,000

Cost of Living: $54,000

Sales Tax: 5.75%

CAPITOL HILL

STANTON PARK
LINCOLN PARK
POTOMAC AVENUE

Boundaries: **North**: H St. NE, H St. NW; **East**: 12th St. NE, 12th St. SE; **South**: South Carolina Ave. SE; **West**: 2nd St. NW, Washington Ave. SW

Location: North of the Washington Navy Yard; east of Judiciary Square and Penn Quarter; south of Union Station rail yards; west of the Southeast Waterfront; north of the Washington Navy Yard

Given the inherent prestige of **Capitol Hill**, many people claim to live there even though their addresses lie well to the south and east of the high ground. There really is a hill. Known as Jenkins Hill before the Capitol was built here, Capitol Hill also boasts the Supreme Court, the Library of Congress, and the offices of national newsmakers ranging from the

Heritage Foundation to the Sierra Club. Members of Congress and their staffers live on the Hill, of course, as do lobbyists and journalists—but plenty of people live here just because they love the well-maintained townhouses from the late 19th and early 20th centuries.

These vintage homes are delightful—many feature exposed brick, hardwood floors, molded plaster, and even some working gaslights. On practically every block, there are a few homes bearing nameplates identifying them as historic landmarks. Naturally, residents pay dearly to live so close to the Capitol—often close to a million dollars. Groups of recent graduates—or even freshman members of Congress—share houses in order to save on rent, and prices drop a bit on the north side of the neighborhood, around **Stanton Park** east of Union Station. Capitol Hill, like many D.C. neighborhoods, is an area where housing prices and quality of life can vary dramatically in the space of a few blocks. H Street NE, a few blocks north of Stanton Park, is just now beginning to recover from the race riots of 1967. Even street corners in the shadow of the Capitol are not immune to late-night drug deals and gang activity, and if you read the police reports in Thursday's *Washington Post,* you'll see more muggings around the Hill than in most comparably wealthy neighborhoods.

Almost every corner has a little market or convenience store, and there are plenty of eateries. Hill residents work long hours and eat out a lot, and Pennsylvania Avenue and 8th Street SE are lined with neighborhood restaurants. Taverns are a popular place to unwind—ask any lobbyist or congressional aide for directions to the Dubliner, Politiki, Tunnicliff's, or the Hawk & Dove. Those who do cook at home shop for groceries at Eastern Market, a cavernous red-brick hall along 7th Street SE north of Pennsylvania Avenue. Here greengrocers, butchers, dairy farmers, and fishermen have been hawking their goods since 1873. Across the street is a weekend flea market, and the neighboring blocks are lined with funky little shops and delis. For upscale shopping and dining, go to Union Station, www.unionstationdc.com, on Massachusetts Avenue NE just a block north of the Capitol. Union Station has been a busy railway station since 1907 and a busy shopping mall since 1988. For many city dwellers, it's a convenient place to see a movie, and it's popular with tired tourists in need of a quick lunch or a sit-down dinner. (Soon after the shopping and dining concourses opened, Union Station dethroned the National Air & Space Museum as the top tourist attraction in the nation's capital.)

Even in this expensive part of town, you can sometimes find a bargain—a fixer-upper townhouse just off the beaten path, near the **Potomac Avenue** Metro station or off **Lincoln Park** on East Capitol Street—and with a five-figure investment over a few years, add six figures to the value of a $300,000 home. Even, or perhaps especially, in areas that have more than their share of muggings and gangs' graffiti "tags," there is a vibrant civic culture dedicated to neighborhood improvement—and it works.

Online Resources: www.capitolhill.org, www.voiceofthehill.com, www.capitalcommunitynews.com/hillrag.cfr, www.stantonpark.org, http://groups.yahoo.com/group/newhilleast

Zip Codes: 20002, 20003

Post Offices: Postal Square, 2 Massachusetts Ave. NE; Southeast Station, 7th St. and Pennsylvania Ave. SE; Union Station Shops

Police Station: First District Substation, 5th & E streets SE, 202-727-4660

Emergency Hospital: Howard University Hospital, 2401 Georgia Ave. NW, 202-865-6100

Libraries: Northeast, 330 7th St. NE, 202-698-3298; Southeast, 403 7th St. SE, 202-698-3377

Public High School: Eastern, 1700 East Capitol St. NE, 202-698-4500

Government: Ward 6

Neighborhood Festival: Barracks Row Festival (October), www.barracks row.org

Parks: Capitol grounds; Folger Park (North Carolina Ave. between 2nd & 3rd streets SE); Garfield Park (off 3rd & G streets SE); Lincoln Park (East Capitol St. between 11th & 13th streets); Stanton Square (C St. NE between 4th & 6th); Seward Square (Pennsylvania & North Carolina avenues SE); Union Station Plaza (between Union Station and the Capitol)

Community Resources: *Eastern Market & Market Five Gallery*, 225 7th St. SE, 202-546-2698, www.easternmarket.net; *Library of Congress* (see **Cultural Life**); *Folger Shakespeare Library* (see **Cultural Life**); *Georgetown University Law Center*, 600 New Jersey Ave. NW, 202-662-9000, www.georgetown.edu; *Capitol Hill Arts Workshop* is a nonprofit facility featuring a theater, darkroom, and studio space for painting, pottery, music, and dance: 545 7th St. SE, 202-547-6839, www.chaw.org.

Public Transportation: Metro: Union Station (Red Line); Capitol South (Blue & Orange lines), 2nd & D streets SE; Eastern Market (Blue & Orange lines), 7th St & Pennsylvania Ave. SE. Metrobus routes: 30-36 (Pennsylvania Ave. SE); 91-97 (1st St.); X8 (Maryland Ave. NE); D6 (C St.). MARC: Union Station (Penn Line, Brunswick & Camden Line). Virginia Rail Express: Union Station (Fredericksburg and Manassas lines)

NEWCOMER'S HANDBOOK FOR MOVING TO AND LIVING IN WASHINGTON D.C.

24

EAST END/ECKINGTON

NoMa
ECKINGTON
LeDROIT PARK

Boundaries: **North**: Rhode Island Ave.; **East**: railroad tracks; **South**: Massachusetts Ave.; **West**: 7th St. NW

Location: north of Penn Quarter; east of Shaw; south of Howard University; west of Gallaudet University

East End, east of the Verizon Center and overlapping with the eastern part of Shaw, is the focal point of big commercial development in the early 21st century. The new convention center opened here in 2003. National Public Radio is headquartered in the area sometimes called **NoMa** (**No**rth of **Ma**ssachusetts Avenue), and XM Satellite Radio and Black Entertainment Television have headquarters across New York Avenue NE in **Eckington**. A new Metro station on the Red Line (New York Avenue) opened here in 2004 to attract more technology firms. Not coincidentally, McKinley Tech, the District's science magnet high school, is in this neighborhood. To the east is Gallaudet University, the world's first four-year university for the deaf.

West of New Jersey Avenue NW, there are a few residential blocks not yet gentrified, so you may be able to find a good deal on a townhouse; some are in excellent shape despite innocuous-looking exteriors. East of New Jersey Avenue, toward North Capitol Street, are some of the most forlorn blocks in the District, with tracts of decaying public housing barely a 15-minute walk from the Capitol.

If you want to live close to this growing technology hub, or to Gallaudet or Howard or even Children's Hospital and Washington Hospital Center, your best bet may be to look north across Rhode Island Avenue. Plain townhouses are still available for under $300,000 here, but property values have grown tenfold in the past 40 years and are still going up. For many longtime residents, as the *Washington Post* pointed out in a 2005 profile of the North Capitol corridor, the trouble is that property taxes rise at least as fast as market values.

This is a frontier of light industry and probably the grayest part of town, lacking the wedges of greenspace that frame most of the residential areas. However, north of **LeDroit Park** is the semi-scenic McMillan Reservoir and its eye-catching old waterworks that look like the battlements of a red brick castle.

Online Resources: www.capitalcommunitynews.com/dcnorth.cfr, http://groups.yahoo.com/group/Eckington, http://groups.yahoo.com/group/mvsna

Zip Codes: 20001, 20002

Post Offices: LeDroit Park, 416 Florida Ave. NW

Police Station: Police Station: Fifth District Headquarters, 1805 Bladensburg Road NE, 202-727-4510

Emergency Hospital: Howard University Hospital, 2401 Georgia Ave. NW, 202-865-6100

Libraries: Watha T. Daniel, 8th St & Rhode Island Ave. NW, 202-671-0212; Sursum Corda, 1st St. & New York Ave. NW, 202-724-4772

Public High Schools: Dunbar, 1301 New Jersey Ave. NW, 202-673-7233; McKinley Technical, 151 T St. NE, 202-281-3950

Government: Ward 2, School District 1

Community Resources: *Capital City Market*, see **Shopping for the Home**

Public Transportation: Metro: New York Ave. (Red Line), entrance on New York Ave. NE east of Florida Ave.; Rhode Island Ave. (Red Line), entrance on Rhode Island Ave. NE east of 5th St. Metrobus routes: 80 (North Capitol St.); 90-93 (Florida Ave.); P6 (New York Ave.); G8 (Rhode Island Ave.)

PENN QUARTER

CHINATOWN
JUDICIARY SQUARE

Boundaries: **North**: Massachusetts Ave. NW; **East**: Louisiana Ave. NW; **South**: Pennsylvania Ave. NW; **West**: 15th St. NW

Location: north of the Mall; east of downtown; south of Mt. Vernon Square; west of Capitol Hill

Penn Quarter is a mostly commercial area with a few luxury condos, but locals and tourists come here for dining, entertainment, and work. The area is largely defined by the Verizon Center and the 7th Street arts district, but also, along H Street NW between 5th and 7th, is **Chinatown**—or what's left of it. A festive Chinese arch still spans H Street outside the Gallery Place-Chinatown Metro station, but the only contemporary nod to the neighborhood's ethnic heritage is Chinese lettering in the windows of the Starbucks, the CVS drugstore, and the burger joints. Most of the Chinese families have long since moved out to the suburbs. There are still

NEWCOMER'S HANDBOOK FOR MOVING TO AND LIVING IN WASHINGTON D.C.

26

plenty of good Chinese restaurants here, however, and the dean of them all is Tony Cheng's—downstairs for Mongolian barbecue cooked in front of you, upstairs for seafood, and in the foyer for photos of every President since Kennedy dining here.

Penn Quarter proper, a triangular area formed by Mt. Vernon Square, the Treasury Department, and the National Archives, emerged in the 1990s as a popular nightspot for the next age bracket past the club scene. Four of the city's most prominent theaters are here—the Warner, the Shakespeare, the National, and historic Ford's—and a hopping restaurant scene nourishes the theater crowds. Popular chain restaurants such as Austin Grill and ESPN Zone are here alongside signature local restaurants, notably Jaleo, which shares the historic Lansburgh department store building at 7th & E with the Shakespeare Theatre and luxury condos. Jaleo doesn't take reservations, and many people are willing to wait an hour for a table to sample the city's most renowned tapas. The meat-and-potatoes crowd goes a block south to the District Chophouse & Brewery, while nouveau cuisine fans head a few blocks west to Red Sage at 12th and Pennsylvania.

Artists and art lovers flock here, too, for the National Portrait Gallery at 7th & F streets and the National Gallery of Art at 7th and Constitution Avenue. The stretch of 7th Street between the two museums is lined with little galleries and studios. The U.S. Navy Memorial and the Martin Luther King Memorial Library (the main D.C. public library) are nearby, and some of the shops and office buildings around 9th and F streets date from the 19th century.

You aren't likely to live in Penn Quarter unless your timing is impeccable; there's not much housing, and vacancies are scarce. If you do find an apartment at the Lansburgh, or at Market Square at 7th & Pennsylvania NW, expect to pay an astronomical price. Despite perennial talk of the need for more downtown housing, no developer wants to pass up this "trophy" real estate where exclusive office towers and hotels—much more profitable than housing—could go.

Between Penn Quarter and the Capitol is **Judiciary Square**, Pennsylvania Avenue to F Street and 4th to 5th streets NW, named for the concentration of federal and local courthouses and Justice Department offices. The Metropolitan Police Department is also headquartered here, and the National Law Enforcement Officers Memorial occupies a broad plaza just outside the Judiciary Square Metro station. At the north end of the square, the National Building Museum, housed in the historic Pension Building, is one of the most underrated museums in Washington—both for its exhibits on architecture and infrastructure and for its intrinsic beauty.

Penn Quarter is part of the **Downtown Business Improvement District (BID)**, www.downtowndc.org, a special tax zone in which business owners have actually *asked* the city to collect a slightly higher tax on commercial property. The added revenue pays for certain extra services, such as private street cleaning contractors, security cameras, and perky "ambassadors" who patrol the sidewalks to greet tourists. Originally the BID tried to shoo homeless people along to some other neighborhood, but more recently the agency has started working with community organizations to help make social services more accessible to the homeless. (The **Golden Triangle BID**, www.gtbid.org, adjoins the Downtown BID to the west and covers the area between Dupont Circle and Pennsylvania Avenue NW.)

Online Resources: www.downtowndc.org

Zip Codes: 20005

Post Offices: Ben Franklin Station, 12th St. & Pennsylvania Ave. NW; Techworld, 8th & K streets NW

Police Station: Metropolitan Police Department Headquarters, 4th & D streets NW, 202-727-1010, http://mpdc.dc.gov

Emergency Hospital: Howard University Hospital, 2401 Georgia Ave. NW, 202-865-6100

Library: Martin Luther King Jr. Memorial, 9th & G streets NW, 202-727-0321

Government: Ward 2, School District 1

Neighborhood Festival: Arts On Foot (September), www.artsonfoot.org

Park: Freedom Plaza/Pershing Park (Pennsylvania Ave. NW between 13th & 15th streets)

Community Resources: *National Portrait Gallery/National Museum of American Art* (see **Cultural Life**); *Ford's Theatre* (see **Cultural Life**); *National Theatre* (see **Cultural Life**); *Shakespeare Theatre* (see **Cultural Life**); *Warner Theatre* (see **Cultural Life**); *U.S. Navy Memorial & Naval Heritage Center,* 7th St. & Pennsylvania Ave. NW, 202-737-2300, www.lonesailor.org; *National Law Enforcement Officers Memorial Visitors Center,* 605 E St. NW, 202-737-3400, www.nleomf.com; *National Building Museum* (see **Cultural Life**); *International Spy Museum* (see **Cultural Life**).

Public Transportation: Metro: Metro Center (Red, Blue, and Orange lines), entrances on G St. NW at 11th, 12th, and 13th streets, and at 12th & F streets NW; Gallery Place-Chinatown (Red, Yellow, and Green lines), entrances on 7th St. NW at F and H streets; Judiciary Square (Red Line), entrances at the National Law Enforcement Officers Memorial and at 4th & D streets NW. Metrobus routes: D1-D6 (K St. NW), S2/S4 (I St. NW), 42 (11th St. NW), 54 (Pennsylvania Ave. NW)

DUPONT CIRCLE

Boundaries: North: S St. NW; **East**: 14th St. NW; **South**: N St. NW, Rhode Island Ave. NW; **West**: Rock Creek

Location: north of downtown; east of Shaw; south of Kalorama and Adams Morgan; east of West End

Dupont Circle is home to dozens of nonprofit advocacy groups, and to many recent college graduates hoping to get paid for their idealism and commitment to social causes. It's also the capital of Washington's large gay and lesbian community, and many stores and restaurants display a pink triangle or rainbow flag in the window. Lambda Rising and Outlook, among other retailers, cater especially to the gay community, as do several bars and cafés along 17th Street NW. Dupont Circle—along with Adams Morgan to the north—is the heart of Washington's nightlife. An array of restaurants and bars, movie theaters, bookstores with long hours, and ample boutique shopping make this a neighborhood where the sidewalks don't roll up at sundown—indeed, not even at midnight.

Kramerbooks & Afterwords was Washington's first combined bookstore/café, and still leads the city's short list for late night dining and spotting political celebrities. Its upstairs bulletin board is a good place to look for short-term sublets or apartment rental postings. The original Teaism teahouse, now a local chain, still draws standing-room crowds to 2009 R Street NW. The Brickskeller, at 1523 22nd Street NW, serves some 800 kinds of beer from all over the world; expect a half-hour wait for a table on weekends. Kramerbooks and other local favorites, including Luna Grill & Diner and Second Story Books, have opened locations in the suburbs.

If you don't want to dine out every night, there's an abundance of gourmet markets, bakeries, and eateries geared toward carryout; and there's a bustling farmers' market on Sunday mornings at the Q Street entrance to the Dupont Circle Metro station. The Safeway supermarket at 17th & R streets is known as the "Soviet Safeway" because of the notoriously long lines. If you're in a hurry, it might actually be quicker to take the No. 42 bus to the Safeway at 1747 Columbia Road.

The Circle itself is a gathering place for bicycle couriers, executives from nearby office buildings, and street people. At lunchtime and early evening, many come to play chess at tables with built-in chessboards, and there's often a small crowd of spectators. Between two concentric rings of benches, which are always crowded, grassy lawns serve as the neighborhood "beach." The fountain in the center of the circle is unique—most circles and squares downtown are dominated by the standard bronze statue of a 19th-century general or admiral. At the other extreme, a tiny patch of grass at 20th Street & New Hampshire Avenue NW was "adopted" by one local citizen and unofficially dedicated as "Sonny Bono Memorial Park." It features one bench, lovingly maintained flowers, and a simple plaque in memory of the entertainer and congressman.

There are some art galleries on Connecticut Avenue and along the side streets north of the Circle, but rising rents have forced some struggling artists to 7th Street NW and Shaw, where zoning "overlays" encourage the development of studios and galleries. South of N Street NW, Connecticut Avenue is lined with office buildings whose storefront restaurants and clothing stores cater to the downtown office crowd. The Improv comedy club is here, at 1140 Connecticut Avenue, and several plain-looking buildings nearby camouflage swanky SoHo-type nightclubs—the kind with fashion police at the door.

Many row houses off the Circle have been converted into apartments of all sizes, and elegant old mansions have been turned into embassies or offices housing nonprofit groups, including Public Citizen and the Church of Scientology. "English basements"—apartments below row houses, with their own separate entrances—make popular rentals for singles and young couples just getting started, but even these fetch $1,000 or more. An efficiency or studio apartment will rent for at least $1,000 in the postwar high-rises along New Hampshire Avenue south of the Circle; in prestigious old apartment buildings to the east, between 14th & 17th streets NW, condo units command even higher rent.

For most young newcomers, the Dupont Circle area is one of the first stops on a house-hunting tour. If you're willing and able to pay a four-figure rent (or to buy a six-figure condo), you'll have a dazzling assortment of restaurants, shops, and nightlife within walking distance.

Online Resources: www.dupont-circle.com, www.intowner.com, http://groups.yahoo.com/group/DupontForum

Zip Codes: 20009, 20036

Post Offices: Temple Heights Station, 1921 Florida Ave. NW; 20th St., 1111 20th St. NW

Police Station: Third District Headquarters, 1620 V St. NW, 202-673-6930

Emergency Hospital: George Washington University Hospital, 901 23rd St. NW, 202-715-4000

Library: West End, 24th & L streets NW, 202-724-8707

Public High Schools: Cardozo, 13th & Clifton streets NW, 202-673-7385; School Without Walls, 2130 G St. NW, 202-724-4889

Government: Ward 2

Neighborhood Festivals: Capital Pride Parade (June), www.capital pride.org; Kramerbooks & Afterwords Block Party (August), 202-387-1400; Halloween High Heels Race

NEWCOMER'S HANDBOOK FOR MOVING TO AND LIVING IN WASHINGTON D.C.

30

Parks: Dupont Circle, Rock Creek (points of access west of 23rd St. NW), Rose (26th & P streets NW), Scott Circle

Community Resources: *Phillips Collection* (see **Cultural Life**); Church Street Theatre (see **Cultural Life**); *D.C. Jewish Community Center* offers a health club, theater, after-school programs, and social activities: 1529 16th St NW, 202-518-9400, www.dcjcc.org. Visit *www.dk museums.com* for a directory of more than a dozen small museums in the Dupont-Kalorama area.

Public Transportation: Metro: Dupont Circle station (Red Line), entrances at Connecticut Ave. & Q St. NW and south side of Dupont Circle at 19th St. NW. Metrobus routes: 42 (Connecticut Ave. NW), G2 (P St. NW), L2 (New Hampshire Ave. NW), N2-N6 (Connecticut Ave. NW downtown, Massachusetts Ave. NW uptown)

KALORAMA

KALORAMA TRIANGLE

Boundaries: **North**: Rock Creek; **East**: Connecticut Avenue NW, Columbia Rd. NW, 19th St. NW; **South**: S St. NW; **West**: Rock Creek

Location: north of Dupont Circle; east of Embassy Row (across Rock Creek); south of Woodley Park (across Rock Creek); west of Adams Morgan

Just up the hill from Dupont Circle, straddling Connecticut Avenue NW, is **Kalorama**, where every home that isn't an embassy or museum is a mansion or luxury apartment. Kalorama, Greek for "beautiful view," is perched on hills above Rock Creek, and many homes offer postcard-perfect views. Indeed, it was a view of the White House—now obstructed by downtown office buildings—that lured affluent Washingtonians to build homes here in the late 19th and early 20th centuries.

Presidents Hoover and Franklin Roosevelt lived in Kalorama before they moved to 1600 Pennsylvania Avenue, and President Wilson retired here. Today, residents include senators, retired Cabinet secretaries, and members of the city council. Nearly a quarter of the houses here are embassies or chanceries, and in 1989, the whole neighborhood was added to the National Register of Historic Places.

Many homes have ballrooms and formal gardens, and some have servants' quarters. Some houses are actually made of parts of European castles or chalets that were moved here. Generally, houses start at half a million dollars, though some are closer to $3 million. Even if money is no object, you will have to watch patiently and move quickly to buy a home here—homes often sell before they're even listed.

Many area apartment buildings were built before World War I and are still among the most elegant residences in town—and the most expensive. Condos often start at a million dollars. If you're lucky, however, you might find an efficiency renting for $900 in the area bounded by Columbia, Calvert, and Rock Creek—the area known as **Kalorama Triangle** in the lingo of real estate classifieds.

If your Kalorama address leaves you a little short on bus fare, you can walk down Connecticut Avenue to shop and dine in Dupont Circle; walk across the Duke Ellington Bridge into Adams Morgan; or walk across the majestic Taft Bridge into Woodley Park. Get used to those walks—pleasant, but hilly—for groceries, videos, and other basics. Kalorama is all residential.

Online Resources: www.intowner.com

Zip Codes: 20008, 20009

Post Offices: Kalorama Station, 2300 18th St. NW; Temple Heights Station, 1921 Florida Ave. NW

Police Station: Third District Headquarters, 1620 V St. NW, 202-673-6930

Emergency Hospital: George Washington University Hospital, 901 23rd St. NW, 202-715-4000

Library: West End, 24th & L streets NW, 202-724-8707

Public High Schools: Cardozo, 13th & Clifton streets NW, 202-673-7385; School Without Walls, 2130 G St. NW, 202-724-4889

Government: Ward 1

Neighborhood Festival: Dupont-Kalorama Museum Walk (June), 202-667-0441, www.dkmuseums.com

Parks: Mitchell (off Massachusetts Ave. NW west of Sheridan Circle); Rock Creek (points of access off Waterside Dr. NW)

Community Resources: *Textile Museum* (see **Cultural Life**); other small museums in the Dupont-Kalorama area are listed at www.dkmuseums.com. The *Woodrow Wilson House,* where the Nobel laureate and ex-President lived, is the only presidential museum in the District: 2340 S St. NW, 202-387-4062, www.woodrowwilsonhouse.org.

Public Transportation: Metrobus routes: L1 (Connecticut Ave. NW); 42 (Columbia Road NW). Walk to Metro, Dupont Circle, or Woodley Park-Zoo stations (Red Line)

NEWCOMER'S HANDBOOK FOR MOVING TO AND LIVING IN WASHINGTON D.C.

32

FOGGY BOTTOM/WEST END

Boundaries: **North**: N St. NW; **East**: 17th St. NW, Connecticut Ave. NW; **South**: Constitution Ave. NW; **West**: Potomac River, Rock Creek

Location: north of the Mall; east of Georgetown (across Rock Creek); south of Kalorama; west of Dupont Circle and downtown

Nestled between the White House and Georgetown, at the foggy bottom of a hill overlooking the Potomac, **Foggy Bottom** is home to the State Department, the International Monetary Fund, and the World Bank. To the north, between Dupont Circle and Georgetown, are the upscale hotels and restaurants of **West End**. Together, these two areas essentially create one neighborhood—a diverse zone of overlap between elite Georgetown, powerful Pennsylvania Avenue, and hip Dupont Circle. George Washington University is here, and so are the headquarters of the American Red Cross, the Federal Reserve, the Pan-American Health Organization, the Bureau of National Affairs, and the General Services Administration—the "landlord" of government office buildings.

Most of the homes here are luxury apartments in modern high-rises, but there are a few blocks of old row houses west of New Hampshire Avenue. Many were built more than a century ago for workers at the Christian Heurich Brewery, which once stood where the Kennedy Center is today. The neighborhood attracts a lot of diplomats and prominent journalists; Mayor Anthony Williams also lives here. At the end of New Hampshire Avenue NW, between the Kennedy Center and the mouth of Rock Creek, is perhaps the most famous address in Washington besides 1600 Pennsylvania Avenue: The Watergate. Scene of the 1972 burglary of the Democratic National Committee headquarters, The Watergate is a towering mixed-use complex with luxury apartments and condominiums, offices, the posh Watergate Hotel, designer boutiques, and four-star restaurants. Justice Ruth Bader Ginsburg, Senator Bob and Secretary Elizabeth Dole, and the most famous White House intern in history have all called The Watergate home. In its shadow, to the north, is the old water gate at the south end of the C&O Canal.

Between the Potomac and George Washington University (GW), you'll find apartments for more varied budgets, but even student-friendly housing isn't exactly cheap. High-rise luxury condos in the vicinity of 22nd and M are not known for their dazzling views, but they do offer a convenient location, lots of space, and modern trimmings. With rooftop pools, concierge services, and carpeted hallways, these buildings look and feel like hotels. Like many urban universities, GW is more like a neighborhood than a distinct campus, and longtime residents of the West End and Foggy Bottom are constantly at odds with the school about student housing, parking, and proposals to expand school facilities. Parking can be a problem here.

Foggy Bottom and West End are just a few minutes' walk from the fine restaurants and clubs of Georgetown, Dupont Circle, and the downtown business district, but there are neighborhood attractions here too: Lulu's nightclub and Blackie's steakhouse, together filling a whole block of 22nd Street; restaurants and taverns that cater to GW students; and Asia Nora.

Some residents continue to fume about the closure of Pennsylvania Avenue NW near the White House, a precaution taken by the Secret Service after several security incidents in the mid-1990s. While a six-lane crosstown thoroughfare was severed, requiring tedious detours around Lafayette Square, the resulting pedestrian zone in front of the White House is popular with sightseers, photographers, street hockey players, and (of course) placard-waving protesters.

Online Resources: http://groups.yahoo.com/group/FoggyBottom Association, www.georgetowner.com

Zip Code: 20037

Post Office: Watergate, 2512 Virginia Ave. NW

Police Station: Second District Headquarters, 3320 Idaho Ave. NW, 202-282-0070

Emergency Hospital: George Washington University Hospital, 901 23rd St. NW, 202-715-4000

Library: West End, 24th & L streets NW, 202-724-8707

Public High School: School Without Walls, 2130 G St. NW, 202-724-4889

Government: Ward 2

Parks: Edward R. Murrow (18th St. and Pennsylvania Ave. NW); Rock Creek (access off 26th & M streets NW); Rose (26th & P streets NW); Washington Circle

Community Resources: George Washington University (see **Higher Education**); *John F. Kennedy Center for the Performing Arts* (see **Cultural Life**)

Public Transportation: Metro: Foggy Bottom-GWU (Blue & Orange lines), 23rd & I streets NW. Metrobus routes: 30-36 (Pennsylvania Ave. NW), D5 (K St. NW), L2 (20th St. NW northbound, 21st St. NW southbound)

NEWCOMER'S HANDBOOK FOR MOVING TO AND LIVING IN WASHINGTON D.C.

34

GEORGETOWN

BURLEITH
FOXHALL

Boundaries: **North**: Whitehaven Pkwy., Whitehaven Park; **East**: Rock Creek; **South**: Potomac River; **West**: Potomac River

Location: north of the Potomac River; east of Palisades; south of Glover Park; west of West End and Dupont Circle (across Rock Creek)

Before upstart colonials dreamed of a nation, let alone a nation's capital, **Georgetown** was a bustling port on the Potomac River at the point where the water becomes too shallow for further navigation. One of the oldest urban neighborhoods in North America, Georgetown remained an industrial center throughout the 19th century and did not become a fashionable address until the 1950s. Today residential Georgetown, with its 200-year-old buildings and cobblestone side streets, boasts a world-renowned university and a disproportionate share of Washington's powerful newsmakers. The commercial strips of Wisconsin Avenue and M Street NW are favorite evening and weekend destinations for tourists, suburbanites, and students from area universities.

Most Georgetown homes are beautiful row houses on tree-lined streets; apartments are rare, other than "English basement" apartments below townhouses. Historic preservation rules limit the alteration of exteriors, but inside most homeowners have added air conditioning and modern kitchens. The appeal here is genuine; the houses, storefronts, and converted industrial buildings are all of a "they don't make 'em like that anymore" quality. Georgetown University adds to the charm, with Gothic stone buildings and the towering steeple of Healy Hall marking the west end of the neighborhood. Not coincidentally, housing is expensive—many homes fetch at least twice the citywide median price. Georgetown University students cram into group houses, rent apartments across the Key Bridge in Virginia, or head uptown.

There is one cluster of 1980s high-rises: Washington Harbour, by the river and the mouth of Rock Creek. The view is worth a million bucks, so the condos here—at half a million—are sort of a bargain. The complex is designed to be accessible by yacht, and boaters come ashore to the waterfront bars and restaurants.

Wisconsin Avenue and M Street feature upscale specialty shops, boutiques, and neighborhood cafés and restaurants; increasingly, however, you'll also find the same Starbucks, Ben & Jerry's and Barnes & Noble stores you'll find in any other city.

No other city has the Chesapeake & Ohio Canal, though. This 19th-century barge canal ran from Georgetown to Cumberland, Md., past rocky stretches of the Potomac. Today, C&O Canal National Historical Park offers some of the best places for cycling and jogging in the Washington area. (See the chapter on **Greenspace** for details.)

Georgetown has its own little suburbs—the posh neighborhoods of **Foxhall** to the west and **Burleith** to the north. These areas feature big homes with big yards behind privacy hedges. In Burleith, one Whitehaven Parkway mansion is the home of Senator Hillary and Bill Clinton. And the Foxhall Village enclave, just west of the university, is an award-winning complex of stucco Tudor houses built in the 1920s.

Know how to make a Georgetown resident laugh? Ask about parking. If you must park here, plan to spend half an hour looking for a space. Better yet, get on the bus.

Online Resources: www.georgetowndc.com, www.georgetowndclife. com, www.georgetowner.com, www.burleith.org, www.foxhall.org, http://groups.yahoo.com/group/burleith

Zip Code: 20007

Post Office: Georgetown, 3050 K St. NW

Police Station: Second District Headquarters, 3320 Idaho Ave. NW, 202-282-0070

Emergency Hospitals: Georgetown University Hospital, 3800 Reservoir Road NW, 202-687-2000; George Washington University Hospital, 901 23rd St. NW, 202-715-4000

Library: West End, 24th & L streets NW, 202-724-8707

Public High Schools: School Without Walls, 2130 G St. NW, 202-724-4889; Duke Ellington School of the Arts, 1698 35th St. NW, 202-292-0123

Government: Ward 2

Parks: C&O Canal (between M St. NW and the Potomac River); Dumbarton Oaks-Montrose (north of R St. NW between Wisconsin Ave. and Rock Creek); Glover Archbold (points of access off 44th St. NW and Reservoir Rd.); Rock Creek (points of access off Pennsylvania Ave. and M St. NW, east of 28th St.); Whitehaven (connecting Dumbarton Oaks and Glover Archbold parks north of T St. NW)

Community Resources: *Georgetown University* (see **Higher Education**); *Junior League of Washington*, 3039 M St. NW, 202-337-2001, www.jlw.org

Public Transportation: Metro: Foggy Bottom-GWU (Blue & Orange lines), 23rd & I streets NW. Metrobus routes: 30-36 (Pennsylvania and

NEWCOMER'S HANDBOOK FOR MOVING TO AND LIVING IN WASHINGTON D.C.

36

Wisconsin avenues NW), D1/D2 and D6 (Q St. NW); G2 (P St. NW westbound, O St. NW eastbound)

UPPER NORTHWEST

EMBASSY ROW
McLEAN GARDENS
AMERICAN UNIVERSITY PARK
FRIENDSHIP HEIGHTS
TENLEYTOWN
SPRING VALLEY
PALISADES
GLOVER PARK

Boundaries: **North**: Maryland; **East**: Reno Rd. NW, 34th St. NW; **South**: Whitehaven Pkwy., Whitehaven Park; **West**: Maryland, Potomac River

Location: north of Georgetown and Burleith; east of the Potomac River; south of Bethesda, Md.; west of the Connecticut Ave. corridor

A classified ad listing a home in **"Upper Northwest"** might mean a spacious colonial in the leafy hills of Foxhall Road, a luxury apartment on the stretch of Massachusetts Avenue known as **Embassy Row**, a brick townhouse in the self-contained residential village of **McLean Gardens**, a detached house with a white picket fence in **American University Park** north of Ward Circle, or an older brick or stone house off the bustling retail corridor of Wisconsin Avenue in **Friendship Heights**. In any case, it is likely to mean an expensive home, but probably more spacious and cheaper per square foot than homes in Dupont Circle or Capitol Hill. It will mean an older home in a stable, upscale neighborhood, and proximity to elite private schools such as Sidwell Friends, St. Alban's, National Cathedral, and the public Duke Ellington School of the Arts, as well as excellent public elementary schools. And unless you live just off Wisconsin or Massachusetts avenues, it will mean a lot of driving—west of American University, even buses are scarce.

East of the university is **Tenleytown**, a commercial strip along Wisconsin Avenue. This is some of the highest ground in Washington, prime real estate for radio and TV towers. NBC, CBS, and Fox have studios nearby, and residents routinely face off against wireless phone companies seeking to add even more towers to the Tenleytown skyline.

In American University Park, south of River Road NW, a nice colonial house with a fenced yard and two or three bedrooms might rent for the price of a one-bedroom apartment on Connecticut Avenue. Across Massachusetts Avenue are posh enclaves in the western corner of the District: **Spring Valley** on the north side of Loughboro Road and **Palisades** on the south. The houses here are spacious, elegant, and shaded by big trees in big yards. Spring Valley lost some of its luster in the 1990s when construction crews unearthed live ammunition and chemical weapons that the Army was testing nearby during World War I. Many residents are concerned about possible effects of long-term exposure to the buried chemicals, though the Army made a major cleanup effort from 1993 to 1995 and maintains that there is no danger to the public. Currently the Army Corps of Engineers is in the process of certifying that each property is free of munitions and harmful chemicals. Despite this sour note, this is still prized real estate that sells quickly when listed.

Heading east along Massachusetts Avenue is Embassy Row, an accurate nickname for the area between Dupont and Westmoreland circles. Japan, the United Kingdom, India, Ireland, New Zealand, Greece, and Finland are just a few of the dozens of countries whose official representatives in the United States are based here. Almost all embassies have visitors' centers and exhibits, and are listed in the business White Pages under "Embassy of . . ." There are a few apartment buildings here, too—big, elegant prewar buildings. Expect to pay $1,000 or more for a one-bedroom rental. West of Embassy Row, the cottages and townhouses of **Glover Park** make affordable rentals for young families and groups of recent graduates.

Ambassadors aren't the only VIPs with official residences in Upper Northwest—there's also the Episcopal Archbishop of Washington, whose house is on the grounds of the National Cathedral, and the Vice President of the United States, whose mansion is on the grounds of the U.S. Naval Observatory. The observatory, on a hill above Massachusetts Avenue NW at 34th Street, is also the home of the Navy's atomic clock, the official timepiece of the U.S. government.

Online Resources: www.palisadesdc.org, http://groups.yahoo.com/
  group/tenleytown

Zip Codes: 20007, 20016

Post Offices: Calvert, Wisconsin Ave. & Calvert St. NW; Friendship,
  4005 Wisconsin Ave. NW; Palisades, 5136 MacArthur Blvd. NW

Police Station: Second District Headquarters, 3320 Idaho Ave. NW
  (39th St.), 202-282-0070

Emergency Hospitals: Georgetown University Hospital, 3800
  Reservoir Rd. NW, 202-687-2000; Sibley Memorial Hospital, 5255
  Loughboro Rd. NW, 202-537-4000

Libraries: Tenley-Friendship, 4450 Wisconsin Ave. NW, 202-282-3090;
  Palisades, 49th & V streets NW, 202-282-3139

NEWCOMER'S HANDBOOK FOR MOVING TO AND LIVING IN WASHINGTON D.C.

38

Public High School: Woodrow Wilson, 3950 Chesapeake St. NW, 202-282-0120

Government: Ward 3

Neighborhood Festivals: Glover Park Day (June); Palisades Fourth of July Parade; Spring Valley 5K to benefit Children's Hospital (September), 202-895-2705

Parks: Battery Kemble (off Chain Bridge Rd. NW between Loughboro Rd. and the Potomac River); C&O Canal (points of access along Clara Barton Pkwy. and Canal Rd. NW); Glover Archbold (east of 44th St. NW between Massachusetts Ave. and the Potomac River); Palisades (Canal Road and Arizona Ave. NW); Wesley Heights (connecting Battery Kemble and Glover Archbold parks south of Garfield St. NW); Whitehaven (south of W St. NW between Wisconsin Ave. and Glover Archbold Park)

Community Resources: *Washington Islamic Center* (see **Places of Worship**); *Washington National Cathedral* (see **Places of Worship**); *Iona House Senior Services*, 4125 Albemarle St., 202-895-9448, www.iona.org/privatecare. The *Capital Crescent Trail* is a Rails-to-Trails bike path along the route of a rail line that once carried coal to the federal power plant serving the Capitol. The commuter-oriented trail connects Georgetown with downtown Silver Spring via Palisades, Bethesda, and Chevy Chase. For information, call 202-234-4874 or visit www.cctrail.org.

Public Transportation: Metro: Tenleytown-AU (Red Line), Wisconsin Ave. and Albemarle; Friendship Heights, Wisconsin and Western avenues NW. Metrobus routes: N2-N8 (Massachusetts Ave. NW), 30-36 (Wisconsin Ave. NW), M4 (Nebraska Ave. NW), D5/D6 (MacArthur Blvd. NW)

CONNECTICUT AVENUE CORRIDOR

WOODLEY PARK
CLEVELAND PARK
VAN NESS
CHEVY CHASE

Boundaries: **North**: Maryland; **East**: Rock Creek; **South**: Taft Bridge; **West**: 34th St. NW, Reno Rd. NW

Location: north of Kalorama; east of Embassy Row, Tenleytown, and Friendship Heights; south of Chevy Chase, Md.

Connecticut Avenue NW from the Taft Bridge over Rock Creek to Chevy Chase Circle at the Maryland line is a charming series of "urban village"

neighborhoods that combine the best elements of urban and suburban living. Most of the homes are in grand old apartment buildings, but there are plenty of single-family houses on tree-lined side streets. The houses here don't all look alike, they have fenced yards, and some are even made of stone. Just off Connecticut Avenue, you'll find many 1930s townhouses with basements converted into separate apartments. Commercial strips punctuate Connecticut Avenue, drawing locals to Woodley Park, Cleveland Park, Van Ness, and Chevy Chase for shopping and dining.

This area attracts a political crowd—a favorite local hangout is Politics & Prose, a bookstore and café that hosts readings by big-name political authors. And more personal checks written to political campaigns bear zip code 20008 than any other zip code outside Hollywood or Manhattan.

From Taft Bridge north to Klingle Valley is **Woodley Park**, whose east-side residents are privy to the early morning sound of trumpeting elephants from the nearby National Zoo. Affordable ethnic restaurants with outdoor seating face the Woodley Park-Zoo Metro station. Around the corner, the city's largest hotel, the Marriott Wardman Park, is perched high above Rock Creek.

North of Woodley Park, Connecticut Avenue crosses a bridge over Klingle Valley Park, a recent addition to the District's extensive park system. Klingle Road, once used as a commuting back door into Mt. Pleasant, was closed in 1990 due to storm damage. While tree removal crews were busy clearing storm debris from residential streets throughout Northwest D.C., residents of Mt. Pleasant and Cleveland Park took the opportunity to use the closed road for walking and jogging. Many residents decided this area served their neighborhood much better as a park rather than as a commuter shortcut, and asked the city not to repair the road.

North of Klingle Valley is **Cleveland Park**, summer retreat of President Grover Cleveland. Cleveland, like many Washingtonians, came to this high ground to enjoy the cooling breezes that bring some relief from the swampy August heat. Many of the 19th-century cottages here were built with wraparound porches to catch the breeze. Some of those vintage homes are palatial, but there are more modest three-bedroom houses on the side streets, with back-alley garages instead of driveways.

Some of the District's best public schools are here, including John Eaton and Oyster Bilingual elementary schools, as well as prestigious private schools such as the Washington International School, Maret, and the National Cathedral School. Consequently, Cleveland Park attracts many families with school-aged children. Students in other neighborhoods compete for limited "out-of-boundary" admission to the top public schools here. (See **Childcare and Education** for more on the process.)

The biggest commercial movie screen in the Washington area is in Cleveland Park, at the vintage Uptown Theater, complete with balcony

NEWCOMER'S HANDBOOK FOR MOVING TO AND LIVING IN WASHINGTON D.C.

40

seats. A commercial strip on Connecticut Avenue between Macomb and Porter streets features two gourmet markets and a health food store, a Petco pet superstore, several coffee bars, two Irish pubs, and an assortment of neighborhood restaurants.

North of Cleveland Park, across another little valley leading to Rock Creek, is the main campus of the University of the District of Columbia. The stores lining Connecticut Avenue here in **Van Ness** are more utilitarian than the destination shops of Cleveland Park—here it's office supplies, photocopying, fast food, and groceries. There's a Pier One Imports home furnishing store, too, and Calvert Woodley Liquors has a nice selection of fine cheeses. Off Connecticut Avenue on Van Ness Street is Howard University Law School.

From Yuma Street north to Chevy Chase Circle is the D.C. neighborhood known as **Chevy Chase**, not to be confused with the neighboring town of Chevy Chase, Md. Just off Connecticut Avenue, you'll find assorted cottages, split-levels, and brick and stone colonials, all beautiful and expensive. Mansions border Rock Creek Park. Some of the District's most desirable schools are in Chevy Chase: Lafayette and Murch elementary schools, Deal Junior High, and the private St. John's and Georgetown Day high schools.

Connecticut Avenue, the commercial main street of Chevy Chase, caters to locals in a high income bracket: gourmet markets, good restaurants, and bookstores, but also video stores, a library, a post office, and Chevy Chase Community Center.

Online Resources: www.clevelandpark.com, http://groups.yahoo.com/group/cleveland-park, www.chevychasecitizens.org

Zip Codes: 20008, 20015

Post Offices: Cleveland Park, 3430 Connecticut Ave. NW; Northwest Station, 5632 Connecticut Ave. NW

Police Stations: Second District Headquarters, 3320 Idaho Ave. NW (39th St), 202-282-0070; Sixth District Headquarters, 100 42nd St. NW (Albemarle St.), 202-727-4520

Emergency Hospitals: Georgetown University Hospital, 3800 Reservoir Rd. NW, 202-687-2000; George Washington University Hospital, 901 23rd St. NW, 202-715-4000

Libraries: Chevy Chase, 5625 Connecticut Ave. NW (Oliver St.), 202-282-0021; Cleveland Park, 3310 Connecticut Ave. NW (Macomb St.), 202-282-3080

Public High School: Woodrow Wilson, 3950 Chesapeake St. NW, 202-282-0120

Government: Ward 3 (except the eastern part of Chevy Chase, which is Ward 4)

Neighborhood Festival: Cleveland Park Day (September)

Parks: Chevy Chase Circle; Klingle Valley (south of Macomb St. NW from Rock Creek west to Woodley Rd.); Melvin C. Hazen (south of Tilden St. NW from Rock Creek west to 34th); Muhlenberg-Fort Reno (off Nebraska Ave. NW just west of Connecticut Ave.); Normanstone (along Massachusetts Ave. NW across from the Naval Observatory); Rock Creek (points of access east of Connecticut Ave. NW and off Military Rd.); Soapstone Valley (south of Albemarle St. NW from Rock Creek west to Connecticut Ave.)

Community Resources: *National Zoo* (see **Greenspace**); *Hillwood Museum & Gardens* (see **Greenspace**); *Loew's Cineplex Uptown Theater,* 3426 Connecticut Ave. NW, 202-333-3456 ext. 799; *University of the District of Columbia* (see **Higher Education**); *Howard University Law School,* 28th & Upton streets NW, 202-806-8000, www.law.howard.edu

Public Transportation: Metro: Woodley Park-Zoo/Adams Morgan (Red Line), Connecticut Ave. & Garfield St. NW; Cleveland Park (Red Line), Connecticut Ave. & Ordway St. NW; Van Ness-UDC (Red Line), Connecticut Ave. & Veazey Terrace NW. Metrobus routes: L1/L2 (Connecticut Ave. NW), H2-H4 (Porter St. NW)

BRIGHTWOOD/PETWORTH

TAKOMA
SHEPHERD PARK
CRESTWOOD

Boundaries: North: Aspen St. NW; **East**: New Hampshire Ave. NW, railroad tracks; **South**: Spring Rd; **West**: Rock Creek

Location: north of Mt. Pleasant; east of the Connecticut Ave. corridor (across Rock Creek); south of Walter Reed Army Medical Center and Takoma Park, Md.; west of the Soldiers' & Airmen's Home

Brightwood is one of the last nice neighborhoods where you can buy a house for under $250,000—if anyone's selling. Some of the sturdy townhouses built before World War II are still occupied by the original owners or their children. Families also cling to the elegant detached houses off 16th Street NW, many also built before the war. The leafy residential belt between 16th Street and Georgia Avenue NW resembles a cross-section of greater Washington: 16th Street is lined with grand Federal and Tudor homes, and just three blocks east, Georgia Avenue is a struggling swath of laundromats, pager stores, and storefront tax preparers. In between the two sections is a quiet, economically diverse residential enclave. There are

NEWCOMER'S HANDBOOK FOR MOVING TO AND LIVING IN WASHINGTON D.C.

42

a few run-down apartment complexes along 14th Street, between Military Road and Walter Reed Army Medical Center, but mostly the side streets resemble the inner suburbs: children at play, people walking dogs and washing cars, and front porches shaded by mature trees. (The historic army hospital is slated to move to Bethesda around 2010.)

In addition to stately homes and embassies, 16th Street hosts a variety of houses of worship, including a selection of Protestant churches, Buddhist and Baha'i temples, a synagogue, Greek and Russian Orthodox churches, and the secular humanist congregation of the Washington Ethical Society. Also here, at 16th Street and Colorado Avenue, is the William H.G. Fitzgerald Tennis Stadium. Beware: Each August brings the Legg Mason Tennis Classic and, along with world-famous athletes, ludicrous traffic jams. Surrounding the tennis stadium is a carpet of soccer fields used by local youth teams. In the woods of Rock Creek Park, behind the fields, the Carter Barron Amphitheatre attracts crowds in the summer and fall to free performances by the Shakespeare Theatre Company, D.C. Blues Society artists, and the National Symphony Orchestra.

The crescent-shaped hill near 13th Street and Georgia Avenue is a remnant of Fort Stevens, which repelled a Confederate attack on Washington during the Civil War. Near the fort, housing is relatively inexpensive—in the shadow of a huge radio antenna reminiscent of the Eiffel Tower, and just beyond walking distance to the Takoma and Georgia Avenue-Petworth Metro stations. Good houses under $250,000 are rare in the District, but you may find them here. Most of the townhouses here are more spacious than they look from outside, and their porches and tiny front yards are nicely landscaped and well maintained.

The triangle of Missouri, Georgia, and New Hampshire avenues is **Petworth**, a vast, mostly residential area. There's a pocket of liquor stores and gang activity along Kennedy Street NW between 5th and 9th streets; 508 Kennedy Street is the Northwest D.C. field office for Medicaid and food stamps. Just a few blocks north, though, you'd hardly notice the depressed strip. The green campus of the U.S. Soldiers' & Airmen's Home, a few blocks east of New Hampshire Avenue, is a retirement community for distinguished enlisted veterans.

North of Brightwood, along Piney Branch Road NW, **Takoma** is a less-expensive version of neighboring Takoma Park, Md., and offers affordable detached houses in every size and shape. There's a waiting list to get into Takoma Village Cohousing, 202-546-4654, www.takomavillage.org, a planned community of some 70 households, just inside the D.C. line. Cohousing is a model of resource-sharing that aims to strike a balance between independent home ownership and a communal lifestyle: Residents live in their own condos, but the community shares certain amenities—one laundry room, one set of home and garden tools, and even some shared cars, computers, and TVs. The community strives for diversity—not just ethnic and economic, but also a balance of young families, singles, and retirees.

West of Takoma and north of the Walter Reed campus is **Shepherd Park**, a stable, leafy neighborhood of detached houses. Some of these colonials and bungalows on curving streets almost feel suburban, and indeed they're closer to downtown Silver Spring than to any shopping or dining in D.C.

Crestwood is an enclave of big, elegant houses nestled between 16th Street and Rock Creek Park south of Colorado Avenue. Old split-levels and colonials line the hillside leading to the park, and there's a cluster of mansions in Tudor and Spanish styles just off 16th and Colorado. Like most of the Brightwood area, this is a secluded and stable community with little turnover.

Online Resources: www.capitalcommunitynews.com/dcnorth.cfr, http://groups.yahoo.com/group/Brightwood_DC, groups.yahoo.com/group/TakomaDC, groups.yahoo.com/group/shepherdpark, http://petworthnews.blogs.com, www.crestwood-dc.org

Zip Codes: 20011, 20012

Post Offices: Brightwood, Georgia Ave. and Piney Branch Rd. NW; Petworth Station, 4211 9th St. NW

Police Station: Fourth District Headquarters, 6001 Georgia Ave. NW, 202-576-6745

Emergency Hospital: Washington Hospital Center, 110 Irving St. NW, 202-877-7000

Libraries: Takoma, 416 Cedar St. NW, 202-576-7252; Petworth, 4200 Kansas Ave. NW, 202-541-6300

Public High School: Coolidge Senior High School, 6315 5th St. NW, 202-576-6143

Government: Ward 4

Parks: Fort Slocum (east of 3rd St. NW between Madison and Oglethorpe streets); Grant Circle; Rock Creek (points of access along 16th St. & Colorado Ave. NW); Sherman Circle

Community Resources: *Carter Barron Amphitheatre* (see **Cultural Life**); *National Museum of Health & Medicine,* Walter Reed Army Medical Center, Georgia Ave. and Butternut St. NW, 202-782-2200; *Rock Creek Park Tennis Center* and *William H.G. Fitzgerald Tennis Stadium,* 16th & Kennedy streets NW, 202-722-5949. *Ft. Stevens & Battleground National Cemetery,* site of the only Civil War battle in the District of Columbia; the fort is at 13th & Rittenhouse streets NW and the cemetery is a few blocks north at 6625 Georgia Ave. NW. President Lincoln dedicated this memorial park for Union soldiers killed in the successful defense of Ft. Stevens. Free and open during daylight hours; for more information, visit www.nps.gov/batt.

NEWCOMER'S HANDBOOK FOR MOVING TO AND LIVING IN WASHINGTON D.C.

44

Public Transportation: Metro: Takoma (Red Line), 4th & Cedar streets NW; Georgia Ave-Petworth (Green Line), Georgia & New Hampshire avenues NW. Metrobus routes: S2-S4 (16th St. NW); 52-54 (14th St. NW); 70-73 (Georgia Ave. NW); 62 (5th St. NW); 64 (New Hampshire Ave. NW); E2-E4 (Kennedy St. NW); K2 (Blair Rd. NW)

MT. PLEASANT

COLUMBIA HEIGHTS

Boundaries: **North**: Piney Branch Park; **East**: 16th St. NW; **South**: Euclid St. NW, Calvert St. NW; **West**: Rock Creek Park

Location: north of Adams Morgan; east of the National Zoo; south of Crestwood; west of Howard University

Mt. Pleasant, west of 16th Street atop Meridian Hill, is the heart of the District's growing Latino community, and it also attracts many recent graduates. Red brick townhouses, many for rent, line the side streets from Hobart to Newton. Quite a few of these homes date from World War I, and some are just as nice inside as those in pricier neighborhoods closer to Dupont Circle. Hardwood floors, exposed brick, and detailed plasterwork are common features here.

This is a favorite neighborhood for groups of young adults sharing a house—it's an easy walk or bike ride to Dupont Circle, where many non-profit employers are located, and landlords here are accustomed to group rentals. Four people can share a four-bedroom townhouse for half the price of a one-bedroom apartment. If you prefer your very own digs, 16th Street and the side streets north of Park Road are lined with charming old apartment buildings. Like a vintage convertible with tail fins and some duct tape on the seats, these buildings might not be in mint condition, but they have character.

Mt. Pleasant Street attracts locals and visitors alike to its dollar stores and *tiendas*, to beloved eateries like Haydee's and Heller's Bakery, and to newer hangouts including The People Garden juice bar and Dos Gringos café, all in a two-block stretch between Kenyon Street and Park Road NW. And the nightlife of Adams Morgan is just around the corner. In addition, no Mt. Pleasant address is more than a few blocks from Rock Creek Park, perfect for walkers and cyclists (see **Greenspace**).

Across 16th Street, **Columbia Heights** stretches east toward Georgia Avenue NW. This is a changing neighborhood—after decades of decline, young homebuyers are buying inexpensive townhouses near the new

Columbia Heights Metro station. The grand old Tivoli Theater at 14th Street and Park Road has been renovated and now houses the Gala Hispanic Theatre troupe as well as shops. Like neighboring Mt. Pleasant, the neighborhood is mostly Latino, and Spanish is the primary language in many of the carry-outs lining 14th Street on the hill down toward Shaw.

Online Resources: www.mtpleasantdc.org, www.innercity.org/columbiaheights, www.intowner.com, http://groups.yahoo.com/group/columbia_heights

Zip Code: 20010

Post Office: Kalorama Station, 2300 18th St. NW

Police Station: Third District Headquarters, 1620 V St. NW, 202-673-6930

Emergency Hospital: Howard University Hospital, 2401 Georgia Ave. NW, 202-865-6100

Library: Mt. Pleasant, 3160 16th St. NW, 202-671-0200

Public High School: Bell Multicultural High School, 3145 Hiatt Place NW, 202-673-7314

Government: Ward 1

Neighborhood Festival: Mt. Pleasant Day (June)

Parks: Lamont (Mt. Pleasant & Lamont streets NW); Piney Branch (points of access off 17th and Mt. Pleasant streets NW); Rock Creek (points of access off Park Rd. and Porter St. NW)

Community Resources: *Gala Hispanic Theatre at Tivoli Square,* 14th St & Park Rd. NW, 202-234-7174, www.galatheatre.org.

Public Transportation: Metrobus routes: 42 (Mt. Pleasant St. NW), S2-S4 (16th St. NW). Walk to Metro, Columbia Heights (Green Line)

ADAMS MORGAN

Boundaries: **North**: Euclid St. NW, Calvert St. NW; **East**: 16th St. NW; **South**: T St. NW; **West**: 19th St. NW

Location: north of Dupont Circle; east of Kalorama; south of Mt. Pleasant; west of Columbia Heights (across Malcolm X Park)

Adams Morgan is a hopping, culturally diverse neighborhood, where locals and visitors can dine out on Ethiopian, West African, Italian, Mexican, Thai, Salvadoran, French, South American, Indian, Chinese, Middle Eastern, and Jamaican cuisine, and adjourn for coffee and dessert at a neighborhood coffeehouse—perhaps Tryst, at 2459 18th Street NW, a couch-and-coffee-table nightspot, or Jolt 'n' Bolt, at 18th & T, featuring a cozy courtyard and a good selection of pastries and fruit smoothies. Little grocery stores, gift shops, and magazine stores catering to the Latino,

NEWCOMER'S HANDBOOK FOR MOVING TO AND LIVING IN WASHINGTON D.C.

46

Ethiopian, and West African communities dot the neighborhood. In addition, the bustling commercial strips along 18th Street and Columbia Road offer the practical basics—a hardware store, a post office, and a Safeway supermarket. City Bikes, at Columbia Road and Champlain Street, is the outfitter of choice for bicycle commuters and couriers.

Adams Morgan got its name when the principals of the predominantly white Adams School and the predominantly black Morgan School called residents together to improve the neighborhood. That 1956 meeting was called "the Adams Morgan Better Neighborhood Conference," and the same cooperative spirit still characterizes the neighborhood today. Many young professionals, especially nonprofit workers from Dupont Circle offices a few blocks south, reside here. Most of the housing here is prewar apartment houses or row houses converted to apartments, and just about every building has a roof deck.

Living in a popular neighborhood has its price: $1,200 for a studio apartment is typical. There are a few blocks south of Columbia Road near 16th Street where rentals are less expensive, but for most young professionals, living in Adams Morgan means sharing an apartment or house.

The enticing shopping and dining strip along 18th Street is always crowded with pedestrians and choked with traffic; however, poorly lit side streets can be unsafe late at night. Muggings are a persistent problem—not an epidemic, statistically, but always a concern for pedestrians. The biggest problem in Adams Morgan, though, is parking—particularly on weekends, which here seem to begin on Thursdays. The chronic parking shortage is being addressed with a new parking garage at 18th and Belmont, out of sight behind the shops. Also, in an attempt to ease the parking problem, "Adams Morgan" was added to the name of the Woodley Park-Zoo Metro station in 1999. The idea was to inspire more people to take public transportation to Adams Morgan, but the station is actually a 15-minute walk away, across Rock Creek Park. Evenings and weekends, there are shuttle buses every 15 minutes from the station and from the U Street-Cardozo station; also, the Dupont Circle station is a short ride away on the crowded No. 42 bus.

Online Resources: http://adamsmorgan.net, www.anc1c.org, www.
  intowner.com, http://groups.yahoo.com/group/AdamsMorgan
Zip Code: 20009
Post Offices: Kalorama Station, 2300 18th St NW; Temple Heights
  Station, 1921 Florida Ave. NW
Police Station: Third District Headquarters, 1620 V St. NW, 202-673-6930
Emergency Hospital: Howard University Hospital, 2401 Georgia Ave.
  NW, 202-865-6100
Library: Mt. Pleasant, 3160 16th St. NW, 202-671-0200
Public High Schools: Bell Multicultural High School, 3145 Hiatt Place

NW, 202-673-7314; Cardozo Senior High School, 1300 Clifton St. NW, 202-673-7385

Government: Ward 1

Neighborhood Festivals: Latino Summer Fiesta (Marie Reed Elementary School, August); Adams Morgan Day (September), www.adamsmorganday.org

Parks: Malcolm X (16th St. NW between W and Euclid streets), Rock Creek (points of access off Harvard St. NW and the Duke Ellington Bridge)

Community Resources: *D.C. Arts Center,* gallery and performance space, 2438 18th St. NW, 202-462-7833; *Meridian International Center,* a nonprofit agency promoting international exchange through the arts, 1630 Crescent Place NW, 202-667-6800, www.meridian.org; *One World Media Center,* a nonprofit video production studio providing equipment and training to amateur filmmakers, 2390 Champlain St. NW, 202-667-9038, www.owmc.org; *Scottish Rite Center for Language Disorders,* Children's National Medical Center, 1630 Columbia Rd. NW, 202-939-4703, www.cnmc.org.

Public Transportation: Metrobus routes: 42 (Columbia Rd. NW), 90-98 (U St. NW)

SHAW

LOGAN CIRCLE

Boundaries: **North**: Florida Ave. NW; **East**: North Capitol St; **South**: Massachusetts Ave. NW; **West**: 16th St. NW

Location: north of Penn Quarter; east of Adams Morgan and Dupont Circle; south of Columbia Heights and Howard University; west of Eckington and NoMa

If you saw Matthew Broderick in *Glory*, you're familiar with Col. Robert Gould Shaw, who commanded the Army's first African-American regiment during the Civil War. The neighborhood that bears his name is vast and diverse, spanning the heart of midtown D.C. This is where jazz legend Duke Ellington made his debut, in an auditorium in the city's first office building designed, built, and owned by African-Americans—the True Reformer Building, which still stands at 13th & U streets NW.

After two decades of decline and middle-class flight, **Shaw** began a slow, steady recovery in the 1990s. Young professionals moved into under-priced townhouses off U Street NW between 7th and 16th, driving property values back up—and driving some long-time residents out. For now,

NEWCOMER'S HANDBOOK FOR MOVING TO AND LIVING IN WASHINGTON D.C.

48

the neighborhood is racially and economically diverse, but lower-income residents and lower-rent businesses are struggling to stay. In the long run, it's a good bet that Shaw will manage to retain its diversity and heritage— old and new residents alike take pride in the community, attend civic association meetings, and do volunteer work. It's not unusual to see someone fixing a bike for a kid next door, or getting up early on Saturday to remove graffiti from a public playground.

Shaw is home to dozens of charitable organizations, most notably the Whitman-Walker Clinic (one of the world's first and largest AIDS clinics, headquartered at 14th and S); Bread for the City, a multi-service center at 7th and P; and Manna, the city's largest nonprofit housing developer. One of the city's biggest playgrounds is here, too: John F. Kennedy Memorial Playground at 7th and O.

The Reeves Center, at 14th & U streets NW, is a municipal office building—the Department of Public Works, the Office of Campaign Finance, the Lottery Commission, and other D.C. agencies are headquartered here. Outside, there are a few sit-down restaurants and many fast-food outlets. A block north, at 2114 14th Street, is one of the city's oldest soup kitchens, Martha's Table. Head east along U Street for trendy nightclubs. Ben's Chili Bowl, the city's sentimental favorite restaurant, is at 12th and U streets NW, next to the historic Lincoln Theatre. To the south are three community theaters: the Source, the Studio, and Living Stage, all on 14th Street NW between P and U streets. Head west on U Street for antique furniture and vintage clothing.

The **Logan Circle** area, around 13th and P, is known as a red light district, though it is also known for grand, expensive brick townhouses and historic mansions. A Fresh Fields supermarket at 14th & P caters to the upscale Logan Circle crowd.

At the south end of Shaw is the new Washington Convention Center, the largest building in the city—three blocks long. Two industrial sump pumps will hum around the clock for decades to come, to keep the underground river displaced by the gargantuan building from gushing into people's basements.

Online Resources: www.shawdc.com, www.logancircle.org, www. intowner.com, http://groups.yahoo.com/group/ustnews, http:// groups.yahoo.com/group/LoganCircleNews

Zip Codes: 20001, 20009

Post Office: T Street Station, 1915 14th St. NW

Police Stations: Third District Headquarters, 1620 V St. NW, 202-673-6930; Traffic Branch, 5th St. and New York Ave. NW, 202-727-4435

Emergency Hospital: Howard University Hospital, 2401 Georgia Ave. NW, 202-865-6100

Libraries: Watha T. Daniel, 8th St. & Rhode Island Ave. NW, 202-671-0212; Sursum Corda, 1st St. & New York Ave. NW, 202-724-4772

Public High Schools: Cardozo, 1300 Clifton St. NW, 202-673-7385; Dunbar, 1301 New Jersey Ave. NW, 202-673-7233

Government: West of 14th St., Ward 2 south of U St. and Ward 1 to the north; east of 14th St., Ward 2 south of S St. and Ward 1 to the north

Neighborhood Festivals: One Common Unity Festival, http://the movement.org

Parks: Logan Circle; Malcolm X (16th St. NW between W and Euclid streets)

Community Resources: *African-American Civil War Memorial*, "Spirit of Freedom" statue and museum, Vermont Ave. & U St. NW, 202-667-2667, www.afroamcivilwar.org; *Howard University* (see Higher Education); *Bread for the City*, 1525 7th St. NW, 202-265-2400, www.breadforthecity.org; *Martha's Table*, 202-328-6608; *Whitman-Walker Clinic*, 202-797-3500, www.wwc.org. The *Shaw EcoVillage Project*, www.shawecovillage.com, trains young people to take leadership roles in improving the quality of life in their neighborhood. Theaters (see **Cultural Life**): *Lincoln Theater, Source Theatre, Studio Theatre, Living Stage. Greater U Street Heritage Trail* is a self-guided tour of historical and cultural sites from the age of Duke Ellington. Free trail guides available from *Cultural Tourism D.C.*, 202-661-7581, www.culturaltourismdc.org. *U.S. Chess Center*, 1501 M St. NW, 202-857-4922, www.chessctr.org.

Public Transportation: Metro: Shaw-Howard University (Green Line), entrances at 7th & S streets NW and 8th & R streets NW; U St-Cardozo (Green Line), entrances at 13th & U streets NW and 10th St. & Vermont Ave. NW; Mt. Vernon Square (Green and Yellow lines), 7th & M streets NW. Note that the "Shaw-Howard University" station is actually more than half a mile downhill from Howard University. Metrobus routes: 52/54 (14th St. NW), 70-73 (7th St. NW), 90-98 (U St. NW)

BROOKLAND

Boundaries: **North**: Providence Hospital; **East**: South Dakota Ave. NE; **South**: Rhode Island Ave. NE, Franklin St. NE; **West**: Catholic University

Location: north of Brentwood and Eckington; east of Catholic University; south of Providence Hospital and Michigan Park; west of Mt. Rainier, Md.

Nuns, monks, and priests are a common sight on the streets of **Brookland**, home of the Catholic University of America and the flagship Roman Catholic Church in the United States, the blue-domed Basilica of

NEWCOMER'S HANDBOOK FOR MOVING TO AND LIVING IN WASHINGTON D.C.

50

the National Shrine of the Immaculate Conception. Across the railroad tracks from campus and the Shrine, Brookland has the look and feel of a suburban town—there are a garden club, lots of settled families, and well-attended community meetings. There are also plenty of opportunities to give back to the community; at Byte Back, for instance, volunteers help homeless adults learn computer skills in order to get jobs. Others help stock the shelves at nearby Capital Area Food Bank, where the city's soup kitchens and shelters do their wholesale shopping.

You'll also find comfortable nightspots close by, including the venerable Col. Brooks' Tavern and Kelly's Ellis Island Pub. On 12th Street NE is a strip of practical shops, including a pharmacy, hardware store, gas station, and eateries. A few blocks away, at 3225 8th Street NE, Dance Place offers classes and recitals.

East of 12th Street, Brookland is a quiet residential neighborhood, with tree-lined streets and an eclectic assortment of houses—Victorians, Georgians, Queen Annes, bungalows, even the occasional ranch house. Many are a century old, and most have bigger yards than the typical D.C. home. Some of the larger houses are actually monasteries or convents.

Brookland's 21st-century claim to fame is the postal anthrax scare of late 2001. Like most of the capital city's mail, the tainted letters were processed at the Brentwood postal facility just across Rhode Island Avenue from here. Hundreds of Brookland residents turned out for candlelight vigils in support of the postal workers.

Walk to the Brookland Metro station for a 10-minute ride downtown, or use the station as an underpass to cross the railroad tracks and take in a concert at the Shrine or the university. As you ride the Metro on elevated tracks toward Capitol Hill, you can see the route of the planned Metropolitan Branch Trail, a commuter-oriented bike path that will eventually link Silver Spring to Capitol Hill.

Online Resources: http://groups.yahoo.com/group/Brookland, www.capitalcommunitynews.com/dcnorth.cfr

Zip Codes: 20017, 20018

Post Office: Brookland Station, 12th and Monroe streets NE

Police Station: Fifth District Headquarters, 1805 Bladensburg Rd. NE, 202-727-4510

Emergency Hospital: Providence Hospital, 1150 Varnum St. NE, 202-269-7000

Library: Woodridge Regional Library, 18th St. & Rhode Island Ave. NE, 202-541-6226

Public High School: Moore Academy, 1001 Monroe St. NE, 202-576-7005

Government: Ward 5

Neighborhood Festival: Brookland Community Day (September)

Parks: Fort Bunker Hill (east of 13th St. NE between Otis and Perry streets); Turkey Thicket (west of Michigan Ave. NE north of Perry St.)

Community Resources: *Byte Back*, 3430 9th St. NE, 202-529-3395, www.byteback.org; *Capital Area Food Bank*, 645 Taylor St. NE, 202-526-5344; *Catholic University of America* (see **Higher Education**); *Dance Place*, 202-269-1600, www.danceplace.org; *Franciscan Monastery* (see **Greenspace**); *National Shrine* (see **Places of Worship**); *Trinity College* (see **Higher Education**)

Public Transportation: Metro: Brookland (Red Line), off Michigan Ave. at the railroad tracks. Metrobus routes: H2-H6 (Michigan Ave.), R4 (Michigan Ave.), G8 (Monroe St)

ANACOSTIA

Boundaries: North: Anacostia River, Pennsylvania Ave. SE; **South**: St. Elizabeths Hospital; **East**: Alabama Ave. SE; **West**: South Capitol St.

Location: north of St. Elizabeths Hospital and Congress Heights; east of the Washington Navy Yard (across the Anacostia River) and Bolling Air Force Base; south of Marshall Heights; west of Hillcrest

Here's a secret: You can visit Anacostia, even live here, and not get shot. Despite its reputation as a tough neighborhood, police statistics show that the number of violent crimes per year in the Anacostia police district is consistently below the citywide average. There are signs of drug trafficking—tiny plastic bags on the sidewalk, the kind of bags used for crack cocaine—but the drug trade and related gang strife seldom involve people who are minding their own business. It's not the ideal place to raise kids, but young adults shouldn't automatically skip real estate listings just because they're "east of the river"—the Anacostia River.

The neighborhoods east of the river are almost exclusively African-American. Though the struggling parts of Southeast D.C. are dotted with pockets of middle-class housing, Anacostia did not benefit from the economic boom of the late 1990s, and even now this area struggles to attract grocery stores and sit-down restaurants to its neglected streets. However, living here is cheap and convenient. It's a 75-cent bus ride to the Anacostia Metro station, and from there, Capitol Hill and the Smithsonian are less than 10 minutes away. For young federal workers at the Transportation, HUD, or Energy departments, it certainly would make commuting easy. And the Navy offices and contractors in the renovated Southeast Federal Center complex are just one Metro stop away, near the Navy Yard station.

NEWCOMER'S HANDBOOK FOR MOVING TO AND LIVING IN WASHINGTON D.C.

52

There's a lot of parkland east of the river, as well as one of the Smithsonian's more obscure museums. The Anacostia Museum in Fort Stanton Park is the Smithsonian's museum of African-American history. And, throughout all the ups and downs of his political career spanning five decades, Marion Barry has lived in Anacostia, not far from the historic home of abolitionist Frederick Douglass. The Douglass estate, Cedar Hill, is a museum of the abolitionist movement. The human rights activist lived here, at 14th & W streets SE, from 1877 to 1895.

The name "Anacostia" is applied loosely to most of Southeast D.C. east of the river. The Anacostia historic district is the area straddling Good Hope Road, overlooking the river. To the south along Martin Luther King Jr. Avenue is St. Elizabeths Hospital, the federal mental institution whose sprawling campus dates back to the Civil War. South of the hospital, at 2737 Martin Luther King Jr. Avenue SE, is Players Lounge, one of the few popular nightspots east of the river.

Again, it's not right for everybody, but worth investigating.

Online Resources: www.capitalcommunitynews.com/eotr.cfr, http://groups.yahoo.com/group/east_of_the_river

Zip Code: 20020

Post Offices: Anacostia Station, 2650 Naylor Road SE; Randle Station, 2306 Prout St. SE

Police Station: Seventh District Headquarters, 2455 Alabama Ave. SE, 202-698-1500

Emergency Hospital: Greater Southeast Community Hospital, 1310 Southern Ave. SE, 202-574-6000

Libraries: Anacostia, 1800 Good Hope Rd. SE, 202-698-1190; Francis Gregory, 3660 Alabama Ave. SE, 202-645-4297

Public High Schools: Anacostia, 1601 16th St. SE, 202-645-3000; Ballou, 3401 4th St. SE, 202-645-3400

Government: Ward 8

Neighborhood Festival: Unifest (May), 202-678-8822

Parks: Anacostia (along the Anacostia River between the Whitney Young Bridge and Bolling Air Force Base); Fort Stanton (off Naylor Rd. SE near 27th St.)

Community Resources: *Anacostia Museum* (see **Cultural Life**); *Frederick Douglass National Historic Site*, 202-426-5961, www.nps.gov/frdo.

Public Transportation: Metro: Anacostia (Green Line), Howard Road & Firth Sterling Ave. SE; Congress Heights (Green Line), 13th St. & Alabama Ave. SE. Metrobus routes: A2-A48 (Martin Luther King Jr. Ave. SE); W1-W8 (Alabama Ave. SE); 90-93 (8th St. SE)

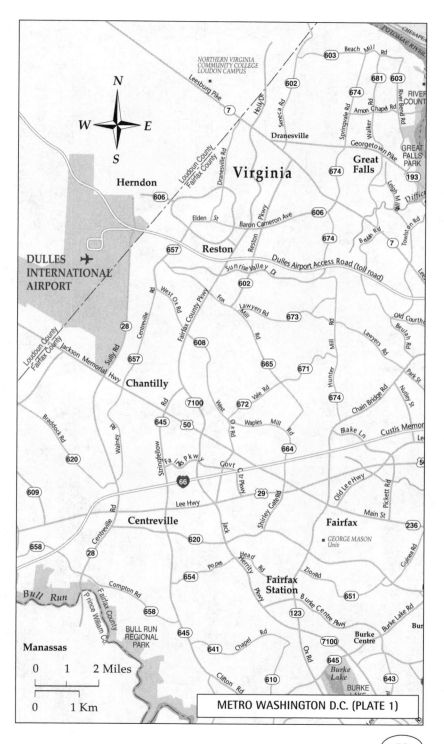

METRO WASHINGTON D.C. (PLATE 1)

53

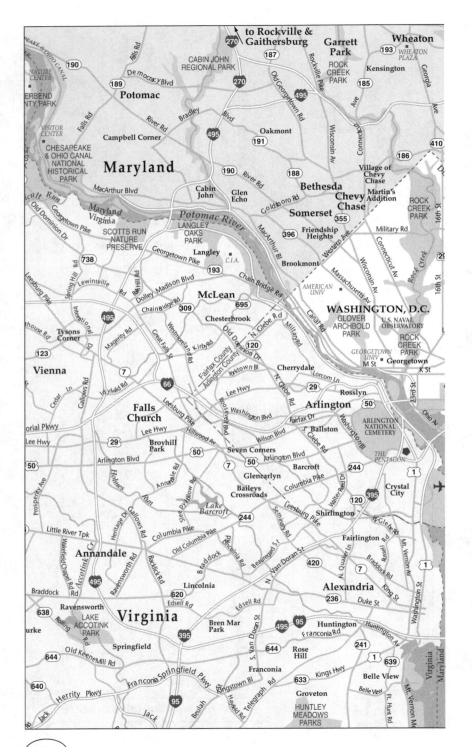

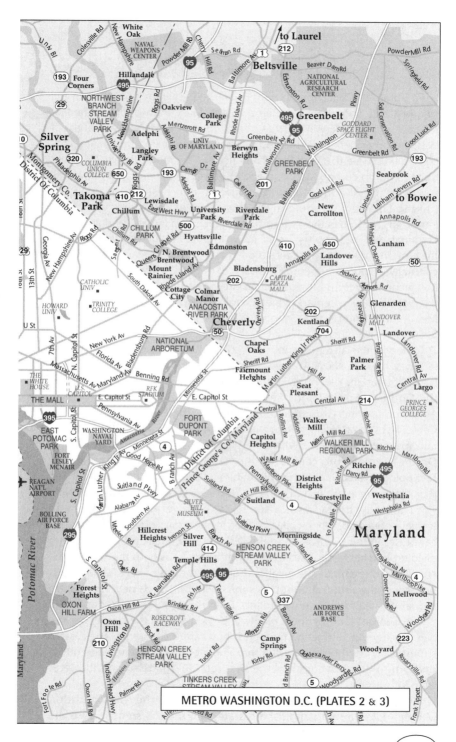

METRO WASHINGTON D.C. (PLATES 2 & 3)

NEWCOMER'S HANDBOOK FOR MOVING TO AND LIVING IN WASHINGTON D.C.

56

MARYLAND

Long before the First Amendment guaranteed religious freedom in the United States, the colonial settlement at St. Mary's City adopted the first religious tolerance law in North America. Today, the Maryland suburbs of Washington are a cultural melting pot, the cosmopolitan population center of a little state that calls itself "America in Miniature." Barely 300 miles from corner to corner, Maryland encompasses coal mines and paper mill towns in the Allegheny Mountains; crab and oyster fishing on the Chesapeake Bay; shipping in the busy port of Baltimore, with most imported cars sold in the eastern United States arriving at Dundalk Marine Terminal; and vast poultry farms, including the Perdue conglomerate on the eastern shore. There are tobacco farms in Southern Maryland— which, culturally, is more southern than much of Virginia; software and information technology firms are clustered in Greenbelt and Columbia; and one of the world's leading centers of biotechnology research, with companies like MedImmune and Human Genome Sciences, lines the I-270 corridor from Bethesda to Frederick.

Maryland is also home to hundreds of square miles of major federal facilities: the U.S. Naval Academy, Andrews Air Force Base, Patuxent River Naval Air Station, Camp David, the National Agricultural Research Center, the Goddard Space Flight Center, the National Institutes of Health, Aberdeen Proving Ground, and Fort Meade. The Naval Surface Warfare Center has several facilities here, including an eye-catching 1,800-foot-long tank just outside Bethesda where the Navy tests scale models of new ships. On the Gaithersburg campus of the National Institute of Standards & Technology, you can visit a small exhibit and see the gray metal block and stick that serve as the nation's official, definitive kilogram and meter.

Naturally, the suburbs attract a lot of government workers and techies—educated, white-collar, middle-income folks employed at federal campuses in the suburbs. As in the District, Rock Creek provides a rough dividing line between upscale neighborhoods, mostly to the west of the creek, and more moderate neighborhoods to the east. There is little abject poverty in the suburbs, although some neighborhoods near the eastern corner of the District are struggling. Even though the demographics in Prince George's County show plenty of buying power, the county has not had an easy time attracting high-end shops and restaurants. The eastern suburbs are often perceived as a stepping stone for those moving out of decaying neighborhoods in the District—an image uncharitable to both jurisdictions.

Beyond the Baltimore-Washington area and the I-270 corridor, Maryland is a farming and fishing state, and there is some industry in Western Maryland and on the upper reaches of the Bay. The culture clash between urban and rural Maryland often leads to tense politics in Annapolis and a divided delegation in Congress. In a traditionally Democratic state, rural conservatives grew increasingly vocal in the 1980s and '90s; some gubernatorial elections were so close, even after recounts, that the losing candidate never did concede. Even within the suburbs, though, the overwhelmingly Democratic county councils wage heated debates about sprawl, highways, mass transit, and the growing pains of a region that is expected to gain another million residents by 2025.

In the cultural sense, you're still "inside the Beltway" here—people actually attend zoning hearings, speak in federal jargon and acronyms, work long hours, and consider themselves devoted public servants and important leaders. And many are.

Capital: Annapolis

Governor: 410-974-3901 or 800-811-8336, www.gov.state.md.us

Maryland General Assembly: 301-970-5400 or 800-492-7122, mlis.state.md.us

Official Web Sites: www.maryland.gov, www.sailor.lib.md.us

Newspaper of Record: *Baltimore Sun*, 410-332-6000 or 800-829-8000; circulation, 410-539-1280; www.baltimoresun.com

MONTGOMERY COUNTY

Montgomery County is one of the most educated places in the world—roughly 90% of residents over age 25 have college degrees. Home to the National Institutes of Health and the National Institute of Standards & Technology, the county is emerging as a center of the biotech industry.

Rapid population growth is changing the county. There are nearly a million people here; about 100,000 arrived in the 1990s, many settling into new townhouse complexes in the northern part of the county. In fact, in the '90s, the population of the outer suburbs here surpassed that of the inner suburbs, and urban sprawl became the dominant issue in local politics. Schools and transportation systems are struggling to keep up with the growth.

Housing, however, is readily available. There are plenty of government workers, military and diplomatic families, scientists, and other mobile types coming and going, putting houses on the market for rent and for sale. Renting here can be a bargain compared to the District—the rent you'd pay for a one-bedroom apartment in Adams Morgan would get you a two-bedroom house in Silver Spring.

Montgomery County stretches from the Potomac River east to the Patuxent, and from D.C. north to Sugarloaf, a little mountain rising 1,300 feet over I-270. At White's Ferry, at the western tip of the county, the last auto ferry making regular trips across the Potomac bears the name of

NEWCOMER'S HANDBOOK FOR MOVING TO AND LIVING IN WASHINGTON D.C.

58

General Jubal Early, whose Confederate troops crossed the river here in 1864 to attack Washington. Across the county, the tiny village of Brookeville proudly reminds visitors that it served as the nation's capital for a day, in 1814, when President Madison retreated there during the British invasion of Washington.

The county takes its name from General Richard Montgomery, who was killed in 1775 leading the Continental Army against the British in Quebec.

Government Information: 240-777-1000, www.montgomerycounty md.gov

County Executive: Executive Office Building, 101 Monroe St., Rockville, 240-777-2500; www.montgomerycountymd.gov

County Council: nine members—five representing districts, four elected at large: Council Office Building, 100 Maryland Ave., Rockville, 240-777-7900, www.montgomerycountymd.gov

Public Schools: 301-279-3000, www.mcps.k12.md.us

Libraries: 240-777-0002, www.montgomerylibrary.org

Police: 301-279-8000, www.montgomerycountymd.gov

Area Codes: 301, 240

Median Home Price: $365,000

Cost of Living: $65,000

Online Guide: www.montgomerycountymd.gov (click on "Residents," then on "Newcomers")

BETHESDA

FRIENDSHIP HEIGHTS
NORTH BETHESDA
SOMERSET
POTOMAC

Boundaries: North: Montrose Rd.; **East**: Wisconsin Ave., Rockville Pike; **South**: District of Columbia; **West**: Seven Locks Rd.

On the west side of Rock Creek, between the old-money citadels of Chevy Chase and the semi-rural estates of Potomac, **Bethesda** is an upscale city of mid-career professionals and their families. Some work nearby as doctors or scientists at the National Institutes of Health or the National Naval Medical Center, both of which occupy huge campuses off Wisconsin Avenue.

The **Friendship Heights** area, which straddles the D.C.-Maryland line, is a shopping and dining destination. This stretch of Wisconsin Avenue is a culinary melting pot full of Mongolian barbecue, local micro-brews, and the Washington area's first Cheesecake Factory. To the north, along Rockville Pike in **North Bethesda**, is a meat-and-potatoes shopping corridor; people flock here for everything from home furnishings and toys to major appliances and cars.

Between Friendship Heights and the naval hospital, Bethesda has its own "downtown," with offices and a bustling restaurant scene near the Metro station. Bethesda even has its own suburb, the little incorporated town of **Somerset**, located between the Chevy Chase Country Club and Little Falls Branch Park. Lining the streets in this little town (population 1,000) are old cottages and colonials. Graced with real Japanese cherry trees, Somerset was one of Maryland's first designated "Tree Cities."

Most of the homes in North Bethesda are standard postwar suburban styles—ramblers, split-levels, bungalows—with garages and ample yards; closer to the District line are older colonials with smaller yards and bigger trees. There are several huge apartment high-rises just off Rockville Pike, and smaller high-rises closer to downtown Bethesda. Bethesda is a safe community with first-rate schools and convenient access to the District, yet housing is more affordable and abundant than you might expect. Thanks to families whose work takes them overseas for a few years at a time, there is a steady rental market here.

Potomac, to the west, is mansion country. This is the Maryland side of the Great Falls area, just as fashionable and pricey as the Virginia side—but Potomac tends to have residents with "newer" money: celebrities, senators, doctors, and lawyers, not the 18th-century families of Northern Virginia. The homes are newer here than across the river, but the yards are just as vast, the winding lanes just as long, and the public transportation just as nonexistent.

Web Sites: www.bethesda.org, www.erols.com/friendshiptsvillage, www.townofsomerset.com

Zip Codes: 20814, 20815, 20817, 20852, 20854

Post Offices: Bethesda, 7400 Wisconsin Ave.; Bethesda Annex, 7001 Arlington Rd.; Friendship Heights, 5530 Wisconsin Ave.; 301-941-2694; West Bethesda, 9601 Seven Locks Rd.

Police Station: Bethesda District, 7359 Wisconsin Ave., 301-657-0119 (commander), 301-279-8000 (Community Concerns Line)

Emergency Hospital: Suburban Healthcare System, 8600 Old Georgetown Rd., 301-896-3100

Libraries: Bethesda Regional, 7400 Arlington Rd., 301-986-4300; Davis, 6400 Democracy Blvd., 301-897-2200; Little Falls, 5501 Massachusetts Ave., 301-320-4880; Potomac, 10101 Glenolden Dr., 301-983-4475

Public High Schools: Bethesda-Chevy Chase, 4301 East-West Highway, 301-649-8280; Walter Johnson, 6400 Rock Spring Dr., 301-571-6900; Walt Whitman, 7100 Whittier Blvd., Bethesda, 301-320-6600; Winston Churchill, 11300 Gainsborough Rd., Potomac, 301-469-1220

NEWCOMER'S HANDBOOK FOR MOVING TO AND LIVING IN WASHINGTON D.C.

60

Government: 8th Congressional District; Montgomery County Council District 1; Somerset Town Hall, 301-657-3211

Neighborhood Festivals: Literary Festival (various locations, April); Imagination Bethesda Children's Arts Festival (Woodmont Ave. & Elm St., June); Bethesda Grand Prix of Cycling (Woodmont Ave., June); Taste of Bethesda (along Norfolk Ave., October); Bethesda Row Arts Festival (Bethesda & Woodmont avenues, October); for more information, call the Bethesda Urban Partnership, 301-215-6660, or visit www.bethesda.org.

Major Parks: Cabin John (off Westlake Dr. south of Tuckerman Lane); C&O Canal (points of access along MacArthur Blvd.); Little Falls Branch (along Little Falls Branch between Bradley Blvd. and the Potomac River); Rock Creek (points of access off Cedar Lane, Grosvenor Lane, and Kensington Parkway); Watts Branch Stream Valley (along Watts Branch between Wootton Parkway and River Rd.)

Community Resources: *Discovery Trail* is a self-guided tour of two dozen works of public art—sculptures, fountains, and murals—in downtown Bethesda. Start at Bethesda Metro Center (outside the Metro station) and follow the signs, or contact the Bethesda Urban Partnership for a map: www.bethesda.org or 301-215-6660. The web site also lists private art galleries and studios in Bethesda. *Capital Crescent Trail* commuter bike path from Georgetown to Silver Spring—for information, call 202-234-4874 or visit www.cctrail.org. Glen Echo, Goldsboro Rd. & MacArthur Blvd.; see **Greenspace** for details. *National Library of Medicine*, 10301 Baltimore Ave.; see **Cultural Life** for details. *The Music Center at Strathmore*, Strathmore Ave. & Rockville Pike; see **Cultural Life** for details. *The Writer's Center* is a facility and a membership organization offering workshops, classes, and special events for local writers. The center also publishes the nation's oldest poetry journal (*PoetLore*, established 1889) and a newsletter for writers: 4508 Walsh St., Bethesda, 301-654-8664, www.writer.org.

Public Transportation: Metro: Bethesda, Medical Center, Grosvenor and White Flint stations (Red Line); Metrobus routes: J1-J3 (Silver Spring, Montgomery Mall), J8-J9 (Gaithersburg), and 14 series (Tysons Corner); Ride On routes: 27-42 & 46 (local), 70 (I-270 corridor), and 92 (free downtown Bethesda loop shuttle)

CHEVY CHASE

**MARTIN'S ADDITIONS
FARMINGTON
VILLAGE OF CHEVY CHASE**

Boundaries: North: Jones Bridge Rd.; **East**: Rock Creek; **South**: District of Columbia; **West**: Wisconsin Ave.

Named for a medieval English battlefield (not the actor), **Chevy Chase** is a patrician bastion of stately homes, big trees, and two of the area's oldest country clubs, Chevy Chase and Columbia. This area, nestled between the District and East-West Highway, is where the "old" families of Washington play tennis and entertain in drawing rooms. Among the nation's wealthiest neighborhoods, Chevy Chase does not feel as ostentatious as you might expect; it's a kid-friendly, dog-walking neighborhood, however pricey.

While Chevy Chase proper is decidedly upscale, there are some more affordable sections closer to Rock Creek. Postwar ramblers and split-levels line the winding streets of the neighborhoods officially called **Martin's Additions** and **Farmington**—but politely just called Chevy Chase.

In addition to picture-perfect houses, there is picture-perfect greenspace here: the Woodend estate, 8940 Jones Mill Road, which belongs to the Audubon Naturalist Society (a local organization not to be confused with the National Audubon Society). The 40-acre grounds bordering Rock Creek Park are a flourishing nature preserve, attracting deer, foxes, owls, and other woodland species to this rich habitat. Annual events at the mansion include a wildlife art show and a holiday fair.

Local government can be confusing here—the separate jurisdictions of the town of Chevy Chase and the incorporated Village of Chevy Chase look and feel the same. The Village is the area between Chevy Chase Country Club and the District, and parts of the area east of Connecticut Avenue.
Web Sites: www.townofchevychase.org, www.ccvillage.org
Zip Code: 20815
Post Office: Chevy Chase Branch, 5910 Connecticut Ave.
Police Station: Bethesda District, 7359 Wisconsin Ave., 301-657-0119 (commander), 301-279-8000 (Community Concerns Line)
Emergency Hospital: Suburban Healthcare System, 8600 Old Georgetown Rd., Bethesda, 301-896-3100
Library: Chevy Chase, 8005 Connecticut Ave., 301-986-4313

NEWCOMER'S HANDBOOK FOR MOVING TO AND LIVING IN WASHINGTON D.C.

62

Public High School: Bethesda-Chevy Chase, 4301 East-West Highway, Bethesda, 301-649-8280

Government: 8th Congressional District; Montgomery County Council District 1; mayor chosen from five-member town council: Town Hall, 4301 Willow Lane, 301-654-7144; Chevy Chase Village Town Hall, 301-654-7300

Major Park: Rock Creek (points of access off East-West Highway and Jones Mill Rd.)

Community Resources: The *National 4-H Center* is a conference facility with the look and feel of a small college campus, and is one of the few visitor destinations in this predominantly residential area: 7100 Connecticut Ave., 301-961-2800 or 800-368-7432, www.4h center.org. *Woodend Mansion* is available for private functions, and the grounds are open to the public. Call 301-652-9188 or visit www.audubonnaturalist.org for seasonal hours and events.

Public Transportation: Metrobus routes: J1-J3 (Montgomery Mall, Silver Spring), L7/L8 (Friendship Heights); Ride On routes: 1 & 11 (Friendship Heights, Silver Spring)

GAITHERSBURG

MONTGOMERY VILLAGE
WASHINGTON GROVE
KENTLANDS

Boundaries: North: Warfield Rd.; **East**: Rock Creek Park, Airpark Rd.; **South**: Darnestown Rd., Shady Grove Rd.; **West**: Seneca Creek State Park

For more than a century, the **City of Gaithersburg**, right in the center of Montgomery County, marked the end of the suburbs and the beginning of the farm belt. By 1990, new subdivisions began springing up in the northern part of the county, and now a majority of the county's population is in Rockville and points north. Gaithersburg is a railroad town, founded in 1878, six years after the arrival of the Baltimore & Ohio Railroad; today, there's a stop on the commuter train line from D.C. to Brunswick, and there are still a few industrial parks along the tracks. The county fairgrounds are here, along the tracks, just west of the authentic Old Town district.

If you live in Gaithersburg and work in D.C., plan for a long commute—you'll need to take a bus, or drive, to the outermost Metro station, where you can settle in for a 35-minute ride downtown. If you work on the Hill, the MARC commuter train can get you there in 45 minutes from the heart of Old Town Gaithersburg, but there are only half a dozen trips a day.

There are plenty of jobs in the Gaithersburg area, though—not just with the biotech research firms in the I-270 corridor, but with some major non-profit employers and federal agencies. The National Geographic Society occupies a big campus here, adjacent to the park-like headquarters of the Izaak Walton League. Between these green spaces and West Diamond Avenue is the vast campus of the National Institute of Standards & Technology (NIST—but still "the Bureau" to those who lived here when it was called the National Bureau of Standards). These sites buffer Muddy Branch Park with plenty of greenspace; if you live nearby, don't be surprised to see an occasional deer in your front yard—or hear an occasional coyote nearby.

Many homes in Gaithersburg are modern townhouse condos or plain, rectangular garden apartments. There are some detached homes, especially between Old Town and Lakeforest Mall, and in the alluring, leafy old village of **Washington Grove** where no two cottages or bungalows are alike. Residents of the village buy fresh meat at an old-fashioned butcher shop, dine at the old Hershey family restaurant, and assist with an all-volunteer children's library.

North of incorporated Gaithersburg, the planned community of **Montgomery Village** offers housing at varied levels of luxury and convenience, but it's still mostly townhouses and garden apartments, and all postwar. Newcomers are lured here by the open space, from Lake Whetstone and the smaller ponds that line Montgomery Village Avenue, to the little parks that link the community golf course with the airstrip at Montgomery County Airpark.

A smaller planned community, **Kentlands**, was built in the late 1980s and early '90s in the southwest corner of Gaithersburg, with a promise of varied housing stock and an economically diverse suburban village. The jury is still out on this emerging neighborhood; while there are some housing bargains, the "village" features more Starbucks and Subway franchises than corner drugstores.

Great Seneca Creek State Park protects a vast forest west of Kentlands. North and west of the park, old farms are giving way to new subdivisions—amid fierce controversy. People move here from the city and inner suburbs in search of open space and quiet surroundings, but so do other people seeking the same, and pretty soon the outer suburbs are as congested as the places the settlers left behind. Everyone, it seems, wants to be the last to arrive.

The future of these communities—especially Kentlands and semi-rural Olney to the east—hinges on the decades-old debate about the proposed Intercounty Connector (ICC) highway, the northern arc of a proposed outer Beltway. The ICC would link northern Prince George's County with

NEWCOMER'S HANDBOOK FOR MOVING TO AND LIVING IN WASHINGTON D.C.

64

the Shady Grove Metro station south of Gaithersburg and, if Virginia law-makers have their way, a new Potomac River bridge. If you're looking for a home anywhere between Gaithersburg and Rockville, ask detailed questions about the latest highway plans—or you could end up living next to a superhighway in a few years.

Web Sites: www.gaithersburgmd.gov, www.kentlandsusa.com, www.washingtongrovemd.org; for official updates about the ICC, visit www.iccstudy.org, but watch for political bias in support of the controversial project

Zip Codes: 20877, 20878, 20879

Post Offices: Gaithersburg, 21 South Summit Ave.; Diamond Farms Branch, 23 Firstfield Rd.; Montgomery Village Branch, 10079 Stedwick Rd.

Police Station: Gaithersburg City Police, 7 East Cedar Ave., 301-258-6400

Emergency Hospitals: Shady Grove Adventist, 9901 Medical Center Dr., Rockville, 301-279-6000; Montgomery General, 18101 Prince Philip Dr., Olney, 301-774-8882

Libraries: Gaithersburg Regional, 18330 Montgomery Village Ave., 301-840-2515; Quince Orchard, 15831 Quince Orchard Rd., 240-777-0200

Public High Schools: Gaithersburg, 314 South Frederick Ave., 301-840-4700; Quince Orchard, 15800 Quince Orchard Rd., 301-840-4686; Watkins Mill, 10301 Apple Ridge Rd., 301-840-3959

Government: 8th Congressional District; Montgomery County Council district 3; mayor and five-member city council: City Hall, 31 South Summit Ave., 301-258-6300; Washington Grove Town Hall, 301-926-2256

Neighborhood Festivals: Olde Towne Gaithersburg Day (along East Diamond Ave., September); Labor Day parade (East Diamond Ave.); Oktoberfest at Kentlands; for information about these and other community events, call the Gaithersburg Arts & Special Events Team, 301-258-6310

Major Parks: Green Farm (off Snouffer School Rd. north of Centerway Rd.); Muddy Branch (along Muddy Branch from I-270 to the Potomac River); Rock Creek (points of access along Needwood Rd. and Muncaster Mill Rd.); Seneca Creek (points of access along Clopper Rd., Great Seneca Highway, and Riffle Ford Rd.)

Community Resources: *Activity Center at Bohrer Park* offers sports and fitness facilities, classes, leagues, and arts activities for all ages, and after-school and summer activities for teens. User fees vary. 506 South Frederick Ave., 301-258-6350. *Free summer concerts* at City Hall Concert Pavilion and at Montgomery Village Lawn Theater, 18850 Montgomery Village Ave.; check newspapers for schedules.

Montgomery County Fairgrounds, off North Frederick Ave., with entrances on Chestnut St. and Perry Pkwy., are a busy venue for commercial and civic events throughout the year—craft fairs, computer shows, concerts, a Fourth of July celebration, and more—in addition to the county fair in August. Check newspapers.

Public Transportation: Metro: Shady Grove (Red Line); MARC: Washington Grove, Gaithersburg, and Germantown stations (Brunswick Line); Ride On: 50 series (Lakeforest Mall), 60 series (Montgomery Village), and 70 series (Germantown)

GARRETT PARK

Boundaries: North: cul-de-sac off Rokeby Ave.; **East**: railroad tracks; **South**: Rock Creek; **West**: west of Kenilworth Ave.

Garrett Park, a leafy little incorporated town nestled between Rock Creek and Rockville Pike, is eccentric and always has been. The town was founded in 1898 for the express purpose of electing a local government to outlaw one high-tech resident's newfangled indoor privy. (That ordinance has since been repealed; in fact, indoor plumbing is strongly encouraged.) In 1982, a year ahead of Takoma Park, the town passed a law boycotting companies that make nuclear weapons—making Garrett Park the world's first official nuclear-free zone. The whole town is a designated arboretum and is listed on the National Register of Historic Places.

Probably the quirkiest of quirks, though, is that Garrett Park doesn't have any mail carrier routes—every residence has a post office box at the old post office down by the railroad tracks. With everyone dropping by to pick up mail, the post office is a natural center of civic life, and it's no surprise that there's a café next door.

Practically every house and garden here is picturesque, and the town is a sampler of architectural styles from old Victorians to postwar bungalows. Long before Bill Gates rediscovered the concept of "bundling," each of the distinctive "Chevy houses" in Garrett Park originally came bundled with a new Chevy in the driveway! If anyone ever decides to move away, just about every home in Garrett Park would fetch half a million dollars. Good luck!

Web Site: www.garrettpark.org

Zip Code: 20896

Post Office: Garrett Park, 4600 Waverly Ave.

Police Station: Bethesda District, 7359 Wisconsin Ave., 301-657-0119 (commander), 301-279-8000 (Community Concerns Line)

Emergency Hospital: Suburban Healthcare System, 8600 Old Georgetown Rd., Bethesda, 301-896-3100

NEWCOMER'S HANDBOOK FOR MOVING TO AND LIVING IN WASHINGTON D.C.

66

Library: Kensington Park, 4201 Knowles Ave., Kensington, 301-897-2211
Public High School: Walter Johnson, 6400 Rock Spring Dr., 301-571-6900
Government: 8th Congressional District; Montgomery County Council District 1; mayor and five-member town council: Town Hall, 10814 Kenilworth Ave., 301-933-7488
Neighborhood Festivals: Pool Opening Picnic (Memorial Day weekend) and Closing Picnic (Labor Day weekend) at Cambria & Knowles avenues; Attic-in-the-Street Sale (various locations, September)
Major Park: Rock Creek (points of access off Knowles Ave. & Beach Dr.)
Community Resources: *Penn Place*, Waverly & Rokeby avenues, houses the post office, Garrett Park Café, and a few shops and offices—it's the one-stop "downtown" Garrett Park
Public Transportation: MARC: Garrett Park (Brunswick Line); Ride On routes 5 (Silver Spring, Twinbrook), 6 (Wheaton, North Bethesda), 38 (Wheaton, Montgomery Mall)

GERMANTOWN

CLARKSBURG

Boundaries: North: Little Bennett Regional Park; **East**: Frederick Rd., Ridge Rd., Kings Valley Rd.; **South**: Seneca Creek State Park; **West**: Clopper Rd., Ten Mile Creek

City slickers dismiss these edge cities in the once-rural upcounty hills as "sprawlville," and indeed they have little history or character—they're manufactured bedroom communities for the growing biotech and aerospace workforce along I-270. The new townhouse subdivisions here are closer to Sugarloaf Mountain in Frederick County than to Rockville.

Although the area is best known for ambitious little biotech firms housed in nondescript office parks with names like Gateway Business Center, many established aerospace companies have big facilities here too—notably Fairchild, Orbital Sciences, and Comsat. (As one recruiting ad in the *Post* put it, you *do* have to be a rocket scientist to work here.)

Germantown, off 270 about five miles north of Gaithersburg, is home to a campus of Montgomery College and more than a million square feet of office space, mostly built since 1980. **Clarksburg**, to the north, was once a rural crossroads on Frederick Road, a two-lane scenic route parallel to the 12-lane interstate; now it's being developed to house 40,000 residents and 20,000 workers.

In 2005, Clarksburg became synonymous with scandal as county code inspectors discovered that developers had run afoul of height limits and other site requirements in hundreds of new townhouses. For a brief but bizarre few weeks, the government actually suspended all building permits throughout the county until new oversight rules were issued. For years to come, in Montgomery County, "Clarksburg"—like "Watergate"— might refer more to an incident than to a place.

Despite the prevalence of beige office parks and cookie-cutter $500,000 townhouses, the 270 corridor is still flanked by rural country and greenspace. Black Hill Regional Park features an artificial lake on Ten Mile Creek, and Little Bennett Regional Park protects one of the biggest woodland areas left in the county. Walk in these woods and, just out of earshot of 270, you might see more deer than people.

Web Site: www.ggchamber.org (Gaithersburg-Germantown Chamber of Commerce)

Zip Codes: 20841, 20871, 20874, 20876

Post Offices: Germantown, 12774 Wisteria Dr.; Clarksburg, 22505 Gateway Center Dr.

Police Station: Germantown District, 20000 Aircraft Dr., 301-840-2650

Emergency Hospitals: Shady Grove Adventist, 9901 Medical Center Dr., Rockville, 301-279-6000; Montgomery General, 18101 Prince Philip Dr., Olney, 301-774-8882

Library: Germantown, 12900 Middlebrook Rd., 240-777-0110

Public High Schools: Seneca Valley, 19401 Crystal Rock Dr., 301-353-8000; Watkins Mill, 10301 Apple Ridge Rd., 301-840-3959; Damascus, 25921 Ridge Rd., 301-253-7030

Government: 8th Congressional District; Montgomery County Council District 2

Major Parks: Black Hill Regional Park (Lake Ridge Dr. off Old Baltimore Rd.); Little Bennett Regional Park (points of access off Frederick Rd. and Clarksburg Rd.); Seneca Creek State Park (see **Greenspace**)

Community Resources: *BlackRock Center for the Arts* offers performance and gallery space, 12901 Town Commons Dr., Germantown, 301-528-2260, www.blackrockcenter.org.

Public Transportation: MARC: Germantown (Brunswick Line); Ride On routes 79 (Shady Grove), 82 (Clarksburg), 83 (Milestone), 97 (Gunners Lake), 98 (Seabreeze Court), 100 (Shady Grove express)

NEWCOMER'S HANDBOOK FOR MOVING TO AND LIVING IN WASHINGTON D.C.

68

KENSINGTON

TOWN OF KENSINGTON
CHEVY CHASE VIEW
FOREST GLEN

Boundaries: North: University Blvd., Decatur Ave.; **East**: Georgia Ave., Wheaton Plaza; **South**: Capital Beltway; **West**: Rock Creek

Almost synonymous with antique dealers clustered along Howard Avenue, historic **Kensington** is a railroad town originally known as Knowles Station; the commercial area grew around a Baltimore & Ohio Railroad station built to serve 19th-century developer George Knowles (rhymes with "moles"). Though modern strip malls line the main drag of Connecticut Avenue, the historic district by the railroad tracks is rivaled only by Old Town Alexandria as the best "antiquing" area inside the Beltway.

The incorporated **Town of Kensington** has a thriving civic scene, with lots of parades and community events and good-natured contested elections. Politically a left-leaning community, Kensington is the western end of a suburban granola belt that winds through Takoma Park to Mt. Rainier and Berwyn Heights. The south part of town is officially the incorporated village of **Chevy Chase View**.

The name "Kensington" is also applied loosely to the unincorporated area between the town and Wheaton, including the hilly enclave of **Forest Glen** along Capitol View Avenue. (Sorry, no Capitol views from here in this century.) Take a wrong turn and you might find yourself in a strange, semi-abandoned storybook village with a Dutch windmill, Swiss chalet, Japanese pagoda and other specimens of far-flung architecture: the campus of the old Forest Park Seminary, originally a 19th-century resort, later a women's school. The campus was last used as a convalescent home for wounded World War II veterans. Now, after years of neglect, the complex is being renovated as a unique housing development.

To the west of the seminary, looming over the south side of Kensington proper, is an even more unusual edifice: the Washington Mormon Temple, a white marble fortress crowned with tall golden spires. On an overcast night, the temple actually reflects enough light to illuminate the clouds.

Web Site: www.tok.org, www.chevychaseview.org
Zip Codes: 20895, 20902
Post Office: Kensington, 10325 Kensington Pkwy.
Police Station: Bethesda District, 7359 Wisconsin Ave. (commander), 301-279-8000 (Community Concerns Line)

Emergency Hospitals: Suburban Healthcare System, 8600 Old Georgetown Rd., Bethesda, 301-896-3100; Holy Cross, 1500 Forest Glen Rd., Silver Spring, 301-754-7000

Library: Kensington Park, 4201 Knowles Ave., 301-897-2211

Public High School: Albert Einstein, 11135 Newport Mill Rd., 301-929-2200

Government: 8th Congressional District; Montgomery County Council District 5; mayor and four-member town council: Town Office, 3710 Mitchell St., 301-949-2424. Chevy Chase View town council, 301-949-9274.

Neighborhood Festivals: Founders Day (May); Town Picnic (June); Labor Day parade and Paint the Town art show; Kite Festival (October). Contact the Town Office for details.

Major Park: Rock Creek (points of access off Knowles Ave.)

Community Resources: *Town Armory* community building, 3710 Mitchell St., available for rent, 301-949-2424. *Forest Park Seminary* grounds usually open for self-guided tours; for information, contact Save Our Seminary at 301-589-1715 or www.saveourseminary.org. *Washington Mormon Temple* visitors center and grounds (see **Places of Worship**).

Public Transportation: MARC: Kensington (Brunswick Line); Metrobus routes L7/L8 (Connecticut Avenue); Ride On routes 5 (Silver Spring, Twinbrook), 6 (Wheaton, North Bethesda), 7 (Wheaton), 33 (Glenmont, Medical Center), 34 (Wheaton, Medical Center)

ROCKVILLE

FALLSMEAD
TWINBROOK

Boundaries: North: Gude Dr.; **East**: Rock Creek Park; **South**: Montrose Rd.; **West**: Lakewood Country Club, Watts Branch Stream Valley Park

The **City of Rockville** is dominated by a little cluster of office towers housing county government offices, and north of downtown Rockville, light industrial sites line the railroad tracks. "Downtown" begins at the north end of the Rockville Pike commercial strip stretching south to Bethesda. "The Pike" here becomes Hungerford Drive, the city's main street—not the pedestrian-friendly kind, but a busy six-lane thoroughfare. In residential **Fallsmead** to the west, and in **Twinbrook**, south along Veirs Mill Road, plain postwar colonials, ramblers, and split-levels made of brick and siding line the winding streets and culs-de-sac of stable neighborhoods. The prices are good as long as you're not too close to the tracks or the constant hum of traffic on I-270, the Pike, or Veirs Mill Road.

NEWCOMER'S HANDBOOK FOR MOVING TO AND LIVING IN WASHINGTON D.C.

70

Rockville is the population center and county seat of the most affluent county in Maryland, and the city's clout in state politics is almost equal to Baltimore's. Not surprisingly, Rockville attracts a government-related crowd—contractors, lobbyists, and ambitious lawyers. Rockville, like most of the Maryland suburbs, is overwhelmingly Democratic, but there's always a referendum or ballot initiative to keep things divisive. From May to November in even-numbered years, campaign signs bloom like weeds in front of many homes.

Web Sites: www.rockvillemd.gov, www.rocknet.org

Zip Codes: 20850, 20851, 20852

Post Offices: Rockville, 500 North Washington St.; Courthouse Station, West Montgomery Ave. & South Washington St.; Pike Station, 143 Rollins Ave.; Twinbrook Shopping Center, 2001 Veirs Mill Rd.

Police Stations: Rockville City Police, City Hall, 111 Maryland Ave., 301-309-3100; Montgomery County Police Department, Rockville District, 1451 Seven Locks Rd., 301-279-1591 (commander), 301-279-1992 (Community Concerns Line)

Emergency Hospitals: Shady Grove Adventist, 9901 Medical Center Dr., 301-279-6000

Libraries: Rockville Regional, 99 Maryland Ave., 240-777-0140; Twinbrook, 202 Meadow Hall Dr., 240-777-0240

Public High Schools: Richard Montgomery (International Baccalaureate magnet providing European-style curriculum), 50 Richard Montgomery Dr., 301-279-8400; Thomas S. Wootton, 2100 Wootton Pkwy., 301-279-8550

Government: 8th Congressional District; Montgomery County Council District 3; mayor and 4-member city council: City Hall, 301-309-3000

Neighborhood Festivals: Rockville's Hometown Holidays (Washington St. & Middle Lane, May) and Spirit of Rockville (Civic Center Park, September), 301-309-3330

Major Parks: Civic Center Park/Norbeck Gardens (Edmonston Dr. off Baltimore Rd.); Rock Creek (points of access off Norbeck Rd. and Avery Rd.); Upper Watts Branch (off Nelson St.)

Community Resources: *Civic Center Park,* off Edmonston Dr. in the northeast corner of the city, includes the F. Scott Fitzgerald Theatre; historic Glenview Mansion, which houses an art gallery and ballrooms available for weddings and other private functions; and acres of woodland park along tributaries of Rock Creek. For more information, call 301-309-3001 or www.rockvillemd.gov. The *Rockville Little Theater Company,* 301-340-1417 or www.rlt-online.org, is based at the F. Scott Fitzgerald Theatre. The Civic Center also houses the Rockville Civic Ballet, Community Chorus, Brass Band, Concert Band, and a Dixieland jazz band. The *F. Scott Fitzgerald Literary Conference* is held every fall at the Rockville campus of Montgomery College; for information, call 301-309-9461 or visit http://peerlessrockville.org/FSF. *The Musical Theater Center at Wintergreen Plaza,* 837-D Rockville Pike, 301-251-5766, www.musicaltheatercenter.org, offers classes in acting, dance, music, and stagecraft for children and adults; two companies in residence perform here and on stages around Washington. *Rockville Arts Place,* 100 East Middle Lane, 301-309-6900, offers classes, camps, exhibits, studio space, and a shop selling works by local artists and craftspeople. *Suto Dance Studio,* 4511 Bestor Dr., 301-871-1000, offers classes in a variety of dance disciplines and skill levels.

Public Transportation: Metro: Rockville and Twinbrook (Red Line); MARC: Rockville station (Brunswick Line); Metrobus routes: Q1/Q2 (Veirs Mill Rd.), Y7 (Norbeck Rd.), and T2 (Falls Rd.); Ride On routes: 48-52 (Olney), 44-47 & 54-59 (local)

SILVER SPRING

Boundaries: North: Dennis Ave., Columbia Pike; **East**: Prince George's County; **South**: District of Columbia, Takoma Park; **West**: railroad tracks, 16th St.

Silver Spring is the name applied loosely to most of southern Montgomery County east of Connecticut Avenue. A real estate listing for Silver Spring might turn out to be half an hour's drive north on U.S. Route 29, in the middle of nowhere, but usually the name refers to downtown Silver Spring—a distinct commercial area capping the northern tip of D.C.—or the postwar suburbs along Sligo Creek.

Downtown Silver Spring, as the home of the American Film Institute and the Discovery Communications family of educational cable channels, is emerging as the capital of the documentary film industry. Many production companies and aspiring filmmakers set up shop here in the nonfiction equivalent of Hollywood. The downtown skyline also features the huge headquarters of the National Oceanic & Atmospheric Administration—the folks who fly research planes into hurricanes. There are apartment towers, too, taller than those allowed in the District.

The AFI and Discovery brought retail and nightlife back to a languishing older suburb. Beloved independent local restaurants hang on against new competition from trendy chains. Commuters eat at Red Lobster; locals go to Crisfield's, a venerable seafood favorite at the busy corner of Georgia Avenue and Colesville Road. Commuters go for grilled panini at Panera Bread; locals go to the vintage Tastee Diner at Georgia and Cameron Street

NEWCOMER'S HANDBOOK FOR MOVING TO AND LIVING IN WASHINGTON D.C.

72

for a "short stack," Key Lime pie, or fries smothered in brown gravy. (In 2000, by popular demand, this 1950s institution was saved from a wrecking ball—the whole diner was physically moved from its original location a few blocks away.) Up Georgia Avenue, near the north end of 16th Street, is Woodside Deli, another classic—crusty rye bread, pastrami, and matzo ball soup, as if transplanted straight from Baltimore. Locals and weekend crowds alike come to shop at Fresh Fields, Borders Books & Music, and Strosnider's hardware store. Up Georgia a few blocks, City Place mall is the only outlet mall inside the Beltway.

The Silver Spring Metro station is a major transit hub. Dozens of Ride On and Metrobus lines converge here, just a few blocks from a MARC/Amtrak stop and a Greyhound station. The free VanGo circulator bus makes a loop through the downtown business district every few minutes.

The Blair Towns townhouse complex at 16th Street & Colesville Road is the first housing project in the Washington area to earn LEED certification (Leadership in Energy & Environmental Design) from the U.S. Green Building Council. The certification is based on energy efficiency, recycled building materials, and a transit-friendly location.

The residential neighborhoods flanking Sligo Creek Park are quintessential suburbs: detached houses built just after World War II, with front and back yards, on tree-lined streets, with lots of kids running around. Most of the houses are colonials, split-levels, and ramblers, but east of Northwest Branch and Columbia Pike there are several pockets of big, stately houses with loop driveways.

If the locals catch you saying "Silver Springs," they'll know you're fresh off the turnip truck—unlike the city in Florida, there's only one silver spring here. (It's in a park near the NOAA complex, and was named for the shiny flecks of mica in the water.) But the Downtown Silver Spring Business District is fond of hanging banners that say "Silver Sprung," as part of the ongoing campaign to keep "u" in Silver Spring.

Web Sites: www.silversprung.com, www.silverspringcenter.com

Zip Codes: 20901, 20902, 20910

Post Offices: Silver Spring, 8616 Second Ave.; Aspen Hill, 14030 Connecticut Ave.; Colesville, 13217 New Hampshire Ave.; Forest Glen, 2460 Linden Lane, 301-295-7594; Silver Spring Centre, 8455 Colesville Rd.; Woodmoor, 110 University Blvd. West

Police Station: Silver Spring District, 801 Sligo Ave., 301-565-7744

Emergency Hospital: Holy Cross, 1500 Forest Glen Rd., Silver Spring, 301-754-7000

Libraries: Silver Spring, 8901 Colesville Rd., 301-565-7689; Long Branch, 8800 Garland Ave., 301-565-7585

Public High Schools: James Hubert Blake (fine arts magnet), 300 Norwood Rd., 301-879-1300; Montgomery Blair (science and communications magnets), 51 University Blvd. East, 301-649-2800; Springbrook, 201 Valley Brook Dr., 301-989-5700

Government: 5th Congressional District; Montgomery County Council District 5

Major Parks: Nolte (points of access off Dale Dr. south of Wayne Ave.); Sligo Creek (points of access off Colesville Rd., Wayne Ave., and Piney Branch Rd.); Woodside (Georgia Ave. and Spring St.)

Community Resources: American Film Institute/AFI Silver Theater & Round House Theater (see **Cultural Life** chapter). *National Capital Trolley Museum* preserves the memory of street railways in Washington and offers rides in vintage streetcars: 1313 Bonifant Rd., 301-384-6088, www.dctrolley.org. *Silver Spring Shared Community ArtSpace* is used by a variety of performing arts organizations and individual performers; at City Place, 8661 Colesville Rd., 301-589-1091.

Public Transportation: Metro: Silver Spring (Red Line); MARC, Silver Spring station (Brunswick Line); major bus system hub served by 26 Metrobus routes and 19 Ride On routes

TAKOMA PARK

LANGLEY PARK

Boundaries: North: Sligo Ave., Piney Branch Rd., University Blvd.; **East**: 14th Ave., New Hampshire Ave.; **South**: District of Columbia; **West**: Chicago Ave.

In the Birkenstocks-and-incense community of **Takoma Park**, the two-party system is Democrats and Greens. City government here boycotts the nuclear industry (so you won't find GE lightbulbs in schools or libraries) and companies that do business in Burma (so no Pepsi machines in municipal buildings). Legal aliens who own or rent homes here are allowed to vote in municipal elections and serve on the city council or school board. In addition, the city has won awards for its recycling efforts and tree conservation, and has been given the nickname "Azalea City" for the colorful bushes that bloom in many front yards in late spring. A thriving food co-op and farmers' market meet the huge demand for natural and organic food, and the neighborhood eateries along Carroll Avenue—an authentic neighborhood main street—are careful to provide vegetarian and vegan selections. Many residential streets have "speed humps" (much bigger than speed bumps, residents explain) to keep traffic from endangering cyclists, pedestrians, and children at play.

NEWCOMER'S HANDBOOK FOR MOVING TO AND LIVING IN WASHINGTON D.C.

74

The town didn't develop its hippie reputation by accident. Takoma Park was built in 1883 as a planned community, and the Seventh-Day Adventist Church—whose adherents are mostly vegetarian—became one of the first and biggest landowners here. With an Adventist hospital, college, bookstore, and churches here, Takoma Park naturally featured some of the Washington area's earliest health food stores, and the Woodstock generation settled here in search of silken tofu and veggie burgers. The town has always been on the leading edge of gay liberation, and many same-sex couples raise families here. Occasionally, a letter to the editor in the *Takoma Voice* reminds residents that there are a few conservatives in town, but most residents don't mind the affectionate references to their community as the "People's Republic of Takoma Park."

In 2005, Takoma Park became the first jurisdiction to adopt instant-runoff voting in local elections. Now, instead of choosing one candidate for mayor, city voters can rank each candidate in order of preference; if no candidate wins a majority of first-choice votes, the second-choice votes are counted. The system is intended to discourage negative campaigning—because candidates will not want to alienate opponents' supporters and lose second-choice votes. (For a complete explanation, contact the Center for Voting & Democracy at 301-270-4616 or www.fairvote.org—a national organization based, not coincidentally, in Takoma Park.)

Except for a few boxy apartment high-rises along Maple Avenue, Takoma Park's hilly, winding streets are lined with nice houses in varied styles: cozy bungalows, clapboard Victorians, and duplexes or big cottages that have been broken up into apartments. Annual building inspections ensure that landlords (and tenants) keep their rental units in good shape. Shaded with mature trees, the typical block is charming; in the spring and summer many yards burst with colorful blooms, particularly forsythia and azaleas. Some homes have tidy little watch-pocket yards, while others have Sligo Creek Park for a backyard.

Takoma Park straddles the original line between Montgomery and Prince George's counties; until 1996, the town government had to deal with courts, police departments, fire marshals, and other agencies in two counties. With hard-won permission from the state legislature, the town held a referendum on "unification" and voted to join Montgomery County.

Takoma Park has its own city police department and a fairly low crime rate, but the huge Salvadoran gang MS-13 is not unknown here. Crime and gang activity is a bigger concern across University Boulevard in **Langley Park**, in apartment complexes politely described as "affordable housing" and strip malls dominated by liquor stores.

The heart of Langley Park, the corner of University Boulevard and New Hampshire Avenue, is an inhospitable place to walk—it's notorious for pedestrians getting hit by cars—but if you're driving, it's a good place to shop for international groceries. It's mostly Latino (in particular Salvadoran, Honduran, Dominican), but it's also the home of Udupi Palace, 1329 University Boulevard East—always crowded with U of M students and Indian immigrants clamoring for the cheap, authentic vegetarian Indian fare and the carryout dessert counter.

Web Site: www.takomaparkmd.gov

Zip Code: 20912

Post Office: Takoma Park, 6909 Laurel Ave.

Police Station: Municipal Building, 7500 Maple Ave., 301-270-8724 (routine) or 301-270-1100 (emergency); or call 911 and the dispatcher will refer the call to municipal police based on the address

Emergency Hospital: Washington Adventist, 7600 Carroll Ave., Takoma Park, 301-891-7600

Libraries: Takoma Park, 101 Philadelphia Ave., 301-270-1717 (municipal library; nearest county library is Long Branch, 8800 Garland Ave., 301-565-7585)

Public High School: Montgomery Blair (science and communications magnet), 51 University Blvd. East, Silver Spring, 301-649-2800

Government: 5th Congressional District; Montgomery County Council District 5; mayor and six-member city council: Municipal Building, Philadelphia & Maple avenues, 301-270-1700

Neighborhood Festivals: Jazz Festival (Takoma Ave. & Fenton St., May); Folk Festival (Municipal Building and grounds, September); Takoma Park Street Festival (along Carroll Ave., October); see **A Washington Year** for details. Also Fourth of July parade (Maple Ave.).

Major Parks: Long Branch (along Long Branch between Wayne Ave. and New Hampshire Ave.); Sligo Creek (points of access off Maple Ave., Piney Branch Rd., and Park Valley Rd.)

Community Resources: *Institute of Musical Traditions* sponsors a concert series and special events, call 301-587-4434 or visit www.imt folk.org. The Institute is a spinoff of the House of Musical Traditions, 7040 Carroll Ave., 301-270-9090, www.hmtrad.com. "HMT" sells hard-to-find instruments, recorded music and related books and videos from around the world, and provides referrals to local music teachers. A *Tool Library* run by the Department of Housing & Community Development provides city residents with free access to hand and power tools; for more information, call 301-589-8274.

Public Transportation: Metro: Takoma (Red Line); Metrobus routes: 52-54 (L'Enfant Plaza), 62 (Georgia Ave.), F1/F2 (Cheverly), K2 (local); Ride On routes: 12-16 & 24/25 (local)

NEWCOMER'S HANDBOOK FOR MOVING TO AND LIVING IN WASHINGTON D.C.

76

WHEATON

GLENMONT

Boundaries: North: Randolph Rd.; **East**: Northwest Branch; **South**: Dennis Ave., Plyers Mill Rd.; **West**: Georgia Ave., Veirs Mill Rd.

Wheaton is the archetypal suburb: grids of similar single-family houses built quickly after World War II. Wheaton Plaza was one of the Washington area's first shopping malls, and it anchors the commercial "downtown" Wheaton. Built around the triangle of Georgia Avenue, University Boulevard, and Veirs Mill Road, Wheaton is home to a good selection of restaurants and specialty stores, including four used bookstores. (The basement of Wheaton Regional Library is a vast catacomb of used books for sale, cheap. Proceeds benefit the county library system.) A trip to Chuck Levin's Washington Music Center, 11151 Veirs Mill Road, is a rite of passage for practically every kid in southern Montgomery County taking music lessons.

If you've heard that Wheaton has a great roots rock and blues scene, sorry, you're a few years too late. Most of the clubs that were old haunts of local boy Danny Gatton ("the world's greatest unknown guitar player," according to *Guitar World* magazine) closed around the turn of the new century, as Wheaton's nightlife drifted from music to dining—especially at inexpensive, smoky Salvadoran *pollo la brasa* grills and good Chinese restaurants in various specialties.

Most of the homes in Wheaton are single-family detached houses that resemble a child's drawing of "a house"—a simple brick box with a tree in the front yard, picket fence optional. Many streets are looping courts or culs-de-sac, making neighborhoods cozy and safe—but the nearest bus stop may be a 10-minute walk, and some blocks don't have sidewalks. East of Georgia Avenue there are a few low-rise apartment complexes—simple, affordable 1960s rectangles in beige and brown. North of Randolph Road, in **Glenmont**, there's more of the same.

Wheaton Regional Park is a 500-acre oasis at the headwaters of Sligo Creek, just south of Randolph Road. There's an ice rink, nature center, stables, a huge playground, a miniature train ride for kids, a lake, even a little campground. Brookside Gardens, a section of the park devoted to formal gardens, conservatories, and picture-perfect gazebos dotting a series of fish ponds, is one of the most romantic spots in the Washington area, and indeed it's booked for outdoor weddings almost every weekend from April to September.

If you know any subway buffs, invite them to visit you here: the Wheaton Metro station on the Red Line has the longest escalator in the western hemisphere, 508 feet; the next station to the south, Forest Glen, is even deeper underground—21 stories beneath Georgia Avenue, accessible only by high-speed elevators.

Web Site: www.wheatonnet.com

Zip Code: 20902

Post Office: Wheaton Branch, 11431 Amherst Ave.

Police Station: Wheaton District, 2300 Randolph Rd., 240-773-5500 (emergency), 240-773-5525 (routine calls)

Emergency Hospital: Holy Cross, 1500 Forest Glen Rd., Silver Spring, 301-754-7000

Library: Wheaton Regional, 11701 Georgia Ave., 301-929-5520

Public High Schools: Albert Einstein, 11135 Newport Mill Rd., Kensington, 301-929-2200; John F. Kennedy, 1901 Randolph Rd., Silver Spring, 301-929-2100; Wheaton, 12601 Dalewood Dr., 301-929-2050

Government: 8th Congressional District; Montgomery County Council District 5

Neighborhood Festival: Taste of Wheaton (Grandview and Ennalls avenues, May), 240-777-8122

Major Parks: Sligo Creek (points of access off Dennis Ave., University Blvd., and Arcola Ave.); Wheaton Regional (points of access off Arcola Ave., Kemp Mill Rd., and Glenallan Ave.)

Community Resources: *Brookside Gardens & Nature Center,* 301-949-8230, www.mc-mncppc.org/parks or www.brooksidegardens.org.

Public Transportation: Metro: Wheaton and Glenmont (Red Line); Metrobus routes: C2 (Greenbelt), L7 (Friendship Heights), Q1/Q2 (Rockville), Y7/Y9 (Olney); Ride On routes: 6 (North Bethesda), 7 (Kensington), 8/9 (Silver Spring), 34-38 (Bethesda), 48 (Rockville)

PRINCE GEORGE'S COUNTY

Prince George's County has a bad reputation, and residents are justifiably defensive. A few pockets of crime around the eastern corner of D.C. taint the county's image in the minds of many Washingtonians. As a result, even the nicer neighborhoods—and there are plenty, mostly in the north end of this largely rural county—are much more affordable than comparable places in Montgomery County. The tradeoff is a shortage of restaurants and practically no upscale shopping.

Most of the older communities here grew up with the railroads: the little towns along U.S. Route 1 just outside Northeast D.C.—such as Mt. Rainier, Hyattsville, Riverdale Park, and Bladensburg. The old mill towns of Laurel and Bowie to the east have long histories, and the houses don't all

NEWCOMER'S HANDBOOK FOR MOVING TO AND LIVING IN WASHINGTON D.C.

78

look alike. In many places, these neighborhoods aren't pedestrian-friendly; if you want to find a house where you can walk to the grocery store, the bank, or a neighborhood pizza joint, you may have a long search ahead. If you don't mind relying on a car or public transportation, though—and if you think of your home as a place to live, not mainly as an investment— northern Prince George's County is one of the few real bargains in the Washington area.

The county stretches from the Potomac to the Patuxent, and from Laurel south to the heart of Maryland's tobacco country. Giant C-5 cargo planes churn the sky above the Beltway on their way to Andrews Air Force Base, home of Air Force One. Government scientists study crops and soil in Beltsville, wetlands in Laurel, and satellite telemetry in Greenbelt. Local high schools offer special science and technology concentrations to take advantage of those resources. A new extension of the Blue Line of the Metro to Largo serves FedEx Field, the suburban home of the "Washington" Redskins, and Six Flags America, the closest amusement park to D.C.

Civic boosters get especially annoyed when people refer to the place as "P.G." County. Since the county doesn't seem to get enough respect from retail businesses, homebuyers, or its neighboring jurisdictions, residents appreciate at least hearing the three-syllable name unabbreviated. (The name refers to Prince George of Denmark, whose wife, Queen Anne of Great Britain, chartered the first European colonies here in the early 18th century.) Prince George's County residents can be very touchy about this, so don't waste your time pointing out that District of Columbia residents don't mind people referring to "D.C."

Government Information: County Administration Building, 14741 Governor Oden Bowie Dr., Upper Marlboro, www.co.pg.md.us

County Executive: 301-952-4131, www.co.pg.md.us

County Council: nine members, each representing a council district; 301-952-3600, www.co.pg.md.us/council

Public Schools: 301-952-6300, www.pgcps.pg.k12.md.us

Libraries: 301-699-3500, www.prge.lib.md.us

Police: 301-772-4740, www.co.pg.md.us

Area Code: 301

Median Home Price: $222,000

Cost of Living: $51,000

Online Guide: www.co.pg.md.us/about

BOWIE

OLD BOWIE
SOUTH BOWIE/MITCHELLVILLE

Boundaries: North: Duckettown Rd., Bowie State University, Patuxent River; **East**: U.S. Route 301; **South**: Central Ave.; **West**: Church Rd., Collington Branch, Hillmeade Rd.

By far the largest city in the Maryland suburbs, **Bowie** offers old and new housing in old and new neighborhoods. A sprawling old railroad town, Bowie even has its own professional baseball team—the Baysox, a minor-league affiliate of the Baltimore Orioles.

On a map, Bowie looks like a cane, and the handle is **Old Bowie**, the 19th-century stomping ground of railroad barons. The modern city of Bowie grew to the south along the tracks, and it was still horse country when Oden Bowie's trains rolled through the rail junction off Chestnut Avenue.

Today, strip malls and modern subdivisions line Annapolis Road, and office parks cluster along U.S. Route 50, known locally as the John Hanson Highway; to the south, you can find attractive bargains. The Mitchellville area, from Allen Pond Park south to Central Avenue, is an upscale enclave where spacious houses on big lots sell for considerably less than comparable homes in Montgomery County. Good luck finding one for rent. There are still a few semi-rural pockets here, but developers are moving in quickly; some low-rise luxury apartments off Mitchellville Road have rental rates approaching those in the District.

The southern part of town, known locally as "**South Bowie**" and technically a part of **Mitchellville**, has the highest average household income in the county. When affluent African-American families left the District in droves in the early 1990s, this is where many settled. Despite this evidence of ample purchasing power, Prince George's County officials complain that upscale retail chains continue to flock to Montgomery County.

By the way, it's pronounced BOO-ee.

Web Site: www.cityofbowie.org
Zip Codes: 20715, 20716, 20720
Post Office: Bowie, 6710 Laurel-Bowie Rd.
Police Station: District II Station, 601 Crain Highway, 301-390-2100
Emergency Hospital: Bowie Health Center, 15001 Health Center Dr., 301-262-5511
Library: Bowie, 15210 Annapolis Rd., 301-262-7000

NEWCOMER'S HANDBOOK FOR MOVING TO AND LIVING IN WASHINGTON D.C.

80

Public High Schools: Bowie, 15200 Annapolis Rd., 301-805-2600; Tall Oaks Vocational, 2112 Church Rd., 301-390-0230

Government: 5th Congressional District; Maryland General Assembly District 23; Prince George's County Council Districts 4 and 6; mayor and six-member city council: City Hall, 2614 Kenhill Dr., 301-262-6200

Major Parks: Allen Pond (Mitchellville Rd. & Northview Dr.); Black Sox (off Mitchellville Rd. south of Mt. Oak Rd.); Collington Branch Stream Valley (along Collington Branch between U.S. Route 50 and Central Ave.); Foxhill (Collington Rd. & Faith Lane); White Marsh (off Route 3 south of Annapolis Rd.)

Community Resources: *Artist of the Month* exhibit at City Hall (see above under Government); *Belair Mansion* is the historic home of colonial Governor Samuel Ogle, circa 1745; open from 1 to 4 p.m., Thursday-Saturday, free: 12207 Tulip Grove Dr., 301-809-3089. *Belair Stable Museum* was part of the Belair Stud Farm; when it closed in 1957, it was the oldest continuously working horse farm in the country; located at 2385 Belair Dr., 301-809-3089. *Bowie Playhouse/ Theatre in the Woods,* White Marsh Park, offers performances by the Bowie Community Theater Company. For information, call 301-805-0219. *Bowie Railroad Station & Huntington Museum* honors Oden Bowie, railroad executive and governor of Maryland in the early 20th century; open noon to 4 p.m., weekends, free. Located at 11th St. & Chestnut Ave., 301-809-3089. *Bowie City Gymnasium,* 4100 Northview Dr., 301-809-3009; other public athletic facilities include the *Bowie Ice Arena,* 301-809-3090, and *Bowie Senior Center,* 301-809-2300. *Prince George's Genealogical Library* is at 12219 Tulip Grove Dr., 301-262-2063. *Radio-Television Museum* (see **Cultural Life** chapter).

Public Transportation: MARC: Seabrook and Bowie State stations (Penn Line); Metrobus routes: B21-B29 & C28 (New Carrollton), C29 (Addison Rd.)

CHEVERLY

Boundaries: North: Landover Rd.; **East**: U.S. Route 50; **South**: U.S. Route 50; **West**: Baltimore-Washington Parkway

Cheverly is a leafy oasis surrounded by industrial parks along the railroad. For a small municipality, Cheverly has a lot of neighborhood parks, which are hardly distinguishable from the town's broad, grassy medians and big residential front lawns. This is lawnmower-and-lemonade territory, and it's a bargain.

A planned community built in 1918, Cheverly carefully avoided the prefabricated look and feel of most planned communities. Distinctive cottages and bungalows line winding streets and lush hillsides. Many locals consider this to be one of the most attractive suburban towns in the area, and you can still find a nice prewar house for under $300,000.

Bumper stickers indicate a gay-friendly community, but it's not Dupont Circle hip. The town web site includes links to the garden club, the homemakers' club, and the women's club. This is a settled suburb for families and couples; young renters—especially a group sharing a house—may be greeted with a bit of suspicion.

The southern part of Cheverly and neighboring Tuxedo Park, along U.S. Route 50, is industrial—wholesale warehouses cluster around the railroad tracks just outside the District.

Route 50 between Washington and Annapolis is called the John Hanson Highway—Maryland's John Hanson was, in a manner of speaking, the first president of the United States. (The Constitution was adopted nine years after the American Revolution, and in those early years, the U.S. Articles of Confederation gave executive power to the president of the Senate—Hanson.) And yet, from the bridge where Cheverly Avenue crosses the tracks, it's not the Hanson Monument you can see in the distance.

Web Site: www.cheverly.com

Zip Code: 20785

Post Office: Landover Branch, 3312 Dodge Park Rd.

Police Stations: Cheverly Police Department, Town Hall, 301-773-8362; Prince George's County Police Department, District I Station, 5000 Rhode Island Ave., Hyattsville, 301-699-2626

Emergency Hospital: Prince George's Hospital Center, 3001 Hospital Dr., 301-618-2000

Library: Bladensburg, 4820 Annapolis Rd., 301-927-4916

Public High School: Fairmont Heights High School (biotech magnet), 1401 Nye St., Capitol Heights, 301-925-1360

Government: 4th Congressional District; Prince George's County Council District 5; mayor and six-member town council: Town Hall, 6401 Forest Rd., 301-773-8360

Neighborhood Festival: Cheverly Day (June), www.cheverlyday.com

Major Park: Anacostia River (points of access west of Kenilworth Ave.)

Community Resources: *Publick Playhouse,* a restored Art Deco performance hall featuring local and touring theater companies and live jazz, gospel, and world music; 5445 Landover Rd., 301-277-1710.

Public Transportation: Metro: Cheverly (Orange Line); MARC: New Carrollton (Penn Line); Metrobus routes: F1/F2 (Takoma), F8 (Langley Park), F12/F13 (New Carrollton); The BUS route 23 (Addison Rd.)

NEWCOMER'S HANDBOOK FOR MOVING TO AND LIVING IN WASHINGTON D.C.

82

GREENBELT/BELTSVILLE

Boundaries: North: Muirkirk Rd., Laurel-Bowie Rd.; **East**: Patuxent Research Refuge, Good Luck Rd.; **South**: Capital Beltway; **West**: Interstate 95

Much larger than any local city except the District of Columbia, the National Agricultural Research Center in Beltsville is a major complex of U.S. Department of Agriculture laboratory farms. If you get lost on the facility's service roads—like Sheep Road or Soil Conservation Road—you might come across a herd of government cows, some fitted with plastic portholes in their sides to give scientists access to samples of their stomach contents. Sounds like an urban legend, but it's true, and it's here.

Beltsville is a newer suburb—siding, not red brick, and fewer mature trees than some older communities in Prince George's County. It has no downtown area.

As Beltsville is synonymous with the USDA facility, neighboring **Greenbelt** is synonymous with the Goddard Space Flight Center, one of NASA's main satellite tracking stations. Goddard hosts a model rocket competition every year in honor of the center's namesake, the first actual rocket scientist. Not coincidentally, Greenbelt is home to a public magnet school emphasizing science and technology: Eleanor Roosevelt High School. Students at nearby DuVal High School, meanwhile, have designed experiments carried by NASA on space shuttle missions.

Old Greenbelt, along Crescent Road, was one of three federal planned communities built by FDR's Resettlement Administration under the New Deal. An experiment in social engineering, the original homes were awarded to applicants screened not only to ensure diverse levels of income but a high level of civic participation. Even today, the town has many cooperative institutions, including a nursery school, supermarket, and a 250-acre, 1,600-unit housing co-op. (To buy a home in Old Greenbelt, you join Greenbelt Homes Inc. and purchase the right to live in one of the co-op's homes. You can earn and sell equity in that home, but the title remains with the member-owned nonprofit corporation. For details, call 301-474-4161 or visit www.greenbelthomes.net.)

The modern sections of Greenbelt, east of the Baltimore-Washington Parkway and west of Kenilworth Avenue, are a little "downtown" with high-rise office buildings, though it's not the most pedestrian-friendly place—even the Metro station is hard to reach on foot.

Web Sites: www.ci.greenbelt.md.us, www.greenbelt.com, www. beltsville.com

Zip Codes: 20770, 20705

Post Offices: Beltsville, 11301 Rhode Island Ave.; Greenbelt, 119 Centerway Rd.

Police Stations: Greenbelt Police Department, 550 Crescent Rd., 301-474-7200 (routine), 301-474-5454 (emergency); Prince George's County Police, District VI Station, 4321 Sellman Rd., Beltsville, 301-937-0910

Emergency Hospitals: Laurel Regional Hospital, 7300 Van Dusen Rd., Laurel, 301-725-4300; Doctors Community Hospital, 8118 Good Luck Rd., Lanham, 301-552-8118

Libraries: Beltsville, 4319 Sellman Rd., 301-937-0294; Greenbelt, 11 Crescent Rd. 301-345-5800

Public High Schools: Eleanor Roosevelt (science magnet), 7601 Hanover Parkway, Greenbelt, 301-513-5400; High Point, 601 Powder Mill Rd., Beltsville, 301-572-6400; DuVal, 9880 Good Luck Rd., Lanham, 301-918-8600

Government: 5th Congressional District; Prince George's County Council Districts 1 and 4; Greenbelt Mayor serves on five-member town council: Town Office, 25 Crescent Rd., 301-474-8000

Neighborhood Festival: Greenbelt Day (various locations, June); Labor Day parade (Crescent Rd.) and festival (various locations)

Major Parks: Greenbelt (points of access off Greenbelt Rd. and Good Luck Rd.)

Community Resources: *National Agricultural Library* (see **Cultural Life**). The *USDA National Visitor Center* offers tours of the 7,000-acre Beltsville agricultural lab. Call 301-504-9403 for reservations or visit www.ars.usda.gov/is/nvc. *Goddard Space Flight Center* offers tours and exhibits at its Visitor Center off Greenbelt Rd. Annual public events include Space Day, with model rocket contests and interactive exhibits, and Community Day, with opportunities to meet astronauts and mission scientists. For information, call 301-286-8981 or visit http://pao.gsfc.nasa.gov. *Greenbelt Community Center* includes a gym, stage, co-op nursery school, dance studio, ceramics studio, city museum, and meeting rooms: 15 Crescent Rd., 301-397-2208; for information about art classes, call the Greenbelt Association for the Visual Arts, 301-474-2192, and for the Greenbelt Concert Band, 301-552-1444.

Public Transportation: Metro: Greenbelt (Green Line); MARC: Seabrook (Penn Line), Greenbelt and Muirkirk stations (Camden Line); Metrobus routes: C2 (Wheaton), R3 (Fort Totten), T15-T17 (New Carrollton), Z series (Silver Spring), 81-86 (Rhode Island Ave.), 87-89 (Laurel); The BUS routes: 11 (local), H (Laurel)

NEWCOMER'S HANDBOOK FOR MOVING TO AND LIVING IN WASHINGTON D.C.

84

LAUREL

SAVAGE
ODENTON
MONTPELIER
KONTERRA

Boundaries: North: Patuxent River; **East**: Patuxent River; **South**: Muirkirk Rd.; **West**: Interstate 95

Historic Laurel has its share of stereotypical postwar suburban tracts: one cookie-cutter subdivision after another, with plain townhouses built quickly in the 1950s to house the young families of World War II veterans— and Army intelligence "spooks" at nearby Fort Meade. In the northern part of town, though, some houses along Main Street were built for 19th-century mill workers.

This is one of the oldest industrial sites in the Washington area—Welsh Quakers arrived here in 1658 and set up ironworks and cotton mills, trading on the Patuxent River when ships were smaller and the river, now filled with sediment, was bigger. When the town was incorporated in the 1870s, it was known as Laurel Factory.

Some of the homes from that era have been carefully restored, with pine floors and leaded-glass windows. They don't change hands often, but when they do, you might be able to steal one for half the price of a comparably historic home in the District. You would not only have a house that could pass for Georgetown or Old Town Alexandria, but a location ideal for couples employed both in Washington and Baltimore.

Laurel's factory days are over, and the big local industries are cryptology and horse racing. Fort George G. Meade, five miles east in **Odenton**, is the home of the NSA—the National Secur- uh, "No Such Agency." It's one of those "secrets" that everyone knows: this is where the Army makes and breaks encryption codes, and there is a military and civilian complement of 34,000 here to do it. You can see some of their exploits at the National Cryptologic Museum on the base; the free exhibits include an Enigma encryption machine captured from the Nazis.

Between the town and the base, Laurel Racetrack has its own train station on the MARC line from Capitol Hill to Baltimore's Camden Yards. Just across the Baltimore-Washington Parkway, the 13,000-acre Patuxent Research Refuge is the federal government's main scientific facility involved in wildlife conservation. Here the U.S. Fish & Wildlife Service studies forest, meadow, and wetland ecosystems, including migratory birds and nesting bald eagles.

A few miles up U.S. Route 1 is the town of **Savage**, where historic Savage Mill produced bolts of canvas from 1822 to 1947: sails for Baltimore clipper ships, tents for the Union army, backdrops for early movie sets, and Army cloth during both World Wars. Now the complex is an arts center and antiques mall, drawing weekend crowds in search of distinctive furniture, collectibles, and works by local artists.

South of Laurel, **Montpelier** and the planned city of **Konterra** are modern subdivisions. Konterra, mostly an office park, was envisioned in the 1990s to take advantage of the planned Intercounty Connector (ICC) superhighway. The ICC remains a topic of hot debate—whether to build it and, if so, where—so Konterra might be little more than an office park for years to come.

Web Sites: www.laurel.md.us, www.odenton.org, www.ftmeade. army.mil

Zip Code: 20707

Post Office: 324 Main St.; Montpelier Branch, 12625 Laurel-Bowie Rd.

Police Stations: Laurel Police Department, 350 Municipal Square, 301-498-0092; Prince George's County Police, District VI Station, 4321 Sellman Rd., Beltsville, 301-937-0910

Emergency Hospital: Laurel Regional Hospital, 7300 Van Dusen Rd., Laurel, 301-725-4300

Library: Laurel, 507 7th St., 301-776-6790

Public High School: Laurel, 8000 Cherry Lane, 301-497-2050

Government: 5th Congressional District; Prince George's County Council District 1; mayor and five-member city council: Municipal Center, 8103 Sandy Spring Rd., 301-725-5300

Neighborhood Festivals: Main Street Festival (May); Montpelier Spring Festival (May—see Montpelier under "Community Resources" below); Riverfest (Riverfront Park, October)

Major Park: Patuxent (points of access off Laurel-Bowie Rd. north of the B-W Parkway and along Brooklyn Bridge Rd. west of I-95)

Community Resources: *Patuxent Research Refuge*—North Tract and the National Wildlife Visitor Center are open daily, 10 a.m. to 5:30 p.m. The Visitor Center, offering tours and exhibits, is located off Powder Mill Rd. between Maryland Route 197 and the B-W Parkway. For more information, call 301-497-5760. *National Cryptologic Museum* at Ft. Meade, 301-88-5849, www.nsa.gov/museum. *Montpelier Mansion & Cultural Arts Center* is the 18th-century Georgian home of Maj. Thomas Snowden, crowning a 70-acre estate. You can tour the preserved mansion and rent banquet rooms where George Washington and Abigail Adams once were guests. The Arts Center, open daily 10 a.m. to 5 p.m., shows juried exhibits of local, national, and international works, and the work of artists in residence. Classes and performances are

NEWCOMER'S HANDBOOK FOR MOVING TO AND LIVING IN WASHINGTON D.C.

86

also held here. Entrance to the grounds is off Muirkirk Rd. just west of Laurel-Bowie Rd. (Maryland Route 197). For more information, call 301-953-1376 (mansion) or 301-953-1993 (Arts Center), or visit www.pgparks.com. *Savage Mill* is open daily; 8600 Foundry St., Savage, 800-788-6455, www.savagemill.com.

Public Transportation: MARC: Muirkirk, Laurel, and Laurel Racetrack stations (Camden Line) and Odenton station (Penn Line); Metrobus routes: 87 & 89 (Greenbelt), 88 (New Carrollton); The BUS routes: A-C (local), D (Burtonsville), E (Columbia), F (Fort Meade), H (Greenbelt)

PORT TOWNS

COLMAR MANOR
COTTAGE CITY
BRENTWOOD
MT. RAINIER
NORTH BRENTWOOD
EDMONSTON
BLADENSBURG
HYATTSVILLE

Boundaries: North: East-West Highway; **East**: Baltimore-Washington Parkway: **South**: Eastern Ave.; **West**: Queens Chapel Rd., Northwest Branch

The D.C.-Maryland line across Rhode Island Avenue is unceremonious, noticeable mainly because traffic lights are painted gray in the District and yellow in the suburbs. But the cluster of old suburban communities along U.S. Route 1 from D.C. to East-West Highway is a diverse area where young University of Maryland graduates and junior federal workers from the USDA facilities in Beltsville, or the NASA facilities in Greenbelt, can actually afford to own a home—with trees in the yard and the obligatory white picket fence.

Don't try to follow this without a map: Clustered just outside the District are the towns of **Mt. Rainier**, from Queens Chapel Road east to Rhode Island Avenue; **Cottage City**, from Rhode Island Avenue east to Bladensburg Road; and **Colmar Manor** east to the Anacostia River. **Brentwood** is just north of Mt. Rainier, extending to the Northwest Branch of the Anacostia and east to the railroad tracks. **Hyattsville** stretches from the Northwest Branch north to Route 410 and east to the tracks; **Edmonston** straddles the Northeast Branch; and **Bladensburg** stretches from the Anacostia east to the Baltimore-Washington Parkway.

Collectively, these are the "Port Towns" that grew up around the colonial-era limit of navigation on the Anacostia River. (The river is smaller after two centuries of construction in its watershed, and a small recreational marina in Bladensburg is all that remains of the historic port.)

These are all similar communities, but each is an incorporated town with its own little police and fire departments and town council. The homes may look the same from one town to the next—some plain modern homes mixed in with plenty of bungalows and cottages built before World War I—but most of these towns have distinct histories. Cottage City is, to the chagrin of longtime residents, known mainly as the home of the child about whom *The Exorcist* was based. Tiny **North Brentwood**, population 500, was the first predominantly African-American town in Prince George's County, founded on land purchased by black Civil War veterans from their commanding officer. And "Historic Bladensburg" may sound like a silly pretense—the town doesn't look especially old—but in fact Bladensburg is the only place where the United States was ever successfully invaded. During the War of 1812, the British navy made it all the way to the site of the present-day Prince George's Marina and put troops ashore to march on Washington. They burned the Capitol and the White House while Dolley Madison smuggled the Constitution out of the city in a trunk of clothes. A stone cross at the junction of U.S. Route 1 and Landover Road marks the landing site; few of the commuters who pass the memorial every day are aware of its significance.

Nearby Mt. Rainier attracts the area's biggest granola contingent outside Takoma Park. Neighborhood amenities include the Glut Food Co-op, under the sign of the giant carrot at 4005 34th Street, and a strip of alternative medicine shops, New Age bookstores, and storefront churches just off Rhode Island Avenue.

Hyattsville is a larger town with its own commercial districts—along Hamilton Street and Ager Road and the south end of Queens Chapel Road—and a mall, Prince George's Plaza, across Route 410. To the south, along a commercial spur of Route 1, an old general store, Franklin's, has been renovated as a microbrewery and restaurant.

Web Sites: www.bladensburg.com, www.hyattsville.org, www.mount rainiermd.org, www.porttowns.org

Zip Codes: 20710, 20712, 20722, 20781, 20782

Post Offices: Brentwood, 4314 41st St.; Hyattsville, 4325 Gallatin St.; Kenilworth Station, 6270 Kenilworth Ave.; Mt. Rainier, 3709 Rhode Island Ave.; Prince George's Plaza; West Hyattsville

Police Stations: District I Station, 5000 Rhode Island Ave., Hyattsville, 301-699-2626; each municipality has its own small police force—call the town hall at the number listed below under "Government."

NEWCOMER'S HANDBOOK FOR MOVING TO AND LIVING IN WASHINGTON D.C.

88

Emergency Hospitals: Doctors Community Hospital, 8118 Good Luck Rd., Lanham, 301-552-8118; Prince George's Hospital Center, 3001 Hospital Dr., Cheverly, 301-618-2000

Libraries: Bladensburg, 4820 Annapolis Rd., 301-927-4916; Hyattsville, 6532 Adelphi Rd., 301-985-4690; Mt. Rainier, 3409 Rhode Island Ave., 301-864-8937

Public High School: Bladensburg, 5160 Tilden Rd., 301-985-1470

Government: 5th Congressional District; Prince George's County Council District 3. Each municipality has a mayor and town council—contact the town hall for more information: Berwyn Heights, 5700 Berwyn Rd., 301-474-5000; Bladensburg, 4229 Edmonston Rd., 301-927-7048; Brentwood, 4300 39th Place, 301-927-7395; Colmar Manor, 3701 Lawrence St., 301-277-4920; Cottage City, 3820 40th Ave., 301-779-2161; Edmonston, 5005 52nd Ave., 301-699-8806; Hyattsville, 4310 Gallatin St., 301-985-5000; Mt. Rainier, 1 Municipal Place, 301-985-6585; North Brentwood, 4507 Church St., 301-699-9699

Neighborhood Festivals: Maryland Day (various locations at the University of Maryland, April), www.marylandday.umd.edu; West Hyattsville Street Festival (September) and Hyattsville Halloween Party, www.hyattsville.org

Major Parks: Anacostia River (access off Bladensburg Rd. on the west side and Kenilworth Ave. on the east side); Northeast Branch (points of access along Kenilworth Ave.); Northwest Branch (along Northwest Branch between Route 1 and the Metro bridge on the Green Line)

Community Resources: *Mt. Rainier Nature Center* offers interpretive programs and guided nature walks: 4701 31st Place, 301-927-2163. *Mt. Rainier Community Tool Shed,* 301-799-0133.

Public Transportation: Metro: West Hyattsville and Prince George's Plaza stations (Green Line); Metrobus routes: C8 (Glenmont), F1/F2 (Takoma Park), F4/F6 (New Carrollton), R3 (Greenbelt, Fort Totten), R4 (Brookland), 80 series (Rhode Island Ave.); The BUS routes: 12/13 (local)

COLLEGE PARK

RIVERDALE PARK
BERWYN HEIGHTS
UNIVERSITY PARK

Boundaries: North: Capital Beltway; **East**: Kenilworth Avenue; **South**: East-West Highway; **West**: Adelphi Rd.

The main campus of the University of Maryland, with its own zip code and 33,000 students, defines the city of **College Park**: a college-town commercial strip along U.S. Route 1 with a lot of bookstores, delis, liquor stores, laundromats, and travel agencies. There are some apartment buildings, but most of the housing stock is detached houses on quiet residential streets. Student group rentals are quite common. So are bicycles, as the "College Park" Metro station (Green Line) is nowhere near campus. It's a 10-minute shuttle ride away, serving the residential east side of town. If you drive, note that the city and the university both rely on parking tickets for a certain percentage of their annual revenue, and here you do have to feed the parking meters on weekends.

College Park Airport, a tiny airstrip off Calvert Road near the Metro and MARC stations, is the oldest working airport in the world: it was built by Wilbur Wright in 1909 as the first flight school for the Army.

Right across the railroad tracks from College Park is the town of **Berwyn Heights**, a leafy suburb where junior faculty members might buy a home. It's also a granola enclave—a strip of cottage businesses along Berwyn Road includes an organic café and funky consignment shops. There's an REI outdoor sporting goods co-op off Route 193 on a fragment of Rhode Island Avenue that doesn't connect to the road of the same name leading into D.C.

University Park, nestled between the University of Maryland and East-West Highway and between Adelphi Road and U.S. Route 1, is a strictly residential enclave—all detached homes, mostly red brick, and no commercial buildings. In the 1990s, the town closed the north end of Queens Chapel Road to through traffic, ending commuter shortcuts through the neighborhood. It's an oasis of high SAT scores, active civic culture, and half-million-dollar houses; still, it's in image-challenged Prince George's County, not fashionable Montgomery County, where comparable homes in comparable neighborhoods fetch $700,000.

Across Route 1 is **Riverdale Park**, an older suburb straddling the railroad tracks—many residential streets have grade crossings. Catering to student group rentals, this neighborhood includes some large houses with many small rooms—note, though, a nine-bedroom house might include some lofts and some very tiny or irregularly shaped rooms. Older maps of this area just show "Riverdale"; voters added "Park" to the town's name in 1998.

Street names can be confusing here. Many suburban roads change names as they pass through different communities; to be on the safe side, ask for directions using route numbers. Maryland Route 410 is known as East-West Highway from Bethesda to Langley Park; in Takoma Park, it becomes Ethan Allen Avenue and then Philadelphia Avenue; after another stretch as East-West Highway, it crosses the B-W Parkway and becomes Riverdale Road. Likewise, Route 1 between D.C. and the Beltway is known variously as Rhode Island Avenue, Bladensburg Road, and Baltimore

NEWCOMER'S HANDBOOK FOR MOVING TO AND LIVING IN WASHINGTON D.C.

90

Avenue; and Route 193 is called University Boulevard west of Route 1, and Greenbelt Road to the east. Seriously, you'll need a good map.

Web Sites: www.ci.college-park.md.us, http://berwyn-heights.com, www.ci.riverdale-park.md.us, www.upmd.org

Zip Codes: 20740, 20742, 20737

Post Offices: College Park, 9591 Baltimore Blvd.; Riverdale, 6411 Baltimore Ave.

Police Stations: District I Station, 5000 Rhode Island Ave., Hyattsville, 301-699-2626; each municipality has its own small police force—call the town hall at the number listed below under "Government."

Emergency Hospitals: Doctors Community Hospital, 8118 Good Luck Rd., Lanham, 301-552-8118; Prince George's Hospital Center, 3001 Hospital Dr., Cheverly, 301-618-2000

Libraries: Hyattsville, 6532 Adelphi Rd., 301-985-4690

Public High School: Bladensburg, 5160 Tilden Rd., 301-985-1470

Government: 5th Congressional District; Prince George's County Council District 3. Each municipality has a mayor and town council—contact the town hall for more information: Berwyn Heights, 5700 Berwyn Rd., 301-474-5000; College Park, 4500 Knox Rd., 301-864-8666; Riverdale Park, 5008 Queensbury Rd., 301-927-6381; University Park, 6724 Baltimore Ave., 301-927-2997

Neighborhood Festivals: Maryland Day (various locations at the University of Maryland, April), www.marylandday.umd.edu

Major Parks: Greenbelt (points of access off Greenbelt Rd. and Good Luck Rd.); Northeast Branch (points of access along Kenilworth Ave.); Paint Branch/Berwyn Stream Valley (east of the railroad tracks between Berwyn Rd. and Calvert Rd.)

Community Resources: *College Park Aviation Museum* features vintage aircraft including one of the Wright Brothers' first military planes. Interactive exhibits include flight simulators, a wind tunnel, and live audio monitors from the control towers at regional airports; 1985 Cpl. Frank Scott Dr., College Park, 301-864-6029, www.pgparks.com. *Riversdale* mansion and estate was built in the early 19th century for George and Rosalie Calvert, whose family founded Maryland. The historic site is open for tours and rentals: 4811 Riverdale Rd., Riverdale Park, 301-864-0420, www.pgparks.com. The *University of Maryland-College Park* offers many cultural events open to the public, including recent movies at a low cost in the Hoff Theater. Check the film, stage, and exhibit listings in the Weekend section of Friday's *Washington Post*, pick up the U of M *Diamondback* on campus, or visit the Campus Activities or Student Union pages at www.inform.umd.edu/Student.

Public Transportation: Metro: College Park station (Green Line); MARC: Riverdale and College Park stations (Camden Line); Metrobus routes: C8 (Glenmont), F1/F2 (Takoma Park), F4/F6 (New Carrollton), R3 (Greenbelt, Fort Totten), R4 (Brookland), 80 series (Rhode Island Ave.); The BUS routes: 12/13 (local)

VIRGINIA

The Commonwealth of Virginia is the oldest settlement of European people in the Western hemisphere, and the names on the state road map sound like the index of an American history book: Lee Highway, Dolley Madison Boulevard, Jefferson High School, Lake Braddock, Wilson Boulevard, George Mason University, and even Jefferson Davis Highway. Virginia schoolchildren learn to think of their state as the "Birthplace of Presidents," and indeed, in its first two centuries, nearly one in five of our nation's chief executives was born here, including Washington, Jefferson, Madison, Monroe, and Wilson.

Virginia, the "Old Dominion," is a conservative state by any standard. A state holiday, Lee-Jackson Day, honors two Confederate generals, and until recently, the Martin Luther King Jr. holiday was combined with it— observed as "Lee-Jackson-King Day"! Head west on I-66 a little over five miles past the Beltway, and you can visit the National Rifle Association museum and headquarters. Even in cosmopolitan Northern Virginia, the two biggest employers—the Pentagon and the information technology sector—attract a conservative set.

While horse farms may still occupy large expanses, the state's leading private industry is information technology. Network Solutions, AOL, Sprint/Nextel, GTS, Primus Telecommunications, BTG, and Microstrategy have headquarters in a growing high-tech corridor from Tysons Corner to Dulles Airport. The aerospace industry is well represented too, with General Dynamics, Fairchild, Orbital Sciences, SpaceHab, and several airlines based here. These company names flank the entrances to modern office parks and corporate campuses in the outer suburbs. Closer to the Potomac, big homes with big yards in airy, modern, elegant subdivisions house descendants of families that have lived in the area for generations as well as some of the newest high-tech millionaires. Closer still, Arlington and Alexandria are little cities themselves, with downtowns and varied residential areas and commercial strips blooming with nightlife.

Populous and urban Northern Virginia is a far cry from the rolling hills of tobacco country and apple orchards throughout most of the state. From Hampton Roads to Massanutten Mountain, from colonial Jamestown to the new National Air & Space Museum annex at Dulles Airport, Virginia relies heavily on tourism—especially on visits from Washingtonians on day trips or weekend getaways.

NEWCOMER'S HANDBOOK FOR MOVING TO AND LIVING IN WASHINGTON D.C.

92

Capital: Richmond
Governor: 804-786-2211, www.governor.virginia.gov
Virginia General Assembly: 804-698-7410 (Senate), 804-698-1500
(House), 800-889-0229 (comment line); http://legis.state.va.us
Online Guide: Virginia Information Providers Network, www.vipnet.org
Newspaper of Record: Richmond Times-Dispatch, 800-468-3382,
www.timesdispatch.com

CITY OF ALEXANDRIA

HUNTINGTON
SPRINGFIELD
ANNANDALE

Boundaries: North: King St., Quaker Ln., South Glebe Rd.; **East**:
Potomac River; **South**: Capital Beltway; **West**: culs-de-sac west of Van
Dorn St. and Holmes Run

The tall, pointy tower looming over Alexandria is the Washington
Monument—the other one. Many of the founders were Freemasons, and
the George Washington National Masonic Memorial here houses General
Washington's own gavel, which he used in the Masonic ceremony dedicat-
ing the cornerstone of the Capitol. Across the railroad tracks from the monument, **Old Town Alexandria** stretches east to the Potomac, and from
the Beltway north to Potomac Yard, an old rail terminal site now is occupied by more big-box chain stores than boxcars.

George Washington shopped in Alexandria, and the historic district is
so well maintained that he wouldn't seem out of place strolling through the
cobblestone streets and the historic buildings—though he might be eating
Ben & Jerry's ice cream or drinking a Starbucks latte. Many homes and
stores bear bronze historical plaques, and woe unto any owner who tries to
alter an original facade. Owning a house in Old Town is an expensive
endeavor, and even some new townhouses here start in the high six figures.

Ladies' Home Journal, in its annual ranking of the 200 "Best Cities for
Women," consistently puts Alexandria in or near the top 10 in several cate-
gories, and in 2002 it was the magazine's No. 1 city for education and
childcare. Alexandria also makes the top 10 in the magazine's rankings for
economy (reflecting job market trends, cost of living, incomes, and property values) and lifestyle (reflecting "more than a dozen measures, including: culture, climate, commute time, air and water quality, voting
percentages, marriage-divorce ratio, divorce rate, number of single men
compared to single women, weather factors affecting a woman's hair and
skin, even the number of toilets"). It should be noted, however, that D.C.

itself was ranked 7th in education, based on graduation rates, per-pupil spending, class sizes and attainment—yet few District residents, teachers, or elected officials would consider their school system one of the best in the country.

For the over-30 crowd, after graduating from the taverns of neighboring Arlington, Old Town is the center of nightlife on the Virginia side of the river. Bistros and bars line the streets, and one of the riverboat restaurants on the Potomac, the *Dandy,* is docked here. Antique stores, boutiques, and art galleries attract weekend crowds. The Torpedo Factory Art Center, once an actual torpedo factory, dominates the waterfront. The cavernous building now houses dozens of artists' suites with galleries in front and studios in back. Many classes are offered here, but it's educational just to sit and chat with the painters, sculptors, weavers, potters, jewelers, and other artists in residence, many of whom are happy to let visitors watch them work. The complex also houses a small museum devoted to Alexandria history and archaeology.

North of Potomac Yard, brick row houses off Glebe Road and Mt. Vernon Avenue are relatively cheap for Alexandria. The Birchmere, at 3701 Mt. Vernon Avenue, is the Washington area's preeminent folk music venue, with bluegrass every week and the best Irish, country, and folk singer-songwriters.

Just off Quaker Lane and I-395 is Park Fairfax, a complex of townhouse condominiums built just after World War II. As newcomers, Richard Nixon and Gerald Ford lived here.

West of the monument, Alexandria does have some low-income housing and scattered pockets of crime. Redevelopment plans for the industrial strip that follows Cameron Run along Eisenhower Avenue and the Beltway include the future home of the Patent & Trademark Office. The incorporated city of Alexandria works hard on public safety and the underlying social tensions, and has never experienced the middle-class flight that hurt D.C. in the late 1980s and early '90s. Today Alexandria, like most of the suburbs, has its share of gang activity; in recent years, local authorities and the Department of Homeland Security have rounded up hundreds of local members of the nationwide gang MS-13. But little or no gang violence is directed against strangers—it's almost all internal.

Alexandria's own suburbs, **Huntington** to the south and **Springfield** and **Annandale** to the west, are vast residential areas consisting mainly of single-family homes. Between the Beltway and Mt. Vernon, expect to find stately old colonials; west of Van Dorn Street, newer split-level homes with large bay windows and skylights are placed in sprawling subdivisions. One of the nation's first public magnet schools for math and science, Thomas Jefferson High School, is here, on Miner Lane off Braddock Road.

NEWCOMER'S HANDBOOK FOR MOVING TO AND LIVING IN WASHINGTON D.C.

94

The Hollin Hills development in Huntington, near the bird-watchers' paradise of Dyke Marsh by the Potomac, is one of the few postwar developments near Mt. Vernon. These low houses nestled in rolling hills were cited in a 1951 issue of *Life* magazine as among the "best houses for under $15,000." Today they sell for half a million dollars—if at all.

Two noise warnings: the north side of Alexandria is close to National Airport, and if you live near Mt. Vernon, you might occasionally hear the 21-gun salute rendered by any U.S. Navy ship that passes by the home of the first Commander-in-Chief.

Web Site: www.ci.alexandria.va.us

Zip Codes: 22003, 22301, 22302, 22304, 22311, 22314

Area Code: 703

Post Offices: Alexandria, 1100 Wythe St.; Belle View, 1626 Belle View Blvd.; Community Branch, 7676 Richmond Hwy.; Engleside, 8758 Richmond Hwy.; Franconia, 5221 Franconia Rd.; Jefferson Manor, 5834 North Kings Hwy.; Lincolnia, 6137 Lincolnia Rd.; Memorial Annex, 2226 Duke St.; Park Fairfax Station, 3682 King St.; Potomac Station, 1908 Mt. Vernon Ave.; Trade Center Station, 340 South Pickett St.

Police Station: Alexandria Police Department, 2003 Mill Rd., 703-838-4444; http://ci.alexandria.va.us/police

Emergency Hospital: Inova Alexandria Hospital, 4320 Seminary Rd., 703-504-3000

Libraries: Charles E. Beatley Jr. Central Library, 5005 Duke St., 703-519-5900; for branch information, call the central library or visit www.alexandria.lib.va.us.

Public High Schools: T.C. Williams, 3330 King St., 703-824-6800; school district, 703-824-6600, www.acps.k12.va.us

Government: 8th Congressional District; mayor and six-member city council; City Hall, 301 King Street, 703-838-4500; www.ci.alexandria.va.us/city/amacc

Neighborhood Festivals: Alexandria Red Cross Waterfront Festival (June), 703-549-8300; Alexandria Birthday (various locations, July), 703-838-4200

Major Parks: Cameron Run (Eisenhower Ave. west of Telegraph Rd.); Daingerfield Island (George Washington Pkwy. south of Four Mile Run); Dyke Marsh (George Washington Pkwy. south of Belle View Blvd.); Holmes Run (along Holmes Run between Columbia Pike and Duke St.)

Community Resources: *The Birchmere*, 3701 Mt. Vernon Ave. (see **Cultural Life**). *Torpedo Factory Art Center*, 105 North Union St., 703-838-4565, www.torpedofactory.org (see **Cultural Life**). *George Washington National Masonic Memorial* is open daily, 9 a.m. to 4

p.m.; tours available. The monument includes ceremonial rooms, a museum, library, and auditorium. For information, call 703-683-2007 or visit www.gwmemorial.org.

Public Transportation: Metro: Braddock Road & King Street (Blue & Yellow lines), Van Dorn Street (Blue Line), Eisenhower Avenue (Yellow Line); VRE: Alexandria (Fredericksburg & Manassas lines), Franconia/ Springfield (Fredericksburg Line), Backlick Road (Manassas Line); Metrobus routes: 9A/9E (Pentagon, Fort Belvoir), 10A/10E (Rosslyn), 10B-10D (Falls Church), 11Y (Fort Belvoir, Farragut Square), 28 series (Tysons Corner), 21 series (Pentagon, Landmark Mall), 25 series (Ballston), 29 series (Little River Turnpike), P13 (Pentagon); Fairfax Connector routes: 101-109 (local); ART shuttle routes (local)

Median Home Price: $500,000

Cost of Living: $61,000

Property Tax Rate: 91.5 cents per $100

ARLINGTON COUNTY

On a map, D.C. looks like somebody took a bite out of a perfect square. The missing "bite" is Arlington County, and indeed, it once was part of the District. The Constitution gives Congress control over "such District (not exceeding ten miles square) as may, by Cession of particular States, and the Acceptance of Congress, become the Seat of the Government of the United States." So Maryland and Virginia each donated land to Congress in 1791. The District was then divided into several smaller jurisdictions: the City of Washington, the City of Georgetown, and Washington County—collectively, the area now known as the District of Columbia—and, across the Potomac, "Arlington, D.C." Half a century later, it turned out that the residents of Arlington didn't identify with the city across the river, the federal government wasn't using much land in Arlington, and tensions were heating up between the North and South, which were separated more clearly by the Potomac than by the Mason-Dixon Line. In 1846, Congress agreed to let Arlington residents hold a referendum to choose whether their county would remain in D.C. or be "retroceded" to Virginia; retrocession won.

Arlington is inside the Beltway, and it's the only county in the Washington suburbs that doesn't have a problem with sprawl—because there's no room to grow.

Government: Arlington County Board, 703-228-3130, www.co.arlington. va.us

Area Code: 703

Public Schools: 703-228-6008, www.arlington.k12.va.us

Libraries: 703-228-5990, www.co.arlington.va.us/lib

NEWCOMER'S HANDBOOK FOR MOVING TO AND LIVING IN WASHINGTON D.C.

96

Police: 703-228-4252, www.co.arlington.va.us/police
Online Guide: www.co.arlington.va.us (click on "New Residents")
Median Home Price: $465,000
Cost of Living: $64,000
Property Tax Rate: $1 per $100

ARLINGTON

NORTH ARLINGTON
SOUTH ARLINGTON
ROSSLYN
CLARENDON
BALLSTON
PENTAGON CITY
CRYSTAL CITY
FAIRLINGTON
SHIRLINGTON

Boundaries: North: U.S. Route 29; **East**: Potomac River; **South**: Four Mile Run, Quaker Ln., King St.; **West**: George Mason Dr.

Arlington offers some of the best views of the Washington skyline, and most of the signature photos of the Capitol, the Jefferson Memorial, the Washington Monument, and the Lincoln Memorial are taken from the Arlington banks of the Potomac.

North Arlington and **South Arlington** are separated by Arlington National Cemetery, the Pentagon, Fort Myer, and the Marine Corps Memorial—more commonly known as the Iwo Jima Memorial. North Arlington's concrete jungle stretches along Wilson and Clarendon boulevards, and from "downtown" Rosslyn to more suburban Clarendon. South Arlington, just west of Reagan National Airport, includes Pentagon City, Crystal City, and Shirlington. Street names indicate north or south relative to the cemetery and Arlington Boulevard (U.S. Route 50).

Rosslyn, just north of the Pentagon, is dominated by the metallic skyscraper known to locals as "the USA Today building" (until 2001, publishing giant Gannett was headquartered here). At the base of the skyscraper is a memorial plaza honoring slain journalists. The building has had a few close calls with low-flying planes landing at Reagan National Airport. Other office high-rises attract military contractors and some offices are leased by the armed forces—even the vast Pentagon can't house everybody. The Rosslyn area is almost all commercial and closes by 7 p.m.; weekends, forget it.

Up the hill from Rosslyn, Courthouse Square in **Clarendon** takes its name from the presence of the Arlington County courts and municipal complex. Scattered among major employers like SRA and Verizon, there are high-rise apartments—some offering spectacular views, costing up to 30% more than those that don't—and some prewar brick houses and modern townhouses. The weekday lunch and happy-hour crowds keep a variety of good restaurants hopping—Italian, Thai, Indian, Southwestern, Middle Eastern, and all-American. Clarendon is emerging as a nightspot, thanks to neighborhood clubs like Whitlow's and Iota, and its retail strips, which include several thrift stores, bookstores, and a growing number of coffee bars.

Beyond Clarendon, marking the northwest corner of commercial Arlington, the **Ballston** neighborhood is dominated by Ballston Common Mall and big-box stores including REI and Barnes & Noble, most clustered along Wilson Boulevard and Fairfax Drive. A few modern apartment complexes off Wilson Boulevard attract mostly young workers looking for a convenient location; many eventually head for South Arlington or Alexandria to raise a family.

South of the Pentagon, whose 17.5 miles of corridors and four zip codes make it a city in itself, is the vast building's own little suburb, **Pentagon City**. It's mostly retail; a small pocket of apartments attracts some of the 23,000 military personnel and civilians who work in the 3.8 million square feet of offices in the world's largest office building.

Between National Airport and U.S. Route 1 is **Crystal City**, a cluster of office high-rises, hotels, and tall apartment buildings surrounding the original complex of three dozen golden brick buildings. Because of the proximity to the airport, many conventions and trade shows are held here. And of course there are lots of defense contractors and military offices. Here's the surprising part: most of the principal buildings in Crystal City are connected by a vast network of pedestrian tunnels, which are lined with shops and restaurants. If you live and work in Crystal City, you never have to go outside.

Once the dominant civilian employer in Crystal City, the U.S. Patent & Trademark Office moved south in 2005 to its huge new headquarters campus off Eisenhower Avenue. The concrete rabbit warrens of Crystal City are still home to thousands of patent lawyers, and some ambitious young associates take advantage of the underground amenities to set their bodies to an artificial day/night cycle, to maximize the hours they can work without sleep!

To the west, the rest of Arlington is more traditional—an old, established residential area with substantial colonials and little subdivisions with brick townhouses sold as condos. Between 1900 and 1910, there were 70 subdivisions built in Arlington County, and not the dull beige boxes so

NEWCOMER'S HANDBOOK FOR MOVING TO AND LIVING IN WASHINGTON D.C.

98

familiar in the outer suburbs. These older subdivisions are shaded by mature trees, and strips of sturdy brick homes are separated more by grassy commons and walkways than by streets and parking lots. Among others, lawmakers, journalists, and high-ranking military officers reside here. In 2005, the City of Arlington won an award from Virginia Clean Cities in recognition of the fact that more than 530 county vehicles (40%) run on clean biodiesel fuel.

In the small section of Arlington south of Four Mile Run, **Shirlington** is becoming the suburban annex of Dupont Circle. In the past decade, cafés, late-night dining, and a substantial gay and lesbian community have filtered in. It's more affordable for young professionals than comparable neighborhoods in D.C.—but partly because it's not the most convenient location. Although it's a short distance from the 14th Street Bridge via Interstate 395, it's a struggle at rush hour.

South of I-395, **Fairlington** attracts young families to affordable low-rise apartment complexes. Southeast Asian immigrants settled here after the Vietnam War, perhaps because many of them had ties to the military; some eventually moved to the outer suburbs, but not before opening a plethora of Asian restaurants and establishing one of the area's few genuine ethnic neighborhoods. Pho noodle houses are a particular hallmark of South Arlington.

The Gunston Arts Center, on Arlington Ridge Road off South Glebe Road, is a unique facility for the performing arts. The center comprises two theaters and rehearsal space, scene shops, and costume shops, all serving local performing companies and offering classes for children and adults. On any given day, there might be opera signers rehearsing in one room and tap dancers practicing next door.

Arlington supports its mom-and-pop stores too. Locals are devoted to the Heidelberg Pastry Shoppe on North Culpeper Street; on Wilson Boulevard, Attila himself will serve your falafel at Attila's; and at Gene's Deli on North 14th Street, Gene always remembers his regular customers.

Web Site: www.co.arlington.va.us, www.clarendon.org

Zip Codes: 22201–22213, 22216

Post Offices: Arlington, 3118 Washington Blvd.; Buckingham Station, 235 N. Glebe Rd.; Courthouse Station, 2043 Wilson Blvd.; Crystal City Station, 1735 Jefferson Davis Hwy.; Eads Station, 1720 S. Eads St.; Rosslyn Station, 1101 Wilson Blvd.; Shirlington Annex, 2850 S. Quincy St.; South Station, 1210 S. Glebe Rd.

Police Station: Arlington County Police Department, 1425 N. Courthouse Rd., 703-228-4252

Emergency Hospital: Arlington Hospital, 1701 N. George Mason Dr., 703-558-5000

Library: Arlington County Central Library, 1015 N. Quincy St., 703-228-5990, www.co.arlington.va.us/lib

Public High Schools: Wakefield, 4901 S. Chesterfield Rd., 703-228-6700; Washington-Lee, 1300 N. Quincy St., 703-228-6200; Yorktown, 5201 N. 28th St., 703-228-5400

Government: 8th Congressional District; five-member county board; county offices at Courthouse Square, 2100 Clarendon Blvd., 703-228-3130

Neighborhood Festival: Neighborhood Day (various locations, May), 703-228-7710; Clarendon Day (October), www.clarendon.org

Major Parks: Four Mile Run (along Four Mile Run between I-66 and the Potomac River); Gravelly Point (George Washington Pkwy. just north of National Airport); Lady Bird Johnson (George Washington Pkwy. at Memorial Bridge); Roaches Run Waterfowl Sanctuary (south end of Boundary Channel Dr.)

Community Resources: *Arlington National Cemetery* is open daily, 8 a.m. to 7 p.m. April–September, 8 a.m. to 5 p.m. October–March. For information, call 703-695-3250 or visit www.arlingtoncemetery.org. *Commuter Store* locations in Rosslyn and Crystal City (see **Transportation**). *Gunston Arts Center,* 2700 S. Lang St., 703-228-6960. Attracted by Gunston Arts Center, there are a dozen professional and amateur theater companies based in Arlington, a community symphony orchestra and opera company, barbershop chorus, half a dozen dance companies, and several private galleries and visual arts studios. For a community arts directory, visit www.arlingtonarts.org or call the Arlington Cultural Affairs Division at Gunston Arts Center.

Public Transportation: Metro: Rosslyn (Blue & Orange lines), Court House, Virginia Square, Ballston-Marymount University (Orange Line), Arlington Cemetery (Blue Line), Pentagon, Pentagon City, Crystal City, National Airport (Blue & Yellow Lines); VRE: Crystal City station (Fredericksburg & Manassas lines); the Pentagon is a major bus system hub served by 73 Metrobus routes.

FAIRFAX COUNTY

Fairfax County is the old stomping ground of George Washington, George Mason, Patrick Henry, J.E.B. Stuart, and the Lees, from Lighthorse Harry to Robert E., as well as quite a few slaves—around 40% of the population at the time the Constitution was ratified. This is where Clara Barton set up her field hospital during the Civil War, inspiring both the American Red Cross

NEWCOMER'S HANDBOOK FOR MOVING TO AND LIVING IN WASHINGTON D.C.

100

and the MASH unit. John Mosby's Rangers waged guerilla war against the Union supply lines here, and Bull Run looks much the same today as it did to Stonewall Jackson.

This was tobacco country until the soil was depleted; after the Civil War, dairy farming took over for a few generations, and then suburban sprawl. There are still semi-rural estates here, the remnants of colonial plantations, but Fairfax County also ranks among the nation's leading jurisdictions in internet use—one of the first jurisdictions in the country where a majority of homes were online, well before the turn of the century.

The county stretches from Watkins Island in the Potomac south to Mason Neck (the wetlands surrounding historic Gunston Hall), and from Arlington west to Bull Run and the Occoquan River. On the northwest county line, where corporate campuses give way to rolling farms, Dulles International Airport occupies as much land as all the cities in Fairfax County combined. The Steven V. Udvar-Hazy Center, the cavernous annex of the National Air & Space Museum, opened here in 2003 on the 100th anniversary of the Wright brothers' first flight. The first space shuttle, *Enterprise,* is on display here, as well as the first Boeing jetliner; the *Enola Gay,* the B-29 that dropped the atomic bomb on Hiroshima; and the fastest plane ever built, the knifelike SR-71 Blackbird spy plane.

The names of entrepreneur John McLean and Senator Stephen Elkins also show up on the map. They built a trolley line connecting the Old Dominion Railroad to Great Falls and later to Herndon, and built housing along the route; unwittingly, perhaps, they invented sprawl. Today, with Fairfax County population just over a million, up 20% in 15 years, many schoolchildren attend class in "portable classrooms" (trailers).

The school system here is good, and the county claims to be the "birthplace of the internet"—a claim it shares with the inner reaches of neighboring Loudoun and Prince William counties. Apart from the advent of the internet, the defining event in the county's modern character came in the mid-1990s, when Disney sought to build an American history theme park just across the county line in Manassas National Battlefield Park. Disney was run out of town by a coalition of Civil War re-enactors, environmentalists, former city slickers seeking peace and quiet, 10th-generation horse farmers, Native Americans whose ancestors lived here for millennia, and descendants of slaves and Civil War veterans. Land use and related quality-of-life issues have dominated Fairfax County politics ever since.

The county must be doing something right: as the government web site boasts, "Out of approximately 32,000 counties and cities in the United States, Fairfax County is one of only 29 with three Triple A bond credit ratings — the highest credit rating possible."

Government: www.co.fairfax.va.us

County Board of Supervisors: 10 members, nine representing dis-

tricts and chair elected at large; 703-324-2000; www.co.fairfax.va.
us/government/board

Public Schools: 703-246-2502, www.fcps.k12.va.us

Libraries: 703-324-3100, www.co.fairfax.va.us/library

Police: 703-691-2131, www.co.fairfax.va.us/ps/police

Online Guide: www.co.fairfax.va.us; newcomer's guide, www.fairfax
county.gov/newtofairfax; recorded information, 703-324-4636; also,
Community Resident Information Services (CRiS) information kiosks
are located at most libraries and government buildings

Area Code: 703

Median Home Price: $413,000

Cost of Living: $68,000

Property Tax Rate: $1 per $100

FAIRFAX

FAIRFAX STATION
CENTREVILLE
CHANTILLY
BURKE

Boundaries: North: Interstate 66; **East:** Pickett Rd., Long Branch;
South: Braddock Rd.; **West:** Route 645

The City of Fairfax is just about the only place in the suburbs west of the
Beltway where you can find high-rise apartments as well as condos, some
under $100,000, and plenty of rentals. There's upscale housing here too—
detached houses and luxury condos in a variety of styles—but Fairfax is an
oasis of affordable living in one of the nation's most expensive counties.

There has been a town here since the early 1700s, but the old town
was ravaged by the Civil War, so most of the historic district, along Main
Street, between East and West streets, dates from the late 19th century. A
monument at Chain Bridge Road and Main Street honors Captain John
Quincy Marr, the first Confederate officer killed in the Civil War. The history
page of the town web site says, "Note that the cannons are facing north, as
do all cannons at Confederate monuments."

The Fairfax mailing address extends west of town to include the
county government complex off West Ox Road and Interstate 66. The
Fairfax County Government Center here houses county offices, and the
courtyard of the horseshoe-shaped building is the venue for the annual
Fairfax Fair in June.

If you have a million dollars and good luck, you might find a home
along the secluded wooded country roads of **Fairfax Station**, south of

NEWCOMER'S HANDBOOK FOR MOVING TO AND LIVING IN WASHINGTON D.C.

102

town off Route 123. These are beautiful houses in eclectic styles, many on several acres of woodland.

Centreville to the west and **Chantilly** to the northwest are modern outer suburbs—nice ones, if you like sprawling subdivisions and lots of driving. **Burke**, to the south, is similar, but it's better served by public transportation and it has several lakes; a few homes sit on lakefront property, and many are within a short walk. These are all pricey areas, though, with spacious designer homes—many with garage space for at least two cars.

Web Sites: www.fairfaxva.gov

Zip Codes: 22030, 22031, 22032

Post Offices: Fairfax, 3951 Chain Bridge Rd.; Turnpike Station, 3601 Pickett Rd.

Police Stations: City of Fairfax Police Department, John C. Wood Municipal Complex, 3730 Old Lee Hwy., 703-385-7960; Fairfax County Police Department, Fair Oaks District Station, 12300 Lee-Jackson Hwy., 703-591-0966

Emergency Hospitals: Inova Fair Oaks, 3600 Joseph Siewick Dr., Fairfax, 703-391-3600; Inova Fairfax, 3300 Gallows Rd., Falls Church, 703-698-1110

Library: Fairfax City Regional, 3915 Chain Bridge Rd., 703-246-2281

Public High Schools: Fairfax, 3500 Old Lee Hwy., 703-219-2200; Woodson, 9525 Main St., 703-503-4600; Robinson Secondary (grades 7-12), 5035 Sideburn Rd., 703-426-2100

Government: 11th Congressional District; mayor and six-member city Council; City Hall, 10455 Armstrong St., 703-385-7855

Neighborhood Festivals: Chocolate Lovers Festival (Old Town Hall, February); Spotlight on the Arts (various locations, April); Blenheim Civil War Encampment (Blenheim, 3610 Old Lee Hwy., May); Fourth of July celebration, various locations; Fall Festival (various locations, October); for information, call 703-385-7855. Fall for the Book literary fair (various locations, September), www.fallforthebook.org; Fairfax Fair (Fairfax County Government Center, June), 703-324-FAIR

Major Parks: Difficult Run (along Difficult Run west of Miller Heights Rd.); Eakin (along Accotink Creek south of Route 50)

Community Resources: *Fairfax Art League* organizes exhibits and special events featuring local artists, and runs a gallery at Old Town Hall, 703-273-2377. For information, call 703-352-ARTS or visit http://nuovo.com/fal. *Old Town Hall* at 3999 University Dr. is available for rentals. Call Historic Fairfax Inc. at 703-385-7858. *Patriot Center* sports and concert arena (see **Cultural Life** and **Sports & Recreation**).

Public Transportation: Metro: Vienna-Fairfax/GMU (Orange Line); VRE: Burke Centre station (Manassas Line); Metrobus routes: 1B-1Z (Ballston), 2A-2G (Ballston), 12 series (Centreville), 17 series

(Pentagon), 20 series (Chantilly), 29K (Alexandria); Fairfax Connector routes 402-404 (local)

GREAT FALLS/McLEAN

LANGLEY

Boundaries: North: Potomac River; **East**: Potomac River; **South**: Arlington County; **West**: Dulles Access Road, Leesburg Pike

The Fairfax County banks of the Potomac are home to genteel, traditional, conservative estates belonging to old money of colonial pedigree and to the political elite. The only time you're likely to find a lot of turnover here is just after an election, when those lawmakers and Cabinet secretaries who aren't joining K Street law firms put their spacious houses and acreage on the market. If your tastes are modest and you shop around, you might find a cottage or luxury townhouse here for as little as a quarter million, but expect to see prices mostly in the high six figures—and sevens, especially for homes with great Potomac River views. After all, it's nice country—this is the Old Dominion, and if you face away from the road you might think the area hasn't changed much in two centuries.

In contrast to Potomac, Md., across the river, the horse fences here aren't just for show. Winding roads follow the terrain, making for picturesque communities, albeit hazardous driving conditions in the rain and snow. And forget about public transportation in this patrician countryside—in fact, some addresses don't even have trash and recycling collection service, and when you drive to the Great Falls dump on Saturday morning, you might run into an entire congressional committee.

The parks along the Potomac protect land that has attracted weekend explorers since John Smith came up from Jamestown in 1608, looking for gold and the legendary Northwest Passage. As it turns out, you can't sail to the Pacific from here—you run into a wall of big rocks across the Potomac where thundering whitewater spills 80 feet down from the piedmont plateau onto the coastal plain. Every year, a few unlucky souls perish here, losing their footing on the slippery rocks, and the place should not be underestimated by climbers and kayakers.

There are plenty of elite private schools in this area, but few schools in the world rival the social prestige of the Madeira School, whose cupola peeks through the treetops on prime real estate overlooking the river.

Downstream toward Arlington, a federal reservation just off Route 123 in **Langley** was known for years as the "Turner-Fairbank Highway Research Center," though everyone knew it was actually CIA headquarters. At some point in the 1980s, a tiny green sign marked the exit "CIA." No vis-

NEWCOMER'S HANDBOOK FOR MOVING TO AND LIVING IN WASHINGTON D.C.

104

itor center, no gift shop, and you're not likely ever to visit the memorial wall of 77 stars each honoring a slain CIA "asset"—many of whose names are still classified. However, according to the agency's web site, www.cia.gov, tours aren't entirely out of the question: there are "an extremely limited number of visits annually for approved academic and civic groups."

The Langley complex isn't the only cloak-and-dagger landmark in the area. Just outside Arlington, Fort Marcy Park is a major stop on the conspiracy buff's tour. Here John Dean handed briefcases full of Nixon campaign money to E. Howard Hunt to buy the Watergate burglars' silence, and here Clinton aide Vince Foster's body was found with a suicide note. Such dramatic episodes reflect the character of the Great Falls and McLean community; this is the home of money, power, and intrigue. Pronounce it right: "McLANE."

Web Site: www.gfcitizens.com

Zip Codes: 22101, 22102, 22066

Post Offices: Great Falls, 748 Walker Rd.; McLean, 6841 Elm St.

Police Station: McLean District Station, 1437 Balls Hill Rd., 703-556-7750

Emergency Hospitals: Reston Hospital Center, 1850 Town Center Pkwy., 703-689-9000; Inova Fairfax Hospital, 3300 Gallows Rd., Falls Church, 703-698-1110

Libraries: Dolley Madison, 1244 Oak Ridge Ave., McLean, 703-356-0770; Great Falls, 9830 Georgetown Pike, 703-757-8560

Public High Schools: Langley, 6520 Georgetown Pike, McLean, 703-287-2700; McLean, 1633 Davidson Rd., 703-714-5700

Government: 11th Congressional District; Dranesville District, Fairfax County Board of Supervisors

Neighborhood Festivals: Taste of McLean (McLean Community Center, 1234 Ingleside Ave., March); McLean Day (various locations, May), 703-790-0123

Major Parks: Great Falls (north end of Old Dominion Dr.); Dranesville (north of Georgetown Pike just outside the Beltway); Langley Oaks/Turkey Run (George Washington Pkwy. just inside the Beltway); Riverbend (Jeffery Rd. off River Bend Rd.)

Community Resources: *McLean Community Center* features art studio space, a theater, a teen center, classes, and recreational programs: 1234 Ingleside Ave., 703-790-0123, www.mcleancenter.org. For information about solid waste disposal and recycling, call 703-324-5040.

Public Transportation: Metrobus routes: 23C (Langley, Crystal City), 23A/B & 23T (Tysons Corner, Crystal City)

HERNDON

Boundaries: North: Herndon Centennial Golf Course, Folly Lick Branch, Herndon High School; **East**: Sugarland Run; **South**: Dulles Access Road; **West**: Loudoun County

If you work in the Dulles corridor, and if planned communities like Reston remind you of *The Truman Show*, Herndon offers the convenience of a Reston location with a less manicured feel. Herndon's main street, Elden Street, is surrounded by older neighborhoods, and offers a good selection of restaurants for a town of 22,000. There are lots of upscale townhouse condos in and around Herndon, some designed to recall the Old Dominion with cupolas and gables. Brick houses still stand in the neighborhoods that grew along the old railroad, which has now been transformed into the Washington & Old Dominion bike trail. Sales and rentals are, as in most of the western suburbs, expensive—but nothing compared to nearby Great Falls, where more homes are inherited than rented.

The Herndon area appeared on colonial charters as early as 1688, but the town wasn't incorporated until 1858. According to local legend, the town founders were debating possible names for the new municipality, and a survivor of a shipwreck proposed that the town be named in honor of Captain William Lewis Herndon, who had gone down with the ship after ensuring the safety of the women and children. Herndon, a former naval officer who helped establish the U.S. Naval Observatory and wrote the first scholarly report on the Amazon, was among more than 400 men who died aboard the packet ship *Central America* in a storm off Cape Hatteras in 1857.

Sixty years after its incorporation, the town was almost as unlucky when a fire destroyed downtown Herndon. Rebuilt in brick, some of the new homes were sturdy prefabricated houses made by Sears & Roebuck and hauled into town on freight trains. Today, these are some of the oldest homes in the Dulles corridor, and most of their occupants work nearby.

Web Sites: www.town.herndon.va.us, http://herndonweb.com
Zip Code: 20070
Post Office: Herndon, 590 Grove St.
Police Station: Herndon Police, 1481 Sterling Rd., 703-435-6846
Emergency Hospital: Reston Hospital Center, 1850 Town Center Pkwy., 703-689-9000
Library: Herndon Fortnightly, 768 Center St., 703-437-8855 (founded by the Fortnightly Club in 1889)
Public High School: Herndon, 700 Bennett St., 703-810-2200

NEWCOMER'S HANDBOOK FOR MOVING TO AND LIVING IN WASHINGTON D.C.

106

Government: 11th Congressional District; Hunter Mill District, Fairfax County Board of Supervisors; Mayor and six-member Town Council; Herndon Municipal Center, 777 Lynn St., 703-435-6800

Neighborhood Festivals: Labor Day Jazz Festival (Town Green), 703-435-6868; Mayor's Cup golf tournament (Herndon Centennial Golf Course, October), 703-471-5769; Herndon Folk Festival (Town Green, October), 703-435-6868

Major Parks: Runnymede/Sugarland Run (along Sugarland Run north of Herndon Pkwy.)

Community Resources: *Entertainment on the Town Green* includes a Thursday evening summer concert series, 703-435-6868, and Friday Night Live performances, 703-437-5556. *Washington & Old Dominion Trail* (see Vienna below).

Public Transportation: Fairfax Connector routes: 551, 901-904, 951/952, 980 (Falls Church), 924 (Dranesville), 927/929 (Chantilly), 941/942, 984 (Tysons Corner)

RESTON

Boundaries: North: Leesburg Pike; **East**: Hunter Mill Rd.; **South**: Fox Mill Rd., Lawyers Rd.; **West**: Herndon, Loudoun County

Reston is a planned community built in the 1960s and named with the initials of its designer, Robert E. Simon. Deliberately eclectic housing stock, with sizes and styles to command a variety of price brackets, surrounds a retail "town center," and residential clusters or "villages" were planned for pedestrians and bicyclists. While planned communities are never quite as charming as they sound in brochures, Reston is more walkable than other modern suburbs, and economically more diverse than most.

The vast community, designed for 70,000 and not quite "full," is sort of a giant condominium: every resident, whether a homeowner or a renter, is a member of the Reston Association and pays mandatory dues—typically $415 per household, less for the few whose property tax assessment is under $83,000 or for households qualifying for certain county tax breaks. These fees maintain 1,300 acres of open space and 125 acres of artificial lakes; 55 miles of pathways with 106 bridges; ballfields, playgrounds, tennis and basketball courts, and fitness trails; Walker Nature Education Center and environmental education programs for all ages; summer camps; special events for children, seniors, and families; 15 swimming pools; a facility for boat and RV storage; community gardens; and a chapel, meeting rooms, and pavilions available for rent.

Residents also agree (by being residents) to abide by certain covenants governing the use, maintenance, and exterior appearance of their homes.

It may sound Orwellian, but in practice it's no different from the zoning ordinances and building codes in any incorporated town in the suburbs; instead of municipal taxes and a town council, Reston—like many smaller subdivisions—has association dues and an elected board of directors. (As this book goes to press, residents are debating whether to take the plunge and incorporate as a new city.)

Streets named after Isaac Newton, Michael Faraday, Roger Bacon, and Samuel Morse underscore the importance of the technology sector in Reston. Many employees from the nearby campuses of America Online, Network Solutions, and Xerox live here. DynCorp and Sallie Mae have headquarters here, along with a slew of smaller computer and telecom companies, and their workforce spills over into neighboring Herndon. Office parks with names like Worldgate, Dulles Technology Center, and Parkway Trade Center loom over the tollbooths of the Dulles Access Road. Virginia Tech has a Reston campus on Isaac Newton Square.

Web Sites: http://reston.org, www.restonweb.com

Zip Codes: 20090, 20091, 20094

Post Offices: Reston 20090, 11110 Sunset Hills Rd.; Reston 20091, 1860 Michael Faraday Dr.

Police Station: Reston District Station, 12000 Bowman Towne Dr., 703-478-0904

Emergency Hospital: Reston Hospital Center, 1850 Town Center Pkwy., 703-689-9000

Library: Reston Regional, 11925 Bowman Towne Dr., 703-689-2700

Public High School: South Lakes, 11400 South Lakes Dr., Reston, 703-715-4500

Government: 11th Congressional District; Hunter Mill District, Fairfax County Board of Supervisors; nine-member Reston Association Board of Directors (four members representing districts, one representing apartment owners, and three elected at large); Reston Association office, 1930 Isaac Newton Square, 703-437-9580

Neighborhood Festival: Reston Festival (north shore of Lake Anne, July), www.restonfestival.com; community events recording, 703-435-6558

Major Parks: Difficult Run (Hunters Valley Rd. off Hunter Mill Rd.); Fox Mill (Fox Mill Rd. south of Lawyers Rd.); Frying Pan (West Ox Rd. east of Centreville Rd.); Lake Fairfax (Lake Fairfax Dr. south of Baron Cameron Ave.)

Community Resources: *Reston Newcomers Club* offers monthly social and informational programs, a newsletter, and a directory for a one-year membership fee of $21, 703-689-3388; for information about any Reston amenities, contact the *Reston Association* office at 703-437-9580 or http://reston.org.

NEWCOMER'S HANDBOOK FOR MOVING TO AND LIVING IN WASHINGTON D.C.

108

Public Transportation: Fairfax Connector routes: 551–557 & 901–905 (Falls Church), 574 (Tysons Corner); RIBS bus service (local)

VIENNA

TYSONS CORNER
WINDOVER HEIGHTS

Boundaries: North: Dulles Access Road; **East**: Dulles Access Road; **South**: Interstate 66; **West**: Hunter Mill Rd., Vale Rd., Nutley St.

Beware: an office with a Vienna mailing address is most likely located in the **Tysons Corner** complex just outside the town of Vienna. If you like big shopping malls and car dealerships, you might like Tysons Corner; otherwise, this permanent traffic jam at the junction of Routes 123 and 7, just outside the Beltway, embodies all the worst stereotypes about congested roads and grim-looking office towers. Thousands of people work here, but practically none live here in this little city that's only open during the day. One Tysons skyscraper, visible from miles away, has twin arches on the roof that resemble a pair of handles; commuters refer to it, with a hint of sarcasm, as "the shopping bag building."

Route 123 south from Tysons leads to Vienna proper, where a few luxurious modern houses sell for a million dollars—often to executives from the technology firms and defense contractors up the road. Most of the homes here are modern suburban designs, but affordable as the Virginia suburbs go—that is, under half a million. There are also a few garden apartment and townhouse complexes, both condos and rentals, at prices comparable to all but the most prestigious neighborhoods in D.C.

Originally called Ayr Hill, Vienna is 22 years older than the United States. Its name was changed when a wealthy doctor from Vienna, N.Y., moved here in the 1850s on the condition that the town change its name.

During the Civil War, Vienna changed hands so many times that many families moved away to escape the continual upheaval. According to the history page of the town web site, a battle at the Park Street railroad crossing was "the first time in history a railroad was used tactically in battle." After the war, the railroad was used for industry, and Vienna boomed with sawmills, blacksmiths, a cannery, and a funeral home, which is now the town's oldest business. Now the railroad is a rails-to-trails bike path making an off-road paved link from rural Purcellville to Mt. Vernon.

In the **Windover Heights Historic District**, off Maple Avenue and Lawyers Road, a preservation review board must approve exterior changes to the historic homes and businesses. Throughout Vienna, an architectural review board ensures that construction "is not bizarre or garish and is harmonious and compatible with existing buildings." Young Tysons techies may be adversely affected by the fact that, by law, group houses are limited to no more than four unrelated adults.

On the drawing boards, to be completed around 2015, is MetroWest, a high-density complex of homes, retail space, and offices clustered around the Vienna Metro station. Developers envision 6,000 people living in 13 skyscrapers at the western terminus of the Orange Line—and easing the pressure on homebuilders to sprawl farther out into the Northern Virginia countryside.

Web Site: www.ci.vienna.va.us

Zip Codes: 22043, 22180, 22182

Post Office: Vienna, 200 Lawyers Rd. NW

Police Station: Vienna Police Department, 215 Center St. South, 703-255-6366

Emergency Hospitals: Inova Fair Oaks, 3600 Joseph Siewick Dr., Fairfax, 703-391-3600; Inova Fairfax, 3300 Gallows Rd., Falls Church, 703-698-1110

Library: Patrick Henry Community Library, 101 Maple Ave. East, 703-938-0405

Public High Schools: Madison, 2500 James Madison Dr., 703-319-2300; Oakton, 2900 Sutton Rd., 703-319-2700

Government: 11th Congressional District; Providence District, Fairfax County Board of Supervisors; mayor and 6-member town council; Town Hall, 127 Center St. South, 703-255-6300

Neighborhood Festival: Fourth of July celebration, Cherry & Center streets

Major Parks: Wolf Trap Farm (off the Dulles Access Road west of Leesburg Pike); Wolftrap Stream Valley (along Wolftrap Run between Old Court House Rd. and Westwood Country Club)

Community Resources: *The Women's Center* provides affordable counseling to women, men, and families, and sponsors an annual women's leadership conference, 133 Park St. NE, 703-281-2657, www.thewomenscenter.org. *Vienna Arts Society* sponsors exhibits, workshops, classes, and trips to out-of-town galleries, 703-319-3971, www.viennaartssociety.org. *Vienna Community Center,* 120 Cherry St. SE, 703-255-6360. *Washington & Old Dominion Trail* is a 45-mile paved bike path from Arlington, where it meets the Mt. Vernon Trail along the Potomac, to rural Loudoun County. For information and maps, contact the Northern Virginia Regional Park Authority at 703-729-0596, www.nvrpa.org/wod, or Friends of the W&OD Trail at www.wodfriends.org. *Wolf Trap Farm Park for the Performing Arts* (see **Cultural Life**).

NEWCOMER'S HANDBOOK FOR MOVING TO AND LIVING IN WASHINGTON D.C.

110

Public Transportation: Metro: Vienna-Fairfax/GMU and Dunn Loring/Merrifield (Orange Line); Metrobus: 1B/1D (Ballston), 2 series (Ballston, Fair Oaks Mall), 3A (Annandale), 3B-3F (Rosslyn), 3W/3Z (Falls Church), 12 series (Centreville), 14 series (Bethesda), 20 series (Chantilly); 23 series (Crystal City); Fairfax Connector bus hub with 19 routes serving Tysons Corner and Metro stations

CITY OF FALLS CHURCH

SEVEN CORNERS
BAILEYS CROSSROADS

Boundaries: North: Route 703, Interstate 66; **East**: Arlington County; **South**: Washington St. South, Hillwood Ave.; **West**: Route 703

An independent city since 1948, Falls Church was first colonized in 1699. According to a pamphlet published for the community's tricentennial, the site once was a busy intersection of native Tauxenent trails—now marked by Leesburg Pike and Lee Highway—for 12,000 years. The city takes its name from a colonial church whose congregation included George Washington and the author of the Bill of Rights, George Mason; the church, in turn, was named for its location along the ancient trail leading to Great Falls.

The National Arbor Day Foundation consistently gives Falls Church an annual Tree City USA award, and Leesburg Pike has a "Main Street" look and feel. Some local businesses are identified with signs dating from the late '50s, and you almost expect to see the parking lot full of big convertibles with tail fins; on the other hand, in 2004, the vintage bowling alley was torn down to make way for luxury condos. The city of about 10,000 people has a median household income close to $100,000 and most adult residents are college graduates. Falls Church also has the highest property tax rate of any jurisdiction in this book, $1.08 per $100 of assessed value.

That's within the little city. The name Falls Church is loosely applied to the suburbs west to the Beltway and south to Holmes Run. Along commercial Leesburg Pike, the retail districts of **Seven Corners** and **Baileys Crossroads** are the places where your neighbors in the inner Virginia suburbs go for practical shopping; Pentagon City and Tysons Corner are good for luxuries and gifts, not for lawnmowers. There are some reasonably priced apartments and condos off Leesburg Pike too, and upscale condos and detached modern houses to the south near Lake Barcroft.

Falls Church is one of the sites chosen for a federal pilot program testing clean-fuel buses. The local GEORGE bus line connects downtown Falls Church to the East and West Falls Church Metro stations using low-emission buses. (For more information, visit the GEORGE page of the city government web site.)

Web Site: www.ci.falls-church.va.us

Zip Code: 20046

Post Office: Falls Church, 301 West Broad St.

Police Station: Falls Church Police Department, City Hall, 703-241-5053 (questions) or 703-241-5050 (emergency)

Emergency Hospitals: Arlington Hospital, 1701 N. George Mason Dr., 703-558-5000; Inova Fairfax, 3300 Gallows Rd., 703-698-1110

Library: Mary Riley Styles Public Library, 120 North Virginia Ave., 703-248-5030; www.falls-church.lib.va.us

Public High Schools: George Mason, 7124 Leesburg Pike, 703-248-5500 (Falls Church City Public Schools, www.fccps.k12.va.us); Falls Church, 7521 Jaguar Trail, 703-207-4000; Marshall, 7731 Leesburg Pike, 703-714-5400; J.E.B. Stuart, 3301 Peace Valley Lane, 703-824-3900 (Fairfax County Public Schools)

Government: 8th Congressional District; mayor serves on seven-member city council; City Hall, 300 Park Ave., 703-248-5014

Major Parks: Four Mile Run (along Four Mile Run south of I-66)

Community Resources: *Falls Church Recreation & Parks Division*, 703-248-5077, www.ci.falls-church.va.us; the *Northern Virginia Center*, 7504 Haycock Rd., is a satellite campus shared by Virginia Tech and the University of Virginia, specializing in continuing education and high tech career development (see **Higher Education**). *Washington & Old Dominion Trail* (see Vienna above).

Public Transportation: Metro: East Falls Church and West Falls Church-VT/UVA (Orange Line); Metrobus routes: 3A-3F (Rosslyn), 3W/3Z and 24T (Tysons Corner), 10C (Alexandria); Fairfax Connector routes: 421/427 (Tysons Corner), 551 & 901-980 (Herndon), 552-557 and 585 (Reston); GEORGE bus (local circulator)

Median Home Price: $527,000

Property Tax Rate: $1.08 per $100

OUTER SUBURBS

People do commute from Washington's sprawling outer suburbs to jobs inside the Beltway. It's universally considered an ordeal and a major lifestyle decision, but the cost of housing in D.C. and the inner suburbs is so high that a growing number of people settle an hour's drive or more out of town. Many people try it and decide that a big mortgage payment is better than a 2-hour commute each way.

On the other hand, if you are moving to the Washington area with a job lined up in the outer suburbs, you might find one of the following

NEWCOMER'S HANDBOOK FOR MOVING TO AND LIVING IN WASHINGTON D.C.

112

communities more convenient than those around the Beltway. Refer to the **Transportation** chapter for contact information about long-distance commuter transit: MARC and Virginia Railway Express (VRE) commuter trains and Maryland Transit Authority (MTA) and OmniRide buses.

MARYLAND

ANNAPOLIS (ANNE ARUNDEL COUNTY)

The capital city of Maryland and the home of the U.S. Naval Academy is about 45 minutes from the Beltway—by road, which is the only way to get there. (On land, anyway.) The Chesapeake Bay and the Severn River make Annapolis a boater's paradise, and broad, sleepy creeks provide ample marina space and waterfront property.) You can find spacious cottages here at much lower prices than in Washington, and there are brokers who specialize in waterfront homes. The colonial-era old town, between the city docks and the green dome of the nation's oldest statehouse, attracts weekend window-shoppers and still feels like a colonial fishing village. There are period homes, cobblestone streets, and oysters on the half shell available on every corner, and minutes uptown, the strip malls along Route 2 and Route 70 meet modern shopping needs.

Web Sites: www.ci.annapolis.md.us, www.co.anne-arundel.md.us
Government Information: 410-263-1183
Newspaper: *The Capital*, 410-268-5000; circulation, 410-268-4800, www.hometownannapolis.com
Getting There: MTA bus route 921 from New Carrollton Metro station or route 922 from Union Station

BALTIMORE

Just 45 miles away but a world apart, Baltimore is a working port city whose tall skyline is a downtown financial district. There have been many efforts to connect Baltimore and Washington economically and culturally, but it has never worked—Baltimore is a blue-collar city and Washington is elitist. As a Washingtonian, you might spend a lot of time in Baltimore on business or in search of good crab cakes, Irish pubs, Italian restaurants, Jewish delis, and the Fells Point seafood joint made famous by thousands of green-and-white bumper stickers that say "Eat Bertha's Mussels." The touristy Inner Harbor area and the midtown arts district around the University of Baltimore are both easily accessible from D.C. by a one-hour MARC train ride. Once you're there, Baltimore has a mixed-bag public transportation system: there's one Metro line, one light rail line, and buses;

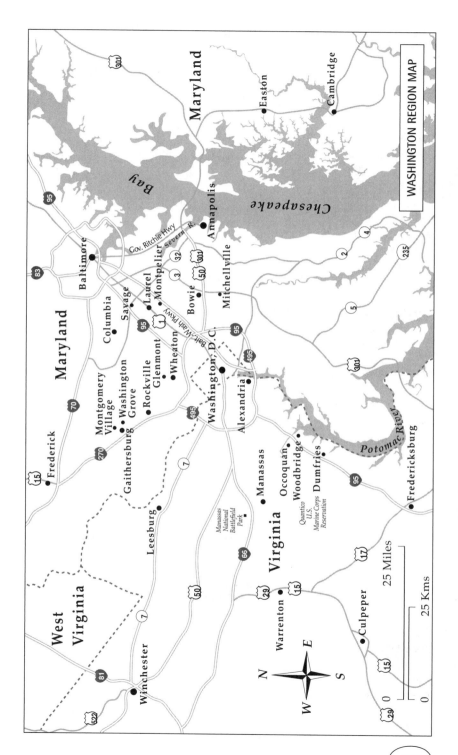

WASHINGTON REGION MAP

NEWCOMER'S HANDBOOK FOR MOVING TO AND LIVING IN WASHINGTON D.C.

114

every trip is a flat $1.60, and it's simple and reliable—if your destination happens to be on one of those few routes.

The **Baltimore Neighborhood Indicators Alliance**, www.bnia. org, provides extensive information about 55 neighborhoods, and the Neighborhoods page of the city web site includes neighborhood profiles and links to civic organizations. Housing is considerably cheaper than in D.C., with 3-bedroom homes (mostly townhouses) available under $300,000. There may even be a few uptown condos under $200,000. Search real estate listings at www.sunspot.net or www.citypaper.com—or the Baltimore page of Craigslist, www.craigslist.org.

Web Site: www.ci.baltimore.md.us

Government Information: 410-396-3100 (government switchboard) or 410-837-4636 (visitor information)

Newspaper: *Baltimore Sun*, 410-332-6000 or 800-829-8000; circulation, 410-539-1280, www.sunspot.net

Getting There: MARC Penn Line from Union Station via New Carrollton Metro station; MARC Camden Line from Union Station via Greenbelt Metro station

COLUMBIA (HOWARD COUNTY)

Columbia, Md., like Reston, is a planned community whose 14,000 acres were divided into nine "villages"—mapped out in the 1960s by developer James Rouse, who went on to design most of the mid-Atlantic region's biggest shopping malls. As in most planned communities, a huge percentage of the town is parkland and recreational amenities; most kids can walk to school; and there is diverse modern housing stock, from efficiency apartments to lakefront bungalows, intended to attract an economically diverse population. Columbia is unique, though, for its location: halfway between Washington and Baltimore along Interstate 95, it was supposed to be a bridge between the two cities. It hasn't quite worked out that way—rather than identifying with both cities, Columbia is remote from either. Many little high-tech firms have offices in Columbia's sprawling "flex" parks, where offices and light industrial outfits share utilitarian, hangar-like buildings, but mostly Columbia interests couples with one job in Washington and one in Baltimore.

Web Sites: www.columbia-md.com, www.co.ho.md.us

Community Information: 410-992-6099

Newspaper: *Columbia Daily Tribune*, 410-997-8000

Getting There: MTA bus route 915 from Washington Navy Yard via Metro center and Silver Spring Metro stations; route 929 from Capitol Hill via Dupont Circle and Silver Spring Metro stations

FREDERICK (FREDERICK COUNTY)

Just north of Montgomery County, and accessible by MARC commuter trains, Frederick has been "on the map" since 1765, when colonial citizens rallied in Court House Square to burn the announcement of the Stamp Act of the British government. Today it is the northern anchor of the 270 Corridor, a biotech industry capital stretching 35 miles south along I-270 to Bethesda. A few telecommunications companies are major employers here, too—notably Bechtel and, in upper Montgomery County, Comsat. If you want to live in a city and work in the 270 Corridor, it's certainly much cheaper to live 15 miles north of your office than 15 miles south. Many of the brick townhomes here are at least a century old, and some survived the Civil War. Visit Frederick's historic district for the antiques and a breath of clean air, upwind from most of the Washington area's exhaust and illegal levels of smog-producing ozone, and decide whether it's too remote or just right. Don't expect much nightlife, though—local teens refer to their town as "Fredneck."

Web Sites: www.cityoffrederick.com, www.co.frederick.md.us

Government Information: 301-360-3842

Newspaper: *Frederick News-Post,* 301-662-1177, www.fredericknews post.com

Getting There: MTA bus route 991 from Shady Grove Metro station; MARC shuttle bus from Point of Rocks station (Brunswick Line)

VIRGINIA

LOUDOUN COUNTY

LEESBURG
ASHBURN

Historic **Leesburg,** where you and your car can still cross the Potomac River on a cable ferry to Poolesville, Md., is just upstream from Fairfax County along Route 7 or the Washington & Old Dominion bike trail. The 18th-century old town is surrounded by varied housing, from historic townhouses to modern detached houses in subdivisions, much more affordable than comparable homes closer to the Beltway. Many homes here still sell for $250,000 and rent for $1,000. Not coincidentally, sprawl has pushed many employers out here, including the main offices of the Federal Aviation Administration, and the population of Leesburg—around 35,000—has more than doubled since 1990.

NEWCOMER'S HANDBOOK FOR MOVING TO AND LIVING IN WASHINGTON D.C.

116

The eastern corner of the county is dominated by Dulles International Airport, and the companies housed in office parks along the Dulles Access Road sometimes refer to their place of business as "Dulles," even though there's no such town. (The Loudoun County side of the airport is in **Ashburn** and the Fairfax County side is **Chantilly**.)

Web Sites: www.co.loudoun.va.us, www.leesburgva.org, http://lees burgva.com

Government Information: 703-777-2420

Newspaper: *Leesburg Today*, 703-771-8800, www.leesburg2day.com

Getting There: Washington Flyer and other Dulles Airport shuttle services

PRINCE WILLIAM COUNTY

OCCOQUAN
QUANTICO
WOODBRIDGE
DUMFRIES
MANASSAS

To most Washingtonians, the area south of Bull Run and the Occoquan River conjures images of discount shopping at Potomac Mills outlet mall or "antiquing" in **Occoquan**. (It's pronounced AHH-kuh-kwahn.) It's also the home of **Quantico** Marine Corps Base—6,600 Marines, 33,000 acres—and the bedroom suburbs of **Woodbridge** and **Dumfries**, both on the Virginia Railway Express line. A rural area just 20 years ago, booming population growth makes it feel increasingly like the older suburbs. The *Washington Post* reported in 2005 that 13% of the Washington area's 83,000 Salvadoran immigrants live in Prince William County, and the Embassy of El Salvador recently opened a new consulate in Woodbridge.

Manassas, best known as the scene of two Civil War battles, marks the western edge of urban sprawl. A few horse-country diehards commute to D.C.—an hour by VRE train and, depending on traffic, much longer by Interstate 66. On a clear night, the lights of Manassas can be seen from the mountains of Shenandoah National Park, 60 miles west. It's a modern suburb, with strip malls and inexpensive subdivision housing—you can rent a three-bedroom townhouse for $1,500 or buy a townhouse for under $200,000, impossible half an hour's drive east of here. For employees of Lockheed Martin and other companies in the western Dulles corridor, it's a short commute; but the main attraction here is the genuine countryside, including the starry skies above the 5,000-acre Manassas National Battlefield Park.

Prince William County campaigns hard to attract businesses to its major corridors along I-95 and I-66. There are modern subdivisions here with plenty of townhouse condos and garden apartments, but don't expect to find many detached houses changing hands.

Web Sites: www.co.prince-william.va.us, www.manassascity.org, www.manassas.com, www.cityofmanassaspark.us, www.occoquan.com

Government Information: 703-792-4660

Newspaper: *Manassas Journal Messenger,* 703-368-3101; circulation, 703-368-3134, www.manassasjm.com

Getting There: VRE Manassas Line from Union Station via L'Enfant Plaza Metro station; VRE Fredericksburg Line via Woodbridge and Quantico; OmniRide buses to Manassas from Foggy Bottom Metro station, to Dumfries from L'Enfant Plaza Metro station, and to Woodbridge from Franconia-Springfield Metro station

STAFFORD COUNTY

FREDERICKSBURG
AQUIA HARBOUR

On the Rappahannock River 50 miles south of D.C. on I-95, modern **Fredericksburg** surrounds the 40-block historic district where George Washington grew up. Because of its age and pedigree, Fredericksburg is the only area within potential commuter range of D.C.—almost 90 minutes by VRE train—with housing prices as high as the District's. Historic Fredericksburg is replete with stately old Victorian cottages and gabled colonials that can sell for half a million or more; even the more modern homes weren't built yesterday and are nicer, sturdier, and more expensive than most homes in outlying areas. Nearby **Aquia Harbour** features big modern homes near secluded marinas off the lower Potomac. Stafford County advertises itself as a "pro-business community," meaning low taxes and little patience with the "smart growth" movement seeking to limit sprawl in other parts of the outer suburbs. GEICO, Intuit, and Coca-Cola have major facilities here, and Stafford Regional Airport caters to executive charters.

Web Sites: www.fredericksburgva.gov, www.fredericksburgvirginia.net, www.co.stafford.va.us

Government Information: 540-372-1010

Newspaper: *Free Lance-Star,* 540-374-5002, www.fredericksburg.com

Getting There: VRE Fredericksburg Line from Union Station via L'Enfant Plaza Station

I N MOST CITIES, THE HOUSING MARKET TENDS TO FOLLOW THE STOCK market and the general economy. In the Washington area, the housing market is more stable and somewhat recession-proof—after all, in any economic conditions, the federal government remains the world's largest employer, consumer, and client.

A quick history of D.C. in the late 20th and early 21st centuries can explain the general real estate trends. In the late 1980s, the crack epidemic and a decline in city services pushed middle-class families out into the suburbs. The suburbs got crowded and congested, young couples and singles started moving into the city again, and their taxes paid for better services. Growing businesses and trendy restaurants discovered neighborhoods that had been neglected since the riots of the 1960s. At the turn of the millennium, the D.C. skyline was dominated by construction cranes.

Result: In hip neighborhoods like Dupont Circle, Adams Morgan, and Mt. Pleasant, rents doubled in five years (1996 to 2001). At the same time, in Georgetown and Capitol Hill, condos were selling for six figures and three-bedroom homes selling for seven, and the *Washington Post* reported that the median price of home sales had increased every year in most of the city's 22 zip codes. In the heart of the city—Shaw, Adams Morgan, Mt. Pleasant, and Columbia Heights—median prices rose by more than 20%; now, a well-kept, spacious townhouse in Adams Morgan or Dupont Circle can command as much rent as a prestigious Georgetown address. The good news is that housing is plentiful—it's much easier to find a home here than in, say, Manhattan or Seattle. A few blocks off the beaten path can make a huge difference in price, too; there are bargains to be found in many of the District's quiet residential neighborhoods. And if you're buying your first home in the District, you may be eligible for a $5,000 tax credit. (See **Assistance for First-time Homebuyers** below.)

NEWCOMER'S HANDBOOK FOR MOVING TO AND LIVING IN WASHINGTON D.C.

120

Here are a few things to watch out for as you search for a place to live:

- **Airport noise:** Reagan National Airport is just across the river from downtown D.C., and air traffic roars over Georgetown and neighboring parts of Maryland as well as Arlington and Alexandria. During business hours, air traffic is constant. There are noise-abatement rules that restrict takeoffs and landings at night, but the only sure bet is to visit a neighborhood several times, at different times of day. In Virginia, the western suburbs—Herndon and Chantilly—have noise problems from Dulles Airport to the west, and the Maryland suburbs just east of D.C. experience noise from huge cargo planes serving Andrews Air Force Base.

- **Civic involvement and public safety:** Find out whether a neighborhood has high turnover or a lot of settled residents. Bonus points for the neighborhood if a lot of residents are active in the local civic association, the PTA, or local politics. Also check with the local police station and interview patrol officers about area safety. Good schools, safe neighborhoods, and sound property investments are found where neighbors care about the community and devote time and effort to its improvement.

- **Termites:** Washington's temperate climate makes it termite heaven. A termite inspection is part of any home sale, and it's advisable to go along on the inspection to make sure it's thorough and to talk with the inspector about any potential problems. See the **Pest Control** section of the **Helpful Services** chapter for more information.

- **Traffic noise:** During rush-hour commutes, when major thoroughfares are crowded, many commuters use residential streets as shortcuts. Some neighborhoods have speed bumps, frequent stop signs, and one-way streets to discourage commuters, but many streets that are tranquil on weekends turn into speedways on Monday morning. Highway noise is a problem for some suburban neighborhoods along the Beltway; concrete walls muffle the roar a bit, but they certainly don't make it go away. Again, the best way to check out noise problems in a prospective neighborhood is to visit several times, at different times of day.

RENTING VS. BUYING

In the long run, buying may be cheaper than renting, and you end up with an asset to show for it; but many newcomers buy a house or condo too soon after moving to town, only to discover that the neighborhood, the commute, or the home itself is more than they bargained for. Property tax rates have been slashed in recent years, but assessed values have skyrocketed and the average tax burden has gone up as a result. (In most local jurisdictions, the property tax rate is between 90 cents and $1 per $100 of assessed value.) In the District, property values can vary dramatically from one block to the next—along with noise, traffic, graffiti, and signs of drug activity. But even inexpensive housing in the Washington area is expensive by nationwide standards. According to 2004 year-end figures reported in the *Washington Times,* the median price of housing is $345,000 in D.C., up $50,000 from a year before, and the median price in the suburbs is $363,000.

If you're not in a hurry to get kids settled into a school, it might be wise to sign a one-year lease to allow time to get to know the city before deciding where to put down permanent roots. Throughout the Washington area, you'll find a good selection of rental houses as well as apartments. Some are owned by local families as investments; others are owned by military or diplomatic families who don't want to leave their permanent homes empty while they're posted overseas. In a typical week, the *Washington Post* Sunday classifieds list hundreds of homes for rent, and the *Washington City Paper* lists dozens of homes for rent and dozens of rooms in shared houses. (And **Craigslist**, www.craigslist.net, shows even more as the real estate market relies increasingly on the web.)

There is some economic good news for renters: in 2005, the real estate research firm Delta Associates reported that the average rent in D.C. is about 60% as much per square foot as a mortgage for the same home— a ratio well below the national average. On the other hand, the market is tight. According to Delta, D.C. has the lowest apartment vacancy rate in the country (in other words, the fiercest competition for rentals), with just 3% of all rental units on the market at any given time.

The rental market is varied enough to suit practically anyone's housing needs: from efficiency apartments in modern high-rises to pedigreed mansions in the country, from postwar suburban duplexes to 19th-century carriage houses. Townhouses, old and new, are especially abundant—tall, narrow houses adjoining similar houses on either side. A common type of rental in D.C. is the "English basement," a basement apartment with its own entrance separate from the townhouse above. Most apartments in D.C. are housed in stately brick apartment buildings built before World War II, but there are plenty of newer high-rises, which tend to have more amenities and less visual charm. In the suburbs, you'll find postwar high-rises and garden apartments—low-rise buildings of two or three stories. There are suburban townhouses, too—in self-contained complexes resembling garden apartment developments. Some townhouses in suburban subdivisions are sold as condo units.

NEWCOMER'S HANDBOOK FOR MOVING TO AND LIVING IN WASHINGTON D.C.

122

RENTING A HOUSE OR APARTMENT

Generally speaking, D.C. is a tenant-friendly jurisdiction. Most renters will find buildings maintained to the high standards required by law. It is difficult for a landlord to evict a tenant, particularly in the winter. And, unless a landlord can give a good reason not to renew a lease when it expires, the tenant has a statutory right to renew it.

The District passed a **rent control** statute in 1975, just a year after it first elected a mayor and city council. The law applies only to major landlords—those who own no more than four units are exempt, unless they have more than three business partners. In addition, certain types of properties are not subject to rent control:

- government-owned or subsidized housing
- new housing (generally, housing built after 1975)
- housing managed or overseen by certain programs of the Department of Housing & Community Development
- foreign-owned housing for embassy staff
- nursing homes and other residential health care facilities
- student housing owned by a college or university
- low-income housing owned by a charitable organization and rented below cost

For all other rental properties, the landlord may raise the rent once a year by the same percentage as the increase in the Consumer Price Index (CPI), calculated by the Bureau of Labor Statistics. (To check the CPI or learn how it is derived, visit http://stats.bls.gov.) The rent ceiling for a vacant unit may be raised by 12% or to the rent ceiling of a comparable occupied unit in the same complex. Landlords may also request an increase in the rent ceiling on the basis of economic hardship (if the current rent ceiling does not allow at least a 12% profit margin), capital improvements, added services, or a voluntary agreement with at least 70% of the tenants affected. The tenant has a right to be notified in writing 30 days in advance of any rent increase. Landlords may not raise the rent for a unit with elderly or disabled tenants on the basis of capital improvements, but may claim an offsetting tax credit instead.

In the suburbs, the only jurisdiction with rent control is Takoma Park. For details, visit www.takomaparkmd.gov/hcd or call 301-270-5900.

Don't assume that rental houses are more expensive than apartments—especially in the suburbs, where houses may be much cheaper per square foot. On the other hand, don't assume that a house will necessarily offer more living space—especially in D.C., where two-bedroom apartments in older buildings are often more spacious and luxurious than modern two-bedroom townhouses. The quoted rent for an apartment often includes utilities, and the quoted rent for a house often doesn't, but always ask. (Keep in mind: If you make an effort to save energy using high-efficiency lighting, water-saving aerators, and a frugal hand on the thermostat, rent that includes utilities can be a rip-off.) In most of the neighborhoods profiled in this book, you should expect to pay $1,000 a month for an efficiency apartment and closer to $1,500 or more for a one-bedroom. In hip neighborhoods like Dupont Circle and Adams Morgan, even an efficiency can fetch $1,500. For a house, expect to pay $600 to $750 per bedroom.

Sound steep? It is. Among the nation's 20 largest metropolitan areas, according to the cost-of-living calculator at www.homefair.com, only four have more expensive rental markets: Boston, Chicago, New York, and San Francisco. But nearly two out of three District residents are renters—some because they don't qualify for a mortgage, yes, but many Washingtonians prefer the freedom and convenience of renting to the major commitments and chores of home ownership.

HOUSE-HUNTING

DIRECT ACTION

Be prepared to pound some pavement. Start by scanning the classifieds, either online or in print, but don't forget to go out and visit prospective neighborhoods and look for "For Rent" signs. Also check for vacancy notices tacked on bulletin boards at neighborhood coffeehouses or grocery stores. In the outer suburbs, follow the "open house" signs on the medians of any main road on any weekend, or call a building's rental office or condo association and simply ask about upcoming vacancies.

Old school and hometown connections can be immensely helpful in choosing a neighborhood and a home. As soon as you know you're moving to Washington, call or e-mail your old college friends or former neighbors who have moved here, or who know someone here, and ask them to keep their eyes and ears open. In this city where almost half the adult population has lived here for less than 20 years, and where old friends and acquaintances often substitute for an extended family, they won't be surprised to hear from you.

Also check with your college alumni office for help finding housing here. Many large universities around the United States have offices in D.C. that can assist alumni; even if you attended a tiny college, its alumni office may be able to put you in touch with a local contact person.

Finally, if you're being transferred to Washington by your employer, or you already have a job lined up here, be sure to ask about any relocation assistance your employer might provide. Many large companies have staff

NEWCOMER'S HANDBOOK FOR MOVING TO AND LIVING IN WASHINGTON D.C.

124

or contractors whose job is to help employees find temporary and permanent housing.

CLASSIFIED ADS

Newspaper classifieds are still the most comprehensive list of homes for sale or rent, but online classified ad sites—especially **Craigslist**—are increasingly vital elements of the hunt for housing. By the time you read a classified ad in the paper, a dozen people might have responded to the listing at www.craigslist.net. The newspapers' own web sites are valuable too: often the classifieds go online the night before the print edition hits the street, and they're searchable.

Still, it's easy and fruitful to browse the print classifieds—especially in May and late August, when students and interns come and go. The listings will give you a good sense of the rental market—the going rate for an efficiency or studio apartment in Adams Morgan, a two-bedroom apartment in Clarendon, a townhouse off Dupont Circle, or a detached house in Wheaton.

- **The *Washington Post*** offers an extensive real estate section on Saturdays, although there are hundreds of houses and apartments listed every day. The Saturday section adds detailed articles about the housing market—trends, styles, changing neighborhoods, and a weekly chart listing mortgage rates at local lenders. *Post* classifieds are searchable online at www.washingtonpost.com. The online apartment guide www.apartments.com is affiliated with the *Post*.
- **The *Washington City Paper*** lists plenty of homes for rent and a few for sale, but is most valuable for those in search of short-term rentals, sublets, house-sitting jobs, a room in a shared house, or a roommate. Check www.washingtoncitypaper.com Tuesday evenings. The paper hits the streets on Thursdays.
- **The *Washington Times*** has daily classifieds and a special Friday "Home Guide" section featuring expanded listings and articles about the real estate market. Listings and related articles can be searched at www.washtimes.com.
- **The *Washington Blade*,** available on Fridays at restaurants, bars, bookstores, and newspaper boxes around town, carries extensive listings of gay-friendly housing to share. Also available at www.washblade.com.
- ***Washingtonian*** magazine lists beach and mountain houses for sale or rent, and a few high-end homes in and around the city. Also available at www.washingtonian.com.
- **Neighborhood papers** listed in the **Getting Settled** chapter are short on actual listings, but carry lots of display ads from real estate

agents specializing in those neighborhoods. It's a safe bet that an agent who buys a half-page ad in, for instance, the *Hill Rag* every month knows a thing or two about the real estate market on Capitol Hill.

- **HomesDatabase**, www.homesdatabase.com, is touted by the D.C. government as "the most comprehensive and up-to-date real estate web site for the Mid-Atlantic region."
- **The Apartment Shoppers Guide** and other glossy catalogs are available for free on racks at Metro stations and busy intersections. The contents are display ads placed by apartment management firms, and the rental rates aren't usually listed, but it's a good way to compare amenities and floor plans in the area's major apartment complexes.

In addition, these web sites provide overviews of apartment complexes and their amenities:

- **The Apartment Shoppers Guide** online, www.apartment guide.com
- **The Apartment Connection**, www.theapartmentconnection.com
- **ForRent.com**, www.forrent.com
- **ProRent Washington, D.C.**, www.apartments-in-washington-dc.net
- **UrbanApartments**, www.urbanapartments.com

REAL ESTATE BROKERS—RENTAL

Most brokers say they're happy to assist people who are looking for rentals, but be realistic: rental commissions are not a real estate broker's bread and butter, and you aren't likely to get the same level of service as clients looking to buy. (Unless you're interested in renting a mansion—and you can, in areas like Potomac and McLean, from owners who go overseas for years at a time.) For help finding a more ordinary house to rent, stick to real estate agencies that specifically advertise rental services. Major brokers with rental divisions in the Washington area include **Weichert** (www.weichert.com or 877-301-7368) and **Avery-Hess** (www.avery hess.com or 800-220-9797).

APARTMENT SEARCH FIRMS

These agencies are funded by property owners to find tenants to fill their buildings—so, like a real estate broker, they work for you for free:

- **Apartment Detectives**, www.apartmentdetectives.com, 202-362-7368
- **Apartment Locators**, 800-999-RENT, 301-585-RENT, www.southern management.com
- **Apartment Search**, www.apartmentsearch.com, 800-APARTMENT

NEWCOMER'S HANDBOOK FOR MOVING TO AND LIVING IN WASHINGTON D.C.

126

SHARING AND SUBLETS

If you're on your own, renting a room in an established group house can be a great way to get acquainted with the city without spending a whole lot on rent. Sometimes a group will get together and find a home, though more often one or two people will rent a house and then seek roommates through advertising, word-of-mouth referrals, or a roommate referral service. There is a brisk market for summer sublets, particularly near colleges and universities. Or, with luck and connections, you might even find a house-sitting position.

Many people find roommates through the bulletin boards in neighborhood bookstores and cafes, and, of course, in main buildings on college and university campuses; however, as with house-hunting, **Craigslist** is increasingly recommended as your first stop. There are also hundreds of listings each week in the *City Paper* under "Housing to Share" and in the *Post* under "Rooms for Rent." Roommate matchmakers advertise in the *City Paper* and usually charge a finder's fee, but you can browse listings on these web sites for free:

- **www.roomiematch.com**
- **www.roommateexpress.com**
- **www.roomster.net**
- **www.thesublet.com**

If you call a group house in response to an ad and you're too late, don't hesitate to ask whether they know of any other vacancies. Especially in neighborhoods like Adams Morgan and Mt. Pleasant, where group houses are common, many vacancies are filled by word-of-mouth referrals.

Group housing is a common practice throughout D.C., where the high cost of living and escalating rents compel many young adults to share a house or large apartment. It's increasingly common to find older singles sharing housing too, and to find group houses in the suburbs—especially Arlington, Takoma Park, and near the University of Maryland.

CHECKING IT OUT

You sign a lease on a cozy efficiency, and two months later, it starts to feel a little *too* cozy. Noise from traffic outside—and from your neighbor's daily soaps—penetrates the thin walls at all hours. The dishwasher is leaking all over the kitchen floor. And there aren't enough washing machines to go around, so you've been hauling your clothes to a laundromat. To minimize the risk of such unpleasant surprises, make a checklist of your musts and must-nots; when you visit a prospective home, allow a few minutes to make a close inspection to be sure its beauty is not just skin deep. A little time and a few questions now can save you a lot of aggravation later on. For example:

- Are the kitchen appliances clean and in working order? Do the stove's burners work? How about the oven? Is there enough counter and shelf space? Will the owner provide you with manuals for any appliances that come with the home, and who is responsible for routine maintenance?
- Do the windows open, close, and lock? Do the bedroom windows face a noisy or busy area? Are there bars on the ground floor windows? Is there a window air conditioner or central air?
- Is there enough storage space? In an apartment building, is there a basement locker room for additional storage? If you have a bike, where can you park it indoors or lock it securely?
- Are there enough electrical outlets, and do they work? In a house, do the circuit breakers or fuses overload often?
- Are there any signs of insects, particularly termites? When was the last termite inspection?
- If the home does not come with a washer and dryer, is there a laundry room in the building?
- Outside, do you feel comfortable? Will you feel safe here at night?
- Is there secure parking? Is there enough? Where do guests park? Does the driveway accommodate two cars side by side, or only with one car blocking the other? Does parking cost extra?
- Is there convenient access to public transportation and shopping? How late do the buses run, and do they run on weekends?

In D.C., a checklist in the official *Tenant's Guide to Safe and Decent Housing* includes relevant legal information about housing codes and leases. (See the section on **Leases & Tenant/Landlord Problems** below.) It can't hurt to look at the checklist even if you're renting in a neighboring jurisdiction.

If you've given the place a thorough inspection, gotten satisfactory answers to all your questions, and everything passes muster, be prepared to stake your claim without delay—before someone else does.

STAKING A CLAIM

True story: A newcomer went for a morning walk before an appointment with a rental agent, and didn't have time to change out of her sweat suit before looking at luxury apartments. She was given the cold shoulder and grudging service—until, when probed, she stated her income bracket. Suddenly she got red-carpet treatment. Unbeknownst to the rental agent, the newcomer was the new editor of an influential local newspaper. The rental agent's judgmental attitude was the subject of a column a few days later.

NEWCOMER'S HANDBOOK FOR MOVING TO AND LIVING IN WASHINGTON D.C.

128

It pays to be aware that landlords and property managers are human, and will make judgments based upon your appearance and demeanor. Yes, such discrimination is illegal—but an experienced landlord can always find a watertight reason to turn you down. The impression you want to make is that of a responsible and conscientious tenant who will pay the rent on time. With that in mind, also come prepared with checkbook (often it is the first person to come with a deposit who gets the apartment), and have ready access to your references—both credit and personal—and your bank account information.

Almost all landlords or property managers will require a security deposit, usually equal to a month's rent, which, less any damages, will be refunded to you, with interest, when you move. Most landlords require an additional deposit from tenants with pets—often a nonrefundable deposit (a polite way to say "fee") anywhere from $50 to $200. Also, application fees of $10 to $25 are sometimes charged as a way to discourage frivolous rental applications. The fee is usually credited toward your deposit if your application is approved.

Some landlords—especially individuals who own only one or two rental properties, as opposed to full-time professional property managers—will ask for personal references, and most will want to check with your bank or your employer. If you've just arrived and you have few local contacts, explain your situation and offer references from your hometown; it's not unusual. In larger apartment buildings, the application process is likely to be simpler and more objective: you'll have to show that the rent is no more than a certain fraction of your income, usually one-third.

LEASES & TENANT/LANDLORD PROBLEMS

The standard one-year lease in D.C. and most surrounding jurisdictions is a renewable contract that, at the end of the term, automatically reverts to a month-to-month lease unless renewed for a definite period. A month-to-month lease remains in effect until the landlord or tenant gives 30 days' notice of termination.

Typically, a lease specifies the address to which rent should be mailed or delivered; late payment penalties; terms of the security deposit, including interest; rules and deposits regarding pets; policy on subletting, maintenance, and repairs; right of entry for the landlord and contractors; and mandatory tenant's insurance. Read carefully for these details, and remember that the lease is most likely a standard form—you and your landlord can make any agreed-upon changes. Just be sure you both initial any handwritten changes and you both possess signed copies of exactly the same agreement.

Be sure to do a "walkthrough" with the landlord to inspect the property for any pre-existing damage that should not be blamed on you. You and the landlord should sign a list of all existing damages and both keep a copy.

Federal law requires the owner of rental housing to disclose any lead-based paint hazards to all tenants, and to provide an approved pamphlet explaining that housing built before 1978 may contain lead-based paint. Lead in dust and chips from such paint can be a health hazard, especially to young children. In the District, if you want to have your child tested for lead poisoning, call the Childhood Lead Poisoning Prevention Program at 202-535-2690. If test results warrant, the Housing Regulation Administration (HRA) will inspect the property for lead-based paint and order abatement measures.

Rental housing codes are fairly uniform throughout the Washington area, but here's the deal in the District: The law requires landlords to maintain rental properties in "clean, safe, and sanitary condition, in good repair, and free from rodents or vermin." (However, if rodents or vermin show up after you move into a rented single-family home, they're legally your problem, not the landlord's.) If you bring a problem to the landlord's attention and repairs do not get under way within a reasonable time, you can ask the HRA to intervene—call 202-442-4610. Of course, "reasonable" means one thing when the problem is a broken furnace in the winter and another thing when it's a hole in a window screen.

The landlord is required to maintain a minimum indoor temperature of 68°F from 6:30 a.m. to 11 p.m. and 65°F at night. There are no exceptions; even if a tenant fails to pay rent or utility bills, the landlord cannot turn off the heat in an occupied unit during the winter. If air conditioning is provided, the landlord must keep it in good repair such that it can cool the indoor air by at least 15°F.

If a D.C. landlord threatens you with the "E" word, you can usually be sure it's an empty threat. Eviction is a rare and extreme remedy in the tenant-friendly District. With legal counsel, almost any tenant can tie an eviction proceeding up for months or years. Many small-time landlords neglect the provision of D.C. Code Section 45-1406 that requires eviction notices to be served in English and Spanish, even if the tenant only speaks Farsi. Once the authorities show up to execute an eviction order, however, the only way to stop the eviction is to pay the full amount of rent or damages due in cash or by money order. In the suburbs, courts tend to look more favorably on owners' rights, and you'll need to get legal aid as soon as you receive a "notice to quit."

The informative 35-page *Tenant's Guide to Safe and Decent Housing* is available from the HRA—pick up a free copy at 941 North Capitol Street NE

NEWCOMER'S HANDBOOK FOR MOVING TO AND LIVING IN WASHINGTON D.C.

130

or download the PDF version at http://dcra.dc.gov. In addition to details about landlord and tenant rights and responsibilities, the booklet includes a checklist for prospective homes; a detailed explanation of grievance and hearing procedures; and a list of low-cost legal aid services.

Contact the landlord-tenant affairs agency in your jurisdiction if you have any questions about the terms of the lease and your rights and responsibilities. The following agencies can answer your questions and mediate landlord/tenant disputes:

- **D.C. Department of Consumer & Regulatory Affairs**, Housing Regulation Administration, 202-442-4620, http://dcra.dc.gov
- **Alexandria Office of Housing**, Landlord-Tenant Relations Division, 703-838-4545, www.ci.alexandria.va.us/city/housing
- **Arlington County Housing Information Center & Tenant Landlord Commission**, 703-228-3765, www.co.arlington.va.us/cphd
- **Fairfax County Tenant-Landlord Commission**, Department of Cable Communications & Consumer Protection, 703-222-8435, www.co.fairfax.va.us/dcccp
- **Montgomery County Department of Housing & Community Affairs**, Commission on Tenant-Landlord Affairs, 240-777-3670, www.montgomerycountymd.us (click on "Departments")
- **Prince George's County Department of Housing & Community Development**, 301-883-5500, www.goprince georgescounty.com (select "Housing & Community" from the Agencies menu)

For more information about landlord and tenant rights and responsibilities, visit the online legal resources www.nolo.com or www.rentlaw.com. These sites include statutes and case citations from D.C. and every state, and Nolo sells a number of plain-English legal handbooks for tenants—notably *Every Tenant's Legal Guide* and *Renter's Rights: The Basics*, both by Janet Portman & Marcia Stewart.

If you must break a lease (for reasons you can't blame on the landlord), you should expect to take a financial hit. At a minimum, you will lose your security deposit. Depending on the amount of rent at stake—the time remaining in the lease and the amount per month—your landlord might not bother to sue, especially if it's a good time of year to put a unit on the rental market (ideally, late spring or late summer). You could, in theory, be sued for the full amount of rent you would pay throughout the remainder of the lease, but in practice, it's a lively rental market and landlords seldom bother chasing down a leasebreaker for more than one or two months' rent. Keep in mind, though, your next rental application will ask for contact information for your most recent landlord—so you will be much better off if you get a lawyer's advice and negotiate an amicable deal. (One way to placate a jilted landlord is to recruit a new tenant yourself, to save on the cost of advertising the vacancy.) At www.nolo.com, you can download a kit entitled "Break Your Lease without Breaking the Law."

RENTER'S/HOMEOWNER'S INSURANCE

Upon signing a lease, your next step should be to get renter's insurance; in fact, most leases here require it. Depending on your possessions, renter's insurance won't likely cost more than $150 a year. Fine jewelry, electronics, or other special items will require additional coverage. A renter's insurance policy typically covers damages to your belongings and personal liability in the event of theft, fire, water damage, or injury. Structural damage to the property is not covered. (Note that most leases become null and void if a fire or other catastrophe makes the home uninhabitable.)

The ideal renter's or homeowner's policy provides "replacement value" coverage, but inflation has made replacement value policies hard to find in recent years; instead, many insurance companies offer coverage for 120% to 125% of the face value of your house and belongings. If disaster strikes, you will be glad you shopped around for a replacement value policy.

Visit these web sites to get quotes and advice about the insurance market:

- **www.choicetrust.com**
- **www.insure.com**
- **www.insuremarket.com**
- **www.quotesmith.com**

To find an insurance agent in your neighborhood, check the Yellow Pages, where agencies are listed by town, or go online to find a local agent of one of these national companies:

- **Allstate**, www.allstate.com
- **Hartford**, www.thehartford.com
- **Nationwide**, www.nationwide.com
- **State Farm**, www.statefarm.com
- **Travelers**, www.travelerspc.com

Homeowner's insurance premiums will be affected by the house's claim history, no matter who owned it at the time of a claim. According to Bankrate.com, buyers can be denied insurance—and thus denied a mortgage—if a home's record on file with the insurance industry's Comprehensive Loss Underwriting Exchange (CLUE) shows major or frequent claims. A history of water damage or mold can be especially serious red flags to insurers. **Choice Point Asset** sells five-year claim reports for $13 at www.choicetrust.com.

NEWCOMER'S HANDBOOK FOR MOVING TO AND LIVING IN WASHINGTON D.C.

132

BUYING

Buying a house, condo, or co-op is a complex and time-consuming process, but the resources listed here—and the professionals in the community—can help you at every step: calculating your budget, choosing the right home in the right neighborhood, finding and obtaining a mortgage, protecting your investment with adequate insurance, moving in, and making repairs and improvements. To get a sense of the current real estate market, study the Real Estate section of Saturday's *Washington Post*—and not just the classified ads. Every week, the *Post* features an in-depth profile of a different neighborhood; a chart showing, by zip code, the number and median price of home sales in a local jurisdiction in the past year; current mortgage rates at area lenders; and a Q&A column. Also, in the weekly *Washington Business Journal*, you can peruse a list of every real estate transaction in the Washington area valued at $200,000 or more and every building permit issued for a new home. The *Washington Times*, which also publishes an expanded real estate section on Fridays, sponsors *Your New Home*, a half-hour real estate TV tour on Channel 7 (WJLA) on Sunday mornings.

Of course, finding the perfect home is just the beginning of the process. Your purchase will cost more than the price of the home. Add up the fees for the title search, title insurance, and other legal services; the inspection and land survey; recording tax; mortgage origination (points). Then add the property tax payment and homeowner's insurance premiums you'll be required to place in an escrow account. In all, expect to pay 5% to 8% more than the purchase price. Assuming you are not paying cash, but seeking a mortgage from a bank, you can usually figure on borrowing up to three or four times your annual income, no more. Be prepared for a thorough examination of your credit history, finances, and employment status. The required down payment is usually 20% of the purchase price, though it can be as low as 10% if you pay higher origination fees. The lender is required to give you a good-faith estimate of closing costs.

The search for a house or condo begins in the same place, whether you're buying or renting: word of mouth, legwork, and the classified ads. Most people in the market for a house enlist the services of a real estate broker—a buyer's agent who knows the market and the neighborhood. And you might benefit from the services of a mortgage broker—a financial advisor who helps you get the best possible mortgage. At no charge to you, a broker will examine your financial situation (age, income, assets, debt load, etc.) and the property you want to buy and recommend the most appropriate lender and the best type of mortgage for your needs. A good broker knows the local banks and can guide you at every step in the process. For a list of mortgage brokers serving the Washington area, visit www.dcpages.com/Real_Estate. Also, if you are purchasing an older home, consider hiring a real estate lawyer who can help you with the special hurdles involved in buying a home that is, or could be, declared historic. For tips on applying for a mortgage, see the section on **Banking & Credit Resources** in the **Money Matters** chapter.

Before a home sale can be completed, termite inspection is mandatory, and most prospective homeowners will hire a building engineer to make a thorough inspection of the structure, heating and cooling systems, plumbing, roof, and major appliances. Should an inspector's report find that major repairs will be likely within a few years, you may be able to negotiate thousands of dollars off the purchase price—or you might decide to keep looking.

The purchase of a condo is a bit simpler. Here, you are buying a unit in a larger complex; the unit is yours to use, rent, or sell. Annual or monthly condo fees cover the expenses of a condo association, which takes care of the building and grounds, laundry room, parking lots or garages, swimming pool, and any other shared amenities. Condo fees can be steep, and when looking at prospective units, it's not enough to have the annual fee quoted. Check past records to find out how often the fees have been raised and by how much. You will also want a lawyer, or a real estate agent specializing in condos, to examine the condominium's prospectus and financial statement, so you don't buy into a financially unstable property.

There are a few cooperative apartment buildings (co-ops) in D.C. and scattered around the suburbs. Buying into a co-op means purchasing a share in a building—the share allows you the exclusive use of a particular unit, but you do not own that unit outright. Prospective buyers must be approved by the existing shareholders (or their board, in a larger building). If you wish to sell or rent your apartment, the buyer or tenant must be approved by the same process. It may be difficult to get a mortgage for a small co-op, since a small number of shareholders collectively possess a relatively high risk of default. Also, keep in mind that co-op maintenance fees, which pay for upkeep of the building and common areas, can be steep, and only the portion of such fees earmarked for property tax payments is tax-deductible.

ASSISTANCE FOR HOMEBUYERS

Many major lenders offer special rates for first-time homebuyers below a certain income level—often $70,000 a year. Ask your lender or mortgage broker whether you might qualify for a reduced down payment or below-market interest rate.

If you have not owned a home in D.C. at any time during the past year, you're considered a first-time homebuyer for the purposes of the

NEWCOMER'S HANDBOOK FOR MOVING TO AND LIVING IN WASHINGTON D.C.

134

D.C. Homebuyer Tax Credit. If you're a single taxpayer earning no more than $70,000 a year, you get a $5,000 tax break when you buy a home in D.C. for your primary residence; likewise if your tax status is "married filing jointly" and you and your spouse have a combined income of no more than $110,000 a year. A partial credit is available up to the income limits of $90,000 for single taxpayers and $130,000 for joint taxpayers. To claim the credit, download Form 8859 from www.irs.gov or request it by phone at 800-829-3676. This tax credit is subject to annual reauthorization by Congress, so the details may change from year to year.

The **Home Purchase Assistance Program**, a project of the Greater Washington Urban League, provides interest breaks on mortgages for low- and moderate-income homebuyers in the District. A family of four can qualify for some assistance if household income is $91,100 or less; for a couple, the income limit is $72,850. (That's officially "moderate" income in D.C.) Depending on household size and income, participants may borrow up to $20,000 interest-free. You'll need to rent a home in D.C. before you apply—the program is open to District residents meeting the income guidelines. For details, contact the Urban League at www.gwul.org or 202-265-8200. (The Urban League also offers homebuyer counseling in Prince George's County at 301-985-3519.)

Two financial aid programs are available from the D.C. Department of Housing & Community Development for purchasers of "fixer-upper" homes in exchange for a commitment to improve the property and raise its assessed value. The **Homestead Housing Preservation Program** sells foreclosed homes for a nominal price (typically $250) to buyers who agree to live in the home for at least five years and, within that time, restore it to comply with building codes. Participants must take a course in home ownership and may qualify for deferred loans to help with improvements. The **Single Family Residential Rehabilitation Program** provides low-interest mortgages to buyers who agree to renovate houses in targeted areas—"Enterprise Communities" or "Community Development Areas." (Naturally, these homes aren't in Georgetown or Kalorama.) For details about these programs, download brochures from the **Resident Resource Center** at www.rrc.dc.gov or call DHCD at 202-442-7200.

For information about similar opportunities in the suburbs, contact the **Maryland Department of Housing & Community Development** at www.dhcd.state.md.us, 410-514-7700, or the **Virginia Housing Development Authority**, www.vhda.com, 800-968-7837 or 804-782-1986. In Maryland, you can also browse promotional mortgage rates at www.marylandmortgageshop.com.

In an effort to promote public transportation and encourage homebuyers to move to transit-friendly locations, lenders participating in the **Smart Commute Initiative** will count your potential savings on commuting expenses as additional income to qualify you for a mortgage. Generally, if you're buying a home within a quarter mile of a bus stop or half a mile from a Metro station or train station, you can apply for an additional $200/month ($250/month for two-income households) and also make a smaller down payment than usual. For more information and a list of participating lenders, contact the **Metropolitan Washington Council of Governments** at 202-962-3200 or www.mwcog.org (click on Housing & Planning).

HomeFree USA is a nonprofit organization providing evening and weekend classes for homebuyers and new homeowners. Topics include "Finding a Home/Working With a Realtor," "Home Inspections," "Closing & Settlement," "Life as a New Homeowner," "Down Payment & Closing Cost Assistance," "Credit Enhancement," "Buying a Home on a Shoestring Budget," and "Homeowner's Insurance & Security." Most classes are open to members only; membership plans range from $11 for one month to $80 for a full year. Members also get free counseling on strategies to find (and get) the best mortgage. For more information, call 202-526-2000 or 866-696-2329 or visit www.homefreeusa.org.

Finally, download or order a series of free publications from the **Fannie Mae Foundation** at www.homebuyingguide.org—"Knowing and Understanding Your Credit," "Opening the Door to a Home of Your Own," "Choosing the Mortgage that's Right for You," and "Borrowing Basics: What You Don't Know Can Hurt You." These excellent overviews are available in nine languages.

REAL ESTATE BROKERS

There is no substitute for the advice of a local real estate broker. Brokers are trained, licensed professionals who keep a close eye on the neighborhoods they serve. A knowledgeable broker may know the college admission rate at the local high school, the crime rate in the local police beat, how many minutes it takes to drive to the Beltway, and—most important—the long-term and recent trends in property values right down to a given block. A good broker will also interview you in detail about your needs and interests—not just your preferred price range, but every detail of your lifestyle. Are you planning to have any more children? Do you need space in the basement to set up your electric trains? Do you want to plant a garden, or would you prefer an ivy-covered lawn that needs no maintenance? Will you ride a bike to the Metro station every day? The more information you provide, the better your broker can match you with a home.

So how do you find a broker who knows the neighborhood where you want to live? Most real estate agencies claim to serve the entire Washington area, and indeed, most agencies can offer at least some valu-

NEWCOMER'S HANDBOOK FOR MOVING TO AND LIVING IN WASHINGTON D.C.

136

able assistance with any home on the market. Naturally, however, an agency is best qualified to show you homes in the neighborhood where it is located—so in the Yellow Pages, agencies are listed by neighborhood. Also, most neighborhood newspapers carry lots of advertising from individual brokers boasting their intimate knowledge of the community. Online, www.realtor.com and http://home-locator.com provide links to specific real estate brokers serving the neighborhoods or cities you select.

Here are some of the major real estate agencies representing buyers in neighborhoods profiled in this book—just a place to start, by no means a substitute for the real estate services advertised in the latest edition of the neighborhood paper where you're looking:

DISTRICT OF COLUMBIA

CAPITOL HILL
- **Century 21 Ashby & Associates**, www.century21.com, 202-543-8060
- **John C. Formant Real Estate**, www.johncformant.com, 202-544-3900
- **Pardoe**, www.pardoe.com, 202-547-3525
- **Re/Max Capital Realtors**, www.thelocalgiant.com, 877-947-5600 or 202-547-5600

CHEVY CHASE
- **Long & Foster**, www.longandfoster.com, 800-762-0782 or 202-363-9700
- **Pardoe**, www.pardoe.com, 202-362-5800
- **Laughlin-Miller**, www.wcanmiller.com, 202-966-1400
- **Weichert**, www.weichert.com, 202-326-1300

CLEVELAND PARK
- **Weichert**, www.weichert.com, 202-326-1100

DOWNTOWN
- **Federal City/Mowbray**, Logan Circle, 202-483-5035
- **Tutt, Taylor & Rankin**, www.tutttaylorrankin.com, 202-234-3344

DUPONT CIRCLE
- **Federal City/Mowbray**, Dupont Circle, 202-745-0700
- **Randall H. Hagner & Co.**, www.hagner.com, 202-857-4300
- **Weichert**, www.weichert.com, 202-326-1010

FOXHALL/SPRING VALLEY
- **Cathie Gill**, www.cathiegill.com, 202-364-3066
- **Laughlin-Miller**, www.wcanmiller.com, 202-362-1300

FRIENDSHIP HEIGHTS
- **Evers & Co.**, www.eversco.com, 202-364-1700

GEORGETOWN
- **Long & Foster**, www.georgetowndchomes.com, 202-944-8400
- **Pardoe**, www.pardoe.com, 202-333-6100
- **Re/Max Capital Realtors**, www.thelocalgiant.com, 877-398-8900 or 202-338-8900
- **Rod Johnston Real Estat**e, www.georgetownrealty.com, 202-333-6749
- **Tutt, Taylor & Rankin**, www.tutttaylorrankin.com, 202-333-1212

TENLEYTOWN
- **Coldwell Banker Stevens**, Washington, www.coldwellbanker.com, 202-686-5000
- **Re/Max Capital Realtors**, www.thelocalgiant.com, 877-963-9800 or 202-363-9800

MARYLAND

ANDREWS AIR FORCE BASE
- **Century 21 Advantage**, www.century21.com, 800-221-8054 or 301-449-9100
- **Coldwell Banker Stevens**, Camp Springs, www.coldwellbanker.com, 301-899-7100
- **Coldwell Banker Stevens**, Oxon Hill, www.coldwellbanker.com, 301-839-4100
- **Long & Foster**, Fort Washington, www.fortwashingtonmd.com, 301-292-0700
- **Weichert**, Andrews, www.weichert.com, 301-423-9200

BETHESDA
- **The Buyer's Edge**, www.buyersagent.com, 800-207-6810
- **Long & Foster**, Elm Street (Downtown), www.bethesda-md.com, 866-215-6444
- **Long & Foster**, One Democracy Center (North Bethesda), www.bethesdahouses.com, 301-654-4900
- **Luxury Home**s, Montgomery, luxuryhomes-md-va.com, 800-711-7988

NEWCOMER'S HANDBOOK FOR MOVING TO AND LIVING IN WASHINGTON D.C.

138

- **Pardoe**, www.pardoe.com, 301-718-0010
- **Prestige Properties**, www.prestigepropertiesintl.com, 301-320-4002
- **Laughlin-Miller**, www.wcanmiller.com, 301-229-4000
- **Weichert**, www.weichert.com, 301-656-2500

BOWIE

- **Coldwell Banker Stevens**, www.coldwellbanker.com, 301-262-6800
- **Long & Foster**, Bowie, www.bowiehomes.com, 301-262-6900
- **Weichert**, www.weichert.com, 301-262-3100

CHEVY CHASE

- **Gerlach Real Estate**, www.gerlachrealestate.com, 301-656-8686
- **Realty Network**, www.realtynetwork.com, 888-765-3148 or 301-951-0581
- **Weichert**, www.weichert.com, 301-718-4000

COLLEGE PARK

- **Long & Foster**, www.collegeparkhomes.com, 800-446-9498

GAITHERSBURG

- **Avery-Hess**, www.averyhess.com, 888-402-7200 or 301-948-7200
- **Coldwell Banker Stevens**, www.coldwellbanker.com, 301-921-1040
- **Long & Foster**, www.gaithersburghomes.com, 800-341-7355 or 301-975-9500
- **Weichert**, www.weichert.com, 301-417-7700

GREENBELT

- **Coldwell Banker Stevens**, Lanham, www.coldwellbanker.com, 301-474-5700
- **Weichert**, www.weichert.com, 301-345-7600

LAUREL

- **Century 21 H.T. Brown**, www.htbrown.com, 800-368-2551
- **Coldwell Banker Stevens**, www.coldwellbanker.com, 800-673-2433 or 301-725-5278
- **Prince George's County Realtors**, www.homes-prince-georges-maryland.com, 800-711-7988

POTOMAC

- **Long & Foster**, www.potomacvillagemd.com, 888-899-2218 or 301-983-0060

- **Pardoe**, www.pardoe.com, 301-983-020
- **Laughlin-Miller**, www.wcanmiller.com, 301-299-6000
- **Weichert**, www.weichert.com, 301-718-4100

ROCKVILLE
- **Avery-Hess**, www.averyhess.com, 800-927-0425 or 301-984-9700
- **Century 21 All Properties**, www.c21all.com, 301-294-0990
- **Llewellyn**, www.llewellynrealtors.com, 800-729-7355 or 301-424-0900
- **Weichert**, www.weichert.com, 301-468-1600

SILVER SPRING
- **Weichert**, Burtonsville, www.weichert.com, 301-681-0444
- **Weichert**, White Oak, www.weichert.com, 301-681-0400

WHEATON
- **Weichert**, Aspen Hill, www.weichert.com, 301-681-0550
- **Weichert**, Wheaton, www.weichert.com, 301-681-0500

VIRGINIA

ALEXANDRIA
- **Century 21 New Millennium**, www.century21.com, 800-708-7085 or 703-549-0600
- **Coldwell Banker Stevens**, www.coldwellbanker.com, 703-212-8000
- **Long & Foster**, www.mtvernonhomes.com, 800-336-6164 or 703-960-8900
- **Luxury Homes, Alexandria**, www.luxuryhomes-md-va.com/alexandria, 800-711-7988
- **McEnearney Associates**, www.mcenearney.com, 703-549-9292
- **Pardoe**, www.pardoe.com, 703-518-8300
- **Re/Max Horizons**, Seminary Road, www.thelocalgiant.com, 800-736-6645 or 703-824-4800
- **Re/Max Horizon**s, Old Town, www.thelocalgiant.com, 703-549-9200
- **Weichert**, Belle View, www.weichert.com, 703-765-4000
- **Weichert**, Old Town, www.weichert.com, 703-549-8700

ANNANDALE
- **Century 21 Howell & Associates**, www.century21.com, 800-422-2556 or 703-941-1300
- **Coldwell Banker Stevens**, www.coldwellbanker.com, 703-941-1600

NEWCOMER'S HANDBOOK FOR MOVING TO AND LIVING IN WASHINGTON D.C.

140

- **Re/Max Horizons**, www.thelocalgiant.com, 703-354-9800
- **Weichert**, www.weichert.com, 703-941-0100

ARLINGTON

- **Buck & Associates**, www.buckrealtors.com, 703-528-2288
- **Coldwell Banker Stevens**, www.coldwellbanker.com, 703-524-2100
- **Long & Foster**, www.arlingtonvahomes.com, 800-760-7282 or 703-522-0500
- **McEnearney Associates**, www.mcenearney.com, 703-525-1900
- **Weichert**, www.weichert.com, 703-527-3300

FAIRFAX

- **Better Homes**, www.betterhomesva.com, 703-385-3003
- **Blue Heron**, www.blueheronrealty.com, 703-451-6670
- **Buyer's Agents Fairfax County**, www.homes.com, 800-903-2997
- **Coldwell Banker Stevens, Fairfax**, www.coldwellbanker.com, 703-691-1400
- **Coldwell Banker Stevens, Fairfax Station**, www.coldwell banker.com, 800-431-4663 or 703-250-1000
- **ERA Elite Group**, www.eraelitegroup.com, 800-441-5420, 703-359-7800
- **The Nellis Group**, Re/Max, www.nellisgroup.com, 800-344-7253 or 703-503-4375
- **Pardoe**, www.pardoe.com, 703-921-0600
- **Re/Max Premier**, www.dulleshomes.com, 800-297-8382 or 703-818-9603
- **Weichert, Burke**, www.weichert.com, 703-569-7870
- **Weichert, Fairfax,** www.weichert.com, 703-691-0555
- **Weichert, Fair Oaks**, www.weichert.com, 703-934-0400

FALLS CHURCH

- **Times Development**, www.timesdevelopment.com, 703-533-8100

GREAT FALLS

- **Coldwell Banker Stevens**, www.coldwellbanker.com, 800-368-3465 or 703-759-4202
- **Weichert**, www.weichert.com, 703-759-6300

HERNDON

- **New Homes Realty**, www.newhomesrealty.com, 703-709-8288
- **Weichert**, www.weichert.com, 703-709-0101

McLEAN

- **The Buyer Brokerage**, www.thebuyerbrokerage.com, 800-903-2297
- **Coldwell Banker Stevens**, www.coldwellbanker.com, 800-555-3095 or 703-356-7000
- **Laughlin-Miller,** www.wcanmiller.com, 703-356-0100
- **Long & Foster**, www.longandfoster.com, 800-819-9971
- **McEnearney Associates**, www.mcenearney.com, 703-790-9090
- **Pardoe**, www.pardoe.com, 703-734-7020
- **Weichert, McLean Center**, www.weichert.com, 301-893-1500
- **Weichert, Dolley Madison Boulevard**, www.weichert.com, 703-760-8880
- **Weichert, Old Dominion Drive,** www.weichert.com, 703-821-8300

RESTON

- **Coldwell Banker Stevens**, www.coldwellbanker.com, 800-856-8440 or 703-476-8440
- **Long & Foster,** www.restonvirginia.com, 800-316-7355 or 703-437-3800
- **Pardoe**, www.pardoe.com, 703-471-7220
- **Weichert**, www.weichert.com, 703-264-0000

SPRINGFIELD

- **Avery-Hess**, www.averyhess.com, 800-220-9797 or 703-451-9797
- **Coldwell Banker Stevens, Burke,** www.coldwellbanker.com, 703-451-2500
- **Re/Max**, www.thelocalgiant.com, 703-642-3380
- **Weichert**, www.weichert.com, 703-569-9700

TYSONS CORNER

- **Avery-Hess**, www.averyhess.com, 800-659-0729 or 703-821-5005
- **Weichert**, www.weichert.com, 703-893-2510

VIENNA

- **Coldwell Banker Stevens**, www.coldwellbanker.com, 703-938-5600
- **Fairfax County Real Estate**, www.homes-fairfax-county.com, 800-711-7988
- **Luxury Homes**, Fairfax, www.luxuryhomes-md-va.com/fairfax, 800-711-7988
- **Re/Max Preferred Properties**, www.thelocalgiant.com, 800-828-9698 or 703-255-9700

NEWCOMER'S HANDBOOK FOR MOVING TO AND LIVING IN WASHINGTON D.C.

142

- **Summerwood Realty**, www.summerwoodrealty.com, 888-917-9191 or 703-255-6500
- **Vienna Real Estate,** www.viennarealestate.com, 703-242-1460
- **Weichert**, www.weichert.com, 703-938-6070

FOR SALE BY OWNER

When you buy a home directly from the owner, you can negotiate for a portion of the savings on the agent's commission. **EconoBroker**, www.econobroker.com or 888-989-4657, lists such homes on the Multiple Listing Service used by real estate agents nationwide. Other sites listing "Fisbos" (homes "For Sale By Owner") include:

- **www.fisbos.com**
- **www.FSBOnetwork.com**
- **www.homesbyowner.com**
- **www.owners.com**

RESOURCES FOR HOMEBUYERS

These web sites and free publications available around town are devoted to listings of homes for sale in the Washington area:

- **Homes & Land**, 800-277-7800, www.homesandland.com
- **The Real Estate Book**, 800-841-3401, www.realestatebook.com
- **Washington, D.C. Homebuyer's Journal**, 800-344-1052, www.homebuyersjournal.com

Also, the **U.S. Department of Housing & Urban Development** lists properties for sale due to foreclosure on government-backed mortgages. Visit www.hud.gov/homes or call 202-708-1112.

Among nationwide resources, the **National Association of Realtors**, www.realtor.com, should be your first stop on the web. This extensive site features nationwide property listings, neighborhood profiles and statistics, virtual tours, loan calculators, and extensive information about mortgage lenders, relocation, contractors and, of course, real estate agents. Other helpful national sites include:

- **www.cyberhomes.com**
- **www.homeseekers.com**
- **www.homestore.com**
- **www.realtylocator.com**

Check **www.scorecard.org** to find out about toxic waste issues in or near your prospective neighborhood. This site, sponsored by the Environmental Defense Fund, is a database of polluters by zip code; the Washington area has practically no heavy industry, but plenty of trash incinerators and waste transfer stations—and anything the Potomac brings down from the paper mills and coal mines of Western Maryland.

To determine how your cost of living will change when you move to Washington, check out the online salary calculator at **www.homefair. com**. A similar tool on the **Coldwell Banker** web site, www.coldwell banker.com, shows the price of comparable homes in different cities.

In addition to the loan resources listed in the **Money Matters** chapter and the housing resources listed above, these web sites offer information about mortgages and interest rates, loan calculators, fair lending practices, and more:

- **www.bankrate.com**
- **http://my.countrywide.com**
- **www.freddiemac.com**
- **www.mtgprofessor.com**

Finally, **WRC-TV** offers a good compilation of real estate "news you can use" online at www.nbc4.com/realestate. See **Moving and Storage** for more relocation tips and tools.

B EFORE YOU START YOUR NEW LIFE INSIDE THE BELTWAY, YOU AND your worldly possessions have to get here. That can be expensive and complicated or cheap and simple, depending on how much stuff you've accumulated, where you're coming from, and how much of the heavy lifting you plan to do. If you're traveling light or you already have friends or family in Washington, you can save a lot of money by driving your own rented moving van; if you're moving everything but the kitchen sink and there are no extra hands waiting on this end of the trip, you'll need to hire movers—chosen carefully on the basis of reputation.

TRUCK RENTAL

If you plan to move your own belongings with the help of a few friends, you can simply rent a vehicle and hit the road. Look in the Yellow Pages under "Truck Rental" or online at www.vanlines.com or www.united rentals.com, and then call around for quotes. Even if you're dealing with a nationwide company, call the location nearest you. If you need a truck between May and September—peak moving season—be sure to reserve one at least a month in advance, especially for one-way rentals. In fact, if you make arrangements during the winter to move in the summer, you may be able to pay the cheaper winter rate.

Once you're on the road, keep in mind that your rental truck may be a tempting target for thieves. If you must park it overnight or for more than a couple of hours, try to find a well-lit place where you can keep an eye on it, and don't leave anything valuable in the cab.

Here are the major national van lines:

- **Budget**, 800-527-0700, www.budget.com
- **Hertz**, 888-999-5500, www.hertztrucks.com
- **National**, 888-628-5826, www.nationalvanlines.com
- **Penske**, 800-467-3675, www.pensketruckleasing.com

NEWCOMER'S HANDBOOK FOR MOVING TO AND LIVING IN WASHINGTON D.C.

146

- **Ryder**, 800-297-9337, www.ryder.com
- **U-Haul**, 800-468-4285, www.uhaul.com

If you just need a minivan or a small trailer, get quotes from a regular car rental company (listed in **Transportation**). If you don't want to hire movers or drive a truck, there's a third option: you can hire a commercial freight carrier to bring a truck or trailer to your house and then drive it to your destination after you load it. Contact **ABF U-Pack Moving** at 800-355-1696 or www.upack.com.

MOVERS

Start with the Yellow Pages, but get references. For long-distance moves, the **American Moving & Storage Association**, www.moving.org, keeps a list of certified movers honoring the organization's code of conduct; also check out the most recent *Consumer Reports* index at a public library or www.consumerreports.org to find any helpful articles or surveys.

Interstate movers are licensed by the **Federal Motor Carrier Safety Administration**. The agency reported to Congress in 2001 that a few movers have been known to hold customers' possessions for "exorbitant, unexpected fees" (a polite way to say "ransom") or to charge four times as much as the initial estimate. It pays to check a company's record before you sign a contract.

First, look for the federal motor carrier (MC) number on the company's advertising and promotional literature. Contact the FMCSA at 800-832-5660 or www.fmcsa.dot.gov to make sure the number matches the company's name, the license is current, and the company has a current insurance certificate. As with any other big transaction, remember the consumer protection resources listed in **Shopping for the Home**—plus the scams unique to the moving industry, listed at **MovingScam.com**. Also, keep these tips in mind:

- *Keep a record of the names of everyone you deal with at the moving company*—the sales representative, the estimator, the driver, and the movers. And be nice to them. Tip the movers if they do a good job, and offer to buy them lunch while they load or unload.
- *Before you move, take inventory of all of your possessions.* Even though the movers will put numbered labels on everything, you should also make your own list of every item and the contents of every box. Take photos of anything valuable. Don't sign anything after the move until you've checked everything off the list at your destination, and even then, keep the list until you're absolutely sure nothing was damaged. (A household inventory is a good thing to have anyway, for insurance purposes.)
- *When you ask for an estimate, give accurate and thorough information.* Mention any stairs, driveways, vegetation, long paths or sidewalks, or any

other obstacles the movers will have to contend with. And be wary of any company that wants you to pay for an estimate. Ask for a "not to exceed" price—a guaranteed maximum—even though it may require a visit from the movers to look at your stuff ahead of time. Be wary of any mover giving a quote by volume; the industry standard is to charge by the hour.

- *Be ready for the truck on both ends of the trip*—don't make the movers wait. It will cost you goodwill and money. On the other hand, understand your shipment can be delayed for reasons beyond the mover's control, such as bad weather or heavy traffic.

- *Ask about insurance.* The standard policy covers 60¢ per pound—not enough to replace most household goods. If you have homeowner's or renter's insurance, check to see whether it covers your belongings during transit. If not, you might want to buy *full replacement* or *full value* coverage from the moving company. If it's expensive, ask about a plan with a deductible of a few hundred dollars.

- *Be prepared to pay the bill in cash* upon delivery. If the sales rep says the movers accept credit cards, get it in writing—many don't. You may be required to pay the movers in cash or with a cashier's check, money order, or traveler's checks in order to get your stuff off the truck.

Above all, ask questions; if you're concerned about something, ask for an explanation and get it in writing. And listen to your movers—they're professionals and can give you expert advice to make the job easier for everybody.

If something does go wrong, you can file a complaint with the FMCSA—or, for a local move that doesn't cross a state line, the usual consumer protection agencies listed in **Helpful Services**.

PACKING & ORGANIZING

Don't wait until the last minute to think about packing. You'll need plenty of boxes, tape, and packing material. Moving companies sell boxes, but most grocery stores or liquor stores will let you take some empty boxes. For foam "peanuts," bubble wrap, and other materials to protect fragile items, look in the Yellow Pages under "Packaging Materials"; if you have some especially fragile and valuable items, you might also want to look under "Packaging Service."

If you have a lot of stuff and don't know where to begin, call a moving consultant. These experts help you sort your belongings, get rid of unwanted items, unpack, arrange the furniture, and handle change-of-address paperwork. The D.C. chapter of the **National Association of Professional Organizers** makes referrals at 202-362-6276 or www.dc organizers.org, and *Washingtonian* magazine lists personal organizing consultants under Shopping & Services at www.washingtonian.com.

NEWCOMER'S HANDBOOK FOR MOVING TO AND LIVING IN WASHINGTON D.C.

148

STORAGE

Most communities have commercial storage facilities where you can rent a secure, climate-controlled self-storage locker—your own little warehouse—to keep items that don't fit in your home or that you only use occasionally. These can also be convenient places to store your belongings temporarily while you find a new home, and many have moving vans for rent. Find a storage facility through Storage Locator at 800-236-7362 or www.storage locator.com; at www.123movers.com; or in the Yellow Pages under "Storage —Households & Commercial."

If you plan to open your storage locker only twice—the day you fill it and the day you empty it—then consider a suburban location that will be cheaper than facilities closer to the heart of a city. If you need more frequent access to your locker, location will matter, and so will access fees. Also note that some storage facilities only allow daytime access. Others have gates that only open when a car or truck triggers a weight-sensitive lock, which can be a problem if you don't own a car. Ask about billing and security deposits, too, and don't be late with payments: if you fall behind, the storage company will not dump your stuff on your doorstep—they'll auction it off.

More convenient, and more expensive, than self-storage is mobile or modular storage. The company delivers a large container to your door, you load it, and the company hauls it away until you call for it. This can save you a lot of time and effort (it's one less round of unpacking and re-packing), but it's not good for easy access.

The biggest storage company in the Washington area is **Public Storage**, with more than 30 locations plus modular service. Call 877-788-2028 or visit www.publicstorage.com for locations and quotes. Here are some other storage companies that have convenient locations in the city and inner suburbs:

- **Capital Self Storage**, 202-543-1400
- **Downtown Storage Center**, 202-635-0714
- **H Street Self Storage**, 202-543-9080
- **National Self Storage**, 202-636-8282
- **R Street Self Storage**, 202-529-7867
- **Shurgard Storage**, 866-866-6199, www.shurgard.com
- **Storage USA**, 800-786-7872, www.sus.com
- **Store to Door** (modular), 888-867-2800, www.storetodoor.com
- **U-Haul Self Storage**, 800-468-4285, www.uhaul.com
- **U-Store**, 202-783-2990 or 202-547-7500, www.u-store.com
- **Uncle Bob's Self Storage**, 800-242-1715, www.unclebobs.com
- **Uptown Self Storage**, 202-541-1555, www.uptownselfstorage.com

TAX DEDUCTIONS

If you move for work-related reasons, some or all of your moving expenses may be tax-deductible—so keep the receipts for those expenses. Generally, you can deduct the cost of moving if your new job is at least 50 miles away from your current home and you work at the new site for at least 39 weeks during the first 12 months after you move. If you take the deduction and then fail to meet the requirements, you will have to pay the IRS back, unless you were laid off through no fault of your own or transferred again by your employer. You'll need to file IRS Form 3903 (available at www.irs.gov or a public library), and it's a good idea to consult a tax expert.

RELOCATION RESOURCES

These web sites feature moving tips and links to movers, real estate leads, and other relocation resources:

- **First Books**, www.firstbooks.com, relocation resources and information on moving to Atlanta, Boston, Chicago, Los Angeles, Minneapolis-St. Paul, New York, San Francisco, Seattle, and Washington, DC, as well as London, England. Also publisher of the *Newcomer's Handbook® for Moving to and Living in the USA* as well as *The Pet-Moving Handbook*.
- ***How to Survive A Move***, edited by Jamie Allen and Kazz Regelman, is a **Hundreds of Heads** guide (www.hundredsofheads.com). Divided into sections ranging from planning a move to packing tips, moving with kids, and worst moves ever, this easy-to-digest book provides the wisdom, dispensed mostly in single-paragraph bites, of hundreds of people who've lived through the experience.
- **American Moving & Storage Association**, www.moving.org: referrals to interstate movers, local movers, storage companies, and packing and moving consultants
- **Employee Relocation Council**, www.erc.org: If your employer is a member of this professional organization, you may have access to special services. Nonmembers can use the online database of real estate agents and related services.
- **HomeFair**, www.homefair.com, provides realty listings, moving tips, cost-of-living calculators, and more from the National Association of Realtors.
- **Moving.com**, formerly Monster Moving, is a comparison shopping site for movers' fees.
- **U.S. Postal Service Relocation Guide**, www.usps.com/moversnet, includes a detailed checklist and tips to help you avoid common mistakes that can delay your mail after you move.

CHILDREN

Moving can be hard on children. Kids moving to a new and faraway city are suddenly isolated from their friends and have to start over in an unfamiliar school and community. According to an American Medical Association study, children who move often are more likely to suffer from such problems as depression, aggression, and low self-esteem. Often their academic performance suffers as well. Aside from avoiding unnecessary moves, there are a few things you can do to help your children cope with these stressful upheavals:

- *Talk about the move with your kids.* Be honest but positive. Listen to their concerns. Involve them in the process as fully as possible.
- *Make sure the children have their favorite possessions* with them on the trip; don't pack "blankey" in the moving van.
- *Have some fun activities planned* on the other end. Your children may feel lonely in their new surroundings, and some ready-made activities can ease the transition.
- *Keep in touch with family and loved ones* as much as possible. Photos, phone calls, and e-mail are important ways to maintain links to the important people you have left behind.
- *If your children are of school age, take the time to involve yourself* in their new school and in their academic life. Don't let them get lost in the shuffle.

The Moving Book: A Kids' Survival Guide by Gabriel Davis is available from First Books, www.firstbooks.com. For younger children, First Books offers *Max's Moving Adventure: A Coloring Book for Kids on the Move*. And for parents, there's *Smart Moves: Your Guide Through the Emotional Maze of Relocation* by Nadia Jensen, Audrey McCollum, and Stuart Copans (Smith & Krauss).

PETS

Moving live animals across the country is stressful on everyone involved, and you might want to leave it to the professionals. **WorldCare Pet Transport** will make all the arrangements with airports, airlines, and the licensing authorities at your destination—and, of course, they'll move your pet in accordance with the Animal Welfare Act and USDA specifications. Call 631-286-9104 or visit www.worldcarepet.com. The *Pet-Moving Handbook* by Carrie Straub, available from First Books (www.first books.com), provides practical answers for all your pet-moving questions and covers domestic and international moves via car, airplane, ferry, etc.

AS SOON AS YOU FIND A PLACE TO HANG YOUR HAT, YOU WILL want to find a home for your money. For major deposits, shop around for interest rates, but for routine checking and savings, you'll be more interested in ATM fees, online banking options, and direct deposit services—an increasingly common alternative to getting a paycheck in the mail or on your desk. Remember that a bank in the Maryland or Virginia suburbs might not have branches in the District; if you do most of your banking at lunchtime or on the way to work, this could be a concern.

BANK ACCOUNTS & SERVICES

By the 21st century, most local banks had been acquired by regional or national giants, so it's possible that your old bank has a branch in your new neighborhood. All major banks offer a variety of checking accounts to fit a variety of personal banking habits: if you write a lot of checks and keep a low average balance, you will want to pay attention to per-check fees and service charges that kick in when your balance drops below a certain minimum; if you use your checking account only to pay your monthly bills, you might want an interest-bearing checking account with some fees instead of a free checking account that doesn't pay interest. Be sure to ask about fees for debit cards and overdraft insurance. Also inquire about the average and maximum time between a deposit and the availability of funds.

All major banks also offer money market accounts and certificates of deposit, with terms and interest rates displayed in the lobby or the window, as well as regular passbook savings accounts.

Here are some of the largest banks in the Washington area. (If you prefer a smaller community bank, check out **City First,** 202-332-5002, www.cityfirstbank.com; **Adams,** 202-466-4090, www.adamsbank.com; or **Industrial,** 202-722-2000, www.industrial-bank.com.)

NEWCOMER'S HANDBOOK FOR MOVING TO AND LIVING IN WASHINGTON D.C.

152

- **Bank of America**, 800-932-2265, www.bankofamerica.com
- **BB&T**, 800-226-5228, www.bbandt.com
- **Chevy Chase**, 800-987-BANK, www.chevychasebank.com
- **Citibank**, 800-627-3999, www.citibank.com
- **Mellon**, 800-635-5662, www.mellon.com
- **PNC**, 888-762-2265, www.pncbank.com
- **Sandy Spring**, 800-399-5919, www.ssnb.com
- **SunTrust**, 800.786.8787, www.suntrust.com
- **Wachovia**, 800-922-4684, www.wachovia.com

CHECKING ACCOUNTS

A typical checking account application will ask the name and address of your employer, two forms of current government-issued ID, proof of address, and an opening deposit. This amount will usually be debited for the cost of your first order of checks, but some checking accounts with a monthly fee or a high minimum balance include free checks. Be sure to ask for enough starter checks to get you through the two weeks or more it will take to get your new checkbook—but note, too, that some merchants will not accept starter checks and you may need to buy money orders.

Most banks now issue debit cards, usually at no cost, which electronically deduct money from your checking account. They are accepted anywhere credit cards are accepted, including the internet; just be sure to ask your bank about card security policies. A stolen debit card, unlike a credit card, gives a thief access to your actual money in the bank.

SAVINGS ACCOUNTS

Opening an ordinary savings account is as simple as opening a checking account, and most banks allow you to link it to your checking account so you can transfer funds between checking and savings instantly by ATM, phone, or internet. Usually, all of your accounts at a particular bank—passbook savings, CDs, money market funds, individual retirement accounts, medical savings accounts, and checking—can be combined to determine your eligibility for discounts and special services offered to customers with a certain total balance on deposit. Note that most savings accounts charge monthly fees if the balance falls below a certain minimum.

CREDIT UNIONS

Credit unions provide an inexpensive alternative to consumer banking. Compared to many large banks, credit unions offer lower fees and more personalized service, and they keep your assets "in the family," so to speak, enhancing the collective economic security of their members. In an era of banking megamergers, you can be sure a credit union will stay close to its roots. Membership is usually limited to employees of certain companies or residents of a certain area. In most cases, if you or a member of your immediate family can show eligibility, you can join for a $5 fee and a $5 opening deposit—and membership is for life, even if you move or change jobs.

Most government agencies, public school districts, and counties and municipalities provide credit unions for their employees, as do many large companies such as Marriott and Lockheed Martin. Employees of smaller companies might be eligible to join a regional credit union serving a select group of public, private, and nonprofit employers; ask your supervisor or benefits administrator. Or you can contact the **Credit Union National Association** at 800-358-7510 or www.creditunion.coop to find a credit union serving your community or industry.

CREDIT CARDS

Washingtonians rely so heavily on plastic—and not just for online, phone, and mail-order shopping—that one regional chain of furniture stores no longer accepts cash! You might point out that it's illegal to refuse cash, the only "legal tender for all debts, public and private," but if a sales clerk stands frozen and dumbfounded at the sight of green paper and gray metal, you'll just have to reach for the more familiar 3" x 2" card.

- **American Express,** 800-528-4800, www.americanexpress.com
- **Diner's Club,** 800-234-6377, www.dinersclub.com
- **Discover/Novus,** 800-347-2683, www.discovercard.com
- **MasterCard,** 800-622-7747, www.mastercard.com
- **VISA,** 800-847-2911, www.visa.com

Also, most department stores and other major retail chains issue charge cards, sometimes with lines of credit. Usually these accounts are issued automatically and instantly if you already have a VISA or MasterCard account. Store charge accounts may have lower fees, or none, and lower interest rates than major credit cards; and perks may include advance notice of sales, access to special services, and cardholder discounts.

You can also buy **prepaid charge cards** tied to a credit card or bank account. These work like debit cards, so you can give them to a teenager or use them for internet shopping and know that you can't lose any more money than is already encoded on the card.

BANKING & CREDIT RESOURCES

For a list of articles about trends in banking, and links to the Federal Trade Commission and other consumer protection agencies, visit the **National**

NEWCOMER'S HANDBOOK FOR MOVING TO AND LIVING IN WASHINGTON D.C.

154

Institute for Consumer Education web site at www.nice.emich.edu. To look up current interest rates on deposits, check out **www.rate.net** or **www.bankrate.com**. **CardWeb**, www.cardweb.com, is an online directory of credit cards; search or browse by interest rates, fees, special offers, or affinity features such as frequent-flyer miles or charity donations based on the amount you charge. The same information can be retrieved by phone at 800-344-7714.

If you're buying a car or boat, renovating your new fixer-upper, or sending the kids to college, you can still shop for loans the old-fashioned way, using the Yellow Pages and the financial section of the newspaper, but the internet can make the job a lot easier. Online loan calculators let you experiment with different payment plans—check out **www.loan lizzard.com**, **www.411-loans.com**, **www.eloan.com**, and **http:// financialpowertools.com**, just for example. You can also find the current interest rates at dozens of local financial institutions at a glance at **www.interest.com/washington_dc**.

Lenders suggest that you "pre-qualify" for a loan—in other words, meet with your potential lender to determine a realistic range of financing. Go prepared with documentation of your financial history, and contact the three major **credit bureaus** to make sure your credit history is accurate. (You will need to provide your name, address, previous address, and Social Security number with your request. Contact each company for specific instructions, or visit www.annualcreditreport.com for online access to all three.) You can get a free report if you've been denied credit within the last 30 days, and federal law allows you one free report per year; beyond that, you may be charged a fee.

The major credit bureaus are:

- **Equifax,** P.O. Box 105873, Atlanta, GA 30348, 800-685-1111
- **Experian** (formerly TRW), P.O. Box 2104, Allen, TX 75002-2104, 888-397-3742
- **TransUnion,** P.O. Box 390, Springfield, PA 19064-0390, 800-916-8800

Your credit rating will be reported as a FICO score, a number from 300 to 850, based on a formula developed by Fair Isaac Corp. For detailed information about the factors considered in your credit score, along with advice about maintaining good credit and preventing identity theft, contact the consumer division of Fair Isaac at 800-319-4433 or www.myfico.com.

If you discover any inaccuracies, you should contact the credit bureau immediately and request that it be corrected. By law they must respond to your request within 30 days.

TAXES

SALES TAX

The D.C. sales tax is 5.75% on consumer goods and 14.5% on hotel bills—a surtax to pay for the Verizon Center and the Washington Convention Center. Groceries are not taxed. The sales tax on restaurant bills is 10%, parking garage space 12%, and bottled liquor 9%.

In Maryland, the sales tax is 5%, with no tax on groceries. Virginia sales tax is 5% (actually 4% state tax plus 1% local sales tax); food is taxed at 1.5% and over-the-counter medications are exempt. The sales tax on restaurant meals and hotel bills varies by county, but is generally around 10%.

Most local jurisdictions are experimenting with a designated "Back to School Week," suspending the sales tax for up to nine days in August. Since these programs are subject to legislative renewal every year, watch your local newspaper for details.

FEDERAL INCOME TAX

D.C. license plates bear the sarcastic motto "Taxation Without Representation," a reminder that District residents pay federal income tax but do not have a vote in the Congress that levies the income tax and decides how to spend it. While some residents would be more than willing to pay their fair share in exchange for equal representation, others would gladly do without representation in exchange for tax breaks.

Federal, District, and state tax forms are available at any library or post office, but don't wait until April 14—indeed, such places may run out of the more common forms by early March, and may not have more esoteric forms at all. Most libraries have a book of tax forms available for photocopying. You can also **download tax forms** at www.irs.gov. And you now live in the same city as the IRS, so you can always drop by and pick up tax forms from the belly of the beast: IRS headquarters, 1111 Constitution Avenue NW.

Don't be afraid to call the IRS and ask for help. You may be placed on hold for a long time, but you will get your questions answered by a real person. The IRS Tax Help Line is 800-829-1040, and at 800-829-4477, you can hear a variety of recordings to help you. Of course, there are plenty of accountants listed in the Yellow Pages and, under "Tax Return Preparation," you'll find dozens of firms, including the giants: H&R Block, www.hrblock.com, and Jackson Hewitt, www.jacksonhewitt.com, specializing in federal tax filings and high-interest instant cash advances against your expected tax refund.

NEWCOMER'S HANDBOOK FOR MOVING TO AND LIVING IN WASHINGTON D.C.

156

STATE INCOME TAX

The Chief Financial Officer of the District of Columbia issues an annual report on tax rates and tax burdens, comparing the District to the largest city in each state. The 2004 report showed D.C.'s taxes to be the 14th highest of the 51 cities profiled for a household with an annual income of $50,000, and 15th for a household earning $100,000.

Most cities this size—the District's population is around 530,000—have a reciprocal tax agreement with the state, allowing the city to collect income tax from suburbanites who work in the city, but the D.C. Home Rule Charter, granted by Congress in 1973, expressly prohibits any form of "commuter tax." So if you live in one jurisdiction and work in another, your employer is required to withhold income taxes for the state or territory where you live.

As with federal tax forms, most of the filing materials you'll need are available at your local library or government office. In addition, the District and both neighboring states offer online tax filing options, electronic transfer of tax payments and refunds, forms by mail or download, and extensive taxpayer assistance on the web.

- **D.C. Chief Financial Officer**, 202-727-2476, www.cfo.washington dc.gov
- **Maryland Comptroller of the Treasury**, 800-MD-TAXES, http://individuals.marylandtaxes.com
- **Virginia Department of Taxation,** 804-367-8031 (information), 888-268-2829 (forms), www.tax.state.va.us

ONLINE FILING & ASSISTANCE

Filing your taxes electronically can save you time, especially if you already keep your personal financial records on software such as TurboTax or MacInTax. Visit www.irs.gov/elec_svs for details, including a list of companies that make tax software.

If your taxable income is $50,000 or less and you are not self-employed, you may be eligible to file your federal taxes by touch-tone phone—visit www.irs.gov/elec_svs or call 800-829-1040 to find out.

Visit **www.taxhelponline.com**, **www.taxresources.com**, or **www.taxlinks.com** for answers to practically any question about federal taxes—or go straight to the extensive **IRS help page** at www.irs. gov/tax_edu. From instructions for Form 1040EZ to the minutiae of Executive Order 13084, "Consultation and Coordination with Indian Tribal Governments," this site probably has the answer.

STARTING OR MOVING A BUSINESS

Washington is, let's face it, the world's leading manufacturer of red tape, and it's no surprise that the city government has a long and justified reputation as a bureaucratic labyrinth. The permits and fees involved in setting up a business in D.C. are enough to keep a special breed of lawyers busy: "expediters" are educated errand runners who know their way around the **D.C. Department of Consumer & Regulatory Affairs** (DCRA). In recent years, the District has made a conscious effort to streamline the DCRA experience. Unless you're trying to build an eight-story hotel, you won't need to hire an expediter. If you start a small business, just go to the DCRA office at 941 North Capitol Street NE and plan to spend a few hours there. You can download business license applications at www.dcra.org.

INCORPORATION

- **D.C. Department of Consumer & Regulatory Affairs**, 202-727-1000, www.dcra.org
- **Maryland Department of Assessments & Taxation**, 888-246-5941 or 410-767-1340, www.dat.state.md.us
- **Virginia State Corporation Commission**, 800-552-7945 or 804-371-9967, www.state.va.us/scc
- **Internal Revenue Service**, 800-829-1040, www.irs.gov (for employer ID number)

BUSINESS & PROFESSIONAL LICENSING

- **D.C. Department of Consumer & Regulatory Affairs**, 202-727-1000, www.dcra.org
- **Maryland Department of Labor, Licensing & Regulation**, 888-218-5925 or 410-230-6231, www.dllr.state.md.us
- **Virginia Department of Professional & Occupational Regulation**, 804-367-8500

ECONOMIC DEVELOPMENT AGENCIES

- **D.C. Office of the Deputy Mayor for Planning & Economic Development**, 202-727-6365, www.dcbiz.dc.gov
- **Maryland Business Information Network**, 800-541-8549, www.mdbusiness.state.md.us
- **Virginia Economic Development Partnership**, 804-371-8100, www.yesvirginia.org

NEWCOMER'S HANDBOOK FOR MOVING TO AND LIVING IN WASHINGTON D.C.

158

- **Small Business Administration**, U.S. Department of Commerce, www.sba.gov

CHAMBERS OF COMMERCE

County and municipal chambers of commerce are listed in the *Washington Business Journal Book of Lists*, available at most public libraries or at www.bizjournals.com/washington, 703-875-2200.

NOW THAT YOU'VE FOUND THE HOME OF YOUR DREAMS, OR AT least a place to hang your hat, you'll need to turn on the lights, hook up the cable and internet, register your car, register to vote, and find a doctor for yourself and a vet for your pet. And get a library card. And subscribe to the newspaper. And maybe install a security system. And . . . well, moving in is just the first step to getting settled in your new city.

UTILITIES

The electricity and natural gas markets opened up to private competition at the beginning of the 21st century; consumers in the District, Maryland, and Virginia may now choose a private energy company as an alternative to the local public utilities. Why? Competition is intended to help keep prices down, and environmentally conscious consumers can choose to buy from companies that produce energy from renewable sources.

Private electric and gas companies must be licensed by the **public service commission**, which is also the agency to go to for consumer information about energy choice and to report disputes or complaints. Contact the PSC where you live for a current list of licensed energy providers:

- **D.C. Public Service Commission**, 202-626-5100, www.dcpsc.org
- **Maryland Public Service Commission**, 410-767-8028 or 800-492-0474, www.psc.state.md.us
- **Virginia State Corporations Commission**, 804-371-9967 or 800-552-7945, www.state.va.us/scc

Even before you move here, you can make arrangements online to start your new electric, phone, and cable service, as well as renter's insurance and mail forwarding, at **www.movedc.com**. The service claims to provide the best deals available from each of the utility companies, but if you

NEWCOMER'S HANDBOOK FOR MOVING TO AND LIVING IN WASHINGTON D.C.

160

want to explore all of the options available, you might want to deal directly with the utilities themselves.

ELECTRICITY

Two public utility companies provide electricity in the Washington area, and a few private companies have entered the market. The public utilities don't charge hookup fees, and unless your home is brand new and barely finished, you can have your power turned on almost immediately when you call to set up your account.

In D.C. and suburban Maryland, the public utility is the **Potomac Electric Power Company, Pepco** for short. Call 202-833-7500 or visit www.pepco.com. In Virginia, the local utility is **Dominion Virginia Power**, 888-667-3000 or www.dom.com.

The local utility company is still the sole distributor supplying power to homes and maintaining power lines, but you can purchase electricity— delivered through the common grid—from a small but growing number of licensed energy producers. As with long distance companies, you have legal protection if your electric company is changed without your consent. If a private electric company fails to deliver, the public utility will automatically supply your power without interruption.

All three PSCs in the area have special web sites and hotlines devoted to energy choice:

- **D.C.**: 202-895-0950, www.dciselectric.com
- **Maryland**: 800-800-4491, www.md-electric-info.com/questions
- **Virginia**: 877-937-2004, www.yesvachoice.com

NATURAL GAS

Many houses and apartments in Washington do not use gas at all; some have a gas stove but an electric water heater and electric heat. At the other extreme, a few townhouses in Georgetown and off Dupont Circle still have working gaslights, gas heat, and clothes dryers. As with electricity, natural gas deregulation in the late 1990s opened the door to private competition, providing alternatives to consumers. The public utility, which serves the entire Washington area, is **Washington Gas**, www.washgas.com. Call 703-750-1000 to have gas service activated. There are no hookup fees unless you are converting electric amenities to gas, which requires a house call. Contact the same PSCs listed above for information about alternative natural gas companies.

Before you do any digging or building on your property, call the "Miss Utility" hotline at 800-257-7777 to have the gas company mark the location of buried gas lines.

TELEPHONE

Verizon (formerly Bell Atlantic) provides most of D.C.'s local phone service, although Starpower, AT&T, and a growing array of newcomers are in the local market as well. Verizon, www.verizon.com, provides basic residential phone service for about $23 a month including taxes. Services such as call waiting, caller ID, voice mail, and call forwarding cost extra. All features are explained in the Customer Guide section of the local White Pages. Verizon requires first-time customers to pay a $50 security deposit, refunded with interest (or credited to your account) after one year. If your home is already wired to suit your needs, you'll only need to call to have service activated; if you need a Verizon technician to do any wiring, you will be charged for the time and labor.

To start or stop Verizon service, visit www.verizon.com or be prepared to spend about 20 minutes with an agent when you call:

- **D.C.**, 202-954-6263
- **Maryland**, 301-954-6260
- **Virginia**, 703-954-6222

Competition in the local phone service market is aimed mostly at business customers, but a few companies provide residential lines; look in the Yellow Pages under "Telecommunications Companies" or check with the public service commission.

INTERNET PHONE SERVICE (VOIP)

VOIP, or voice-over-internet protocol, is a combination of subscriber service and hardware that enables you to use a computer data line to make regular voice phone calls. It's a flat (and low) rate for unlimited long distance, and you can usually choose an area code that isn't necessarily where you live—so it's cheaper for your friends and family back home to keep in touch with you here in D.C. There is one serious downside, though: VOIP phone lines will not work during a power failure (and the Washington area does experience weather-related power failures). Police and fire officials therefore caution against relying exclusively on a VOIP line.

Most of the major internet service providers offer VOIP service, and so do some telecom companies, including:

- **Skype**, www.skype.com
- **Speakeasy**, www.speakeasy.net, 800-556-5829
- **Viatalk**, www.viatalk.com, 866-626-7150
- **Vonage**, www.vonage.com, 800-986-4866

NEWCOMER'S HANDBOOK FOR MOVING TO AND LIVING IN WASHINGTON D.C.

162

For a good list of current providers and deals, check out www.order voip.com. Oh, and obviously, you'll need a computer with the latest operating system and a fast broadband connection.

AREA CODES

There are certain complications that come with a territory that spans two states and a federal colony. If you come from a place where phone numbers have only seven digits, you'll need to get used to area codes: even local calls require an area code here.

The District has only one area code, **202**. In Maryland, area codes **301** and **240** are both used in areas west of the Patuxent River, from the Washington suburbs to the mountains of Western Maryland, and the area code alone does not reveal whether a Maryland number is a long-distance call from Washington. Gaithersburg to the north and Waldorf to the south are the approximate limits of the local calling area, although some residents and most businesses throughout neighboring counties pay extra to have a metro-area phone number. In Virginia, area code **703** covers the suburbs and not much else. Beyond the suburbs, Virginia uses area codes **540** to the west and **804** to the south; in Maryland, area codes **410** and **443** are found to the east.

Within the Washington area, you must always dial the area code if it is different from your own, even if it's a local call. (In some parts of Maryland beyond the immediate suburbs, you have to dial the area code for all calls, period.)

LONG DISTANCE SERVICE

For a helpful comparison of long distance services from an independent clearinghouse not funded by the telecommunications industry, contact the **Telecommunications Research and Action Center** at 202-263-2950 or www.trac.org.

The major long-distance players in the Washington market include:
- **AT&T**, 800-222-0300, www.att.com
- **MCI WorldCom**, 800-950-5555, www.mci.com
- **SBC**, 877-430-7228, www.sbctelecom.com
- **Sprint**, 800-877-7746, www.sprint.com
- **Starpower**, 877-782-7769, www.starpower.net
- **Verizon**, 800-343-2092, www.verizon.net

Working Assets Long Distance, 800-788-0898, www.workingfor change.com, donates a percentage of your long distance bill to environmental and human rights groups and, although you won't be needing it here, the company gives free long distance time to customers calling their federal lawmakers.

Every convenience store and corner market sells **prepaid calling cards** in denominations of $5 to $25, some claiming rates of 1.2 cents a minute. These rates apply to actual talking time, though—with dialing charges and a surcharge for using a pay phone, a lot of short calls will deplete the card quickly. Still, it's cheaper than most long distance services, and the only catch is that the local number you dial to access your prepaid long distance account might give you an occasional busy signal.

WIRELESS PHONE SERVICE

Washingtonians are addicted to their cell phones, and a growing number of residents actually go without regular landline service and use their cellular or digital PCS phones at home. Some restaurants try to enforce a "no cell phones" policy, and on most commuter trains there's a designated "quiet car," but the only place in Washington where you can expect to be free of ringtones and one-sided conversations is in a theater or a house of worship. (And even that's not guaranteed.) In the District, it is illegal to talk on a wireless phone while driving unless using a hands-free attachment; in Maryland, drivers under age 18 may not use cell phones behind the wheel except to call 911. Also, some elementary and secondary schools prohibit cell phones during the school day.

Check the Yellow Pages for a complete list of cellular and PCS providers, and check **www.point.com** for the latest deals on service plans. The major players in the Washington area include:

- **Cingular**, 866-246-4852, www.cingular.com
- **Sprint/Nextel**, 800-777-4681, www.sprintpcs.com.
- **T-Mobile**, 800-866-2453, www.t-mobile.com
- **USA Mobility**, 800-333-4722, www.usamobility.com
- **Verizon Wireless**, 800-922-0204, www.verizon.com

INTERNET SERVICE

Exploring your new environs can be much easier with the help of the web. Get online to check store hours, look at maps and bus schedules, learn about community organizations, manage your bank accounts, and shop at midnight, all from the convenience of your own home. Here are some of the major internet service providers in the area:

- **America Online**, 800-827-6364, www.aol.com
- **AT&T WorldNet**, 800-967-5363, www.att.net
- **Cox Communications**, 703-378-8422, www.cox.net
- **Earthlink**, 800-327-8454, www.earthlink.net

NEWCOMER'S HANDBOOK FOR MOVING TO AND LIVING IN WASHINGTON D.C.

164

- **Microsoft Network**, 800-426-9400, www.msn.com
- **NetZero**, 877-665-9995, www.netzero.net
- **Verizon Internet**, 800-638-2026, www.verizon.net

Also, you can surf for free (in 15-minute time slots) at most public libraries and recreation centers in D.C., or at:

- **Howard University Community Technology Center**, 2006 Georgia Ave. NW, 202-234-3657
- **Harry Thomas Community Service Center**, 1801 Lincoln Rd. NE, 202-541-7499
- **Southeast Tennis & Learning Center** (venue for athletic and academic youth programs), 701 Mississippi Ave. SE, 202-645-6273
- **Judiciary Square One-Stop Career Center**, One Judiciary Square, 202-727-9726
- **Naylor Road One-Stop Career Center**, 202-645-3413

Many coffeehouses and hotel lobbies are **wi-fi** zones where a properly equipped laptop can access the internet. Dupont Circle, much of Capitol Hill, Farragut Square, Old Town Alexandria, and the Freedom Plaza–Pershing Park area along Pennsylvania Avenue NW are also wi-fi areas. For the latest list of free internet terminals and wi-fi zones, visit http://cityofaccess.dc.gov.

WATER

In the District, water and sewer bills are addressed to "occupant"—so you don't need to set up an account, just make sure service is turned on. The **D.C. Water & Sewer Authority** distributes water from Army Corps of Engineers reservoirs—mainly the Dalecarlia Reservoir near the western tip of the District, fed by an underground aqueduct from the Potomac River. The McMillan Reservoir, near Howard University, and the Georgetown Reservoir provide backup during dry spells. In a moderate drought, authorities will call for voluntary limits on the use of water for lawn care and car washing; if conditions get worse, as in 1999, such activities might be limited to certain days or even prohibited.

Most residents of suburban Maryland get their water from the Triadelphia Reservoir, impounded by Brighton Dam, and the T. Howard Duckett Reservoir, impounded by Rocky Gorge Dam, both on the Patuxent River. The Virginia suburbs draw their water from the Potomac and Occoquan rivers—except Arlington, which buys water from the same Corps of Engineers division that supplies water to the District.

Call the local water utility to start service:

- **District of Columbia**: D.C. Water & Sewer Authority, 202-354-3600, www.dcwasa.com

- **Maryland**: Washington Suburban Sanitary Commission, 301-206-4001 or 800-634-8400, www.wssc.dst.md.us
- **Arlington County**: Department of Public Works, 703-228-3636, www.co.arlington.va.us/dpw
- **Fairfax County**: Fairfax County Water Authority, 703-698-5800, www.fcwa.org
- **Alexandria**: Virginia-American Water Co., 703-549-7080; www.vawc.com/alex
- **Falls Church**: Public Utilities Division, 703-248-5071, www.ci.falls-church.va.us

Each of these utilities issues an annual report on water quality, available online or by mail. Tap water in D.C. is always nasty tasting and occasionally dangerous—in the late 1990s, the EPA issued several "boil water" alerts, fearing unlawfully high levels of cryptosporidium. The official advisories have been lifted, but many residents—especially those with young children, the elderly, or those with compromised immune systems—rely on bottled water or water filters.

In the suburbs, the tap water is generally better, though Brita filters are popular throughout the region. These inexpensive filters remove the taste and odor of chlorine, which can be strong at times, but they don't eliminate most pollutants. Heavy-duty water filters that remove almost all microbes, lead, chlorine, and other toxic trace elements from tap water are available by mail from Gaiam, 800-869-3446 or www.gaiam.com, and area department stores carry a few models.

For information about local water utilities, including a record of violations and enforcement actions, call the **EPA Safe Drinking Water Hotline** at 800-426-4791 or visit www.epa.gov/safewater. The EPA also publishes consumer pamphlets and factsheets on home filtration systems, home water testing, conservation tips, and the Safe Drinking Water Act of 1974.

If you have doubts about the quality of your tap water, you can buy testing kits at large hardware stores or look in the Yellow Pages under "Laboratories - Testing." Test kits—and advice for improving test results—are also available from the nonprofit **Water Quality Association**, 630-505-0160 or www.wqa.org.

You can also lease an office-grade water cooler and get bottled water delivered on a weekly or monthly basis; look in the Yellow Pages under "Water - Bottled & Bulk."

CONSUMER PROTECTION—UTILITY COMPLAINTS

Public utility companies providing electricity, natural gas, water, and local telephone service are regulated by the state or D.C. public service commis-

NEWCOMER'S HANDBOOK FOR MOVING TO AND LIVING IN WASHINGTON D.C.

166

sion listed above. These commissions set maximum rates, investigate consumer complaints, and license alternative service providers setting up to compete with public utilities. Contact the PSC if you have a question or concern that the utility company cannot resolve.

The **D.C. Office of People's Counsel**, 202-727-3071 or www. dcpsc.org, handles consumer complaints about proposed rate increases and other changes in utility service.

If you have a billing dispute with your long distance provider, and your local phone company cannot help, the next step is to file a complaint with the **Federal Communications Commission** at 888-225-5322, www.fcc.gov, or the **Federal Trade Commission** at 202-382-4357, www.ftc.gov.

These agencies oversee cable TV providers:

- **D.C. Office of Cable Television & Telecommunications**, 202-671-0066
- **Montgomery County Office of Cable Communications**, 240-773-2288
- **Prince George's County Cable Television Commission**, 301-952-3990
- **Arlington County Cable Administration**, 703-228-3242
- **Fairfax County Department of Cable Communications and Consumer Protection**, 703-324-5902
- **Alexandria Citizen Assistance Office**, 703-838-4533

If you have a problem with a local business, see the Consumer Resources section in the **Shopping for the Home** chapter and Consumer Protection in **Helpful Services**; for landlord or property issues, check the chapter on **Finding a Place to Live**.

GARBAGE, RECYCLING, COMPOSTING

Except in a few outlying suburbs where you actually take your trash to a local dump, Washington area trash collection is a county or city service. If you live in an apartment, your landlord or condo association will arrange for trash and recycling pickup. In most D.C. neighborhoods, each house is issued a sturdy plastic "Supercan"—a big trashcan on wheels—owned by the Department of Public Works. In some neighborhoods, trash and recycling are collected in a back alley, and in others at the front curb; just ask a neighbor, or see where people keep their trashcans and recycling bins.

In some suburban cities and towns, trash and recycling are collected by a municipal service rather than the county agency; to find out, call the municipal phone number listed in the **Useful Phone Numbers and Web Sites** chapter. Some suburban jurisdictions provide trashcans; in others you'll need to buy a trashcan with a lid to keep out rats and raccoons as well as neighborhood dogs. Most jurisdictions provide plastic bins or color-coded plastic bags for recyclables.

Unfortunately the Washington area is not one of the parts of the country where households are charged by the bag or the pound for trash pickup. Here homeowners pay for waste management as a percentage of their property taxes, regardless of their efforts to reduce, reuse, and recycle. However, almost all jurisdictions in the Washington area have mandatory curbside recycling, and provide bins for your glass, cans, and plastic containers. These may be commingled in the same bin, and you do not need to sort glass by color. Newspapers are collected separately, and must be bundled with twine or in paper grocery bags; in some jurisdictions, cardboard, magazines, junk mail, and other mixed paper are also collected at curbside.

Call the local environmental services agency for details about recyclables, and to find out when trash and recyclables are collected in your neighborhood:

- **D.C. Department of Public Works**, 202-727-1000, http://dpw.dc.gov
- **Montgomery County Solid Waste Services Division**, 240-777-6400, www.montgomerycountymd.gov/solidwaste
- **Prince George's County Department of Environmental Resources**, 301-883-5810, www.goprincegeorgescounty.com
- **Arlington County Department of Environmental Services**, 703-228-4488, www.arlingtonva.us
- **Fairfax County Department of Public Works & Environmental Services**, 703-802-3322, www.co.fairfax.va.us/dpwes
- **Alexandria Department of Transportation & Environmental Services**, 703-751-5130, http://ci.alexandria.va.us/tes

The same solid waste agencies collect raked leaves in the fall. In some areas, leaves must be bagged; in others, vacuum trucks sweep up the piles raked to the curb. Christmas trees are collected at curbside in early January in most jurisdictions.

In all jurisdictions, backyard composting of kitchen scraps (vegetable matter only) is allowed as long as neighbors don't complain of a nuisance. A properly managed compost pile does not smell bad or attract pests, but the compost pile must be properly aerated and maintained. City dwellers without yards might consider indoor composting, letting worms turn kitchen scraps into soil in a specially designed bin. For an introduction to backyard and indoor composting, visit www.nrcs.usda.gov or call the nearest **USDA Natural Resources Conservation Service** office:

- **D.C.**, 202-535-2242
- **Maryland**, 301-590-2855
- **Virginia**, 703-324-1460

NEWCOMER'S HANDBOOK FOR MOVING TO AND LIVING IN WASHINGTON D.C.

168

DRIVER'S LICENSE, NON-DRIVER'S ID

If you expect the Department of Motor Vehicles to greet you with long lines and inefficient, complicated paperwork, you won't be disappointed. However, D.C. residents are finding DMV lines moving faster than they once did, and in Maryland express offices handle routine license renewals, so you only need to go to a full-service office for a new license or vehicle registration. DMV offices also issue official photo ID cards ("non-driver's ID") for residents not licensed to drive. These ID cards are not mandatory, but they are universally accepted as a substitute for a driver's license for identification and proof of age.

New residents of D.C., Maryland, and Virginia have 30 days to obtain a local driver's license and vehicle registration. If your current out-of-state or foreign driver's license has not expired, you can get a local license without taking a road test or a written test if your previous state or country offers registration reciprocity with your new jurisdiction. Just bring your current license and proof of residence, such as a recent utility bill, voter registration card, or a copy of your lease or mortgage statement; in Maryland and Virginia, you also need to bring an official copy of your birth certificate. In the District, if you have any unpaid parking tickets or other administrative debts of more than $100, you will have to pay them in order to get a driver's license. Then you just take an eye test and pay a fee.

If your previous state or country does not have reciprocity with your new jurisdiction, you may have to take a road test, a written test, or both; if you have a foreign license that is not printed in English, you may be required to provide a translation on embassy letterhead or bearing the raised seal of a certified translator.

If you do not have a current driver's license, you will have to get a learner's permit and schedule a road test at a later date. You will need to show a government-issued photo ID; proof of residence; and your original Social Security card or a bank statement, IRS document, or pay stub bearing your Social Security number. (In Virginia, you also need to show a second form of ID and proof of U.S. citizenship or valid immigration status.) Then you take a written test and eye test, pay the fee, and make an appointment for the road test. You provide your own vehicle for the road test; also, since a learner's permit does not allow you to drive alone, you need to be accompanied by a licensed driver.

Contact your motor vehicle agency (listed below) for details about learner's permits and first-time applicants for a driver's license. The District, Maryland, and Virginia all require first-time applicants to take a certified driver education course, log a certain number of hours of supervised driving, or both. In Maryland, rookie drivers under 18 years old are subject to certain restrictions—most notably, no cell phones while driving and, during the first five months of licensure, no passengers under age 18 except family members.

To obtain a non-driver's ID card, you'll need to show proof of identity—a comparable card from another state, a birth certificate, a passport, or military ID—and pay a small fee.

In D.C., the fee for a driver's license is $39; a learner's permit or non-driver's ID is $15. In Maryland, the fee is $45 for a license, $50 for a learner's permit, and $15 for ID. In Virginia, the driver's license fee is $4 per year (your license will expire on your birthday the next time your age is divisible by 5), plus $3 extra for a learner's permit; $10 for ID.

DRIVER'S LICENSE OFFICES

D.C. Department of Motor Vehicles, 202-727-5000, http://dmv. washingtondc.gov:
- 95 M St. SW
- 1233 Brentwood Rd. NE
- 3214 Pennsylvania Ave. SE
- Shops at Georgetown Park (renewals only)

Maryland Motor Vehicle Administration, 800-950-1682, www. mva.state.md.us:
- 15 Metropolitan Grove Rd., Gaithersburg
- 11760 Baltimore Ave., Beltsville
- 10251 Central Ave., Largo
- Beltway Plaza, 6000 Greenbelt Rd., Greenbelt (renewals only)

Virginia Department of Motor Vehicles, 866-368-5463, www. dmv.state.va.us:
- 2681 Mill Rd., Alexandria
- 6306 Grovedale Dr., Alexandria
- 4150 South Four Mile Run Dr., Arlington
- 1968 Gallows Rd., Vienna
- 14950 Northridge Dr., Chantilly
- Fair Oaks Mall, Fairfax
- Springfield Mall, Springfield

OWNING A CAR

AUTOMOBILE REGISTRATION

Visit the same DMV office as above to register your vehicle within 30 days after your arrival. You will need to show the title, proof of insurance, and proof of a safety inspection; you'll be charged a registration fee, and a one-time excise tax based on the vehicle's book value.

NEWCOMER'S HANDBOOK FOR MOVING TO AND LIVING IN WASHINGTON D.C.

170

In D.C., there is only one inspection facility, and lines are long. It's located at 1001 Half Street SW, open weekdays 6 a.m. to 6 p.m. and Saturdays 7 a.m. to 3 p.m. (During the summer, on days when the ozone pollution level reaches "code red," the station closes at 1 p.m.) Excise taxes (as a percentage of book value) and annual registration fees are based on vehicle weight:

Class	Tax	Fee
Under 3,500 lbs.	6%	$72 ($36 hybrids and clean fuel vehicles)
3,500–4,999 lbs.	7%	$115
5,000 lbs. or more	8%	$155

Along with the registration fee, you will be charged $25 for the **inspection** and $15 for a **residential parking permit**. You may choose to register your vehicle for two years—doubling each of these amounts. Minimum **insurance** coverage is $25,000/person and $50,000/accident for bodily injury, $10,000 for property damage.

You must convert your old driver's license to a D.C. license before you register a vehicle in the District. For temporary residents, a six-month parking permit is $250; a student parking permit is $338/year. Reciprocity parking permits are $10/year for military personnel and members of Congress, $15/year for diplomats. For more information, call the DMV at 202-727-5000.

IN MARYLAND

The excise tax in Maryland is 5% of the actual sale price or the minimum book value ($640), whichever is greater; if your vehicle is titled in a state with an excise tax equal to Maryland's or greater, and you register within 60 days after moving to Maryland, the tax is $100.

Mandatory **safety inspections** are performed at service stations or repair shops displaying a state-issued sign marking them as an authorized inspection station. Minimum **insurance** coverage is $20,000 for bodily injury (one person), $40,000 for bodily injury (two or more people), and $15,000 for property damage; personal injury, $2,500.

Vehicles registered in Maryland (except some hybrids) are subject to annual **emissions testing**. You will be notified by mail when your vehicle is due for an emissions test, and you have two months to go to an emissions test station, pay the $14 fee, and take the test. Test stations are open 8 a.m. to 5:30 p.m. Mondays, Wednesdays, and Fridays; 7 a.m. to 7 p.m. Tuesdays and Thursdays; and 7 a.m. to 1 p.m. Saturdays. Locations are:

- 2121 Industrial Parkway, White Oak (off U.S. Route 29 near New Hampshire Ave.)

- 7407 Lindbergh Dr., Gaithersburg (central Montgomery County)
- 15910 Chieftain Ave., Derwood (northern Montgomery County)
- 7213 Old Alexandria Ferry Rd., Clinton (near Andrews Air Force Base)
- 7401 Jefferson Ave., Glenarden (near the Beltway and U.S. Route 50)

Hybrid vehicles are exempt if their city mileage is at least 50 mpg according to the federal Fuel Economy Guide (www.fueleconomy.gov). For more information, call 800-638-8347 or visit www.marylandmva.com (click on MVA Programs).

IN VIRGINIA

Vehicles must pass an **emissions test** before being registered in Northern Virginia (Arlington, Fairfax, Loudoun, Prince William, and Stafford counties and Alexandria). Any authorized service station can perform an emissions test; for locations, call the **Department of Environmental Quality** at 703-583-3900 or 800-275-3844 or visit www.virims.com/stations. Testing fees vary, but the DMV says they "should not" exceed $28. If you are moving from a state that performs emissions tests and you have a valid test certificate less than a year old, Virginia may honor your current certificate—check the DMV web site for a list of states with reciprocity.

The excise tax is 3% of the sale price, or $35, whichever is greater, and there is a $10 titling fee. Minimum **insurance** coverage is $25,000 for bodily injury or death of one person; $50,000 for bodily injury or death of two or more persons; and $20,000 for property damage; uninsured motorists may register a vehicle for an additional fee of $500/year. The registration fee is based on vehicle weight:

Class	Fee
Under 4,000 lbs.	$29.50
4,001 lbs. or more	$34.50
Pickup trucks (6,501–7,500 lbs.)	$40.50

LOCAL REGISTRATION & PARKING PERMITS

And you thought you were done! In Virginia, you have to register your vehicle with the county as well as the state, and some municipalities in Maryland require you to buy a residential parking decal. (See **Useful Phone Numbers & Web Sites** for county and municipal government phone numbers.) If you live in a subdivision, condominium, or apartment complex, check with the property manager about parking permits for yourself and your guests.

NEWCOMER'S HANDBOOK FOR MOVING TO AND LIVING IN WASHINGTON D.C.

172

In Virginia, you will receive a local registration decal as a receipt for payment of the tax on your car. Contact the local tax authority to pay for your registration decals in person or by mail—or, if you're on active duty in the armed services, to get your tax-exempt decals:

- **Arlington County** vehicle registration decals cost $24/year, payable to the Treasurer of Arlington County at 2100 Clarendon Blvd., Suite 200. You can register by mail if you do not have any unpaid parking tickets or property tax bills, and if you are not a student, diplomat, or NATO staff member. Vehicles owned solely by U.S. military personnel on active duty are exempt; you will need to mail in photocopies of your military ID and transfer orders. Call 703-228-3135 or pay online at http://payment.arlingtonva.us.

- **Fairfax County** vehicle registration decals cost $25/year for most passenger vehicles, payable to Fairfax County, Department of Tax Administration, 12000 Government Center Pkwy., Suite 223, Fairfax, VA 22035. You must register your vehicle within 60 days after moving into the county. Vehicles owned by military or diplomatic personnel are exempt, and decals are free (with payment of property tax) for certain categories of veterans and police, fire and rescue personnel, and for antique cars. Call 703-222-8234 or download a form at www.co. fairfax.va.us/dta.

- **Alexandria** vehicle registration decals cost $25/year for most passenger vehicles, payable to the Alexandria Department of Finance, Revenue Division, P.O. Box 178, Alexandria, VA 22313. You must register your vehicle within 30 days after moving into the city (but if you live in an area where a residential parking permit is required, there is no 30-day grace period). You can register in person at City Hall, Room 1410; bring your state registration, the title or bill of sale, and your driver's license. To register by mail, call 703-838-4560 or download a form at http://alexandriava.gov/#.

PARKING

In D.C. and some suburban municipalities, parking tickets are an important source of public revenue. The city decided to turn most of its parking meters over to private contractors in the 1990s after a bizarre crime wave in which hundreds of parking meters were stolen. Contractors just operate the meters themselves—tickets are still issued by the Metropolitan Police Department, http://mpdc.dc.gov. While thousands of D.C. residents have diplomatic immunity and can park wherever they like, the city doesn't miss any opportunity to ticket those who don't have magic "DPL" tags.

If you park at a meter that is malfunctioning, call 202-541-6030 to report the number of the meter. Your license tag number will be recorded, and you will be allowed to remain parked at the broken meter for the maximum amount of time the meter would normally allow. (You might still get a ticket, but you will have a valid defense against it.)

The procedures for paying or contesting a ticket are printed on the back of the citation. You have 15 days to pay or demand a hearing; after that the fine is doubled. After 30 days, the ticket is considered delinquent and you lose the right to contest it; if you have two or more delinquent tickets at any time, your car may be booted, and you will have to pay $50 plus all outstanding tickets in order to get the boot removed.

For more information about parking tickets and paying fines, contact the DMV at 202-727-5000 or http://dmv.dc.gov. In the suburbs, follow the instructions on the ticket if you choose to pay by mail or in person, or if you want to contest the citation.

PARKING GARAGES & LOTS

Parking in downtown D.C. is an expensive and often difficult proposition, and a compelling incentive to use Metrorail and buses. If you must commute by car, monthly passes are available from parking garages—daily rates can easily run $10, and the "daily" rate can apply to anything longer than two or three hours. (Many garages only deal in monthly passes and don't even offer daily parking.) If you drive downtown in the evening, skip the commercial lots and look for parking meters—most metered parking spaces are free after 6 p.m. and on weekends. Public parking garages are located every few blocks, but most close around 7 p.m.

TOWING

If your vehicle is towed in D.C., call 202-727-5000 to find it—usually it's at Blue Plains Vehicle Impoundment Lot at 5001 Shepherd Parkway SW. Before you can retrieve your car, you must pay all outstanding fines plus a towing fee of $100 and a storage fee of $20 per day. Go to the **DMV Adjudication Services** office, 301 C Street NW (Judiciary Square Metro station). The office is open 8:15 a.m. to 4 p.m. Tuesday through Saturday. You can also pay online (or check the status of a towed vehicle) at http://dmv.dc.gov.

The Blue Plains lot is served by Metrobus routes A4/A5 from Anacostia Metro station. If your car is registered in the name of your spouse, parent, employer, etc., you must show a notarized statement from the owner authorizing you to pick it up; if the vehicle is leased, you must show the lease.

In the suburbs, call these numbers for instructions if your car is towed:
- **Alexandria Code Enforcement Bureau**, 703-838-4360
- **Arlington County Police**, 703-228-4040

NEWCOMER'S HANDBOOK FOR MOVING TO AND LIVING IN WASHINGTON D.C.

174

- **Fairfax County Police Traffic Division**, 703-280-0587
- **Montgomery County Police**, 301-840-2454 or 301-279-8000
- **Prince George's County Police**, 301-772-4740

AUTOMOBILE SAFETY

Drunk drivers in D.C., Maryland, and Virginia killed 679 people in 2003, up from 521 in 1999—a period during which the nationwide rate of drunk driving fatalities declined.

In the District, if you are convicted of **driving while intoxicated** (DWI) or **driving under the influence of alcohol** (DUI), your license will be revoked for at least six months. In Maryland, a first conviction for DWI can result in revocation of your license, fines up to $1,000, and up to a year in jail; a DUI can result in suspension of your license, fines up to $500, and up to 60 days in jail. In Virginia, if you're convicted of an alcohol-related driving offense, you may be ordered to have your vehicle equipped with a special lock that opens only when you pass a Breathalyzer test. Maryland prosecutors are allowed to notify a jury if you refuse to take a Breathalyzer test. And in all three jurisdictions, the DMV can suspend your license through administrative hearings even if you are not convicted in court. The legal threshold for DWI is a blood alcohol content of 0.08 in D.C. and both neighboring states; in the District, a driver can be charged with DUI with *any* measurable blood alcohol content.

All three jurisdictions require federally approved **car seats** or **booster seats** for children under age 6; D.C. requires them up to age 8, and Maryland requires car seats for children under 40 pounds. Safe Kids Worldwide, the certifying body for child passenger safety technicians, recommends using car seats or booster seats for all children under 4 feet 9 inches tall. All drivers and passengers are required to wear seatbelts at all times—even in taxicabs—and in D.C. and Maryland, seatbelt laws are sometimes enforced even in the absence of other violations. Contact Safe Kids at 202-662-0600, www.usa.safekids.org, for details about the proper use of child passenger restraints and a schedule of free, voluntary car seat inspections.

VOTING

Now that you live in the capital of democracy, you might want to partici-pate in it. These contacts will help you register to vote, learn the political landscape of your new community, and find out for yourself who's who in local politics.

VOTER REGISTRATION

Voter registration deadlines in the District, Maryland, and Virginia are 30 days prior to any general or primary election. D.C. and Maryland hold closed primaries—in order to vote in a party's primary election, you must be a registered member of that party. In Virginia, voters with no party affiliation may vote in the Democratic or Republican primary.

In each jurisdiction, mail-in voter registration forms are available at libraries, community centers, and other public buildings. You can also register to vote at DMV offices or with your state or local board of elections:

- **D.C. Board of Elections & Ethics**, 202-727-2525, www.dcboee.org
- **Maryland State Board of Elections**, 800-222-8683, www.elections. state.md.us
- **Montgomery County Board of Elections**, 240-777-8500, www. montgomerycountymd.gov; 24-hour information line, 240-777-8683
- **Prince George's County Board of Elections**, 301-952-3270, www.co.pg.md.us; 24-hour information line, 301-627-2814
- **Virginia State Board of Elections**, 800-552-9745, www.sbe. state.va.us
- **Alexandria Office of Voter Registration**, 703-838-4050, www. alexandriavoter.org
- **Arlington County Registrar of Voters**, 703-228-3456, www. arlingtonva.us
- **Fairfax County Electoral Board & General Registrar**, 703-222-0776, www.co.fairfax.va.us/eb; 24-hour information line, 703-324-4700

POLITICAL PARTIES

In D.C., there are 38 political parties recognized by the Board of Elections & Ethics; three are officially considered "major" parties and are entitled to hold primaries—the Democratic, Republican, and D.C. Statehood Green parties. (The D.C. Statehood Party and the D.C. Green Party merged in 1999.) In addition, the Umoja, Socialist Workers, and Libertarian parties have placed candidates on the ballot in recent years. In Maryland and Virginia, state election authorities recognize several major and minor parties.

DISTRICT OF COLUMBIA
- **Democratic Party**, 202-223-2113, www.dcdsc.org
- **Republican Party**, 202-289-8005, www.dcgop.com
- **D.C. Statehood Green Party**, 202-232-1724, www.dcstatehood green.org

NEWCOMER'S HANDBOOK FOR MOVING TO AND LIVING IN WASHINGTON D.C.

176

MARYLAND

- **Democratic Party**, 410-269-8818, www.mddems.org
- **Republican Party**, 410-269-0113, www.mdgop.org
- **Constitution Party**, 877-487-8847, www.cpmaryland.com
- **Green Party**, 410-867-7626, www.mdgreens.org
- **Libertarian Party**, 800-657-1776, www.md.lp.org

VIRGINIA

- **Democratic Party**, 804-644-1966, www.vademocrats.org
- **Republican Party**, 804-780-0111, www.rpv.org
- **Constitution Party**, 877-487-8847, www.constitutionpartyva.com
- **Green Party**, 703-534-2187, www.vagreenparty.org
- **Libertarian Party**, 800-619-1776, www.lpva.com
- **Natural Law Party**, 540-868-1459, www.va-natural-law.org

VOTING & CAMPAIGN FINANCE RECORDS

Project Vote Smart tracks the voting records and positions of federal, state, and local officials nationwide. Call 888-VOTE SMART or visit www.vote-smart.org. Other web sites useful in comparing candidates include:

- **D.C. Watch**, www.dcwatch.com
- **Center for Responsive Politics**, www.opensecrets.org
- **C-SPAN**, www.cspan.org
- **League of Women Voters**, www.lwv.org
- **Politics1**, www.politics1.com

Also, since you happen to live in the nation's capital, you can stop by the storefront reading room at **Federal Election Commission** headquarters, 999 E Street NW, on any business day, and browse campaign finance records on every presidential and congressional candidate, as well as every PAC that gives them money. For more information, call 202-694-1100 or visit www.fec.gov.

PASSPORTS

A routine application for a U.S. passport takes about six weeks. If you are leaving the country within two weeks or you need foreign visas, call 877-487-2778 to make an appointment at the **Washington Passport Agency**, 1111 19th Street NW, for special processing. Routine applications are accepted at most post offices—contact the **Bureau of Consular Affairs** at http://travel.state.gov to find the nearest location.

You will need to show proof of citizenship (old U.S. passport, birth certificate, naturalization certificate) and proof of identity (driver's license or other government-issued photo ID). The fee for routine processing is $97 for a new passport ($82 for persons under 16) or $67 for a renewal; for expedited service, the Washington Passport Agency charges an additional $60. You also need to provide two identical photos, 1 3/8" x 1 3/4." For this purpose, practically every camera store, travel agency, and copy shop offers "passport photos"—twin photos taken with a two-chambered camera—for about $10.

In most cases, you can renew a passport by mail—download the application forms and instructions from the Bureau of Consular Affairs site. For more information, call the **National Passport Information Center** at 877-487-2778.

LIBRARIES

Library cards are issued free with proof of residence (a current utility bill, a copy of a lease or insurance policy, voter registration card, or ID bearing your address). In some jurisdictions, a parental consent form is required for children obtaining their own cards. The main library in each jurisdiction is listed in the Literary Life section of **Cultural Life**, along with private and special-interest libraries; branch locations are included in the neighborhood profiles. If you want to borrow materials from another jurisdiction's library system, your neighborhood library can arrange an inter-library loan.

MEDIA

TELEVISION

Many Washingtonians would be lost without CNN and C-SPAN; others are content to watch "The West Wing" and Jim Lehrer for free. In addition to the national broadcast networks, there are several public television stations here, and many residents on high ground or with good antennas can pick up Baltimore and Annapolis broadcasts as well.

LOCAL BROADCAST STATIONS
- **Channel 4** WRC/NBC
- **Channel 5** WTTG/FOX
- **Channel 7** WJLA/ABC
- **Channel 9** WUSA/CBS
- **Channel 20** WDCA/UPN
- **Channel 26** WETA/PBS
- **Channel 32** WHUT/PBS
- **Channel 50** WBFF/WB

NEWCOMER'S HANDBOOK FOR MOVING TO AND LIVING IN WASHINGTON D.C.

178

In the outer suburbs in Maryland, you might also receive Baltimore and Annapolis signals: ABC on Channel 2, NBC on 11, CBS on 13, Fox on 45, and UPN on 54.

CABLE & SATELLITE TV SERVICE
* **Comcast**, 800-266-2278, www.comcast.com
* **Cox Communications** (Northern Virginia), 703-378-8422, www.cox.com
* **RCN** (formerly Starpower), 800-746-4726, www.rcn.com
* **DirecTV**, 800-237-5988, www.directv.com
* **Dish Network**, 800-732-6401, www.dishnetwork.com

RADIO STATIONS

From Amy Goodman to G. Gordon Liddy, and from Chuck D to Berlioz to the Dixie Chicks, there isn't much missing from the radio dial in the Washington area. XM Satellite Radio, the first company to provide paying subscribers with hundreds of coast-to-coast radio broadcasts, is headquartered just off New York Avenue NE—but Washington still has plenty of local stations you can hear for free.

NEWS/TALK
* WFED-AM 1050 . . . . Federal News Radio, Nationals games
* WMAL-AM 630 . . . . News
* WMET-AM 1150 . . . . Business news and talk
* WTEM-AM 980 . . . . Sports
* WTOP-FM 103.5 . . . . Weather & traffic "on the eights," CBS news
* WTWP-AM 1500 and
  WTWP-FM 107.7 . . . . Washington Post Radio

MUSIC (COMMERCIAL)
* WARW-FM 94.7 . . . . Classic rock
* WASH-FM 97.1 . . . . Soft rock
* WAVA-FM 105.1 . . . . Christian
* WBIG-FM 100.1 . . . . Oldies
* WGMS-FM 104.1 and 103.9 . . Classical
* WHFS-FM 105.7 . . . . Modern rock
* WHUR-FM 96.3 . . . . Contemporary (Howard University)
* WJFK-FM 106.7 . . . . Syndicated personalities, Redskins games . . . .
* WJMO-FM 99.5 . . . . Modern rock
* WJZW-FM 105.9 . . . . Smooth jazz

- WLZL-FM 99.1 . . . . Latino
- WMMJ-FM 102.3 . . . . R&B
- WMZQ-FM 98.7 . . . . Country
- WPGC-FM 95.5 . . . . Contemporary
- WRQX-FM 107.3 . . . . Pop
- WWDC-FM 101.1 . . . . Hard rock

PUBLIC RADIO
- WAMU-FM 88.5 . . . . NPR and roots music/bluegrass
- WETA-FM 90.9 . . . . NPR & PRI
- WMRA-FM 94.5 . . . . NPR
- WPFW-FM 89.3 . . . . Pacifica Radio and jazz

NEWSPAPERS & MAGAZINES

Washington is the news capital of the world, and it's no accident that the Freedom Forum's museum of journalism, the Newseum, is moving from its Rosslyn headquarters to a place of honor between the Capitol and the White House. Indeed, the new site is just a few doors down from the National Archives, where you can go see the First Amendment itself. Naturally, Washingtonians are news junkies—practically everybody reads the *Post* and the free weekly *City Paper*, and many homes and most offices subscribe to more than one newspaper.

- ***The Washington Post***, 202-334-6100, www.washingtonpost.com; a necessity, even though many find its local news coverage leaves a lot to be desired. If you're looking for a home, job, car, movie review, restaurant review, or practically any kind of consumer news, the *Post* and the *City Paper* are your two essential stops. The *Post* also offers plenty of original (not canned) coverage of national and world affairs; big, intelligent literary, arts, and opinion sections on Sunday; and four pages of daily comics. Conservatives say the *Post* has a liberal bias and liberals say it has a conservative bias, so journalists believe it must be doing something right. Daily, also publishes the ***Express***, a free weekday news tabloid aimed at transit riders.
- ***Washington City Paper***, 202-332-2100, www.washingtoncity paper.com; essentially an arts and entertainment guide, with lots of advertising including a huge and useful classified section. The free *City Paper* does run some ambitious feature stories, and the weekly "Loose Lips" column packs into one page more knowledge of D.C. politics than the *Post* demonstrates in a week. For a real overview of Washington culture, read the personal ads in the *City Paper*, even if you're not looking for a date. Generally available by Thursday evening

NEWCOMER'S HANDBOOK FOR MOVING TO AND LIVING IN WASHINGTON D.C.

180

rush hour; the classified ads are posted on the web site on Tuesday, at least 48 hours before they hit the streets.

- **The Washington Times**, 202-636-3333, www.washtimes.com; not officially a partisan paper, but the *Times* is the preferred daily paper among conservatives. Its owner, Rev. Sun Myung Moon, says he is not involved in editorial decisions, but the editorial pages sometimes make Fox News look like NPR.

- **The Common Denominator**, 202-635-6397, www.thecommon denominator.com; the only local newspaper serving all of the District and just the District, this little biweekly provides solid coverage of D.C. politics and its communities, offering consumer news aimed at an economically diverse audience. Includes homegrown editorial cartoons and a thorough calendar of civic meetings and D.C. government hearings. Published alternate Mondays.

- **The Examiner**, 800-531-1223, www.dcexaminer.com; free weekday paper combining solid local coverage with syndicated national news and veteran local columnists. Heftier than the *Express* but still concise enough to read on a subway ride. District, Maryland, and Virginia editions.

- **Gazette Newspapers**, 301-607-1015, www.gazette.net; Maryland's oldest newspaper, the *Gaithersburg Gazette,* is now part of a regional chain of community papers owned by The Washington Post Company. The Montgomery, Prince George's, and Frederick *Gazettes* still provide in-depth coverage of local news and civic life.

- **Times Community Newspapers**, 703-437-5400, www.times community.com; these local papers serve a dozen suburban communities in Virginia, from Arlington to Chantilly.

NEIGHBORHOOD NEWSPAPERS

These biweekly or monthly papers are available free at Metro stations, bookstores, libraries, restaurants, bars, and other neighborhood establishments. This is the best way to follow real estate markets, zoning and development issues, and politics as they relate to a specific section of D.C.

- **The Georgetowner**, 202-338-4833, www.georgetowner.com
- **Hill Rag**, 202-543-8300, www.hillrag.com
- **The InTowner** serves Adams Morgan, Cleveland Park, Columbia Heights, Dupont Circle, Mt. Pleasant, Shaw, and Woodley Park. 202-234-1717, www.intowner.com
- **Montgomery Sentinel**, 301-838-0788, www.thesentinel.com/mcfolder
- **The Northwest Current** serves D.C. neighborhoods west of Connecticut Ave. NW; in some neighborhoods, it's the *Rock Creek Current*, with some zoned articles. 202-244-7223

- **Prince George's Sentinel**, 301-306-9500, www.thesentinel.com/pgfolder
- **Takoma Voice**, 301-891-6744, www.takoma.com; also publishes the **Silver Spring Voice**, www.takoma.com/ssindex.html
- **Voice of the Hill**, 202-544-0703, www.voiceofthehill.com

SPECIAL-INTEREST NEWSPAPERS
- **Afro-American**, 202-332-0080, www.afro.com
- **Catholic Standard**, 202-281-2410, www.cathstan.org
- **El Pregonero**, 202-281-2440, www.elpreg.org
- **The Hill** (covering Congress), 202-628-8500, www.hillnews.com
- **Legal Times**, 202-457-0686, www.law.com/jsp/dc
- **Progressive Review**, 202-835-0770, http://prorev.com
- **Roll Call** (covering Congress), 202-824-6800, www.rollcall.com
- **Tiempo Latino**, 703-527-7860, http://eltiempolatino.com
- **Washington Blade** (GLBT interests), 202-797-7000, www.washblade.com
- **Washington Business Journal**, 703-875-2200, www.bizjournals.com/washington
- **Washington Diplomat** (covering D.C.'s international community), 301-933-3552, www.washdiplomat.com
- **Washington Informer** (African-American interests), 202-561-4100, http://www.washingtoninformer.com
- **Washington Jewish Week**, 301-360-2222, www.washingtonjewishweek.com

MAGAZINES
- **Washingtonian**, www.washingtonian.com; combines society pages and consumer news to cover the movers and shakers in Washington and the places where they dine, shop, live, go to school, and go on vacation. Annual features include "Cheap Eats," "Best & Worst of Everything," and "10 Charities That Deserve Your Money." Other local glossies have come and gone, but "the Washingtonian" has been a fixture for more than 40 years.
- **Washington, D.C. Style**, www.dcstylemag.com, was launched in 2005 by the publisher of *Philadelphia Style*. It celebrates upscale living and is aimed at a "high net worth" audience.
- **Capitol File**, www.capitolfile-magazine.com, also made its debut in 2005. Sister publication of *L.A. Confidential*, the magazine declares Washington is "home to the world's most powerful people, and Capitol File magazine reaches its most dynamic players."
- **D.C. Pulse**, www.dcpulsemag.com, is a hip little 'zine celebrating local writers and artists.

NEWCOMER'S HANDBOOK FOR MOVING TO AND LIVING IN WASHINGTON D.C.

182

FINDING A PHYSICIAN

If you have a job that includes health benefits, your insurance plan or HMO will provide you with a list of participating doctors. If you're self-employed, self-insured, or a member of Washington's growing ranks of "career temps," you will need to shop around for a doctor.

Ideally, get a referral from a friend or trusted co-worker. Also check out the **Washington Consumers' Checkbook** web site, www. checkbook.org, for ratings of local doctors and dentists, hospitals, health plans, and pharmacies, along with general advice about choosing health services. Or you can call 800-DOCTORS (in D.C., 202-DOCTORS) for a referral; to find a dentist, call 202-547-7613. The American Board of Medical Specialties can tell you whether a particular doctor is board certi-fied—call 866-275-2267 or visit www.abms.org.

Every year, *Washingtonian* magazine asks 5,000 Washington-area physicians to name the top specialists in 31 medical fields—the doctors to whom they would refer their own families. The resulting list is available at www.washingtonian.com.

To check a doctor's credentials and history of lawsuits or professional sanctions, or to make a formal complaint about a doctor or other medical professional, call:

- **D.C. Board of Medicine**, 202-724-4900
- **Maryland Board of Physician Quality Assurance**, 800-492-6836, www.mbp.state.md.us (for information about professional records)
- **Maryland Health Care Alternative Dispute Resolution Office**, 800-492-1951 (for information about malpractice cases)
- **Virginia Board of Medicine**, 804-662-9908 (804-662-7636 for license verifications), www.dhp.state.va.us/medicine

A federal web site, hospitalcompare.hhs.gov, allows users to compare 4,200 hospitals on the basis of various statistics regarding cardiac care and pneumonia.

For alternative health care practitioners—acupuncture, ayurveda, Feldenkrais, herbalism, macrobiotics, reflexology, yoga, and other holistic disciplines—check out *Pathways* magazine, available free at libraries and heath food stores, or visit www.pathwaysmag.com.

PET LAWS & SERVICES

Washington is a great walking city, and walking a well-behaved dog is an easy way to meet people—and to feel safe if you're not accustomed to a big city. Busy Washingtonians support a huge industry of pet sitters, dog-walk-ing services, and even doggie day care. If your neighbors have pets, ask them for recommendations—especially for a good veterinarian and pet food store.

LICENSING

The District and all neighboring counties require dogs to be licensed after the age of four months. A rabies certificate from a vet or shelter must be presented along with the license fee. In most cases you can apply by mail—ask the vet or shelter for an application, or contact your local licensing agency:

- **D.C. Animal Control Shelter**, 202-576-6664
- **Montgomery County Police**, Division of Animal Control & Humane Treatment, 301-279-1249, www.co.mo.md.us/services/police
- **Prince George's County Animal Control Commission**, 301-883-6009
- **Arlington County Office of the Treasurer**, 703-228-3255, www.co.arlington.va.us/treas
- **Fairfax County Department of Tax Administration**, 703-222-8234, www.co.fairfax.va.us/dta
- **Alexandria Police**, Animal Control/Protection Service, 703-838-4774

VETERINARIANS

While it's no substitute for a personal referral, the **American Veterinary Medical Association** web site, www.avma.org, offers advice on finding and choosing a vet. Also visit the health care section of the **Washington Consumers' Checkbook** web site, www.checkbook.org. There are at least 20 veterinary clinics in D.C. and the inner suburbs. Most have 24-hour emergency service or at least a recording with a vet's pager or emergency phone number.

WALKING YOUR DOG

Most neighborhoods in the city and inner suburbs are dog-friendly. Every local jurisdiction requires leashes and scoops. In the outer suburbs, most homes have generous yards or wide, grassy medians on subdivision streets.

In the District, parks favored by dogs and their owners include Rose Park, 26th & P streets NW; Battery Kemble Park, off Loughboro Road; Stanton Square, on C Street NE between 4th & 6th; Lincoln Park, on East Capitol Street between 11th & 13th; Malcolm X Park, on 16th Street NW between W and Euclid streets; and the green wedge bounded by New Hampshire Avenue, 17th Street, and T Street NW. If you have to work long hours, look in the Yellow Pages under "Pet Sitting Services" for midday dog walkers.

For a list of designated off-leash dog parks in the suburbs, contact:

- **Arlington County Department of Parks, Recreation & Community Resources**, 703-228-6525, www.co.arlington.va.us/prcr

NEWCOMER'S HANDBOOK FOR MOVING TO AND LIVING IN WASHINGTON D.C.

184

- **Fairfax County Park Authority**, 703-324-8702 or www.co.fairfax. va.us/parks
- **Alexandria Department of Recreation, Parks & Cultural Activities**, 703-638-4345 or www.ci.alexandria.va.us/recreation
- **Maryland-National Capital Park & Planning Commission** (Montgomery and Prince George's counties), 301-495-2503, www. mc-mncppc.org/parks

PET CARE SERVICES

If you can find a friend or trusted neighbor to look after your pets while you're out of town, it's probably easier on your pets than a boarding kennel. Several companies provide licensed and bonded in-house pet sitters and midday dog walkers, and many animal hospitals offer boarding. "Doggie day care" centers became popular in the late 1990s. These facilities are not kennels, but well-appointed recreational facilities for dogs, with optional grooming services. Pet sitters, dog walkers, day care centers, pet food stores, and grooming salons are listed in the Yellow Pages under "Pet."

CRIME & SAFETY

Every major city in the United States has its "good" and "bad" sections, and every major city has street gangs. Here in D.C., "bad" neighborhoods are those with a concentration of gang-related shootings, and they tend to be highly localized—often a single block or intersection. Statistically, you aren't likely ever to experience violent crime in the Washington area. Most longtime residents know one or two people who have been mugged—in a metropolis of more than 7 million residents and commuters. If you live here long enough, eventually a case of car theft or a "smash-and-grab" (theft of articles from parked cars) may hit close to home.

Watch Your Car is a program offered by the Metropolitan Police Department with federal funding from the Justice Department. If you own a car in D.C. and you don't normally drive between 1 a.m. and 5 a.m., you can register your car at http://mpdc.dc.gov and get a program decal. Cars bearing the decal can be pulled over by the police during those hours without further cause.

Panhandling, or begging, is not a crime unless it's done "aggressively" or on private property. In D.C., the only place where panhandling is consistently discouraged is within designated Business Improvement Districts, where business owners collectively hire private security guards and cleaning crews for their section of downtown.

Bicycle theft is a serious concern for those who rely on a bike for urban transportation. If you're new to a big city, have a bike salesperson give you a few tips on the proper use of U-locks and cables. You'll see people carrying bike seats around all day—which is a deterrent: even if a thief can break a lock, a bike without a seat isn't likely to be taken very far. Call your local police department (see **Useful Phone Numbers and Web Sites**) to register your serial number. **CityBikes**, 202-265-1564 or http://citybikes. com, keeps a registry of stolen bikes.

Finally, Washington has a special place in the history of the world's oldest profession: during the Civil War, a Washington garrison commander rounded up the city's prostitutes and marched them across the Potomac into Virginia. They came back, and they're mostly in the same place—east of Logan Circle—but today they bear the name of that hapless officer, Major General Hooker.

CRIME PREVENTION

As in any big city, pay attention to your surroundings—avoid poorly lit streets and deserted areas, and don't walk alone late at night. Remember that large bills, jewelry, and even maps can attract the wrong kind of attention. Know roughly what time it is—if a stranger asks, you can answer without showing off your watch. And, no, you don't have a cigarette. On a crowded bus or train, watch out for pickpockets and purse-snatchers.

Two common scams to watch out for: at public phones, if you use a calling card, make sure no one can see you dial—someone could steal your account number. And if you pull into a parking space and someone offers to "watch your car" for $5, park somewhere else—the offer could be a thinly veiled threat to vandalize your vehicle.

Call your local police non-emergency number for information about neighborhood watch groups (also known as "Citizens On Patrol" groups or "Orange Hat Patrols") in your area. The police department can also provide pamphlets and workshops on crime prevention.

Here are the home burglar alarm dealers with the highest rating from **Washington Consumers' Checkbook** in 2005; this is by no means a complete list of reputable dealers—see the Yellow Pages under "Burglar Alarm Systems."

- **Allied Alarm Specialists**, 301-733-9589 or 703-329-8660
- **Guardian Protection Service**, 800-776-8328
- **Hofheimer Security & Telephone Systems**, 703-820-0808
- **InterAmerican Security**, 301-840-0004
- **Potomac Security Systems**, 301-983-0907
- **Security Services (ADT)**, 866-746-7238

NEWCOMER'S HANDBOOK FOR MOVING TO AND LIVING IN WASHINGTON D.C.

186

DISASTER PREPAREDNESS & HOMELAND SECURITY

Even before September 11, when the smoke from the Pentagon stretched halfway to the Capitol, Washingtonians had been edgy about the possibility of terrorism. Some locals remember the day in 1982 when a lone terrorist parked a box truck beside the Washington Monument and claimed it was full of dynamite. The first metal detectors appeared in major government buildings here after the 1993 bomb attack at the World Trade Center, and since the Oklahoma City and 1996 Olympics bombings, almost all office buildings in the District have required all visitors to sign in. Some, such as the Ronald Reagan Building and International Trade Center, have security gates like an airport.

The Washington area has its share of natural disasters, too—see the **Weather & Climate** chapter. Emergency management officials recommend that every household keep a disaster kit on hand: at least three gallons of water per person; flashlights, a radio, and plenty of batteries; nonperishable food; first aid supplies and spare medications; warm, weather-resistant clothing; maps; and enough cash to live on for several days.

Every local jurisdiction has an emergency management agency, and most now offer free subscriptions to emergency alerts by phone, e-mail, or text message. Also known as "reverse 911" systems, these alerts include severe weather warnings, changes in the homeland security threat level, amber alerts for missing children, and civil emergencies requiring evacuation or other special instructions. WTOP is the designated primary radio station for official emergency broadcasts; in a disaster (or even a major traffic jam), keep an ear on 103.5 FM, or www.wtopnews.com.

Visit the web site of your local emergency management agency for further advice and updates:

- **D.C.**: http://dcema.dc.gov; for alerts, http://alert.dc.gov
- **Arlington**: www.co.arlington.va.us; for alerts, www.arlingtonalert.com
- **Alexandria**: www.alexandriava.gov/fire (click on Emergency Management)
- **Fairfax County**: www.co.fairfax.va.us/emergency; alerts, www.co.fairfax.va.us/cean
- **Montgomery County**: www.montgomerycountymd.gov; for alerts, http://alert.montgomerycountymd.gov
- **Prince George's County**: www.goprincegeorgescounty.com (click on Emergency Management under the Agencies menu)
  In other jurisdictions, visit:
- **Maryland**: www.gov.state.md.us/homelandsecurity.html
- **Virginia**: www.vaemergency.com
- **Nationwide**: www.ready.gov

WHETHER YOU REALLY ARE A BUSY WASHINGTON VIP OR JUST think you are, time is money here, and it may pay to hire somebody to take care of some time-consuming chores and errands. You can hire someone to stand in line for theater tickets, organize your closet, auction off your old furniture, renovate your house, or get your license tags renewed—do practically anything, for a fee. Mechanics, manicurists, yard workers, housekeepers, caterers, grocers, and other helpful people will come to you, with goods and services in hand, and the meter running.

PERSONAL ASSISTANTS

If you're just plain busy and you need a personal assistant or concierge—a 21st-century Jeeves—to take care of assorted chores and errands, start by looking at *Washingtonian* magazine's list of companies providing custom personal services. Look for bonded and insured professionals to run errands, wait for deliveries, take care of repair calls, shop for gifts, take the dog to the vet, get the car inspected, and pay the bills. Usually the only thing these agencies won't do is transport people—only a licensed taxi or limo service can do that. With fees ranging from $30 to $100 an hour, you probably won't want to hire someone to run out for sandwiches, but sometimes it's worth the expense to have someone else tackle the big errands. Contact **Concierge America**, 301-986-0418, www.concierge america.com, or **The Runaround**, 301-922-0196, www.runaround.com. There's also a list of personal concierge agencies under "Shopping & Services" at www.washingtonian.com, along with insider leads on home repair, organizing, home improvement, "Best of Washington," bargains, flea markets, "Where the Experts Shop," nanny agencies, pet care resources, and more.

NEWCOMER'S HANDBOOK FOR MOVING TO AND LIVING IN WASHINGTON D.C.

188

Couriers are listed in the Yellow Pages under "Delivery Service." Most courier services offer "placeholder" service, too: for about $30 an hour, you can hire someone to stand in line for you. This service caters mainly to lobbyists and junior federal officials who need to attend crowded hearings on the Hill, where seating is scare and cannot be reserved.

RENTAL SERVICES

If you need to furnish a home right away and you don't have time to shop for the perfect furniture and appliances, or if you won't be in town for more than a couple months, you can rent practically anything you need. Be careful, though: if you rent household items for more than a few months, you will almost always end up paying more than if you had bought new furniture—even credit purchases are usually cheaper in the long run than "rent-to-own" plans. Use these services sparingly.

FURNITURE

For a wide selection of new furniture available for short-term rental, lease, or rent-to-own, check out:

- **Aaron Rents & Sells**, 14 Derwood Cir., Rockville, 301-279-5530; 11714 Baltimore Ave., Beltsville, 301-210-0120; 5720 General Washington Dr., Alexandria, 703-941-7195; 4124-A Walney Rd., Chantilly, 703-378-0080; www.aaronrents.com
- **Alperstein's**, 1015 7th St. NW, 202-783-0100, www.alpersteins.com
- **Cort Furniture Rental**, 1100 New York Ave. NW, 202-223-9241; 11711 Parklawn Dr., Rockville, 301-881-7388; 801 Hampton Park Blvd., Capitol Heights, 301-324-8684; 3101 Park Center Dr. #100, Alexandria, 703-379-8846; 5710-A General Washington Dr., Alexandria, 703-354-2600; 14130 Sullyfield Cir., Chantilly, 703-818-2660; www.cort1.com
- **Scherr Furniture Rental**, 12340 Parklawn Dr., Rockville, 301-881-8960

These are established rental outfits, and most offer free next-day delivery on orders above a certain minimum, if the items you need are in stock.

Special needs can be met as well. If you need to host an elegant reception at your gas-lighted Capitol Hill townhouse and you don't even own a punchbowl, you can rent high-end accoutrements from **Antique & Contemporary Leasing**, 709 12th Street SE, 202-547-3030, www.antiqueleasing.com. You can also hire their interior design and installation staff for an hourly fee.

DOMESTIC SERVICES

Cabinet nominees aren't the only people in Washington who hire domestic help. Plenty of people choose not to spend a lot of time doing housework or yard maintenance.

LAUNDRY & DIAPER SERVICES

On the "Shopping & Services" page of www.washingtonian.com, click on "Pay Someone to Do It" for a list of dry cleaners and laundry services that pick up and deliver. There aren't many **diaper services** left, but the few holdouts in this quaint industry have generations of good reputation. Call Dy-Dee at 800-492-9895 or Modern Diaper Service, 301-823-3993 or 703-823-3993.

HOME IMPROVEMENT

For free referrals to licensed repair services with good references, contact **Home Connections**, 800-474-1596, www.homeconnections.com, or read the customer reviews posted at **Angie's List**, www.angieslist.com.

If you own a home but would like the convenience of having a property manager, **Delbe Home Services** will manage your home repairs and maintenance, working on your behalf with contractors and suppliers; call 202-237-0187 or visit www.delbe.com.

HOUSE CLEANING SERVICES

Maid services are listed in the Yellow Pages under "House Cleaning." Agencies employing bonded and insured maids usually say so in display ads. As domestic labor is often a first stop for new immigrants entering the workforce, you may want a copy of *Spanish-English Housekeeping* by Ruth M. Dietz, a phrasebook for employers of Latino domestic workers. For serious cleaning—after accidents, fires, or other disasters—call **Special Forces** at 202-289-6501 or 703-560-2151.

JUNK

Your junk may be someone else's treasure, and the emergence of online trading posts such as Craigslist and eBay makes it easier than ever to find out just whose treasure it is. Locally, there are several chapters of **Freecycle**, www.freecycle.org, whose members swap used goods

NEWCOMER'S HANDBOOK FOR MOVING TO AND LIVING IN WASHINGTON D.C.

190

through online bulletin boards. **The List**, formerly and affectionately known as Levey's List, started out as a personal service of neighborly *Washington Post* columnist Bob Levey. Readers would e-mail Levey when they wanted to donate furniture, office equipment, or other durable goods to a local charity, and he'd pass the list on to charities that requested it. Levey passed the List, along with his column, to John Kelley, who still helps used items (in good condition) find their way to grateful charities. E-mail kellyj@washpost.com.

If all else fails, you can donate just about anything to the **thrift stores** listed in **Shopping for the Home**. Old **cell phones** are accepted at most police and fire stations to be given to senior citizens and residents of shelters for battered women, so they can call 911 in an emergency whether they sign up for cellular service or not.

PEST CONTROL

Roaches love Washington in the summer. On the sidewalk in the evening, under the cheery light of fireflies, you will see dozens of big Asian cockroaches. The best way to keep them outside is to keep your home, especially the kitchen, scrupulously clean and to keep baseboards and kitchen fixtures painted or caulked. Even then, don't be surprised by the occasional six-legged visitor. If you have an infestation, reach for the Yellow Pages to look up "Hardware Stores" for traps, or "Pest Control Services" for chemicals. If you're trying to prevent an infestation, though, little plastic "bait stations" available at any drugstore or hardware store are generally effective. The Gardens Alive catalog sells **nontoxic pest control** supplies such as pantry moth traps, old-fashioned flypaper strips, and natural chemicals that repel or kill ants and roaches. Call 812-537-8651 or visit www.gardens alive.com.

Rats abound here too—as one local politician put it, the four-legged kind as well as the two-legged kind. And don't assume rats stick to unsavory neighborhoods; they're egalitarian pests, just as likely to turn up in elite zip codes. The best deterrent is to keep your trash and recycling areas clean and avoid putting your trash out more than 12 hours before pickup, or get a cat. (It doesn't matter whether your cat will actually chase rodents—the rodents will smell cat.) As with other pests, your best resources for rat control are hardware stores and exterminators listed in the Yellow Pages.

If you have small children, chemical sensitivities, an impaired immune system, or just an aversion to harsh chemicals, visit **www.pestweb.com** for information about natural pest control products and integrated pest management (ecological controls, such as attracting ladybugs to eat aphids or keeping a cat to repel mice). It's an industry site and some of the information is fairly technical, but it's a comprehensive source of good advice.

LAWN CARE

For routine cutting and clipping, there's always an enterprising teenager down the block (in the suburbs) or a neighborhood jack-of-all-trades (in the District). The going rate depends on the neighborhood, but expect to pay around $20 for an average lawn. For comprehensive lawn maintenance, look in the Yellow Pages under "Lawn Maintenance"—or just find a neighbor with a nice lawn and ask for a referral. **Organic lawn care** is available from Bay Country Lawns, 703-204-9000, www.baycountrylawns.com, and Fairway Lawn Care, 301-681-3000, www.fairwaylawncare.com.

POSTAL & SHIPPING SERVICES

MAIL DELIVERY

Mail delivery in D.C. has always been a bit erratic, and the anthrax scares of 2001-'02 didn't help. If you mail ten letters to local addresses all at once, nine will arrive the next day and the tenth might take a week; if it's missing a return address or it looks like it's been opened and resealed, all bets are off. But the problems are easy to exaggerate—the mail is generally so reliable we can take it for granted, and when it disappoints, it really disappoints.

The simplest way to help ensure fast delivery is to use the nine-digit zip code and follow the postal service guidelines for printed addresses: all caps with no punctuation. Call 800-275-8777 or visit www.usps.com for zip codes, postal rates, and other general information.

JUNK MAIL & TELEMARKETING

You've just moved to one of the most affluent cities and, quite possibly, one of the most affluent neighborhoods in the world. You most certainly will be inundated with junk mail and pestered almost every day by telephone solicitors. Most companies will take you off their own lists if you ask them to, but it would be a full-time job to contact every outfit that sends you unsolicited mail or to speak to the supervisor of every telemarketer who interrupts your dinner.

You can curtail junk mail and telemarketers to some extent: first, write a note to the **Direct Marketing Association** (Mail Preference Service, PO Box 643, Carmel, NY 10512), requesting that your address be listed with the Mail Preference Service. (You can also register online at www.dmaconsumers.org, but there's a $5 fee.) Most—not all—business and charities sending junk mail will exclude addresses registered with this

NEWCOMER'S HANDBOOK FOR MOVING TO AND LIVING IN WASHINGTON D.C.

192

service. It will not deter companies that do not buy the preference lists. The major credit bureaus—Experian, Equifax, and TransUnion—share an "automated opt-out" line, 888-567-8688; call to have your name removed from any lists these bureaus sell to direct mail companies.

If all else fails, remember, junk mail is recyclable.

Most commercial telemarketers (not charities or political campaigns) can be stopped by adding your phone number to the **National Do Not Call Registry** maintained by the Federal Trade Commission. Call 800-382-1222 or visit www.donotcall.gov.

MAIL RECEIVING

A post office box might be convenient if you're in a short-term rental or sublet or if you're staying with friends. Also, if you expect to move around a few times while looking for the perfect home, a box will spare you the hassle of changing your address repeatedly. Most post offices have boxes for rent, though there may be a waiting list at busy downtown locations. You can also have mail delivered to **Vantas**, with 24 locations in D.C. and the suburbs, 888-633-4237, www.vantasinc.com, or **Mail Boxes Etc.**, www.mbe.com, with locations in:

* **Silver Spring**, 8639-B 16th St., 301-587-9191
* **College Park**, Stamp Student Union #106, University of Maryland, 301-314-9982
* **Arlington**, 4201 Wilson Blvd. #110, 703-522-4000

SHIPPING

For bulky or heavy items, **Craters & Freighters**, 800-736-3335, www.cratersandfreighters.com, advertises: "Too large for UPS? Too small for movers? We'll ship it!" For conventional packages, the nationwide parcel services are all familiar names:

* **DHL**, 800-225-5345, www.dhl-usa.com
* **FedEx**, 800-463-3339, www.fedex.com/us
* **UPS**, 800-742-5877, www.ups.com
* **U.S. Postal Service Express Mail**, 800-275-8777, www.usps.com

AUTOMOBILES

Nearly a quarter of a million commuters in the Washington area spend more than two hours a day behind the wheel; for more than a million commuters, it's at least an hour a day. Bumper-to-bumper traffic on the Beltway puts a lot of wear on your brake pads. In the winter, salt and slush leave their mark on your paint job. One resident of downtown D.C. found that his ignition wires had been gnawed apart by rats—on several occasions. And then there's parking, one of the city's most treasured commodities.

REPAIRS & MAINTENANCE

By far, the best way to find a trustworthy mechanic is to get recommendations from friends, neighbors, or co-workers, preferably from those with the same make of car. The consumer resources listed in **Shopping for the Home—Washington Consumers' Checkbook**, the **Better Business Bureau**, *Washingtonian* magazine, and **Themail** at www.dc watch.com—can help if you need to start from scratch. (The Shopping & Services page at www.washingtonian.com even has a list of mechanics who make house calls—click on "Make Your Life Easier.") Shop around for a mechanic before you need one; when your car is in urgent need of repairs, you may be tempted to go to the nearest chop shop down the street.

Auto dealerships are generally reliable, if pricey; at least they definitely have the parts, equipment, and expertise to deal with the cars they sell. The Yellow Pages list more than 300 dealerships, so you don't have to go far afield to get expert service for your Lamborghini, Hummer, or Austin-Healy.

D.C. law gives the consumer the right to a **written estimate**, and the final bill cannot exceed the estimate by more than 10% (20% if the estimate is $300 or less). Maryland and Virginia have similar laws.

For a free second opinion about car repairs, you can always call Tom & Ray Magliozzi, better known as Click & Clack, the guys on National Public Radio's "Car Talk." For schedules and contact information, visit http://cartalk.cars.com.

Some auto clubs provide seals of approval or will rate certain local repair shops, but it's a good idea to read the fine print to see whether the shops pay a fee or are listed based on the quality of provided services. The most comprehensive auto club, in terms of services and coverage area, is AAA (contact AAA Mid-Atlantic at 888-859-5161 or go to www.aaamid atlantic.com). The lesser-known Auto Club of America, 800-411-2007, www.autoclubofamerica.com, offers similar services and, unlike AAA, doesn't spend members' money on political lobbying. Many national service station chains and insurance companies also offer road service plans.

HELP WITH RED TAPE

The U.S. Vehicle Registration Service is a private company that can help you navigate the DMV bureaucracy to register vehicles, get residential parking permits, pay parking tickets, get boots removed, and drive your car to and from scheduled maintenance appointments. Call 202-342-2558 or visit http://usvrs.com.

CAREER SERVICES

"Welcome to Washington. What do you do for a living?" Get used to it—and to the more perfunctory "Who are you with?" (meaning your employer, not your date). In a city where people are largely defined by their careers, it's no surprise that a whole industry emerged in the late 20th century to provide services to people seeking to advance their careers.

There are dozens of agencies and solo consultants specializing in resumes and job placement—and not just at entry level. Many executive and management jobs in private companies are filled with the help of out-placement and recruiting agencies, better known as "headhunters." These services can make your career, but be sure you know what you're buying: some headhunters and resume consultants do little more than scan your previous job titles and generate a list of job openings with matching key-words. Anyone serious about helping you advance in a challenging career will start with a personal, in-depth interview. To find an agency, check the Yellow Pages under "Resumes" and "Employment Agencies," and look in the employment classifieds in Sunday's *Washington Post.* Smaller resume shops, which may offer more personalized service, advertise in the *City Paper* classifieds too.

If you move here without a job lined up, you might join the vast ranks of Washingtonians who have taken at least a few assignments through temp agencies. The 20 biggest temporary placement firms alone send more than 5,000 people into hundreds of offices every day—not just secretaries and data entry clerks, but paralegals; writers and editors; computer network administrators; even lawyers and legislative analysts. In the Washington area, temp placement, which is a $300 million industry, can be a good way to get the feel of a company or industry. All kinds of employers use temps—law firms, federal contractors, nonprofits, trade associations, newspapers and magazines, even presidential campaigns. Just make sure you communicate your interests clearly to the agency—some agencies offer lots of short-term assignments, and some prefer to make "temp-to-perm" assignments.

Temp agencies are listed in the Yellow Pages under "Employment Contractors - Temporary Help" and in the Employment section of the *Washington Post.* A more detailed listing of the largest temp agencies, with some information about their specialties, is published in the *Washington Business Journal Book of Lists*, along with a list of the top headhunters, politely called "executive search firms."

Federal jobs are listed at the **Office of Personnel Management** employment site, www.usajobs.opm.gov, along with information about civil service exams and internet tools that let you upload your resume for federal hiring managers to retrieve.

The **Center for Urban Progress** at Howard University provides free career counseling, job placement assistance, and skills training. Call 202-806-4433 or visit www.howard.edu/centerurbanprogress.

The **D.C. Department of Employment Services** operates "One-Stop Career Centers" that provide placement assistance and job banks as well as unemployment benefits. Call 202-724-7000 or visit www.dc networks.org for more information. There are eight centers:

- **Naylor Road**, 2626 Naylor Rd. SE, 202-645-3535
- **South Capitol**, 4049 South Capitol St. SW, 202-645-4000
- **One Judiciary Square**, 441 4th St. NW 202-727-9726
- **Franklin Street**, 1500 Franklin St. NE, 202-576-3050
- **Veterans Affairs**, 1722 I St. NW #335, 202-530-9371
- **Euclid Street**, 1704 Euclid St. NW, 202-671-1725
- **Downtown BID**, 945 G St. NW, 202-724-4541
- **A. Philip Randolph**, 6210 North Capitol St. NW, 202-576-6515

CONSUMER PROTECTION—RIP-OFF RECOURSE

You're a savvy consumer: you read all the fine print, you save receipts and canceled checks, you always write down the name of the customer service rep who answers your call, you make sure contractors are licensed by the **Department of Consumer & Regulatory Affairs**, 202-442-4400, and have clean files with the Better Business Bureau. You even order free pamphlets about industries from the **Federal Consumer Information Center** at 888-878-3256 or www.pueblo.gsa.gov, and you stay up-to-date on the latest tricks at **www.scambusters.org** and **www.consumer.gov**. But you've been ripped off. You negotiate, calmly but firmly, with documents in hand, but to no avail. What can you do?

First, contact the **Better Business Bureau of Metro Washington D.C.** at 202-393-8000 or www.dc.bbb.org. Though this agency will keep a permanent record of unresolved complaints, its first priority is to encourage its affiliated businesses to address all reasonable complaints promptly and thoroughly. The BBB will not get involved until you have exhausted the usual channels of complaint—contacting the supervisor of your sales representative, for example, or the manager or owner. You can also file a complaint with the **Federal Trade Commission** at 877-382-4357 or www.ftc.gov, or the agency responsible for consumer protection where the offending business is located:

- **D.C. Corporation Counsel**, Office of the Attorney General, 202-727-3400, http://occ.dc.gov
- **Maryland Office of the Attorney General**, Consumer Protection Division, 410-528-8662, www.oag.state.md.us

NEWCOMER'S HANDBOOK FOR MOVING TO AND LIVING IN WASHINGTON D.C.

196

- **Virginia Department of Agriculture and Consumer Services**, Office of Consumer Affairs, 804-786-2042 or 800-552-9963, www.vdacs.virginia.gov

Finally, if all else fails, you can go to court. The D.C., Maryland, and Virginia court systems each have offices that provide referrals to court-approved alternative dispute resolution (ADR) agencies, offering legally binding mediation, arbitration, and other out-of-court negotiation services. Both parties must agree to use ADR, and it works best when the dispute is mostly about fault and there is no major disagreement about the underlying facts. The result, in most cases, is a negotiated agreement acceptable to both sides and much less time and hassle than a trial, even in small claims court.

If ADR won't work—for instance, if there is substantial disagreement about facts—or if someone violates the terms of an agreement reached by ADR, you can take the case to small claims court without a lawyer. Call the clerk of the court in the appropriate jurisdiction for details, or download an informational pamphlet at:

- **D.C. Superior Court**, 202-879-1120, www.dccourts.gov; the Small Claims & Conciliation Division hears cases regarding damages or property valued up to $5,000.
- **Maryland District Court**, Montgomery County, 301-279-1500; Prince George's County, 301-952-4080; www.courts.state.md.us/district; the Small Claims Division hears cases regarding damages or property valued up to $5,000 plus interest and court costs.
- **Virginia General District Court**, Arlington County, 703-228-7900; Fairfax County, 703-691-7320; Alexandria, 703-838-4021; www.courts.state.va.us; the Small Claims Division hears cases regarding damages or property valued up to $2,000.

SERVICES FOR PEOPLE WITH DISABILITIES

Among cities its size, Washington is on the leading edge of accessibility. After all, it has more than the usual share of public buildings subject to the Americans with Disabilities Act. Government buildings, museums, monuments, and the Metro system are all fully accessible, and the government and most major private employers make substantial efforts to hire and accommodate workers with disabilities.

Stores and restaurants are not as universally accessible. The Washington D.C. Convention & Visitors Association offers a free fact sheet on the accessibility of area hotels, restaurants, shopping centers, and tourist sites—call 202-789-7093 or visit www.washington.org. Another good web site is www.wiredonwheels.org, which rates restaurants for wheelchair access.

Just north of Capitol Hill, between Florida and New York avenues NE, is **Gallaudet University**, the nation's only university for the deaf and hearing impaired. In addition to a complete and academically respected university curriculum, Gallaudet features a model high school, a conference center, its own cable TV programming, and athletic programs. Gallaudet's football team invented the huddle—to hide its sign-language "audibles" from the other team. For more information, call 202-651-5000 (voice/TDD) or visit www.gallaudet.edu.

GETTING AROUND

Given at least 24 hours notice, most local and national passenger carriers will make any needed accommodations for passengers with special needs. Service animals are welcome practically everywhere, but call to make sure.

Metrorail is fully accessible and most **Metrobus** coaches on major routes are equipped with lifts. Metro stations have Braille signage, and train operators announce each stop; on the newer buses, computerized recordings announce each stop. When a Metro station elevator is out of service, loudspeakers and electronic signs announce that free shuttle service is available from a nearby station. Visit the Accessibility page at www.wmata.com or call for more information about:

- **Metro system accessibility** in general, call 202-962-0128 or TDD 202-638-3780.
- **Disabled Passenger ID** card (for fare discounts), call 202-962-1245 or TDD 202-628-8973.
- **MetroAccess** paratransit service for eligible disabled passengers outside regular bus and rail routes, call 301-562-5360 or TDD 301-588-7535.

RAIL & BUS LINES

Generally accessible, and Greyhound offers free travel for companions of passengers with disabilities. For details, contact:

- **Amtrak**, 800-872-7245 or TDD 800-523-6590; www.amtrak.com (click on "Traveling With Amtrak")
- **MARC & Maryland MTA buses**, 800-325-7245 or TDD 410-539-3497; www.mtamaryland.com/pwd
- **Virginia Railway Express**, 703-684-0401 or TDD 703-684-0551; www.vre.org/programs
- **Greyhound**, 800-752-4841 or TDD 800-345-3109; www.greyhound bus.com

NEWCOMER'S HANDBOOK FOR MOVING TO AND LIVING IN WASHINGTON D.C.

198

CARS

- **Rentals**: the car rental companies listed in **Getting Settled** can accommodate special needs with 48 to 72 hours' notice. **The Boulevard**, www.blvd.com, is a web portal for disability resources that includes a list of companies that rent wheelchair-compatible vehicles.
- **Taxis**: the **Project Action** database at http://projectaction.easter seals.com lists taxi companies and hotel and airport shuttles with accessible vehicles.
- **Parking**: for information about handicapped license plates and parking permits, contact the appropriate motor vehicle agency listed in **Getting Settled**.

AIRLINES

The **U.S. Department of Transportation** publishes a free booklet entitled *New Horizons: Information for the Air Traveler with a Disability*, also available online at http://airconsumer.ost.dot.gov (click on "Travel Tips & Publications"). For more information, call the DOT **Disability Hotline** at 800-778-4838 or TDD 800-455-9880.

TRAVEL RESOURCES

- **Mobility International USA**, 541-343-1284 (voice and TDD), www.miusa.org; publishes *A World of Options: A Guide to International Exchange, Community Service and Travel for Persons with Disabilities*
- **Moss Rehab Hospital Travel Information Service**, 215-456-9603, www.mossresourcenet.org
- **Project Action Accessible Travel Database**, 202-347-3066 or TDD 202-347-7385, http://projectaction.easterseals.com
- **Society for Accessible Travel & Hospitality**, 212-447-7284, www.sath.org

COMMUNICATION

Recording for the Blind & Dyslexic, 202-244-8990, provides books on tape, including academic textbooks. **Metropolitan Washington Ear**, 301-681-6636, www.washear.org, provides newspapers and magazines on tape.

Telecommunications Relay Service allows deaf and hearing persons to communicate with each other by phone through a trained operator using text telephones. The relay operator translates both parties' words verbatim and is required by law to keep all conversations strictly confidential. The service is free. Voice users call **711** and TDD users call:

- **D.C. Relay**, TDD 202-855-1234
- **Maryland Relay**, TDD 800-735-2258
- **Virginia Relay**, TDD 866-246-9300
- **Spanish Relay**, TDD 800-546-7111

HOUSING

Centers for Independent Living can help you find accessible housing or contractors who specialize in making homes accessible. Contact:

- **D.C. Center for Independent Living**, 202-388-0033, TDD 202-388-0277, www.dccil.org
- **Independence Now** (Maryland), 301-277-2839 (for TDD, use Relay), www.innow.org
- **Endependence Center of Northern Virginia**, 703-525-3268 or TDD 703-525-3553, www.ecnv.org

ADDITIONAL RESOURCES

The most comprehensive sources of information for people with special needs are **www.disAbility.gov**, a portal to hundreds of federal government sites and related links, and the **International Center for Disability Resources on the Internet**, www.icdri.org. Other good resources include:

- **Columbia Lighthouse for the Blind**, 202-454-6400 or 877-324-5252, www.clb.org, offers employment training, vocational rehabilitation, and placement services, and runs an Assistive Technology Center providing access to the latest devices aiding blind and visually impaired readers and computer users.
- **Goodwill of Greater Washington**, 202-636-4225, www.dcgood will.org, provides rehabilitation, job placement, and employment for people with disabilities.
- **Mobility Resource**, 800-695-3933, www.disabilityresource.com, distributes monthly advertising card packs promoting resources for people with special mobility needs.
- **National Council on Independent Living**, 703-525-3406, TDD 703-525-4153, is an advocacy group for accessible housing, public spaces, and technology, provides dozens of useful links at www.ncil.org.

NEWCOMER'S HANDBOOK FOR MOVING TO AND LIVING IN WASHINGTON D.C.

200

GAY & LESBIAN LIFE

The free weekly **Washington Blade** and the bulletin board at **Lambda Rising,** 1625 Connecticut Avenue NW, are the two indispensable sources of information about the large and prominent gay, lesbian, bisexual, and transgender community in Washington. The Dupont Circle neighborhood is famous as one of the capitals of gay and lesbian culture in the United States, and businesses along Connecticut Avenue north of the circle and along 17th Street between P and R streets NW cater to "the sexual minority"—as well as plenty of straight folks attracted to the thriving nightlife. But there are rainbow flags and "Queer Nation" bumper stickers throughout residential Washington—and in the suburbs, especially Takoma Park and Shirlington. Among major U.S. cities, D.C. ranks sixth in gay and lesbian population, according to an Urban Institute study reported in the *Washington Post*. By some estimates, "we're here, we're queer" applies to 12% of the D.C. population (not to mention 15% of the city council).

Many private employers here recognize domestic partnership for insurance purposes, and housing discrimination based on sexual orientation is rare. The District and Montgomery County extend spouse benefits to the domestic partners of local government employees, and in 2001, the Maryland legislature outlawed discrimination based on sexual orientation. D.C. is the only jurisdiction to recognize domestic partnership for citizens other than government employees—for details, contact the D.C. Department of Health, Vital Records Division, at 442-9303 or http://doh.dc.gov.

GayDC.net is the most comprehensive online directory of organizations serving the gay, lesbian, bisexual, and transgender (GLBT) community. From the Log Cabin Republicans to the Lesbian Avengers, a quick glance at the list of resources here will attest that the GLBT community is just as diverse as the city at large.

The Metropolitan Police Department has a **Gay & Lesbian Liaison Unit** that supports the GLBT community by investigating hate crimes, patrolling GLBT businesses, providing diversity training to other law enforcement units, and generally helping to make the District a safer place especially for GLBT residents and visitors. For more information, call 877-495-5995 (pager) or 727-5427 (voicemail) or visit www.gaydc.net/gllu.

As in any other city, GLBT persons who experience discrimination should contact:

- **Gay & Lesbian Alliance Against Defamation**, 202-986-1360, www.glaad.org
- **Pride at Work**, Baltimore-Washington, 202-434-1150 ext. 6, www.igc.org/prideatwork

- **Sexual Minorities Youth Assistance League**, 202-546-5940, www.smyal.org

For heterosexual supporters of GLBT rights, there's a D.C. chapter of **Parents and Friends of Lesbians & Gays**, 202-638-3852, www.pflagdc.org.

INTERNATIONAL NEWCOMERS

The Washington area, together with Baltimore, is home to nearly a million immigrants—12% of the region's population overall and the majority in some neighborhoods. Only five metropolitan areas in the country (Los Angeles, New York, San Francisco, Miami, and Chicago) have a bigger foreign-born population. And the District of Columbia even surrounds more than 180 distinct patches of legally foreign soil: embassies and chanceries of diplomatic missions to the United States. Most embassies are open to the public at least a few hours each week, and all are open to provide consular services to their own citizens traveling or living in the United States. For a one-stop list of embassy phone numbers and addresses, go to **www.embassy.org**; most are also listed in the D.C. business White Pages.

International newcomers experiencing culture shock can get a quick overview of American culture, etiquette, expectations, and quirks in the *Newcomer's Handbook for Moving to and Living in the USA* by Mike Livingston, published by **First Books** in 2005. Call 503-968-6777 or visit www.firstbooks.com.

Aliens who need free legal aid in immigration matters should contact:
- **Ayuda**, 202-387-4848, www.ayudainc.org
- **Catholic Charities Immigration Legal Services**, 202-772-4356, www.catholiccharitiesdc.org
- **Central American Resource Center**, 202-328-9799, www.dccare cen.org
- **George Washington University Immigration Clinic**, 202-994-7463, www.law.gwu.edu
- **Human Rights First**, 202-547-5692, www.humanrightsfirst.org
- **Lutheran Social Services of the National Capital Area**, 202-723-3000, www.lssnca.org

MILITARY NEWCOMERS

The Washington area is home, at least for a while, to some 100,000 active-duty military personnel at any given time. In addition to the Pentagon, there's Walter Reed Army Medical Center, the National Naval Medical Center, Andrews and Bolling AFBs, Ft. McNair, Ft. Myer, Ft. Meade, Ft.

NEWCOMER'S HANDBOOK FOR MOVING TO AND LIVING IN WASHINGTON D.C.

202

Belvoir, the Naval Surface Warfare Center, the Army's Harry Diamond Laboratories, the Washington Navy Yard, Henderson Hall, and the U.S. Naval Observatory, as well as military personnel stationed at the White House or housed in nondescript government offices in Arlington. Within an hour's commute, there's also the Naval Academy, Quantico Marine Base, and (shhh) Ft. Detrick, which is none of your business.

The **USO of Metropolitan Washington** will meet you at the airport and start helping you get settled even before you report to your new post. Call 703-696-2628 or visit www.usometrodc.org for general information, or call one of the airport USO offices:

- **Reagan National Airport**, 703-419-3990
- **Marshall BWI Airport**, 410-859-3890
- **Andrews AFB**, 301-981-1854

  For additional resources on the web, visit:
- **http://dcmilitary.com** for links to all of the base newspapers and base guides in the area
- **www.sgtmoms.com** for military family support links
- **www.mdw.army.mil**, the official site of the Military District of Washington
- **www.armymwr.com**, the Army site for morale, welfare, and recreation

THE WASHINGTON AREA CAN BE AN EXCELLENT PLACE TO RAISE A family. In addition to good schools, the area offers countless opportunities to explore the arts and culture, the great outdoors, history, sports, and science, mostly for free. Some children who grow up here are astonished to learn that there are cities where you have to pay to get into a museum. As in any city, however, you will want to take care in choosing the right school and childcare programs, public or private, keeping in mind that even institutions with the best reputations many not be suited to your child's individual needs. Get comfy with the phone book and the web—a lot of research is in order.

CHILDCARE

Two-career couples are prevalent in the Washington area, making childcare a major concern and a major industry. At many government agencies, large companies, and organizations in large office buildings, onsite childcare is a coveted employee benefit. Professional and family childcare facilities—large and small, licensed and unlicensed—abound in the District and suburbs, and they're as diverse in character and price as the city itself. In addition, most public and private schools have afterschool programs. Before you entrust your child to a daycare facility, you will want to research your options, talk to co-workers or neighbors with children, visit facilities and meet with staff, and familiarize yourself with the local regulatory agencies, and area parenting publications.

REFERRAL & RESOURCES

In D.C., daycare facilities must be licensed except for those providing "occasional babysitting in the babysitter's home, informal parent-supervised neighborhood playgroups, care furnished in places of worship dur-

NEWCOMER'S HANDBOOK FOR MOVING TO AND LIVING IN WASHINGTON D.C.

204

ing religious services, or child development centers providing only a before- or after-school child-development program." The regulations set the maximum size of daycare enrollment in each age group (from 8 for toddlers to 30 for preteens), the maximum ratio of children to adults (4 to 1 for toddlers, 15 to 1 for preteens), and standards for physical facilities, safety, snacks, and government inspections.

When visiting prospective daycare centers—and you should visit, at least a couple of times—look for a clean, safe, calm environment, and then start asking questions: what degrees or training do the employees have? Is the center licensed? How frequent is staff turnover? What is the ratio of children to adults? How much time is spent outdoors? Are teachers or other experts involved in designing activities and programs? And pay attention to your gut feeling—the "vibe" you pick up is just as important as the certifications and curriculum.

These government agencies offer listings of licensed providers—along with tips and checklists for choosing one:

- **Office of Early Childhood Development**, D.C. Department of Human Services, 202-671-4200, http://dhs.dc.gov
- **Maryland Committee for Children**, 301-279-1773 (Montgomery County), 301-772-8400 (Prince George's County), 410-625-1111 (statewide), www.mdchildcare.org
- **Virginia Department of Social Services**, 800-451-1501, www.dss.virginia.gov (click on "Choosing Child Care" and download the guide, no matter where you live—it includes a sample interview for screening childcare facilities)
- **Montgomery County Child Care Resource & Referral Center**, 301-279-1260, www.montgomerycountymd.gov
- **Prince George's Child Resource Center**, 301-772-8420, www.childresource.org
- **Arlington County Child Care Office**, 703-228-1685, www.co.arlington.va.us
- **Fairfax County Office for Children**, 703-449-8484, www.co.fairfax.va.us/ofc
- **Alexandria Child Care Information Service**, 703-838-0750, www.ci.alexandria.va.us/dhs

You can call these local regulatory agencies with questions about licensing:

- **D.C. Health Regulation Administration**, Child and Residential Care Facilities Division, 202-442-5929, http://app.doh.dc.gov
- **Office of Child Care**, Maryland State Department of Education, 240-314-1400 (Montgomery County), 301-333-6940 (Prince George's County), 410-767-0600 (statewide), www.dhr.state.md.us/cca

- **Division of Licensing Programs**, Virginia Department of Social Services, 703-934-1505 (Northern Virginia), 804-726-7000 (statewide), www.dss.virginia.gov/division/license

NANNIES

Hiring a nanny is generally the most expensive childcare option, but it can be a very rewarding arrangement for everyone involved. A day nanny can easily cost $20/hour, and for a live-in nanny, room and board expenses are an additional factor. If you hire a nanny directly (not through an agency), you will need to cover payroll taxes and social security, Medicare, and possibly unemployment insurance. For tax questions about employing domestic childcare, contact **Nanitax**, 800-626-4829, www.4nanny taxes.com, or **GTM Associates**, 888-432-7972, www.4easypay.com. Also, keep in mind that most nannies are recent immigrants and you will need to make sure they can legally work in the United States and communicate fluently with you and your family.

Visit **Nanny Network**, www.nannynetwork.com, for a national database of nanny agencies, tax and background check services, training materials, FAQ pages, and other resources to help you find and employ the right caregiver. The **National Alliance of Professional Nanny Agencies**, www.theapna.org, can also help you know what to look for in a nanny service.

Excel Domestics, 703-823-8645, places all kinds of domestic help including nannies, maids, butlers, cooks, and drivers. **Teacher Care**, 888-832-2407, www.teachercare.com, places retired or part-time schoolteachers as nannies, especially for summer help. Other local listings of nannies or nanny agencies include:

- **www.washingtonparent.com** (click on Guides)
- **www.washingtonian.com** (click on Shopping & Services)
- **www.anannyonthenet.com**, 703-248-0400 or 888-436-0222
- **www.4nanny.com**, 866-296-2669
- **www.helpinghandnanny.com**, 410-664-0284
- **www.nannyville.com**

Most agencies run their own background checks, but if you have any doubts or you want a second opinion, you can check online for various services. Type "employment screening" into your search engine for links. Likely services include criminal and driving records and credit information. **Eisenberg Associates**, 800-777-5765, www.eisenbergassociates.com, provides health insurance and other fringe benefits for nannies.

NEWCOMER'S HANDBOOK FOR MOVING TO AND LIVING IN WASHINGTON D.C.

206

AU PAIRS

Au pairs are young adults, usually college-age women, visiting the United States with a special visa status that allows them to provide childcare and light housekeeping services in exchange for room and board, airfare, and a stipend (usually $260 per week). The host family benefits from the cultural exchange as well as the relatively inexpensive childcare—but the placement only lasts one year. Also, an au pair might not offer the same level of maturity and experience as a career nanny; as one Potomac family told *Washingtonian* magazine, when childcare duties cut into an au pair's free time, "What you have is a teenager who sulks in two languages."

Au pair placement agencies are regulated by the State Department—for details, contact the **Bureau of Educational & Cultural Affairs** at 202-203-5096 or www.exchanges.state.gov/education. These national au pair agencies will connect you with a local placement coordinator:

- **Au Pair in America**, 800-928-7247, www.aupairinamerica.com
- **AuPairCare**, 800-428-7247, www.aupaircare.com
- **Au Pair USA/InterExchange**, 800-287-2477, www.aupairusa.org
- **Cultural Care Au Pair**, 800-333-6056, www.efaupair.org
- **EurAuPair**, 800-901-2002, www.euraupair.com

BABYSITTING

The perfect babysitter is usually the responsible high school or college student whose parents are your friends, neighbors, or co-workers. Ask around about the going rate, and be prepared to pay more when giving short notice or on holidays. (Of course, you might also be charged extra based on your child's reputation among neighborhood sitters.)

If you don't know any suitable young people, you might try classified ads or the bulletin board at a local supermarket or coffeehouse. Many places of worship run daycare programs or provide good referrals, and they are happy to help regardless of your religious affiliation or faith. Apartment complexes and neighborhood associations might have listings in a newsletter or even an organized babysitting exchange.

If your sitter calls in sick at the last minute, or you haven't yet found a reliable sitter, most nanny agencies (see above) provide sitters on short notice, at a premium.

Most colleges and universities post job listings for students interested in babysitting on a regular basis. Contact the student employment office at the institution nearest you:

- **American University**, 202-885-1861; www.studentconfederation.org/jobcorps
- **Catholic University**, 202-319-5623, http://careers.cua.edu

- **George Mason University**, 703-993-2370, http://careers.gmu. edu/patriotjobweb
- **Georgetown University**, 202- 687-4187, seo.georgetown.edu
- **Howard University**, 202-806-7513, www.howard.edu/careerservices
- **Montgomery College**, 301-353-1920, www.montgomerycollege. edu/departments/studemp
- **Northern Virginia Community College**, 703-845-6245, www. nvcc.edu/careerstart
- **Prince George's Community College**, 301-322-0831, http://pg web.pg.cc.md.us
- **University of the District of Columbia**, 202-274-6251, www.udc. edu (click on Student Life)
- **University of Maryland**, 301-314-7225, www.careercenter. umd.edu

For a current list of private babysitter agencies, visit **www.washington parent.com** (under Guides) or **www.4sitters.com**.

PARENTING & CHILD SAFETY RESOURCES

- *Washington Parent* is a monthly tabloid whose ads are just as helpful as the articles. Available free at libraries, or online (with archives and resource listings) at www.washingtonparent.com.
- The **Family Services Agency** is a public-private partnership in Maryland providing parenting education, child development information, and links to parenting resources. Call 301-840-2000 or visit www.familyservicesagency.org
- **Safe Kids Worldwide** provides information about child passenger safety, home childproofing, and prevention of drowning, fire, falls, poisoning, and choking. Accidental injury is the no. 1 killer of children 14 and under. Call 202-662-0600 or visit www.safekids.org.

CPR & FIRST AID TRAINING

Most area hospitals offer CPR and first aid courses, and you can also search for an instructor or training program through any of the major CPR certifying organizations:

- **American Heart Association**, 800-242-4277, www.american heart.org
- **American Red Cross**, 202-303-4498, www.redcross.org/services/hss
- **American Safety & Health Institute**, 800-682-5067, www.ash institute.org/trainingcenter.asp
- **National Safety Council**, 800-875-4770, www.nsc.org/training

NEWCOMER'S HANDBOOK FOR MOVING TO AND LIVING IN WASHINGTON D.C.

208

CAR SEAT ASSISTANCE

An estimated 82% of car seats are installed or adjusted incorrectly; even worse, half of the children killed in car crashes were not restrained at all. The local **Safe Kids** coalitions offer free car seat inspections by nationally certified Child Passenger Safety Technicians and provide free or low-cost car seats to low-income families as supplies permit. Visit www.usa.safekids.org or contact Safe Kids at:

- **Children's National Medical Center**, 202-884-4993
- **Montgomery County Fire & Rescue Service**, 240-777-2222
- **Prince George's County Fire & EMS**, 301-883-3422
- **Inova Fairfax Hospital**, 703-776-2260

SCHOOLS

There are approximately 1,200 public and private schools in the Washington area; choosing the right one for your child can be complicated and time-consuming. The public school systems in the District and most neighboring jurisdictions have a growing number of magnet programs and specialty schools; add private schools and privately operated public charter schools into the mix and the range of options is extraordinary.

The *Washington Post* publishes a quarterly **education review** in January, April, July, and October, packed with ratings of area public schools and ads for private schools. Articles from the education review and regular news sections are specially archived on the Schools page at www.washington post.com. Also on the web, the **American School Directory** offers general information about almost every K-12 school in the United States at www.asd.com. At local bookstores and libraries, check out *Georgia Irvin's Guide to Schools: Metropolitan Washington* (Cooper Square Publishers) or *Washington School & Daycare Guide* by Andrew Fogaty (Morris Publishing). *Washingtonian* magazine's annual directory of area private schools is published in November and archived at www.washingtonian.com/schools. Finally, visit the education page at www.checkbook.org for advice from **Washington Consumers' Checkbook** about choosing a school, public or private.

In the city and suburbs alike, a key to students' prospects for success is the level of parent and community involvement in the school. Dropout rates, truancy, and disciplinary problems are all consistently lower in schools with active PTAs and accessible, responsive teachers and principals. So perhaps the most important step in choosing a school is to talk to parents, teachers, neighbors, school district officials, and the principal; find out whether parents play an active role in efforts to improve the school.

Visit a prospective school—public or private—and ask yourself:

- Am I comfortable here? Will my child be comfortable here?
- Does the school feel safe? Are the bathrooms clean and free of graffiti?
- Do the students seem to be engaged? Is student work on display?
- Are adults present throughout the building and grounds? Are parents encouraged to volunteer?
- Are classrooms crowded? Do teachers appear to be overworked?
- Are instructional materials, desks, and computers plentiful and new?
- Does the school offer academic and extracurricular opportunities for students to explore their own special interests (such as art, music, sports, or science)?
- Does the school have a clear mission statement? Do teachers seem to teach with that mission in mind? Can teachers articulate the school's educational philosophy?
- In an elementary school, pay attention to the way children are moving around—are they interacting naturally, but staying on task? In a secondary school, notice how students interact with each other and with teachers at the beginning and end of class, and in the halls.

Pay attention to your gut feeling about a school, as well as to the wealth of perspectives you can get from parents and teachers. And, to paraphrase JFK, ask not only what the school can do for your child, but what you can do for your child's school.

PUBLIC SCHOOLS

In the Washington area, you will find some of the finest public schools in the country, and some of the most desperate. As in many big cities, inner-city schools here have metal detectors at the doors and uniformed security guards patrolling the halls. Most high schools—in the suburbs as well as the city—have at least a few gangs ("crews"), whose activities vary from teenage mischief to serious involvement with drugs and weapons. Still, the District and surrounding counties produce a consistently large number of National Merit Scholars, Advanced Placement graduates, and high SAT scores.

DISTRICT OF COLUMBIA

D.C. public schools have a per-pupil budget that is much higher than the national average, yet the schools are struggling; many have chronic shortages of desks, books, and other basic materials—teachers have been known to reach into their own pockets to buy supplies. The main culprit is the cost of maintaining the city's aging school buildings, most of which were built in the first half of the 20th century—some even earlier.

NEWCOMER'S HANDBOOK FOR MOVING TO AND LIVING IN WASHINGTON D.C.

210

It's important to know the recent history of school board politics: In 1997, the start of the school year was delayed because too many school buildings were in hazardous condition, and a judge ordered major repairs to be completed before students returned. Congress stepped in and placed an emergency oversight board in charge of the District's schools, returning power to local officials in 2001. Not surprisingly, the school system has been plagued with blame games. Parents were starkly divided over a referendum in 2000 that changed the structure of the D.C. school board, replacing some elected seats with mayoral appointees and changing the geographic constituencies of the remaining elected seats. The close vote underscored the city's economic divide, with the more affluent precincts west of Rock Creek approving the changes and the precincts east of Rock Creek voting to preserve the fully elected board. Supporters of the reform hoped the new structure would result in a board with fewer politicos and more blue-ribbon experts; opponents argued that it would make the school system less accountable to the community. The jury is still out.

Nevertheless, there are plenty of good educational opportunities available to D.C. students. The city has a prestigious arts magnet, the **Duke Ellington School**, www.ellingtonschool.org, in Georgetown, and an academic magnet, **Benjamin Banneker High School**, www.benjamin banneker.org, near Howard University, 202-673-7322. **School Without Walls**, www.swwhs.org, in Foggy Bottom emphasizes experiential learning, taking advantage of the city's cultural resources; like a magnet, "Walls" requires an entrance application. Visit **www.dcschoolsearch.com**, a service of the District government, for a complete directory of D.C. schools, or call the superintendent's office at 202-724-4222.

The District also allows **public charter schools**—public schools run autonomously by a board of trustees approved by the government, outside the jurisdiction of the superintendent of schools. Some charter schools offer a regular curriculum, but promise closer oversight and smaller classes than regular public schools; others offer specialized curricula, such as the Cesar Chavez Public Charter School for Public Policy or the Marriott Hospitality High School. Contact the **D.C. Public Charter School Board** at 202-328-2660 or www.dcpubliccharter.com for more information about charter schools.

Even regular public schools vary in character from one neighborhood to another. Some schools have adopted mandatory school uniforms, especially in neighborhoods with large numbers of low-income households; school officials hope children will be relieved of peer pressure to keep up with fashion. Some neighborhoods have middle schools, grades 6–8; others have junior high schools, grades 7–9. And many schools have had their budgets for athletics, arts, and extracurricular activities drastically cut since the mid-1990s, and the range and quality of activities often depends on the ability of concerned individuals to buy enough baked goods and M&Ms to fund band uniforms or soccer cleats.

Your child has a right to attend your neighborhood school. If you can provide the transportation, however, your child may attend any public school in the District, if space permits. Many parents wait in long lines for "out-of-boundary" applications to enroll their kids in schools with well-funded extracurricular programs.

For more information about the Board of Education, school boundaries, special programs, and policies and reforms, contact **D.C. Public Schools** at 202-724-4222 or visit www.k12.dc.us. The main offices are located at 825 North Capitol Street NE.

HOW TO ENROLL IN D.C. PUBLIC SCHOOLS

Schooling is compulsory for D.C. residents from age 5 to 18. Children should be enrolled in kindergarten in the fall of the calendar year in which they turn 5, and may be enrolled in pre-K in the fall of the calendar year in which they turn 4.

To register your children, go to the school you want them to attend; if you want to enroll a child in an "out-of-boundary" school, you need permission from the principal of that school. Generally, principals accept out-of-boundary requests in late January and February for the following school year, and allow enrollment as space permits. Call the school district or ask your local school for the exact dates each year.

Once you have chosen your neighborhood school or secured space in an out-of-boundary school, you must provide proof of residence and, for each child, proof of age and immunization records.

- Proof of residence: you must provide three documents showing that you currently live in D.C. One of these documents must also show your tax status—you can provide a current tax withholding statement or proof of payment of D.C. personal income tax, or ask the school for a release you can sign to authorize the school to verify your tax status. For the other two documents, you can use a driver's license or non-driver's ID, your vehicle registration, the deed or lease to your home, your voter registration card, or utility bills with receipts or canceled checks showing payment within the past two months. For more information, call the Student Residency Office at 202-442-5215. If you are registering more than one child, you only need to show proof of residency once at each school. Also, the school is not permitted to ask you any questions about your citizenship or immigration status when you register.
- Proof of age: show an embossed copy of the child's birth certificate or copy of official records from your old school district.
- Immunization records: your child must be immunized against diphtheria/pertussis/tetanus; polio; measles/mumps/rubella; hemophilus

NEWCOMER'S HANDBOOK FOR MOVING TO AND LIVING IN WASHINGTON D.C.

212

influenza type B; hepatitis B; and, for children who have not had chicken pox, varicella. A tuberculosis screening is also required, and students entering grade 5 or above should have a diphtheria/tetanus booster if they have not been immunized within the past five years. For a list of clinics providing free and low-cost immunizations, call 202-576-7130; for general information about immunization requirements, call 202-442-5141.

- Students entering middle school, junior high school, or senior high school at the beginning of the school year must attend an orientation program in late August. Orientation schedules will be mailed to registered students.

The D.C. school day is 8:45 a.m. to 3:15 p.m. at all grade levels.

THE SUBURBS

Suburban school districts generally have one huge advantage over D.C. schools: in the suburbs, local government isn't a novelty. Because the District has had a school board since only 1973 and a legislature since 1974, the D.C. school board still attracts a lot of ambitious politicos who use it as a stepping-stone to a more prestigious office in the neighboring counties; in the suburbs it's more likely that the average school board member is dedicated first and foremost to education.

Of course, the suburbs present their own challenges. After a quarter century of sprawl and population boom, with no end in sight, many schools are overcrowded and capital budgets are strained by frantic construction of new schools. And even in affluent suburban neighborhoods, high schools are hardly immune to the nationwide problems of gangs and drugs. However, county schools in the area have dropout rates 50% to 75% lower than D.C.'s, and despite crowding, most school districts manage to keep the average class size around a respectable 20.

Each local jurisdiction has magnet schools offering special curricula to students who have demonstrated a particular aptitude—in math and science, the arts, vocational skills, or other areas of emphasis. Also, every local jurisdiction allows students from other jurisdictions to attend public school by paying non-resident tuition. This little-known option enables all students to take advantage of the region's best public schools.

HOW TO ENROLL IN COUNTY OR CITY PUBLIC SCHOOLS

In every jurisdiction in suburban Maryland and Northern Virginia, schooling is compulsory for ages 5–16. As in D.C., most students should be enrolled in the school closest to home unless applying for admission to a countywide magnet school with a special academic emphasis. (An exception is Montgomery County high schools, where students may choose among several nearby schools on the basis of different academic specialties.) Contact the local school district at the phone number or web site below for details about school boundaries and magnet schools.

Registration procedures are fairly uniform throughout the Washington area—go to the appropriate school and present proof of residence (usually a lease, deed, property tax bill, or current utility bill); proof of age (birth certificate, passport, or affidavit); school transcript, unless your child is enrolling in kindergarten for the first time; and immunization records. Contact the school district for the exact list of required immunizations and other documents to bring. Also request, or download, an academic calendar. If you move here during the summer, note that most schools have an August registration fair for new students. Finally, contact the school district for instructions if you need to register a child whose primary language is not English or who has other special needs.

The school day in most jurisdictions is 9 a.m. to 3 p.m. for elementary and 8 a.m. to 3:15 p.m. for high schools. Middle schools, junior high schools, and intermediate schools (grades 7-8) may vary, but generally, students have to get up earlier as they get older.

Contact your county or city school district for more information:

- **Montgomery County**, 850 Hungerford Dr., Rockville, 301-309-6277, www.mcps.k12.md.us
- **Prince George's County**, 14201 School Lane, Upper Marlboro, 301-952-6001, www.pgcps.pg.k12.md.us
- **Arlington County**, 1426 N. Quincy St., Arlington, 703-228-6000, www.arlington.k12.va.us
- **Fairfax County**, 10700 Page Ave., Fairfax, 703-246-2991, www.fcps.k12.va.us
- **Alexandria**, 2000 N. Beauregard St., 703-824-6600, www.acps.k12.va.us
- **Falls Church**, 803 West Broad St., 703-248-5600, www.fccps.k12.va.us

PARENT ORGANIZATIONS

To find your local PTA and regional council of PTAs, contact:
- **D.C. Congress of PTAs**, 202-543-0333
- **Maryland PTA**, 410-760-6221, www.mdpta.org
- **Virginia PTA**, 866-482-5437, www.vapta.org
- **National PTA**, 202-289-6790, www.pta.org

Other organizations working to improve students' D.C. public school experience include:
- **D.C. Action for Children**, 202-234-9404, www.dckids.org
- **D.C. Voice**, 202-986-8535, www.dcvoice.org

NEWCOMER'S HANDBOOK FOR MOVING TO AND LIVING IN WASHINGTON D.C.

214

- **Parents United for the D.C. Public Schools**, 202-518-3667, www.dcwatch.com/parents
- **Communities In Schools**, 202-367-1041, www.cisnet.org/capital

PUBLIC SCHOOL EVALUATIONS

D.C. schools are evaluated by the Stanford-9 Achievement Test, and average test scores at each school are used to calculate funding and staffing priorities. For information about each school's Stanford-9 scores, visit www.k12.dc.us/dcps or call 202-724-4222. The annual Maryland Report Card on public schools is available from the State Department of Education at www.mdreportcard.org or by calling 888-246-0016. In Virginia, controversial high-stakes Standards of Learning tests can determine the future not only of schools, but of individual students and teachers. For more information, go to www.pen.k12.va.us and select SOL Testing under Most Requested Information or call 800-292-3820. Each school district's web site and main switchboard can also provide information on benchmarks and plans for compliance with the federal No Child Left Behind Act.

PRIVATE & PAROCHIAL SCHOOLS

Every jurisdiction in the Washington area has a range of private elementary and secondary schools, both religious and secular. Many parents, religious or not, prefer the academic and disciplinary rigor of Catholic, Jewish, and other parochial schools. Others seek alternative secular approaches to education, including Waldorf and Montessori methods, the International Baccalaureate program recognized throughout Europe, or a bilingual or multicultural setting.

Private school tuition ranges from $1,000 a year to the high 20s, depending on a school's academic reputation and social prestige. Most private schools offer some need-based scholarships, but get in line and don't count on it. In D.C., a controversial pilot program awards tuition vouchers to a few needy families, and the credit is good toward tuition at any accredited private school, but it doesn't take a huge bite out of the tuition at the best schools.

For the text of state and local regulations governing academic and safety standards for private schools, visit the **U.S. Department of Education** web site at www.ed.gov/pubs, or contact the **National Library of Education** at 202-205-5015 or www.ed.gov/NLE. Local private schools are listed in the *Independent School Guide for Washington, D.C. and Surrounding Area*, available at www.washingtonbk.com or by calling 703-212-9113.

For more information about private schools, including links and contact information for most area schools, contact:

- **Association of Independent Schools of Greater Washington**, 202-625-9223, www.aisgw.org
- **Association of Independent Maryland Schools**, 301-858-6311, www.aimsmd.org
- **Virginia Association of Independent Schools**, 804-282-3592, www.vais.org
- **National Association of Independent Schools**, 202-973-9700, www.nais.org

Parents Council of Washington is the private-school equivalent of a regional council of PTAs; call 301-767-2385 or visit www.parentscouncil. org. And **Washington Families** magazine, www.washingtonfamilies. com, publishes a good list of **preschools**.

HOMESCHOOLING

Parents who have misgivings about urban public schools have the right to take their children's education into their own hands. Many parents believe that they are best suited to design an educational program that will engage and challenge their children, responding to each child's unique psychological and intellectual traits. Homeschooling is especially popular among strongly religious parents who object to the secular nature of public schools, and among liberal parents who object to the public schools' increasing reliance on educational materials provided by corporate sponsors.

Teaching is not easy—you will need a lot of time and energy to plan and execute a study program that will enable your children to earn a high school diploma at home—but there are plenty of organizations and resources to help you. Check out **Homeschooling Today** magazine online at www.homeschooltoday.com for dozens of useful links.

TUTORS

For a referral to afterschool tutors, contact your local school district at the number or web site above. In D.C., the number for tutor referrals is 202-442-5155. Your child's teacher should also be able to recommend appropriate tutors for specific skills. Private tutoring services are listed in the Yellow Pages and on Craigslist. **TutorFind** represents hundreds of experienced tutors in every subject and grade level—call 800-648-8867 or visit www.tutorfind.com.

NEWCOMER'S HANDBOOK FOR MOVING TO AND LIVING IN WASHINGTON D.C.

216

CAMPS & SUMMER PROGRAMS

In addition to the listings (and ads) in *Washington Parent* and *Washington Families,* plan to meet with summer camp representatives at the annual **Camp & Summer Programs Expo** at White Flint Mall in Bethesda, usually held in late January. Check the *Montgomery Gazette*, www.gazette.net, or call White Flint at 301-231-7467 for more information. Also note that most of the larger museums, galleries, and theater companies have summer programs for kids.

APART FROM METRO STATIONS, THE LEADING HUBS OF TRAFFIC and development in the Washington area are shopping malls. Tysons Corner, a busy cluster of office high-rises in Northern Virginia, was originally a shopping mall and a cluster of car dealerships; now it's a recognized suburb in its own right. Likewise, you might hear people say they live in White Flint or Seven Corners or Pentagon City—all neighborhoods that grew up around malls of the same name. The vast Potomac Mills discount mall in Woodbridge, Va., draws more visitors than any tourist attraction in the Washington area.

While area malls have lost some traffic, in recent years, to "big-box" stores—destination stores like Wal-Mart, PetSmart, Sports Authority, Borders, and Pottery Barn—Washingtonians still spend $4 billion a year at the area's 10 largest malls. And then there are the ubiquitous strip malls in the suburbs, which typically include a grocery store and a big-box outlet. Rockville Pike, between North Bethesda and downtown Rockville, is practically a two-mile-long strip mall.

In downtown D.C., most of the big, elegant, free-standing department stores closed in the early 1990s—many after a century or more. Stores today are smaller and more specialized—furniture boutiques abound in Adams Morgan and along U Street NW, and clothing stores line Connecticut Avenue NW between Dupont Circle and the White House. You can find just about anything in Georgetown, along Wisconsin Avenue and M Street NW, from distinctive local shops to popular national chains.

Retail hours here cater to a workaholic climate and busy two-career couples. Almost all stores are open seven days a week, and many—especially in malls—are open until 10 p.m. six days a week and 6 p.m. on Sundays. Increasingly, "bricks-and-mortar" retailers know they need to compete with Amazon.com and eBay.

Although consumer prices here are high, Washington is fertile ground for bargain hunters. There are always people coming and going, not just

NEWCOMER'S HANDBOOK FOR MOVING TO AND LIVING IN WASHINGTON D.C.

218

after an election—military and diplomatic families get deployed, college students head off to school, graduates move here to launch careers—all contributing to an endless supply of inventory for thrift stores, consignment shops, and yard sales. Classified ads, too, are replete with $25 sofas and $50 stereos in good condition.

Unless otherwise noted, stores listed here are in D.C.

SHOPPING MALLS

The handful of malls in the District are fashionable, pricey, and relatively small. Suburban malls range from upscale fashion meccas to utilitarian discount centers. At most of the larger malls, you'll find a good mix of the luxurious and the practical; for a general idea of a mall's character, though, check the list of the major department stores at each mall against the descriptions under "Department Stores" below.

DISTRICT OF COLUMBIA

- **Chevy Chase Pavilion**, 5335 Wisconsin Ave. NW (Metro: Friendship Heights), 202-686-5335, www.ccpavilion.com; 30 stores including The Cheesecake Factory, J. Crew, Pottery Barn
- **Mazza Gallerie**, 5300 Wisconsin Ave. NW (Metro: Friendship Heights), 202-966-6114, www.mazzagallerie.com; 60 stores including Neiman Marcus, Saks Fifth Avenue, Filene's Basement
- **Shops at Georgetown Park**, 3222 M St. NW (Metrobus: routes 30-36 from Farragut West), 202-298-5577, www.shopsatgeorgetown park.com; 105 stores including Anthropologie, J. Crew
- **The Shops at National Place**, 1331 Pennsylvania Ave. NW (Metro: Metro Center), 202-783-9090; 40 specialty stores and restaurants including Five Guys, Corner Bakery
- **Union Station**, 50 Massachusetts Ave. NE (Metro: Union Station), 202-289-1908, www.unionstationdc.com; 130 specialty stores and restaurants including Discovery Store, Appalachian Spring

MARYLAND

- **Beltway Plaza**, 6000 Greenbelt Rd., Greenbelt (Metrobus: routes T15-T17 from Greenbelt), 301-345-1500, www.beltwayplazamall.com; 120 stores including Burlington Coat Factory, Marshall's, Target
- **Boulevard at Capital Centre**, off the Capital Beltway & Central Ave., Largo (Metro: Largo Town Center), 301-333-2583; 70 stores including Sports Authority, Linens 'n Things, Borders

- **Capitol Plaza Mall**, 6200 Annapolis Rd., Landover Hills (Metrobus: routes A11-A15 from Landover), 301-773-6611; 65 stores including Montgomery Ward
- **City Place**, 8661 Colesville Rd., Silver Spring (Metro: Silver Spring), 301-589-1091; 65 stores including Burlington Coat Factory, Marshall's, Nordstrom Rack, Ross
- **Congressional Plaza**, 1300 Rockville Pike, Rockville (Metro: Twinbrook), 301-998-8395, www.congressionalplaza.com; 40 stores including Whole Foods, Tower Records, Appalachian Spring
- **Lakeforest Mall**, Route 355 & Montgomery Village Ave., Gaithersburg (Ride-On: routes 57-58 from Shady Grove), 301-840-5840, www.shop lakeforest.com; 160 stores including JC Penney, Lord & Taylor, Sears
- **Laurel Mall**, 14828 Baltimore Ave., Laurel (Metrobus: route 89 from Greenbelt), 301-953-3300, www.shoplaurelmall.com; 105 stores including Hecht's, JC Penney, Burlington Coat Factory
- **Milestone Center**, Route 355 & Shakespeare Blvd., Germantown (Ride-On: route 79 from Shady Grove), 301-631-7510; 10 stores including Toys 'R' Us, Kohl's, Home Depot, Target, Wal-Mart, PetSmart
- **Montgomery Mall**, Democracy Blvd. & Westlake Dr., Bethesda (Metrobus: routes J1-J3 from Silver Spring), 301-469-6025, www.west field.com/montgomery; 200 stores including Hecht's, JC Penney, Nordstrom, Sears
- **Prince George's Plaza**, 3500 East-West Hwy., Hyattsville (Metro: Prince George's Plaza), 301-559-8844, www.princegeorgesplaza.com; 120 stores including Target, JC Penney, Old Navy
- **Wheaton Plaza**, 11160 Veirs Mill Rd., Wheaton (Metro: Wheaton), 301-942-3200, www.westfield.com/wheaton; 140 stores including Giant Food, Hecht's, JC Penney, Target
- **White Flint**, 11301 Rockville Pike, North Bethesda (Metro: White Flint), 301-231-7467, www.shopwhiteflint.com; 125 stores including Borders Books & Music, Bloomingdale's, Dave & Buster's, Lord & Taylor

VIRGINIA

- **Ballston Common Mall**, 4238 Wilson Blvd., Arlington, 703-243-8088, www.ballston-common.com; 100 stores including The Commuter Store, Hecht's
- **Dulles Town Center**, Routes 7 and 28, Dulles, 703-404-7120, www.shopdullestowncenter.com; 170 stores including Nordstrom, JC Penney, Lord & Taylor, Sears
- **Fair Lakes Center**, 6 Fair Lakes Pkwy., Fairfax (Metrobus: route 12S from Vienna), 703-227-0883, www.fairlakes.com/evillage/retail; 50 stores including Target, Wal-Mart, PetSmart

NEWCOMER'S HANDBOOK FOR MOVING TO AND LIVING IN WASHINGTON D.C.

220

- **Fair Oaks Mall**, I-66 and U.S. Route 50, Fairfax (Metrobus: route 2G from Vienna), 703-359-8300, www.shopfairoaksmall.com; 180 stores including JC Penney, Lord & Taylor, Sears
- **Fashion Centre at Pentagon City**, 1100 South Hayes St., Arlington (Metro: Pentagon City) 703-415-2400, www.fashioncentrepentagon. com; 160 stores including Macy's, Nordstrom
- **Landmark Mall**, 5801 Duke St., Alexandria (Metrobus: routes 29K-29N from King St.), 703-354-8405, www.landmarkmall.com; 150 stores including Lord & Taylor, Sears
- **Potomac Yard Center**, Jefferson Davis Hwy. & Reed Ave., Alexandria (Metrobus: routes 9A, 9E from Pentagon), 703-548-9770; 15 stores including Barnes & Noble, Target, T.J. Maxx
- **Seven Corners Center**, 6201 Arlington Blvd., Falls Church (Metrobus: routes 4B, 4H from Rosslyn), 703-986-2200; 40 stores including Barnes & Noble, Home Depot, Jo-Ann Fabrics
- **Tysons Corner Center**, 703-893-9403, www.shoptysons.com and **Tysons Galleria**, 703-827-7700, www.tysonsgalleria.com, Dolley Madison Blvd. and International Dr., McLean (Metrobus: routes 3W, 3Z from West Falls Church); 340 stores including Bloomingdale's, L.L. Bean, Lord & Taylor, Macy's, Neiman Marcus, Nordstrom, Saks Fifth Avenue
- **Springfield Mall**, I-95 and Franconia Rd., Springfield (Fairfax Connector: route 401 from Franconia-Springfield), 703-971-3600, www.springfieldmall.com; 230 stores including JC Penney, Macy's, Target—plus a working merry-go-round

OUTLYING AREAS

These malls are outside the area covered in this book, but their huge selections or discount outlets draw thousands of Washingtonians on weekends:
- **Annapolis Mall**, off U.S. Route 50 in Annapolis, 410-266-5432, www. westfield.com/annapolis; 160 stores including JC Penney, Lord & Taylor, Sears, Nordstrom
- **Arundel Mills**, Route 100 & Route 713 near Marshall BWI Airport, 410-580-9050, www.millscorp.com/arundel; 200 discount outlets including Burlington Coat Factory, Old Navy, Saks Fifth Avenue outlet
- **Columbia Mall**, 10300 Little Patuxent Parkway, Columbia, Md., 410-730-3300, www.themallincolumbia.com; 190 stores including Nordstrom, JC Penney, Lord & Taylor, Sears, L.L. Bean
- **Leesburg Corner Premium Outlets**, on Route 7 in Leesburg, 703-737-3071, www.premiumoutlets.com; 60 discount stores including Crate & Barrel, Kenneth Cole, Williams-Sonoma
- **Manassas Mall**, 8300 Sudley Road, Manassas, 703-368-0181, www. manassasmall.com; 120 stores including JC Penney, Sears, Target

- **Potomac Mills**, off I-95 in Woodbridge, 703-496-9301, www. potomacmills.com; 230 discount stores including Saks Fifth Avenue Outlet, Nordstrom Rack, Ikea, Marshall's
- **Prime Outlets Hagerstown**, off I-70 in Hagerstown, Md., 888-883-6288, www.primeoutlets.com; 90 discount outlets including L.L. Bean, Rockport, Adidas
- **Prime Outlets Queenstown**, U.S. Route 50 & U.S. Route 301 in Queenstown, Md., 410-827-8699, www.primeoutlets.com; over 60 discount stores including Bass, The Gap, L.L. Bean
- **St. Charles Towne Center**, U.S. Route 301 in Waldorf, Md., 301-870-6997; 130 stores including JC Penney, Kohl's, Target, Sears

DEPARTMENT STORES

- **Bloomingdale's**, www.bloomingdales.com: renowned for its furniture collections and model rooms, "Bloomies" stores are great for browsers looking for decorating ideas. White Flint, 301-984-4600; Tysons Corner Center, 703-556-4600
- **The Hecht Company**, 800-424-9205, www.hechts.com: You might see a few of the May Company's upscale "Hecht's" stores, but they're being phased out and rebranded as Macy's and Bloomingdale's.
- **JC Penney**, 800-322-1189, www.jcpenney.com: all over town, selling everything from washing machines and lawnmowers to jewelry and cosmetics. Lakeforest Mall, Prince George's Plaza, Wheaton Plaza, Dulles Town Center, Fair Oaks Mall, Springfield Mall
- **Kohl's**, 866-887-8884, www.kohls.com: relatively new in town, Kohl's competes with Sears and JC Penney. 12024 Cherry Hill Rd., Silver Spring; 9871 Washingtonian Blvd., Gaithersburg; 20918 Frederick Rd., Germantown; Corridor Marketplace, Laurel; 4200 Mitchellville Rd., Bowie; 5701 Kingstowne Blvd., Springfield
- **Lord & Taylor**, 800-348-6940, www.lordandtaylor.com: this "white glove" store still carries clothing and accessories for the traditional set, and small, select gift items. 5255 Western Ave. NW, Lakeforest Mall, White Flint, Dulles Town Center, Fair Oaks Mall, Landmark Mall, Tysons Corner Center
- **Macy's**, 800-289-6229, www.macys.com: attracts fashion-conscious men and women, and it's also attractive to gourmet cooks looking for fine housewares and delicacies. Wheaton Plaza, Fair Oaks Mall, Pentagon City, Springfield Mall, Tysons Galleria
- **Neiman Marcus**, 888-888-4757, www.neimanmarcus.com: extravagant and eccentric gift items—from the chocolate Monopoly set to the private submarine—made Neiman Marcus famous, but most come here for the elegant designer clothing. Mazza Gallerie, Tysons Galleria

NEWCOMER'S HANDBOOK FOR MOVING TO AND LIVING IN WASHINGTON D.C.

222

- **Nordstrom**, 888-282-6060, www.nordstrom.com: this West Coast retailer is known for superlative service, knowledgeably selling well-made clothing, cosmetics, toiletries and accessories. Dulles Town Center, Montgomery Mall, Pentagon City, Tysons Corner Center
- **Saks Fifth Avenue**, 877-551-7257, www.saksfifthavenue.com: carries top-of-the-line clothing and accessories for men, women, and children; its extensive lines of evening wear attract the charity ball crowd. 5555 Wisconsin Ave., Chevy Chase; Tysons Galleria
- **Sears**, 800-349-4358, www.sears.com: known for Craftsman power tools, Sears is also a mainstay for family clothing, appliances, and home electronics. Lakeforest Mall, Montgomery Mall, Fair Oaks Mall, Landmark Mall, Seven Corners Center

DISCOUNT DEPARTMENT STORES

Many upscale department stores have their own outlets where they sell discontinued, overstocked, or slightly irregular merchandise at reduced prices. Such goods are also sold through discount outlets such as Marshall's, Ross, and T.J. Maxx. Other discount chains—Ames, Caldor, Kmart, and Target—carry name-brand goods, but not the designer labels available at upscale department stores.

- **Filene's Basement**, 1133 Connecticut Ave. NW; Shops at National Place; Mazza Gallerie; 11840 Rockville Pike; 888-843-8474, www.filenes basement.com
- **Kmart/Big K/Super K**, 6411 Riggs Rd., Hyattsville; 8829 Greenbelt Rd., Greenbelt; 6163 Oxon Hill Rd., Oxon Hill, Md.; 4251 John Marr Dr., Annandale; Springfield Mall; 866-562-7848, www.kmart.com
- **Marshall's**, City Place Mall; Landmark Mall; Pentagon City; 5830 Crossroads Center Blvd., Baileys Crossroads; 3100 Donnell Dr., Forestville, Md.; 888-627-7425, www.marshallsonline.com
- **Nordstrom Rack**, City Place; 15760 Shady Grove Road, Gaithersburg; 45575 Eastern Plaza, Sterling, Va.; 888-282-6060, www.nordstrom.com
- **Ross**, 13855 Outlet Dr., Silver Spring; 12270 Rockville Pike, Rockville; 7455 Greenbelt Rd., Greenbelt; 14200 Baltimore Ave., Laurel; 5830 Kingstowne Center, Springfield; 9230 Old Keene Mill Rd., Burke; Landmark Mall; 3562 Main St., Fairfax; 5840 Leesburg Pike, Falls Church; Seven Corners Center; 800-945-7677, www.rossstores.com
- **Syms**, 1900 Chapman Ave., Rockville; 1000 E. Broad St., Falls Church; 800-322-7967, www.syms.com
- **Target**, Wheaton Plaza; Prince George's Plaza; 6100 Greenbelt Rd, Greenbelt; 10500 Campus Way South, Largo, Md.; 3101 Donnell Dr., Forestville, Md.; 3101 Jefferson Davis Hwy., Alexandria; 5115 Leesburg

Pike, Falls Church; 6100 Arlington Blvd., Falls Church; 800-440-0680, www.target.com
- **T.J. Maxx**, 4350 Jenifer St. NW; 1776 E. Jefferson St., Rockville; 18329 Village Mart Dr., Olney, Md.; Milestone Center; 3504 S. Jefferson St., Falls Church; 3451 Jefferson Davis Hwy., Alexandria; 7730 Richmond Hwy., Alexandria; 5950 Kingstowne Towne Center, Springfield; 800-285-6299, www.tjmaxx.com
- **Wal-Mart**, 20910 Frederick Rd., Germantown; 8745 Branch Ave., Clinton, Md.; 3300 N. Crain Hwy., Bowie; 3549 Russett Green East, Laurel; 5800 Kingstowne Blvd., Alexandria; 7910 Richmond Hwy., Alexandria; 13059 Fair Lakes Pkwy., Fairfax; 6000 Burke Commons Rd., Burke; 800-925-6278, www.walmart.com

And don't forget the membership warehouse giants **Costco** and **Sam's Club**. They offer low prices on food, electronics, cameras, small appliances, housewares, automotive supplies, sporting goods, even eyeglasses; membership fees apply, and you don't get—or pay for—the level of service you expect from a regular department store. See the **Food** section for locations.

APPLIANCES, ELECTRONICS, COMPUTERS

For computer experts, the best deals on hardware may be found in classified ads in the Business section of the *Washington Post* on Mondays. If you don't need the latest technology, the classified ads in the *City Paper* are bursting with bargains on used computers. Savings can also be found at the **MarketPro Computer Show & Sale**, a consumer-oriented trade show held almost every weekend, rotating through a series of suburban venues. Dealers sell clearance items for less than half the retail price, and if you find what you want, the savings will certainly cover the $7 admission. See www.marketproshows.com for dates and locations.

For computer stores, check the Yellow Pages under "Computers"; look for other home electronics under "Appliances," "Stereo," and "Television," or try these electronics dealers:
- **Belmont TV**, 12500 Layhill Rd., Wheaton, 301-942-1300; 9101 Marshall Ave., Laurel, 301-498-5600; 4723 King St., Arlington, 703-671-8500; www.belmonttv.com
- **Best Buy**, 4500 Wisconsin Ave. NW; 1200 Rockville Pike, Rockville; 15750 Shady Grove Rd., Gaithersburg; 14160 Baltimore Ave., Laurel; 15800 Collington Rd., Bowie; Pentagon City; Potomac Yard; 5799 Leesburg Pike, Falls Church; Tysons Corner; Springfield Mall; 1861 Fountain Dr., Reston; 888-237-8289, www.bestbuy.com

NEWCOMER'S HANDBOOK FOR MOVING TO AND LIVING IN WASHINGTON D.C.

224

- **Circuit City**, 11160 Veirs Mill Rd., Wheaton; 1501 Rockville Pike, Rockville; 602 Quince Orchard Rd., Gaitherburg; 3551 32nd Ave., Marlow Heights, Md.; 11011 Baltimore Ave., Beltsville; Pentagon City; 8520 Leesburg Pike, Vienna; 1905 Chain Bridge Rd., McLean; 11220 James Swart Circle, Fairfax; 5710 Columbia Pike, Baileys Crossroads; 6640 Loisdale Rd., Springfield; 800-843-2489, www.circuitcity.com
- **CompUSA**, 1776 E. Jefferson St., Rockville; 5901 Stevenson Ave., Alexandria; 12189 Fair Lakes Parkway, Fairfax; 8357 Leesburg Pike, Vienna; 800-266-7872, www.compusa.com
- **Graffiti Audio-Video**, 1219 Connecticut Ave. NW; 4914 Wisconsin Ave. NW; 7810 Old Georgetown Rd., Bethesda; 202-296-8412, www.graffitiaudio.com
- **Murrell's Electronics**, 2140 Wisconsin Ave. NW, 202-338-7730
- **MyerEmco AudioVideo**, 2400 Wisconsin Ave. NW; Montgomery Mall; 2 Bureau Dr., Gaithersburg; 2800 Clarendon Blvd., Arlington; 12300 Price Club Plaza Dr., Fairfax; 3511 Carlin Springs Rd., Baileys Crossroads; 8138 Watson St., McLean; 301-921-0700, www.myeremco.com
- **Office Depot**, 4455 Connecticut Ave. NW; 8515 Georgia Ave., Silver Spring; 11130 New Hampshire Ave., Silver Spring; 3500 East-West Hwy., Hyattsville; 7933 Annapolis Rd., Lanham, Md.; 900 Shoppers Way, Largo, Md.; 1515 N. Courthouse Rd., Arlington; 5845 Leesburg Pike, Baileys Crossroads; 6700 Richmond Hwy., Alexandria; 2901 Gallows Rd., Merrifield, Va.; 800-463-3768, www.officedepot.com
- **Radio Shack**, 1109 F St. NW; 1100 15th St. NW; 1830 K St. NW; 732 7th St. NW; 1150 Connecticut Ave. NW; 1767 Columbia Rd. NW; 3323 Connecticut Ave. NW; 4531 Wisconsin Ave. NW; 442 L'Enfant Plaza SW; 717 D St. SE; 2837 Alabama Ave. SE; 1141 University Blvd., Takoma Park; Prince George's Plaza; 5201 Indian Head Hwy., Oxon Hill, Md.; 6183 Oxon Hill Rd., Oxon Hill; Pentagon City; 1651 Crystal Square Arcade, Arlington; Ballston Common Mall; 3425 King St., Alexandria; 800-843-7422, www.radioshack.com
- **Staples**, 1250 H St. NW; 1901 L St. NW; 6800 Wisconsin Ave., Chevy Chase; 5556 Randolph Rd., Rockville; Congressional Plaza; 9440 Georgia Ave., Silver Spring; 12389 Georgia Ave., Silver Spring; 12008 Cherry Hill Rd., Silver Spring; 8904 62nd Ave., College Park; 8452 Annapolis Rd., New Carrollton; 6139 Oxon Hill Rd., Oxon Hill, Md.; 910 N. Glebe Rd., Arlington; 3301 Jefferson Davis Hwy., Alexandria; 6224 Richmond Hwy., Alexandria; 1104 W. Broad St., Falls Church; 5801 Leesburg Pike, Baileys Crossroads; 800-378-2753, www.staples.com

MAJOR APPLIANCES

- **Appliance Distributors Unlimited**, 729 Erie Ave., Takoma Park, 301-608-2600; 7405 Alban Station Court, Springfield, 703-866-3000; 14909 Bogle Drive, Chantilly, 703-263-2300; www.adu.com
- **ApplianceLand, Etc.**, 10801 Baltimore Avenue, Beltsville, 301-595-7360; 866 Rockville Pike, Rockville, 301-762-5544; www.appliance land.com
- **Bray & Scarff**, 7924 Wisconsin Ave., Bethesda; 831 Rockville Pike, Rockville; 8610 Cherry Ln., Laurel; 11950 Baltimore Ave., Beltsville; 5715 Lee Hwy., Arlington; 6733 Richmond Hwy., Alexandria; 11015 Lee Hwy., Fairfax; 8486 Tyco Rd., Vienna; 301-470-7500, www.brayand scarff.com

FUTONS & MATTRESSES

- **1-800-Mattress**, 7000 Wisconsin Ave., Bethesda; 905 Washington Blvd. South, Laurel; 10233 Southard Dr., Beltsville; 800-628-8737 or 800-824-7777, www.mattress.com
- **Bedroom Factory Outlet**, 9445 U.S. Route 1, Laurel, 800-800-2378; 515 Baltimore Pike, Bel Air, 888-888-5376; www.bfo.com
- **Ellen's Futon Wholesalers**, 4455 Connecticut Ave. NW; 1050 Rockville Pike, Rockville; 931 Washington Blvd., Laurel; 3000 N. 10th St., Arlington; 516 South Van Dorn Street, Alexandria, 703-823-8127; 10142 Lee Hwy., Fairfax; 11106 Lee Hwy., Fairfax; 703-823-8129, www.ellensfutons.com
- **Market Home Furnishings**, 13048 Fair Lakes Center, Fairfax; 703-222-1200, www.markethomefurnishings.com
- **Mattress Discounters**, 40 locations; 800-289-2233, www.mattress discounters.com
- **Mattress Warehouse**, 4555 Wisconsin Ave. NW; 6930 Wisconsin Ave., Bethesda; 8204 Georgia Ave., Silver Spring; 10165 New Hampshire Ave., Silver Spring; 10100 Colesville Rd., Silver Spring; Boulevard at Capital Centre; 1201 S. Joyce St., Arlington; 382 S. Pickett St., Alexandria; 3517 S. Jefferson St., Baileys Crossroads; Seven Corners Center; 800-233-7253, www.sleephappens.com
- **United Futons**, 13929 Baltimore Ave., Laurel, 301-776-0006; 819 Hungerford Dr., Rockville, 301-315-0222
- **Z Futons & Furniture**, 2130 P St. NW; 5620 General Washington Dr., Alexandria; 866-941-5042, www.zfurniture.com

NEWCOMER'S HANDBOOK FOR MOVING TO AND LIVING IN WASHINGTON D.C.

226

CARPETS, RUGS & TILE

If you don't have time to go to a carpet showroom, **Carpet Discounters** will bring samples to your home; call 301-568-5900 or visit www.carpet discounters.net. Most carpet dealers will make free house calls to provide estimates, and most offer their own financing plans.

- **Best Buy Carpet**, 1401 Chain Bridge Rd., McLean, 703-749-0700, www.bestbuycarpet.com
- **Bill's Carpet Fair**, 10980 Lee Hwy., Fairfax, 703-691-1664, www.bills carpetfair.com
- **Color Tile & Carpetland**, 844 Rockville Pike, Rockville, 301-279-0000
- **Custom Carpet Shop**, 5414 Randolph Rd., Rockville, 301-881-7322, http://customcarpetshop.com
- **Georgetown Carpet**, 2208 Wisconsin Ave. NW, 202-342-2262; 7828 Wisconsin Ave., Bethesda, 301-654-0202
- **Georgetown Floorcoverings**, 3233 K St. NW, 202-965-3200, www.georgetownfloorcoverings.com
- **J&J Oriental Rug Gallery**, 1200 King St., Alexandria, 703-548-0000, www.ssbinc.com/jandj
- **Kemper Carpet**, 12145 Rockville Pike, 301-231-6300; 1524 Spring Hill Rd., McLean, 703-467-9297
- **Ken's Carpet Corner**, 2662 University Blvd., Wheaton, 301-949-0550
- **Manoukian Brothers**, 1862 Columbia Rd. NW, 202-332-0700
- **Mark Keshishian & Sons**, 4505 Stanford St., Chevy Chase, 301-654-4044, www.orientalcarpets.net
- **Mill Direct Floor Coverings**, 8446 Lee Hwy., Fairfax, 703-698-0002
- **Parivizian**, 7034 Wisconsin Ave., Bethesda, 301-654-8989; 8065 Leesburg Pike, Tysons Corner, 703-749-9090; Landmark Mall, 703-750-0404
- **Park Carpet**, 4748 Lee Hwy., Arlington, 703-524-7275

FURNITURE

Retailers of traditional fine furniture advertise heavily in the *Washington Post* Sunday magazine and *Washingtonian*. For vintage, funky, or avant-garde styles, check out the Adams Morgan and U Street boutiques that advertise in the *City Paper*.

- **Apartment Zero**, 406 7th Street NW, 202-628-4067, www.apart mentzero.com; sleek, artistic modern furniture
- **Carolina Furniture Gallery**, Georgia & Missouri avenues NW, 202-722-1900; modern styles at moderate prices
- **Danker Furniture**, 1582 Rockville Pike, Rockville, 301-881-6010; 1211 S. Fern St., Arlington, 703-416-0200; 10670 Lee Hwy., Fairfax, 703-691-4333; www.danker-furniture.com; elegant contemporary designs

- **England Custom Furniture Direct**, 10901 Georgia Ave., Wheaton, 301-942-3008; 202 Kentlands Blvd., Gaithersburg, 301-208-2121; www.englandcfd.com; bedding and imported tables
- **Ethan Allen Gallery**, 1800 Rockville Pike, 301-984-4360; 2900 Wilson Blvd., Arlington, 703-971-4504; 8520 Leesburg Pike, Vienna, 703-356-6405; www.ethanallen.com; early American furniture
- **Expo Design Center**, 7111 Westlake Terrace, Bethesda, 301-767-3400; 11181 Lee Hwy., Fairfax, 703-691-2433; www.expo.com; complete rooms and coverings
- **Good Wood**, 1428 U St. NW, 202-986-3640; select vintage and restored wooden furniture
- **Haverty's**, 4510 Mitchellville Rd., Bowie, 464-5415; 11151 Lee Hwy., Fairfax, 703-934-0263; 21085 Dulles Town Circle, 703-444-0944; www.havertys.com; complete furniture and design showroom
- **Home Rule**, 1807 14th St. NW, 202-797-5544; helps trendy Logan Circle residents outfit vintage downtown homes
- **IKEA**, 10100 Baltimore Ave., College Park; 800-434-4532, www.ikea-usa.com; huge selection of inexpensive, stylish, sturdy, mostly wood furniture to be assembled from simple kits
- **Jennifer Convertibles**, 1634 Wisconsin Ave. NW, 202-342-5496; 3302 M St. NW, 202-333-0080; 11520 Rockville Pike, Rockville, 301-984-3490; 18306 Contour Rd., Gaithersburg, 301-670-0793; 8849 Greenbelt Rd., Greenbelt, 301-552-4144; 3230 Donnell Dr., Forestville, Md., 301-420-0425; 8150 Leesburg Pike, Vienna, 703-556-0802; 3501 South Jefferson St., Baileys Crossroads, 703-931-8933; www.jenniferfurniture.com; modular pieces that can be arranged to fit any living room
- **LA-Z-BOY Furniture Galleries**, 5060 Nicholson Ln., North Bethesda, 301-770-1658; 6003 Kingstown Village, Alexandria, 703-971-5065; 10900 Lee Hwy., Fairfax, 703 273-6133; www.lazboy.com; recliners, sofas and sleep sofas
- **Marlo**, 725 Rockville Pike, Rockville; 15450 Baltimore Ave., Laurel; 3300 Marlo Ln., Forestville, Md.; 5650 General Washington Dr., Alexandria; (301) 735-2087, www.marlofurniture.com; traditional and contemporary discount room sets
- **Reincarnations Furnishings**, 1401 14th Street NW, 202-319-1606, www.reincarnationsfurnishings.com; sells carefully restored antique pieces
- **RoomStore**, 1150 Rockville Pike, Rockville, 301-762-6164; 7970 Annapolis Rd., New Carrollton, Md., 301-577-9500; 4350 Branch Ave., Marlow Heights, Md., 301-423-5464; 13055 Lee-Jackson Hwy., Fairfax, 703-378-3147; Seven Corners Center, 703-237-5364; 7031 Columbia Pike, Annandale, 703-941-1800; www.roomstore.com; discount ensembles

NEWCOMER'S HANDBOOK FOR MOVING TO AND LIVING IN WASHINGTON D.C.

228

- **Scan**, 1800 Rockville Pike, Rockville; 7311 Arlington Blvd., Falls Church; 45633 Dulles Eastern Plaza, Sterling, Va.; 800-386-0989, www.scan furniture.com; modern wood furniture in Scandinavian styles
- **Saah's Furniture**, 2330 Columbia Pike, Arlington, 703-920-1500; 5641 General Washington Drive, 703-256-4315; www.saahfurniture.com; unfinished wood pieces awaiting custom stains and treatments
- **Skynear & Co.**, 2122 18th St. NW; 202-797-7160, www.skynearon line.com; funky and elegant modern furnishings, including direct imports at bargain prices
- **Storehouse**, 1526 14th St. NW; 6700 Wisconsin Ave., Bethesda; 8519 Georgia Ave., Silver Spring; 1775 Rockville Pike, Rockville; 13 Grand Corner Ave., Gaithersburg; 1101 S. Joyce St., Arlington; 809 S. Washington St., Alexandria; Tysons Corner; 10986 Lee Hwy., Fairfax; 7505 Leesburg Pike, Falls Church; 888-786-7346, www.storehouse furniture.com; ergonomically advanced leather furniture
- **Theodore's**, 2233 Wisconsin Ave. NW; 202-333-2300, www. theodores.com; sleek, modern designer pieces

HOUSEWARES & LINENS

If the department stores don't have just what you're looking for, these spe-
cialty stores might:
- **Anthropologie**, 11500 Rockville Pike, North Bethesda, 301-230-6520; Tysons Galleria, 703-288-4387; www.anthropologie.com; ornamental pieces and furnishings with a Southwestern flair
- **Appalachian Spring**, 1415 Wisconsin Ave. NW, 202-337-5780; Union Station, 202-682-0505; 1641 Rockville Pike, 301-230-1380; 102 W. Jefferson St., Falls Church, 703-533-0930; fine pottery and wood accessories
- **April Cornell**, 3278 M St. NW, 202-625-7887; 1100 S. Hayes St., Arlington, 703-415-2290; Tysons Corner, 703-448-6972; www.april cornell.com; linens and ornamental pieces
- **The Container Store**, 4500 Wisconsin Ave. NW; Congressional Plaza; 2800 Clarendon Blvd., Arlington; Tysons Corner; 888-266-8246, www.containerstore.com; guess what they sell.
- **Chesapeake Knife & Tool**, Georgetown Park; Montgomery Mall; Lakeforest Mall; Fair Oaks Mall; Springfield Mall; Tysons Corner; Dulles Town Center; National Airport; Dulles Airport; 800-531-1168, www.chesapeakeknifeandtool.com; sells and sharpens fine cutlery. (It's also a gift shop. The airport locations do *not* sell or sharpen cutlery.)
- **Crate & Barrel**, 4820 Massachusetts Ave. NW; Montgomery Mall; Tysons Corner; 2800 Clarendon Blvd., Arlington; 1700 Prince St.,

Alexandria; 800-967-6696, www.crateandbarrel.com; mainly known for housewares, the Tysons Corner store carries modern and country traditional furniture.

- **Dean & DeLuca** (see Food, p.234); the gourmet food store has a good kitchenware department at its Georgetown location.
- **Finewares**, 7042 Carroll Ave., Takoma Park, 301-270-3138, pottery and craft pieces by local artisans on consignment
- **Hinckley Pottery**, 1707 Kalorama Rd. NW; 202-745-7055, www.hinckleypottery.com; fine handmade pottery—and classes
- **Linens 'n Things**, 5333 Wisconsin Ave. NW; 4710 Cherry Hill Rd., College Park; 1201 S. Hayes St., Arlington; 866-568-7378, www.lnt.com; huge line of housewares and accessories at moderate prices (and 20% discount coupons in the *Post* almost every Sunday)
- **Pier One Imports**, 4455 Connecticut Ave. NW; 6801 Wisconsin Ave., Chevy Chase; 8510 Fenton St., Silver Spring; 1590 Rockville Pike, Rockville; 30 Grand Corner Ave., Gaithersburg; 7573 Greenbelt Rd., Greenbelt; Boulevard at Capital Centre; 3401 Ft. Meade Rd., Laurel; 4410 Mitchellville Rd., Bowie; 4349 Duke St., Alexandria; 3901 Jefferson Davis Hwy., Alexandria; 11210 James Swart Circle, Fairfax; 5857 Leesburg Pike, Falls Church; 7253 Arlington Blvd., Falls Church; 8311 Leesburg Pike, Vienna; 6751 Frontier Dr., Springfield; 800-245-4595, www.pier1.com; wide range of housewares and linens
- **Platypus**, Georgetown Park, 202-338-7680; elegant accent pieces including wine racks and fine glassware
- **Pottery Barn**, 3077 M St. NW; Chevy Chase Pavilion; White Flint; 2700 Clarendon Blvd., Arlington; Tysons Galleria; Fair Oaks Mall; 11937 Market St., Reston; 888-779-5176, www.potterybarn.com; comfortable and well-made home furnishings and kitchenware
- **Restoration Hardware**, 1222 Wisconsin Ave. NW; 614 King St., Alexandria; Tysons Corner; 800-910-9836, www.restoration hardware.com; ornamental fixtures and knickknacks as well as old-fashioned tools
- **Rodman's**, 5100 Wisconsin Ave. NW, 202-363-3466; 4301 Randolph Rd., Wheaton, 301-946-3100; www.rodmans.com; sells housewares, small appliances, and groceries under one roof
- **SteinMart**, 5345 Wisconsin Ave. NW; 202-363-7075, www.stein mart.com; discount source of upscale furniture and apparel
- **Tuesday Morning**, 13832 Georgia Ave., Silver Spring, 301-871-6207; Congressional Plaza, 240-221-0606; 353 Muddy Branch Rd., Gaithersburg, 301-921-9542; 15530 Annapolis Rd., Bowie, 301-262-0853; 131 Bowie Rd., Laurel, 301-953-7907; 6140 Rose Hill Dr., Alexandria, 703-922-5718; 3501 Carlin Springs Rd., Baileys Crossroads,

NEWCOMER'S HANDBOOK FOR MOVING TO AND LIVING IN WASHINGTON D.C.

230

703-845-3710; 136 Maple Ave. W, Vienna, 703-938-6707; 6230 Rolling Rd., Springfield, 703-866-0379; www.tuesdaymorning.com; housewares discount outlet

- **Williams-Sonoma**, Mazza Gallerie; White Flint; Pentagon City; Fair Oaks Mall; Tysons Corner; Tysons Galleria; 2700 Clarendon Blvd., Arlington; 825 S. Washington St., Alexandria; 11897 Market St., Reston; 877-812-6235, www.williams-sonoma.com; high-end cookware and hard-to-find utensils
- **World Market**, 11818 Rockville Pike, Rockville; 20904 Frederick Rd., Germantown; 1301 S. Joyce St., Arlington; Kingstowne Towne Center, Alexandria; Dulles Eastern Plaza, Sterling; 12993 Fair Lakes Pkwy., Fairfax; 3532 S. Jefferson St., Falls Church; Tysons Corner; 800-267-8758, www.worldmarket.com; like an upscale Wal-Mart, sells elegant furnishings, wine, and gourmet packaged goods

Also visit the **Sugarloaf Crafts Festival**, held three times a year in Gaithersburg, Chantilly, Manassas, and the Maryland state fairgrounds in Timonium (north of Baltimore). More than 300 artisans gather from all over the United States and Canada for this major East Coast craft fair. For schedules and information, call 301-253-9620 or visit www.sugar loafcrafts.com.

For home trimmings such as towel racks, doorknobs, switch plates, curtain rods, and doors, check out **The Brass Knob**, which sells salvaged antique architectural elements, at 2311 18th Street NW, 202-332-3370, www.thebrassknob.com. And **Rugs to Riches** sells high-end vintage home furnishings at 116 King Street, Alexandria, 703-739-4662, www.rugstoriches.com.

HARDWARE & GARDEN STORES

No question, Home Depot superstores command a major share of the hardware and garden market in the Washington area. But don't forget the little neighborhood hardware stores scattered around Washington, where the lights are dim and you'll find more nails and hammers than decorator accessories. Carl's at 5700 Georgia Avenue NW and Adams Morgan Hardware at 2200 18th Street NW are true neighborhood institutions—just for example. Check the Yellow Pages or go for a walk to find a gem near you. Here are the major regional home and garden stores:

- **Behnke Nurseries**, 11300 Baltimore Ave., Beltsville, 301-937-1100; 9545 River Rd., Potomac, 301-983-9200; www.behnkes.com
- **Hardware City**, 10504 Connecticut Ave., Kensington, 301-933-2027; 13711 Annapolis Rd., Bowie, 301-464-9030; http://hardware city.doitbest.com

- **Home Depot**, 901 Rhode Island Ave. NE; 3301 East-West Hwy., Hyattsville; 4700 Cherry Hill Rd., College Park; 6003 Oxon Hill Rd., Oxon Hill, Md.; 150 Hampton Park Blvd., Capitol Heights, Md.; 4121 NE Crain Hwy., Bowie; 400 S. Pickett St., Alexandria; Seven Corners Center; 6555 Little River Turnpike, Annandale; 800-553-3199, www.homedepot.com
- **J.H. Burton & Sons Nurseries**, 5950 Ager Road, Hyattsville, 301-559-1100
- **Johnson's Florist & Garden Center**, 4200 Wisconsin Avenue NW, 202-244-6100; 10313 Kensington Pkwy., Kensington, 301-946-6700; 12201 Darnestown Rd., Gaithersburg, 301-948-5650; 5011 Olney-Laytonsville Rd., Olney, 301-987-1940; www.johnsonsflorists.com
- **Lowe's**, 205 Kentlands Blvd., Gaithersburg; 7710 Riverdale Rd., New Carrollton, Md.; 14300 Baltimore Ave., Laurel; 16301 Heritage Blvd., Bowie; 8755 Branch Ave., Clinton; 6750 Richmond Hwy., Alexandria; 13856 Metrotech Dr., Chantilly; 800-445-6937, www.lowes.com
- **Merrifield Garden Center**, 8132 Lee Hwy., Merrifield, 703-560-6222; 12101 Lee Hwy., Fairfax, 703-968-9600; www.merrifieldgarden center.com
- **Roozen Nursery & Garden Center**, 9513 Georgia Ave., Silver Spring, 301-565-9544; 8009 Allentown Rd., Fort Washington; 7610 Little River Turnpike, Annandale, 301-941-2900
- **Smith & Hawken**, 1209 31st St. NW; 8551 Connecticut Ave., Chevy Chase; 6705 Whittier Ave., McLean; 800-940-1170, www.smith-hawken.com
- **Strosniders**, 6930 Arlington Rd., Bethesda, 301-654-5688; 815 Wayne Ave., Silver Spring, 301-565-9150; 10110 River Rd., Potomac, 301-299-6333; www.strosniders.com

Contact Garden Resources of Washington (GROW) at 202-234-0591 or www.growdc.org for information about local garden clubs. Also, the National Arboretum sponsors gardening classes and plant sales—call 202-245-2726 or visit www.usna.usda.gov/Gardens.

SECONDHAND SHOPPING

Washington isn't quite the revolving door people tend to assume it is, but people do come and go as in any major city, and families do move around locally. There's never a shortage of good used furniture, clothing, toys, and even electronics to be found on Craigslist and in the classified ads; in thrift stores; and at the countless yard sales, church bazaars, and flea markets that pop up on sunny weekends like dandelions. One note of caution: always check **Recalls.gov** for safety notices about any secondhand toys or appliances.

NEWCOMER'S HANDBOOK FOR MOVING TO AND LIVING IN WASHINGTON D.C.

232

ANTIQUE DEALERS

"Antiquing" is a favorite weekend pastime in Washington, especially among Georgetown and Northern Virginia homeowners looking to fill their 19th-century homes with period pieces. Antique stores abound in pedigreed neighborhoods like Georgetown and Old Town Alexandria, and prices reflect the refined surroundings. For more affordable antique dealers, head toward Howard Avenue in Kensington and East Diamond Avenue in Gaithersburg—or, for the real troves of antique furniture and decor, go to the old town sections of Ellicott City, Frederick, and Waldorf in Maryland; to Baltimore's Antique Row on North Howard Street; or to the villages of Sperryville and New Market in Virginia.

For vintage clothing, 1950s funk, conversation pieces, and old glassware and housewares, there are a number of vintage shops on 18th Street NW in Adams Morgan and Carroll Avenue in Takoma Park.

Watch the Weekend section of the *Washington Post* on Fridays for listings of antique shows, and the classified ads in the *Post* and *City Paper* for estate sales.

THRIFT & CONSIGNMENT SHOPS

Almost every neighborhood has at least one resale shop. Some are thrift stores, whose merchandise is donated and whose profits benefit a charitable organization; others are consignment shops.

Small resale shops offer bargains on clothing and housewares in particular, and patient scavengers browse forgotten stacks of books and records. The larger shops listed here also handle furniture and small appliances:

- **Amvets**, 6101 Georgia Ave. NW, 202-291-4013
- **Arlington Resale**, 2919 Columbia Pike, Arlington, 703-486-2362
- **Goodwill Industries**, 2200 South Dakota Ave. NE; 4890 Boiling Brook Pkwy., Rockville; 619 S. Frederick Ave., Gaithersburg; 12655 Laurel-Bowie Rd., Laurel; 10 S. Glebe Rd., Arlington; 4714 Columbia Pike, Arlington; 6136 Arlington Blvd., Falls Church; 202-636-4225, www.dcgoodwill.org
- **Salvation Army**, 1375 H St. NE; 11181 Veirs Mill Rd., Wheaton; 7505 New Hampshire Ave., Takoma Park; 3304 Kenilworth Ave., Hyattsville; 4724 Suitland Rd., Suitland; 10350 Guilford Ave., Savage; 6528 Little River Turnpike, Alexandria; 2421 Centreville Rd., Herndon; 14647 Jefferson Davis Hwy., Woodbridge; 301-277-7878 or 703-642-9270, www.satruck.com

- **Rainbow Christian Services Thrift Shop**, 2620 Wilson Blvd., Arlington, 703-243-0239

  For a complete **directory** of Washington-area resale shops, check out the "Living in D.C." page of www.aafsw.org, the Associates of the American Foreign Service Worldwide. Also check out these specialty resellers:
- **Bid4Assets** is the official online auction house for property seized by the U.S. Marshals Service, the IRS, and many state and local governments; www.bid4assets.com.
- **The Community Forklift**, 4671 Tanglewood Dr., Edmonston, sells building materials and fixtures salvaged from construction site surplus or renovations. Call 301-985-5180 or visit www.communityforklift.com to buy or donate materials.
- **Upscale Resale**, 8100 Lee Hwy., Falls Church, sells high-end furniture and furnishings in good or restored condition; 703-698-8100.

  Pawn shops, which sell forfeited collateral from cash loans, can be a source of good deals on cameras, jewelry, musical instruments, and home electronics. Look in the Yellow Pages under "Pawn." Check to make sure a pawnbroker is licensed and bonded; in the District, look for members of the industry's self-monitoring group, the Pawnbrokers Association of D.C.

YARD SALES & FLEA MARKETS

Every weekend, from April through October, telephone poles are festooned with hand-lettered signs pointing to yard sales. These aren't necessarily junk sales—remember, a lot of government families live here and move around as careers unfold. Some yard sales are listed in the classifieds, especially in the local *Journal* or *Gazette* newspapers; devotees scour these ads and get to the sales early. Furniture, musical instruments, cameras, and other prize items are often sold within the first few minutes of a yard sale.

Community flea markets, church bazaars, and multi-family yard sales are listed in the Weekend section of the *Washington Post*; also, there are permanent flea markets in the spring and summer across from Eastern Market, 7th & C streets SE, and in Georgetown, across from the Safeway at 1855 Wisconsin Avenue NW.

CONSUMER RESOURCES—SHOPPING

Before you shop for a houseful of furniture, appliances, and electronics, check out the reviews local businesses have earned for the quality and the price of their goods and services.
- **Washington Consumers' Checkbook**, www.checkbook.org, 202-347-7283; the regional edition of *Consumers' Checkbook*, published by the nonprofit Center for the Study of Services, is a magazine that rates

NEWCOMER'S HANDBOOK FOR MOVING TO AND LIVING IN WASHINGTON D.C.

234

everything from retail stores and restaurants to HMOs and insurance plans. The companion *Bargains* newsletter lists the best prices in town on specific models of appliances and electronics. Findings are sometimes reported in the Style section of the *Washington Post.* Subscribers can take part in consumer-to-consumer message boards; read the online *Guide to Washington Area Restaurants,* with more than 22,000 customer ratings of hundreds of restaurants; read the biweekly newsletter *CarDeals,* which lists car manufacturers' rebates and incentives; and receive discounts on car-shopping services and publications including *Guide to Top Doctors, Hospital Guide,* and *Federal Employees Guide to Health Insurance.* A two-year subscription is $30 for four issues of *Checkbook* magazine, the *Bargains* newsletter, and access to the online resources. Online access only is $25 for two years. For an additional one-time fee of $25, you can view all archived *Checkbook* reports and ratings online as long as you maintain a subscription.

- **Washingtonian** magazine, www.washingtonian.com, offers recent articles and annual features online, including the latest guide to "Cheap Eats," "100 Very Best Restaurants," "Top Doctors," and "Weekend Getaways."

- **Better Business Bureau of Metro Washington D.C.** is a membership association whose goal is to hold the business community to high ethical standards. You can view an online database at www.dc.bbb.org that shows a "satisfactory" rating for companies that do not have an unusual volume or pattern of customer complaints, are not facing serious legal action, and meet certain standards of conduct in responding to customer complaints referred by the organization. Automated help is available 24 hours a day at 202-393-8000.

- **Local referrals**—there is no substitute for a personal review, positive or negative, of a specific business. In the District, the online newsletter *Themail* is read by hundreds of residents who know the city well and care about their neighborhoods. For a virtual earful about the best and worst places to buy a futon, fresh bagels, a car, or a pet guinea pig, send an e-mail message to themail@dcwatch.com asking for recommendations. (Messages to *Themail* are compiled and distributed to subscribers on Sunday and Wednesday nights.)

FOOD

Washington isn't exactly famous for its restaurant scene, but the city deserves more credit than it gets. The District and, increasingly, the suburbs offer enough culinary choices to please any connoisseur exploring cuisines from all over the world. Individual restaurants come and go, but there's always a new bistro or Thai noodle house or vegetarian Tandoori place step-ping up to face the *Washington Post's* food critic, Tom Sietsema.

Neighborhoods like Adams Morgan, Bethesda, Capitol Hill, Clarendon, Dupont Circle, Silver Spring, and Wheaton can keep the most avid restaurant-hopper busy for years, and there are plenty of city slickers who dine out twice a day, every day, and never get bored.

Zagat's Restaurant Survey, available at www.firstbooks.com, com-piles consumer ratings, while the restaurant reviews in the *Washington Post* (in the Food section on Wednesday and in the Sunday magazine) offer more detailed opinions of new restaurants, or old favorites with new chefs. The **Washington Consumers' Checkbook** web site, www.check book.org, also offers restaurant ratings. For a directory of vegetarian restaurants and grocers, contact the **Vegetarian Society of D.C.** at 202-362-8349 or www.vsdc.org. And don't forget the Yellow Pages, where restaurants are listed by cuisine.

It's not only the restaurant scene that has matured in Washington—gro-cery stores, too, are more diverse and sophisticated than they were 20 years ago. In the heart of D.C., from Shaw to Mt. Pleasant, corner grocery stores carry good selections of Asian, Mexican, Salvadoran, and Caribbean items. If you need some *tef* to make traditional Ethiopian *injera*, you can buy it at an Ethiopian market. In a city where there were only three or four gourmet grocery stores in 1980, today there are half a dozen gourmet chains.

There's good local produce, too. For a directory of farmers' markets, community gardens, community-supported agriculture or "farmshare" programs, and other ways to "think globally, eat locally," visit www. communityharvestdc.org (click on Food Network). The informative web site is maintained by **Community Harvest**, a local nonprofit that pro-motes locally grown food with an emphasis on organic and sustainable production. Dozens of neighborhoods have little farmers' markets once or twice a week, but two big markets remain from the bygone days of cav-ernous market halls: Eastern Market on Capitol Hill, and Montgomery County Farm Women's Co-op in Bethesda. From organic peaches and corn to free-range beef and Chesapeake Bay fish, the stalls of these old-fash-ioned markets are a kaleidoscope of the region's purest tastes and aromas.

Finally, in an international city of 3.5 million people, it's no surprise that it's hard to identify a unique local cuisine. New Orleans has its Cajun food and Baltimore has Chesapeake Bay seafood; Philadelphia has its sig-nature dish, cheesesteaks, and Boston has baked beans. In 2000, *Washington Post* readers were invited to nominate a culinary symbol for the city. Inspired by a favorite dish at Ben's Chili Bowl, 1213 U Street NW, the winner was the Washington half-smoke, a grilled kosher sausage served like a hot dog, topped with sauerkraut if you like. Sure enough, in

NEWCOMER'S HANDBOOK FOR MOVING TO AND LIVING IN WASHINGTON D.C.

236

downtown D.C. and along the Mall, ubiquitous vending trucks do a lively business in half-smoke.

And if the half-smoke is the hallmark of the city's cuisine, then the suburbs' answer is *pollo la brasa*. In every neighboring county, the spicy smoke rises from dozens of strip malls where a neighborhood Salvadoran grill has only two things on the menu: grilled half chicken and grilled quarter chicken, served with fries and slaw. The name means "rubbed chicken," and before grilling, it's been rubbed with pepper and spices until it's black on the outside. These are just about the only places in the suburbs where you can eat hearty for less than $5.

SUPERMARKETS

Giant Food and Safeway supermarkets have dozens of locations in the Washington area, and two big Southern chains, Food Lion and Harris Teeter, are making inroads in Virginia. Whole Foods Market stores, specializing in natural and organic foods, serve Northwest D.C., Montgomery County, and Northern Virginia. Shopper's Food Warehouse supermarkets offer slight discounts in a no-frills, no-nonsense shopping environment. Check the Yellow Pages or the advertising supplements to the *Washington Post* on Sundays and Wednesdays.

Some supermarkets in D.C. have earned nicknames: the "Social Safeway" at 1855 Wisconsin Avenue NW, which has a legendary reputation among Georgetown singles, and the "Soviet Safeway" at 17th and Corcoran streets NW, which is notorious for long lines.

In addition to the major chains, there are plenty of local and independent grocery stores, including countless little markets in apartment buildings or office complexes. Here are some of the larger independent stores and gourmet chains:

- **Balducci's**, 3201 New Mexico Ave. NW; 10323 Old Georgetown Rd., Bethesda; 600 Franklin St., Alexandria; 6655 Old Dominion Dr., McLean; 240-403-2440, www.balduccis.com
- **Brookville Supermarket**, 3427 Connecticut Ave. NW, 202-244-9114
- **Dean & DeLuca**, 3276 M St. NW, 202-342-2500, www.dean deluca.com
- **Eighth Street Market**, 419 8th St. SE, 202-548-4919
- **Greenbelt Co-op** (worker-owned), 121 Center Way, Greenbelt, 301-474-0522, www.greenbeltco-op.com
- **Grosvenor Market**, 10401 Grosvenor Place, Bethesda, 301-493-6217
- **Katz's Kosher Supermarket**, 4860 Boiling Brook Parkway, Rockville, 301-468-0400
- **Magruder's**, 5626 Connecticut Avenue NW, 202-244-7800; 3527 Connecticut Ave. NW, 202-237-2531; 15108 N. Frederick Rd., Rockville,

301-315-0703; 602 Quince Orchard Rd., Gaithersburg, 301-948-2165; 6810 Race Track Rd., Bowie, 301-262-8229; 4604 Kenmore Avenue, Alexandria, 703-562-0362; 2800 Graham Rd., Falls Church, 703-280-0440; 7010 Columbia Pike, Annandale, 703-941-8864; 80 Maple Ave. W, Vienna, 703-938-4700; www.magruders.com

- **Rodman's** Discount Gourmet & Wine, 5100 Wisconsin Ave. NW, 202-363-3466; 4301 Randolph Rd., Wheaton, 301-946-3100; 5130 Nicholson Ln., Kensington, 301-881-6253; www.rodmans.com
- **Roland's of Capitol Hill**, 333 Pennsylvania Ave. SE, 202-546-9592
- **Snider's**, 1936 Seminary Rd., Silver Spring, 301-589-3240
- **Trader Joe's**, 6831 Wisconsin Ave., Bethesda; 12268 Rockville Pike, Rockville; 18270 Contour Rd., Gaithersburg; 10741 Columbia Pike, Silver Spring; 612 N. Saint Asaph St., Alexandria; 9464 Main St., Fairfax; 5847 Leesburg Pike, Bailey's Crossroads; 7514 Leesburg Pike, Falls Church; 11958 Killingsworth Ave., Reston; Springfield Mall; 14100 Lee Hwy., Centreville; 800-746-7857, www.traderjoes.com

Several **online grocers** deliver orders at prices competitive with bricks-and-mortar grocery stores, with reasonable delivery fees. For a minimum order of $50, **Peapod**, www.peapod.com, will deliver your groceries the next day, within a two-hour period you select. Bulk quantities of premium items, such as free-range organic meat, are available from **Horizon**, www.horizonfoods.com, and **King Arthur Flour**, www.kingarthurflour.com, delivers top-quality baking ingredients.

WAREHOUSE STORES

Membership warehouses have low prices on groceries and other household goods, but only in much larger volumes than you would buy at an ordinary grocery store. Don't expect much service, either—some of these stores keep prices low by not hiring baggers, loaders or delivery people. You'll need a membership card to shop at a membership warehouse. Household memberships are available for a fee if you can't get a free card through an employer, union, military base or other institution that has a group membership.

- **Costco**, 10925 Baltimore Ave., Beltsville; 880 Russell Avenue, Gaithersburg, 301-417-1503; 1200 South Fern St., Arlington; 4725 West Ox Rd., Fairfax, 703-802-0372; 7373 Boston Blvd., Springfield; 800-774-2678, www.costco.com
- **Sam's Club**, 610 N. Frederick Ave., Gaithersburg, 301-216-2550; 3535 Russet Green East, Laurel; 888-746-7726, www.samsclub.com
- **Wonder Bread & Hostess Cakes Outlet**, 3110 Hamilton St., Hyattsville, 301-853-2180

NEWCOMER'S HANDBOOK FOR MOVING TO AND LIVING IN WASHINGTON D.C.

238

ORGANIC FOOD & LOCAL PRODUCE

Washingtonians have discovered, over the past decade or two, that good food is worth a little extra money. With the emergence of Whole Foods Markets and Balducci's (which acquired the venerable local Sutton Place Gourmet chain), traditional supermarkets have been forced to expand their offerings of natural and organic foods, though probably not enough for shoppers who put a premium on organic items. If your local supermarket doesn't have everything you need, try these specialty shops:

- **Becraft's Farm Produce**, 14722 New Hampshire Ave., Silver Spring, 301-236-4545
- **Bethesda Co-op**, 6500 Seven Locks Rd., Bethesda, 301-320-2530
- **Cash Grocer Natural Foods**, 1315 King St., Alexandria, 703-549-9544, www.cashgrocer.com
- **Country Boy**, 2211 Randolph Road, Glenmont, 301-942-6355
- **DeBaggio's Herb Farm & Nursery**, 43494 Mountain View Dr., Chantilly, 703-327-6976
- **Ecology Health Food**, 8200 Fenton Street, Silver Spring, 301-589-8474
- **Everlasting Life**, 2928 Georgia Ave. NW, 202-232-1700; 9185 Central Ave., Capitol Heights, Md., 301-324-6900; www.everlastinglife.net
- **Glut Food Co-op**, 4005 34th St., Mt. Rainier, 301-779-1978, www.glut.org
- **The Greenhouse at Washington National Cathedral**, Wisconsin & Massachusetts avenues NW, 202-537-6263, www.cathedral.org/cathedral/shop
- **Heyser Farms**, 14526 New Hampshire Avenue, Silver Spring, 301-384-7859
- **Maryland Food Collective**, Stamp Student Union Building, University of Maryland, College Park, 301-314-8089, www.student org.umd.edu/ffc
- **MOM's (My Organic Market)**, 11711 Parklawn Drive, Rockville, 301-816-4944; 9827 Rhode Island Ave., College Park, 301-220-1100; 3831 Mt. Vernon Ave., Alexandria, 703-535-5980; www.myorganicmarket.com
- **Montgomery County Farm Women's Cooperative Market**, 7155 Wisconsin Ave., Bethesda, 301-652-2291
- **Potomac Adventist Book & Health Food Store**, 12004 Cherry Hill Rd., Silver Spring, 301-572-0700
- **Senbeb Natural Foods**, 5922 Georgia Ave. NW, 202-723-5566
- **Smile Herb Shop**, 4908 Berwyn Road, College Park, 301-474-8791, www.smileherb.com
- **Takoma Park-Silver Spring Co-op**, 201 Ethan Allan Ave., Takoma Park, 301-891-2667; 8309 Grubb Rd., Silver Spring, 240-247-2667; www.tpss.coop

- **Wellness Cafe**, 325 Pennsylvania Ave. SE, 202-543-2266, www.wellness cafedc.com
- **Yes! Organic Market**, 1825 Columbia Road NW, 202-462-5150; 3425 Connecticut Avenue NW, 202-363-1559; 658 Pennsylvania Avenue SE, 202-546-9850

FARMERS' MARKETS

Farmers' markets enable you to skip the middleman and buy fresh produce from the people who grew it. It's all locally produced, a lot of it is organic, and it's usually much less expensive than comparable goods in stores. Dozens of neighborhoods in the District and suburbs have their own weekly farmers' markets, at least from May through November, and so do a few of the larger federal office buildings. **Community Harvest** keeps a list at www.communityharvestdc.org (click on Food Network). One venerable old market deserves special mention: the cavernous red brick hall of **Eastern Market**, 7th & C streets SE, where local farmers, butchers, dairies, and fishermen have peddled their wares since 1873; call 202-544-0083 or visit www.easternmarketdc.com. Also check out the **Maine Avenue Fish Market** on the Southwest waterfront, 202-479-4188.

COMMUNITY GARDENS

If your yard is too small for a vegetable patch, you can sign up for a plot at a community garden. Some offer community-owned tools and some are bring-your-own. Many vacant lots are being converted into shared gardens; contact Garden Resources of Washington at 202-234-0591 or www.grow dc.org for a list or to find out whether any new sites are available near you.

COMMUNITY-SUPPORTED AGRICULTURE

In a community-supported agriculture (CSA) program, consumers buy shares of a year's harvest directly from the farmer. You pay a fee in the spring, and throughout the harvest season, you'll receive a certain volume of just-picked produce every week. In some CSAs, consumers go to the farm to pick up weekly crates; in others, farmers will make drop-offs at central locations in the city or suburbs. Most CSAs sell shares by the bushel, and only the largest households can use a whole bushel of fruits and vegetables every week; but if you split a share with a few neighbors or co-workers, this can be an inexpensive and healthy way to get fresh produce. For a current CSA directory, visit www.communityharvestdc.org and click on Food Network.

W ASHINGTON IS A WORLD CITY, A DIVERSE CAPITAL WITH HIGHER-
than-average levels of education and disposable income, prestigious venues, and influential audiences. Every performing artist
wants to play here and every visual artist wants to be installed here. The
D.C. area also offers the world plenty of homegrown local talent, from the
late Duke Ellington to Fugazi, from the Starland Vocal Band (remember
"Afternoon Delight"?) to Chuck Brown. On canvas, in clay, and in all kinds
of innovative mixed media, local visual artists work their magic in studios in
a converted old torpedo factory in Alexandria and funky galleries off
Dupont Circle or 7th Street NW. World-class symphonies, operas, and bal-
lets grace the Kennedy Center and Wolf Trap, while the works of Vermeer
and Toulouse-Lautrec pass through the National Gallery. Some of the
world's most popular museums and most important libraries are here at
your disposal. Film festivals and repertory houses, including the American
Film Institute, bring the best and the boldest in cinema to D.C. audiences.
And every December, with the President on hand, the nation bestows its
highest tribute to living artists of all kinds: the Kennedy Center Honors,
often described as the American equivalent of knighthood.

All of the major museums, theaters, and arts organizations offer special
programs for children, ranging from hands-on exhibits and kid-friendly
guided tours to afterschool programs and summer day camps. If your kids
show interest in a particular subject or medium, visit the web site of the
related institution and you'll find plenty of stimulating activities; if you want
to scan the full range of children's cultural activities in the area, check out
the "Saturday's Child" pages of the *Washington Post*'s Weekend section.

Best of all, a lot of this is free. The Smithsonian museums, the Festival
of American Folklife, the Library of Congress and dozens of specialty
libraries—all this belongs to you. Screen on the Green, Shakespeare Free for

NEWCOMER'S HANDBOOK FOR MOVING TO AND LIVING IN WASHINGTON D.C.

242

All, Arts On Foot, and other annual events are gifts to the public from sponsoring businesses and government partners. And every day of the year, at 6 p.m., Millennium Stage offers a free performance at the Kennedy Center—just a sample of the rich kaleidoscope of the arts in Washington.

WHAT'S GOING ON

The most complete listings of upcoming events in the performing arts, as well as exhibit openings and closings, are in the Weekend section of the *Washington Post* (published on Fridays) and the *Washington City Paper.* The Weekend section even lists auditions and casting calls, on the "Guide to the Lively Arts" page, and in late May an edition is devoted to the definitive list of every concert scheduled within 100 miles during the summer. For book signings and other literary events, check out the Book World section of the *Washington Post* on Sundays. There are also extensive listings online at www.potomacstages.com and national theater sites such as www.curtainrising.com, www.curtainup.com, and www.theatermania.com.

To help you get your bearings in one of the most historic and diverse cities in the modern world, check out:

- **BeyondGuide**, 866-334-8533, www.beyondguide.com; audio tours of historic sites in D.C. are sent to your cell phone—so you can listen to historic speeches while standing at the sites where they were made, or follow a narrated tour of historic hotels and churches. Free samples available.
- **Cultural Tourism D.C.**, 202-661-7581, www.culturaltourismdc.org; this coalition of arts, history and civic organizations publishes walking tours of historic neighborhoods.
- **National Register of Historic Places**, www.cr.nps.gov/nr; the nation's definitive catalog of important landmarks.

For additional self-guided tours, check out the printed guides listed in **A D.C. Reading List**.

TICKETS

If you go directly to the box office to buy your tickets, you'll save some money on handling fees, but if you want the convenience of buying tickets over the phone or online, there are a few options:

- **TicketMaster** sells tickets to almost every event in town. To order tickets or find a local retail outlet, visit www.ticketmaster.com or call the local number: in D.C., 202-397-7328; Maryland, 410-547-7328; Virginia, 703-573-7328; from other area codes, 800-551-7328.
- **Tickets.com** also sells tickets online to most live performance venues in the area.

- **Ticketplace**, 407 7th Street NW, www.ticketplace.org, sells same-day tickets for half price—a good option if you're flexible and don't mind making last-minute plans. No phone sales; you can buy tickets online between noon and 4 p.m. Tuesday-Friday or at the box office 11 a.m. to 6 p.m. Tuesday-Friday and 10 a.m. to 5 p.m. Saturday. (Sunday tickets are sold on Saturdays, when available.)
- The **Washington Performing Arts Society**, 202-785-9727, www.wpas.org, sells tickets to dozens of special performances in and around Washington and has a membership program offering discounts and VIP ticket services.
- **Fandango** sells movie tickets online, www.fandango.com, and by phone, 800-326-3264, for a small fee.

Most venues offer discounts for students, seniors, and members of the affiliated arts organizations. (You can "join" the Kennedy Center or the Smithsonian, for example; although no membership is required to attend events, members get discounts, preferred seating, VIP receptions, and other insider perks.)

MUSEUMS & GALLERIES

To 19 million visitors each year, Washington is a city of monuments and museums. The monuments need no introduction—you'll recognize them from the coins in your pocket and, with the exception of free timed-entry tickets to the Washington Monument, you can walk right into them any time. The dozens of world-class museums here, however, take some more planning and navigating. All but the smallest offer guided tours, and many offer headsets with recorded narratives on them. And many of the most popular museums are free, so jump in and start exploring.

THE SMITHSONIAN

Philanthropist James Smithson's gift to the United States in 1836 was a fund intended to promote "the increase and diffusion of knowledge among men." Today, the **Smithsonian Institution** operates 17 museums (16 in D.C. and one in New York City), plus the National Zoo; a satellite branch of the Air & Space Museum in Chantilly, Va.; a satellite branch of the American Indian Museum in New York City; and conservation facilities in Suitland, Md., and Front Royal, Va. (Two ways to mark yourself as a permanent tourist and never a real Washingtonian: say "Smithsonian Institute" or ask for directions to "the Smithsonian"—remember, it's not a place, it's an organization. You can ask, or give, directions to a specific museum.)

All of the Smithsonian museums in D.C. are open every day except Christmas, 10 a.m. to 5:30 p.m., and admission is free—after all, you own

NEWCOMER'S HANDBOOK FOR MOVING TO AND LIVING IN WASHINGTON D.C.

244

them. Some special exhibits require "timed entry" tickets to prevent over-crowding, and you can pick up the tickets at the museum the same day or order them in advance for a small fee. Also, there's an admission fee for the large-format IMAX movies and planetarium shows at the Air & Space Museum and the movies at the Natural History Museum.

The Smithsonian is also a record label, publishing a vast catalog of folk and world music; a publishing house, with a thick monthly magazine and thousands of book titles; a tour company, leading culturally sensitive educational trips all over the world; and the organizer of the annual Festival of American Folklife, a lively showcase of cultural heritage held in tent cities on the Mall for two weeks before the Fourth of July. The museums sometimes stay open late for movies, lectures, concerts, or receptions.

For more information about the Smithsonian, call 202-633-1000 (or 202-357-2020 for recorded information) or visit www.si.edu. The Smithsonian facilities in the D.C. area are:

- **Anacostia Museum**: Exhibits about African-American culture in the nation's capital and the Smithsonian Center for African American History & Culture. 1901 Fort Place SE. Note: Unlike the other Smithsonian museums, closes at 5 p.m.
- **Arts & Industries Building**: Originally the National Museum; houses permanent exhibits from the Centennial Exposition in 1876 and temporary exhibits about the Industrial Revolution. South side of the Mall at 9th Street SW.
- **Freer & Sackler Galleries**: The Freer building and the underground Sackler Gallery, connected by an underground passage, jointly house Asian, Middle Eastern, and Egyptian art as well as Charles Lang Freer's collection of the works of James McNeill Whistler. The Freer is on the south side of the Mall at 12th St. SW; direct entrance to the Sackler is at 1050 Independence Ave. SW.
- **Hirshhorn Museum & Sculpture Garden**: The distinctive dough-nut-shaped Hirshhorn building houses contemporary painting, sculpture, and mixed-media artwork, and the Sculpture Garden across Jefferson Drive is a sunken courtyard full of modern installations. (Not to be confused with the National Gallery's sculpture garden across the Mall.) South side of the Mall at 7th St. SW.
- **National Air & Space Museum**: two locations. The original Air & Space Museum on the Mall (between 4th & 7th streets SW) is the most popular museum in the world, housing the Wright Flyer I, the Spirit of St. Louis, the Friendship VII and Apollo XI spacecraft, and a Moon rock you can touch. The Steven F. Udvar-Hazy Center in Chantilly, which opened in 2003 on the 100th anniversary of powered flight, houses the original space shuttle, the SR-71 Blackbird spy plane, the B-29 Enola Gay, and the first passenger jet. Parking at the Udvar-Hazy Center is

$12; there are shuttle buses from the Mall with a round-trip fare of $12 with discounts for seniors and groups. Call 202-633-4629 or visit www.nasm.si.edu for bus schedules and details.

- **National Museum of African Art**: Underground galleries house artwork, pottery, jewelry, and spiritual artifacts from every region of Africa. Entrance on the south side of the Mall between 9th & 10th streets SW.
- **National Museum of American Art**: Houses the federal art collection started in 1829, representing American artists of all periods and styles. 750 9th St. NW
- **National Museum of American History**: Home of the Star-Spangled Banner, Jefferson's writing desk, Lincoln's hat, the inaugural gowns of the First Ladies, and the only surviving gunboat from the American Revolution—plus generations of political memorabilia, industrial technology, and pop culture artifacts including Archie & Edith Bunker's chairs, Dorothy's ruby slippers, The Fonz's jacket, and Kermit the Frog. On the north side of the Mall at 14th St. NW.
- **National Museum of the American Indian**: two locations. The main museum on the Mall (south side at 4th St. SW) houses artifacts from the first peoples of the Americas—and works to repatriate illegally acquired artifacts of a culturally significant nature, such as human remains and religious items, to the first nations. The museum's **George Gustav Heye Center** is in New York City.
- **National Museum of Natural History**: Best known for the Hope Diamond, this is also a classic science museum with dinosaur skeletons, fossils, stone tools, and even a preserved giant squid. Also houses the Orkin Insect Zoo, where you can watch daily scorpion feedings and see roaches that make the local pests look tiny. Under the distinctive green dome on the north side of the Mall at 10th St. NW.
- **National Portrait Gallery**: Home of historic portraits of great Americans, but best known for the Hall of Presidents and Gilbert Stuart's Lansdowne portrait of George Washington. 8th & F streets NW (adjacent to the Museum of American Art).
- **National Zoological Park**: Houses the Smithsonian's collection of live animals and related scientific programs. (See **Greenspace**.) In Rock Creek Park at 3001 Connecticut Ave. NW.
- **Postal Museum**: Houses some 6 million postage stamps, historic letters, and artifacts tracing the history of written communication in the United States. 2 Massachusetts Ave. NE, near Union Station.
- **Renwick Gallery**: American crafts and decorative arts housed in the historic building designed for the city's first art museum. 17th St. & Pennsylvania Ave. NW.

NEWCOMER'S HANDBOOK FOR MOVING TO AND LIVING IN WASHINGTON D.C.

246

- **S. Dillon Ripley Center**: Academic building for Smithsonian research programs and lectures, with some gallery space for temporary exhibits. Located underground near the Castle (see below) with entrance on the south side of the Mall at 11th St. SW.
- **Smithsonian Institution Building**: better known as "the Castle," this red sandstone citadel is the headquarters of the Smithsonian Institution and a good first stop for general information. (The visitor center opens at 8:30 every morning except Christmas.) Receptions and special events are also held here. South side of the Mall at 10th St. SW.

You can easily spend a whole lifetime in Washington and never see all of the Smithsonian's museum exhibits; still, overwhelmingly, there's more. Check out:

- **Smithsonian Folkways** recordings, www.folkways.si.edu
- **Festival of American Folklife**, www.folklife.si.edu (see **A Washington Year**)
- **Smithsonian Journeys**, educational travel, http://smithsonian journeys.org
- **Smithsonian Associates**, membership organization offering special events and discounts at Smithsonian museum shops, www.si.edu/membership

OTHER MUSEUMS & GALLERIES

Unless otherwise noted, these are private museums with either an admission fee or a strongly "suggested" donation. Why no detailed descriptions here? Because you're not a tourist anymore—you live here, and this isn't a tourist guide, it's a relocation guide to help you get settled. So get more information where the locals do: the *Post* and the *City Paper* list temporary exhibits and special programs, and if you want to know more about a particular museum, you have plenty of opportunities to *go*!

- **Alexandria Archaeology Museum**, at the Torpedo Factory Art Center, 703-838-4399, www.alexandriaarchaeology.org
- **Alexandria Black History Museum**, 638 N. Alfred St., Alexandria 703-838-4356, http://oha.ci.alexandria.va.us/bhrc
- **Art Museum of the Americas**, Organization of American States, 201 18th St. NW, 202-458-6016, www.museum.oas.org, free
- **Arts Club of Washington**, 2017 I St. NW, 202-331-7282, http://artsclubofwashington.org
- **Black Fashion Museum**, 2007 Vermont Ave. NW, 202-667-0744, www.bfmdc.org (appointment only)
- **B'nai B'rith Klutznick National Jewish Museum**, 1640 Rhode Island Ave. NW, 202-857-6583, www.bnaibrith.org. Appointment only.

- **City Museum of Washington**, 801 K St. NW, 202-383-1850, www.citymuseumdc.org
- **College Park Aviation Museum**, 1985 Cpl. Frank Scott Dr., College Park, 301-864-6029, www.pgparks.com
- **Collingwood Library & Museum on Americanism**, 8301 East Boulevard Dr., Alexandria, 703-765-1652, www.collingwoodlibrary.com
- **Corcoran Gallery of Art**, 500 17th St. NW, 202-639-1700, www.corcoran.org
- **D.C. Arts Center**, 2438 18th St. NW, 202- 462-7833, www.dcartscenter.org. Free.
- **Discovery Creek Children's Museum**, Glen Echo Park, Bethesda, 202-364-3111, www.discoverycreek.org
- **Fondo del Sol Visual Arts Center**, 2112 R St. NW, 202-483-2777, www.dkmuseums.com/fondo.html
- **Ft. Ward**, W. Braddock Rd., Alexandria 703-838-4848, oha.ci.alexandria.va.us/fortward
- **Friendship Firehouse Museum**, 107 S. Alfred St., Alexandria, 703-838-3891, http://oha.ci.alexandria.va.us/friendship
- **Gadsby's Tavern**, 134 N. Royal St., Alexandria, 703-838-4242, www.gadsbystavern.org
- **Glen Echo Park**, Goldsboro Rd. & MacArthur Blvd. Bethesda, 301-634-2222, www.glenechopark.org
- **International Spy Museum**, 800 F St. NW, 202-393-7798, www.spymuseum.org
- **The Lyceum** (local history museum), 201 S. Washington St., Alexandria, 703-838-4994, http://oha.ci.alexandria.va.us/lyceum
- **Montpelier Cultural Arts Center**, 12826 Laurel-Bowie Rd., Laurel, 301-953-1993, www.pgparks.com
- **National Aquarium**, U.S. Department of Commerce, 14th St. & Constitution Ave. NW, 202-482-2825, www.nationalaquarium.com
- **National Building Museum**, 401 F St. NW, 202-272-2448, www.nbm.org
- **National Capital Trolley Museum**, 1313 Bonifant Rd., Silver Spring, 301-384-6088, www.dctrolley.org
- **National Children's Museum**, slated to open in 2008 at L'Enfant Plaza, 202-675-4120, www.ncm.museum
- **National Cryptologic Museum**, Ft. Meade, Odenton, 301-88-5849, www.nsa.gov/museum. Free.
- **National Gallery of Art**, 202-737-4215, www.nga.gov. East Wing (modern art) is on the north side of the Mall between 3rd & 4th streets NW; West Wing (Enlightenment through 19th century) between 4th & 7th; Sculpture Garden between 7th & 9th. Free.

NEWCOMER'S HANDBOOK FOR MOVING TO AND LIVING IN WASHINGTON D.C.

248

- **National Geographic Museum**, 17th & M streets NW, 202-857-7588, www.nationalgeographic.com/museum. Free.
- **National Museum of American Jewish Military History**, 1811 R St. NW, 202-265-6280, www.nmajmh.org
- **National Museum of Health & Medicine**, Walter Reed Army Medical Center, 6900 Georgia Ave., 202-782-2200, nmhm.washington dc.museum. Free.
- **National Museum of Women in the Arts**, 1250 New York Ave. NW, 202-783-5000, www.nmwa.org
- **Newseum**, slated to open in 2006 at 6th St. & Pennsylvania Ave. NW, 888-639-7386, www.newseum.org
- **Phillips Collection** (American & European art), 1600 21st St. NW, 202-387-2151, www.phillipscollection.org
- **Pierce Mill & Art Barn**, in Rock Creek Park at Beach Drive & Tilden St. NW, 202-895-6070, www.nps.gov/rocr. Free.
- **Radio-Television Museum**, 2608 Mitchellville Road, 301-390-1020, www.radiohistory.org
- **Rockville Arts Place**, 9300 Gaither Rd., Gaithersburg, 301-869-8623, www.rockvilleartsplace.org
- **Lillian & Albert Small Museum of Jewish History**, 600 I St. NW (archives), 3rd & G streets NW (synagogue), 202-789-0900, www. jhsgw.org
- **Charles Sumner School Museum & Archives**, 1201 17th St. NW, 202-442-6046. Free.
- **Textile Museum**, 2320 S St. NW, 202-667-0441, www.textile museum.org
- **Torpedo Factory Art Center**, 105 N. Union St., Alexandria, 703-838-4565, www.torpedofactory.org. Free.
- **U.S. Holocaust Memorial Museum**, 100 Raoul Wallenberg Place SW, 202-488-0400, www.ushmm.org. Free; timed entry tickets required for main exhibit.
- **George Washington National Masonic Memorial**, 101 Callahan Dr., Alexandria, 703-683-2007, www.gwmemorial.org

HISTORIC HOUSES

These are just the most significant landmark homes in the Washington area that are open to the public as museums. Hundreds of historic mansions remain in private use as homes, offices, and rental space for private functions—check out the National Register of Historic Places, www.cr.nps.gov/nr, or ask your local neighborhood association about house tours.

- **Anderson House**, 2118 Massachusetts Ave. NW, 202-785-2040, www.thesocietyofthecincinnati.addr.com; headquarters museum of the Society of the Cincinnati, organization of veterans of the American Revolution. Free.

- **Arlington House (Custis-Lee Mansion)**, Arlington National Cemetery, 703-607-8000, www.arlingtoncemetery.net/arlhouse.htm; seized from the family of Robert E. Lee during the Civil War. Free.
- **Clara Barton House**, Glen Echo Park, Bethesda, 301-492-6245, www.nps.gov/clba; mansion of the founder of the American Red Cross. Free.
- **Mary McLeod Bethune Museum & Archives**, 1318 Vermont Ave. NW, 202-673-2404, www.nps.gov/mamc. Home of the founder of the National Council of Negro Women.
- **Carlyle House**, 121 N. Fairfax St., Alexandria, 703-549-2997, www.nvrpa.org/carlyle.html; British headquarters during the French & Indian War (1755-'63).
- **Frederick Douglass National Historic Site**, 1411 W St. SE, 202-426-5960, www.nps.gov/frdo; last home of the abolitionist leader who inspired Lincoln. Free.
- **Decatur House**, 748 Jackson Place NW, 202-842-0920, www.decaturhouse.org; from 1819 to 1956, home of lawmakers, cabinet members, and future president Martin Van Buren.
- **Dumbarton Oaks**, 1703 32nd St. NW, 202-339-6409, www.doaks.org; birthplace of the United Nations (see **Greenspace**).
- **Christian Heurich Mansion**, 1307 New Hampshire Ave. NW, 202-429-1894, www.brewmasterscastle.com; home of 19th-century beer magnate
- **Hillwood Museum & Gardens**, 4155 Linnean Ave. NW, 202-686-5807, www.hillwoodmuseum.org; home of cereal heiress and art collector Marjorie Merriweather Post
- **Kreeger Museum**, 2401 Foxhall Rd. NW, 202-337-3050, www.kreegermuseum.com; home of art collectors David & Carmen Kreeger
- **Mt. Vernon**, south end of the George Washington Memorial Parkway, 703-780-2000, www.mountvernon.org; home of George Washington
- **The Octagon**, 1799 New York Ave. NW, 202-638-3105, www.archfoundation.org/octagon; temporary Executive Mansion after the White House was burned by the British in the War of 1812, now the museum of the American Architectural Foundation
- **Old Stone House**, 3051 M St. NW, 202-895-6070, www.nps.gov/rocr. Oldest house in the District (1765). Free.
- **Peterson House**, 516 10th St. NW, 202-426-6924, www.nps.gov/foth; better known simply as "the House Where Lincoln Died"
- **Pope-Leighey House**, Woodlawn Plantation, U.S. Route 1 near Mt. Vernon, 703-780-4000, www.popeleighey1940.org; the only Frank Lloyd Wright house in the Washington area

NEWCOMER'S HANDBOOK FOR MOVING TO AND LIVING IN WASHINGTON D.C.

250

- **Riversdale**, 4811 Riverdale Rd., Riverdale Park, 301-864-0420, www.pgparks.com; belonged to the founding family of Maryland
- **Sewall-Belmont House**, 144 Constitution Ave. NE, 202-546-1210, www.sewallbelmont.org; headquarters of the National Woman's Party and museum of the suffrage movement.
- **Tudor Place**, 1644 31st St. NW, 202-965-0400, www.tudorplace.org; home to generations of Martha Washington's descendants
- **The White House,** 1600 Pennsylvania Ave. NW, 202-456-7041 (tours), 202-208-1631 (visitor center), www.whitehouse.gov or www. nps.gov/whho; not only the official residence of every president since John Adams, the White House has its own curatorial staff to preserve and display the mansion's collections of art and historical artifacts.
- **Woodrow Wilson House**, 2340 S St. NW, 202-387-4062, www. woodrowwilsonhouse.org; the only presidential museum in D.C.

PERFORMING ARTS

Enjoy the world-class venues that bring A-list talent to your new home-town, but don't be intimidated by that scene—Washington is also teeming with cozy jazz clubs, free lunchtime concerts, good (and cheap) perform-ances at colleges and universities, edgy community theater, and commu-nity orchestras that give you an excuse to dust off the old trombone you haven't touched since high school.

MAJOR THEATERS & CONCERT HALLS

In addition to these auditoriums, note that many of the major sports ven-ues listed in **Sports and Recreation** double as concert venues—most notably the **Verizon Center**, the **Patriot Center**, and **RFK Stadium**.
- **Arena Stage**, 1101 6th St. SW, 202-488-3300, www.arenastage.org. Home of the Helen Hayes Awards, the D.C. theater scene's highest hon-ors, this complex houses three stages (the Fichandler Stage, the Kreeger Theater and the Old Vat Room) and a fourth, the Cradle, slated to open in 2008. Metro: Waterfront.
- **Carter Barron Amphitheater**, 4850 Colorado Ave. NW, 202-426-6837, www.nps.gov/rocr/cbarron. This outdoor stage in Rock Creek Park is the home of the annual Shakespeare Free for All and a summer lineup of blues, jazz, zydeco, and classical music. Metrobus: routes S2/S4.
- **Constitution Hall**, 1776 D St. NW, 202-628-4780, www.dar.org/conthall. This grand auditorium is located in the headquarters of the Daughters of the American Revolution. Every president since Coolidge has attended performances here. Famous for barring Marian Anderson from its segregated stage in 1939, Constitution Hall later became a

venue for significant moments in racial healing; Anderson herself launched her farewell concert tour here in 1964. Metro: Farragut West.

- **The Folger**, at the Folger Shakespeare Library, 201 East Capitol St. NE, 202-544-7077, www.folger.edu. An authentic replica of the Bard's own Globe Theater. Metro: Capitol South.

- **Ford's Theatre**, 511 10th St. NW, 202-347-4833, www.fords theatre.org (box office) or 202-426-6924, www.nps.gov/foth (general information). Lincoln would recognize the place: a carefully preserved historic landmark under the jurisdiction of the National Park Service, Ford's is also a working theater—you just can't sit in the old presidential box. Theatrically, best known for its annual production of *A Christmas Carol*. Metro: Metro Center.

- **Kennedy Center**, New Hampshire Ave. & Rock Creek Pkwy. NW, 202-467-4600, www.kennedy-center.org. The **John F. Kennedy Center for the Performing Arts** is a complex housing seven distinct performance venues: the **Kennedy Center Opera House**, the **Kennedy Center Concert Hall**, the **Eisenhower Theater**, the **Terrace Theater**, the **Theater Lab**, and **Millennium Stage**. Home of the Kennedy Center Honors, the nation's highest awards in the performing arts, and the Mark Twain Prize in comedy. Arts organizations in residence include the National Symphony Orchestra, the Washington National Opera (under the direction of Placido Domingo), the Washington Chamber Symphony, the Washington Chorus, and the Choral Arts Society of Washington. Metro: Foggy Bottom (free shuttle) or Metrobus route 80.

- **Lisner Auditorium**, 731 21st St. NW, 202-994-6800, www.lisner.org. George Washington University's main venue brings music and dance companies as well as A-list comedians and lecturers to town. Metro: Foggy Bottom.

- **Merriweather Post Pavilion**, off U.S. Route 29 in Columbia, Md., 410-715-5550 , www.merriweathermusic.com. This concert pavilion designed by top-shelf architect Frank Gehry attracts big names in the summer. Sheltered and lawn seating. No public transportation access.

- **National Theatre**, 1321 Pennsylvania Ave. NW, 202-628-6161, www.nationaltheatre.org. Since 1835, top U.S. and international touring performers have stopped here for presidents living three blocks away. Said to be haunted. Metro: Metro Center.

- **Nissan Pavilion at Stone Ridge**, off I-66 in Manassas, 703-754-1288 (box office) or 703-754-6400 (general information), www.nissan pavilion.com. Concert pavilion with lawn seating attracts A-list rock and pop stars. No public transportation access.

- **The Shakespeare Theatre at the Lansburgh**, 450 7th Street NW, 202-547-1122, www.shakespearedc.org. Under the direction of

NEWCOMER'S HANDBOOK FOR MOVING TO AND LIVING IN WASHINGTON D.C.

252

Michael Kahn, the Shakespeare Theatre Company has brought big names and big accolades to D.C. Metro: Gallery Place.

- **Strathmore**, 5301 Tuckerman Lane, North Bethesda, 301-581-5100, www.strathmore.org. The Music Center at Strathmore is the area's newest major venue, a state-of-the-art concert hall that hosts touring performers as well as several arts organizations in residence: the Baltimore Symphony Orchestra, the National Philharmonic, the Washington Performing Arts Society, the Levine School of Music, CityDance Ensemble, and the Maryland Classic Youth Orchestras. Metro: Grosvenor (free shuttle); also Ride-On routes 5, 6, 46.
- **Warner Theater**, 202-783-4000, www.warnertheatre.com. Once a Roaring '20s movie palace, this renovated theater is the D.C. equivalent of Mann's in Hollywood: set in the sidewalk in front are the handprints and autographs of dozens of luminaries who have performed here, including Frank Sinatra and Johnny Cash. Metro: Metro Center.
- **Wolf Trap Farm Park for the Performing Arts**, in Vienna, 703-255-1860, www.wolftrap.org (tickets) or www.nps.gov/wotr (general information). This old farm, run by the National Park Service, has three concert venues: the **Filene Center**, a concert pavilion with sheltered and lawn seating, for headline acts; the **Barns of Wolf Trap**, cozier indoor stage for smaller touring acts; and the outdoor **Theater in the Woods** offering children's programs. Bring a picnic and explore the nature preserve before the show! Metro: West Falls Church (shuttle).

COMMUNITY THEATERS & TROUPES

In addition to these homegrown theater companies, check the Weekend section of the *Post* for listings of college and even high school productions—inexpensive, earnest, and fun. There's serious talent behind the musicals of the Georgetown Law School Gilbert & Sullivan Society and student productions at the Duke Ellington and Eubie Blake arts magnet schools.

- **Actors' Theatre of Washington**, GLBT themes, at the Source Theatre, 800-494-8497, www.atwdc.org
- **Adventure Theater**, children's, at Glen Echo Park (see **Greenspace**), 301-320-5331, www.adventuretheatre.org
- **Capitol Hill Arts Workshop**, 545 7th St. SE, 202-547-6839, www.chaw.org
- **Church Street Theater**, 1742 Church St. NW, 202-265-3748
- **Clark Street Playhouse**, home of the Washington Shakespeare Company, 601 South Clark St., Arlington, 703-418-4808, www.washington shakespeare.org

- **D.C. Arts Center**, experimental, 2438 18th St. NW, 202-462-7833, www.dcartscenter.org
- **Dominion Stage**, at Gunston Arts Center, 2700 S. Lang St., Arlington, 703-683-0502, www.dominionstage.org
- **F. Scott Fitzgerald Theatre**, Rockville Civic Center Park, Rockville, 240-314-8690, www.rockvillemd.gov/theatre
- **Foundry Players**, at Foundry United Methodist Church, 1500 16th St. NW, 202-332-3454, www.nbrconsulting.com/foundry
- **Gala Hispanic Theatre**, at Tivoli Square, 3333 14th St. NW, 202-234-7174, www.galatheatre.org
- **Horizons Theatre**, women's themes, 3700 S. Four Mile Run Dr., Arlington, 703-578-1100, www.horizonstheatre.org
- **Lincoln Theatre**, 1215 U St. NW, 202-328-6000, www.thelincoln theatre.org
- **Little Theatre of Alexandria**, 600 Wolfe St., Alexandria, 703-683-0496, www.thelittletheatre.com
- **The Musical Theater Center**, 837-D Rockville Pike, 301-251-5766, www.musicaltheatercenter.org
- **Olney Theatre**, 2001 Olney-Sandy Spring Road, Olney, Md., 301-924-3400, www.olneytheatre.org
- **Publick Playhouse**, 5445 Landover Rd., 301-277-1710, www. pgparks.com
- **Puppet Company Playhouse**, at Glen Echo Park (see **Greenspace**), 301-320-6668, www.thepuppetco.org
- **Rockville Little Theater Company**, at the F. Scott Fitzgerald Theatre, 301-340-1417, www.rlt-online.org
- **Roundhouse Theater**, two locations: 4545 East-West Highway, Bethesda, and 8641 Colesville Road, Silver Spring, 240-644-1100, www.round-house.org
- **Source Theatre Company**, 1835 14th St. NW, 202-462-1073, www.sourcetheatre.com
- **Silver Spring Stage**, 10145 Colesville Rd., Silver Spring, 301-593-6036, www.ssstage.org
- **Studio Theatre**, 1501 14th St NW, 202-332-3300, www.studio theatre.org
- **Theater J**, D.C. Jewish Community Center, 1529 16th St. NW, 800-494-8497, www.dcjcc.org
- **Warehouse Theater**, 1017 7th St. NW, 202-783-3933, www.warehouse theater.com
- **Washington Storytellers Theatre**, 202-545-6840, www.washington storytellers.org
- **Woolly Mammoth Theatre Company**, 641 D St. NW 202-289-2443, www.woollymammoth.net

NEWCOMER'S HANDBOOK FOR MOVING TO AND LIVING IN WASHINGTON D.C.

254

DINNER THEATERS

- **Lazy Susan**, U.S. Route 1 in Woodbridge, Va., 703-550-7384, www. lazysusan.com
- **Mimi's**, 2120 P St. NW, 202-464-6464, www.mimisdc.com
- **Murder Mystery Dinner Theatre**, Blair Mansion Inn, 7711 Eastern Ave., Silver Spring, 301-588-6646, www.mansionmysteries.com
- **Toby's**, off U.S. Route 29 in Columbia, Md., 301-596-6161, www.tobysdinnertheatre.com

ORCHESTRAS & CLASSICAL ENSEMBLES

- **Alexandria Symphony Orchestra**, 703-845-8005, www. alexsym.org
- **Arlington Symphony Orchestra,** 703-528-1817, www.arlington symphony.org
- **Baltimore Symphony Orchestra at Strathmore**, 877-276-1444, www.bsoatstrathmore.org
- **Fairfax Symphony Orchestra**, 703-642-7200, www.fairfaxsymphony. org
- **Maryland Classic Youth Orchestras**, 301-581-5208, www. mcyo.org
- **National Chamber Orchestra**, 301-762-8580, www.nationalchamber orch.org
- **National Philharmonic**, 301-493-9283, www.nationalphilharmonic. org
- **National Symphony Orchestra**, 202-467-4600, www.kennedy-center.org/nso
- **Washington Chamber Symphony**, 202-467-4600, www.kennedy-center.org/nso
- **Washington Metropolitan Philharmonic**, 703-799-8229, www. washingtonmetrophilharmonic.org

CHORUSES & CHOIRS

- **Alexandria Choral Society**, 703-548-4734, www.alexchoralsociety. org
- **Alexandria Harmonizers** (barbershop), 703-836-0969, www. harmonizers.org
- **Bread & Roses Feminist Singers**, www.geocities.com/mieloerge
- **Cathedral Choral Society** 202-537-5527, www.cathedralchoral society.org

- **Children's Chorus of Washington**, 202-237-1005, cchorus.home stead.com
- **Choral Arts Society of Washington**, 202-244-3669, www.choral arts.org
- **Fairfax Choral Society**, 703-642-3277, www.fairfaxchoral society.org
- **Gay Men's Chorus**, 202-293-1548, www.gmcw.org
- **Lesbian and Gay Chorus of Washington**, 202-546-1549, www. lgcw.org
- **Master Chorale of Washington**, 202-337-7464, http://master chorale.org
- **The Washington Chorus**, 202-342-6221, www.thewashington chorus.org
- **Washington Men's Camerata**, 202-363-1064, www.camerata.com
- **Washington Revels**, 202-723-7528, www.revelsdc.org

OPERA COMPANIES

- **Opera Camerata of Washington**, 202-722-5335, www.opera camerata.org
- **Opera Theatre of Northern Virginia**, 703-528-1433, www.nova opera.org
- **Summer Opera Theatre Company**, 202-526-1669, www.summer opera.org
- **Washington Concert Opera**, 202-364-5826, www.concert opera.org
- **Washington National Opera**, 202-295-2400, www.dc-opera.org
- **Washington Savoyards**, 202-315-1323, www.savoyards.org

DANCE COMPANIES

- **CityDance Ensemble**, 202-347-3903, www.citydance.net
- **Dance Place**, 202-969-1600, www.danceplace.org
- **Liz Lerman Dance Exchange**, 301-270-6700, www.dance exchange.org
- **The Washington Ballet**, 202-467-4600, www.washingtonballet.org

FOLK MUSIC & DANCE

- **American Folklife Center**, Library of Congress, 202-707-5510, www.loc.gov/folklife
- **Folklore Society of Greater Washington**, 202-546-2228, www.fsgw.org

NEWCOMER'S HANDBOOK FOR MOVING TO AND LIVING IN WASHINGTON D.C.

256

- **Glen Echo Park Partnership for Arts & Culture**, 301-634-2222, www.glenechopark.org
- **Institute of Musical Traditions**, 301-587-4434, www.imtfolk.org
- **Maryland Renaissance Festival**, 800-296-7304, www.rennfest.com
- **National Council for the Traditional Arts**, 301-565-0654, www.ncta.net

NIGHTCLUBS

The only book that can list all of the area's nightclubs, coffeehouses, and cabarets is the phone book; for a complete lineup, check out the *Post* Weekend section or the *City Paper*. Listed here are some of the headline clubs known primarily as music venues—not cafés with a stage in the corner, not bars that have a piano, but real concert venues.

Here in Duke Ellington's hometown, it's worth mentioning that **HR-57** is not only a jazz club, but a nonprofit conservatory named after the congressional resolution of 1987 declaring jazz to be a national treasure.

- **The Birchmere**, 3701 Mt. Vernon Ave., Alexandria, 703-549-7500, www.birchmere.com
- **Black Cat**, 1831 14th St. NW, 202-667-7960, www.blackcatdc.com
- **Blues Alley**, 1073 Wisconsin Ave. NW, 202-337-4141, www.blue salley.com
- **Bohemian Caverns**, 2001 11th St. NW, 202-299-0801, www. bohemiancaverns.com
- **Busboys & Poets**, 14th & V streets NW, 202-387-7638, www.busboys andpoets.com
- **Half Moon BBQ**, 8235 Georgia Ave., Silver Spring, 301-585-1290, www.halfmoonbbq.com
- **HR-57**, 1610 14th St. NW, 202-667-3700, www.hr57.org
- **Iota**, 2832 Wilson Blvd., Arlington, 703-522-8340, www.iotacluband cafe.com
- **Jammin' Java**, 227 Maple Ave., Vienna, 703-255-1566, www.jammin java.com
- **Madam's Organ**, 2461 18th St. NW, 202-667-5370, www.madams organ.com
- **Metro Cafe**, 1522 14th St. NW, 202-588-9118, http:// metrocafe.home.att.net
- **9:30 Club**, 815 V St. NW, 202-393-0930, www.930.com
- **State Theater**, 220 N. Washington St., Falls Church, 703-237-0300, www.thestatetheatre.com
- **Twins Jazz**, 1344 U St. NW, 202-234-0072, www.twinsjazz.com
- **Twins Lounge**, 5516 Colorado Ave. NW, 202-882-2523, www.twins jazz.com

- **Velvet Lounge**, 915 U St. NW, 202-462-7625, www.velvetlounge dc.com
- **Whitlow's on Wilson**, 2854 Wilson Blvd., Arlington, 703-276-9693, www.whitlows.com

COMEDY CLUBS & TROUPES

The nation's capital *does* have a sense of humor. Chris Rock heads a comedy writing program at Howard University, and this is the hometown of cartoonists Aaron McGruder and Frank Cho; Muppets creator Jim Henson; and satirist Mark Russell. Two venerable comedy troupes have been staging equal-opportunity political satire for decades: Hexagon, in which members of Congress and Cabinet secretaries take the stage alongside professional comic actors to poke fun at themselves, and the Capitol Steps, which once drew a warning from Surgeon General C. Everett Koop: "The Capitol Steps will cause your sides to split."

- **Capitol Steps**, political satire, 800-733-7837, www.capsteps.com
- **The Comedy Spot/ComedySportz**, Ballston Common Mall, 703-294-5233, www.cszdc.com
- **Headliners**, 14 Plyers Mill Rd, Kensington, 301-929-8686
- **Hexagon**, 202-333-7469, www.hexagon.org
- **Improv**, 1140 Connecticut Avenue NW, 202-296-7008, www.dc improv.com

FILM

For the latest Hollywood fare at the local multiplex, check the newspaper or www.fandango.com. The listings here are special movie theaters, either because they're grand old big-screen movie houses of a dying breed or because they specialize in art films and other limited releases. In addition to these commercial and repertory theaters, there are large-format IMAX theaters at the National Air & Space Museum (both locations), National Museum of Natural History, and the U.S. Navy Memorial visitors center, and many other museums offer movie screenings.

- **American Film Institute Silver Theatre & Cultural Center**, 8633 Colesville Rd., Silver Spring, 301-495-6720 (inquiries) or 301-495-6700 (recorded information), www.afi.com. The definitive conservatory of U.S. film moved from the Kennedy Center to this vintage Silver Spring movie palace in 2003.
- **Arlington Cinema 'N' Drafthouse**, 2903 Columbia Pike, Arlington, 703-486-2345, www.arlingtondrafthouse.com; restaurant and saloon shows recent movies at bargain prices on a big screen.

NEWCOMER'S HANDBOOK FOR MOVING TO AND LIVING IN WASHINGTON D.C.

258

- **The Avalon**, 5612 Connecticut Ave. NW, 202-966-6000; one of the last few commercial big screens.
- **Landmark Bethesda Row Cinema**, 7235 Woodmont Ave., Bethesda, 301-652-7273, and **E Street Cinema**, 11th & E streets NW, 202-452-7672, www.landmarktheatres.com; first-run independent, foreign, and art films.
- **Mary Pickford Theater**, Library of Congress – Madison Bldg., 101 Independence Ave. SE, 202-707-5677, www.loc.gov/rr/mopic. Screenings from the nation's own motion picture collection.
- **The Uptown**, 3426 Connecticut Ave. NW, 202-333-3456 ext. 799; vintage movie palace with wraparound screen two stories tall.

FILM FESTIVALS

- **Comcast NIH Film Festival**, August, www.filmfestnih.org; recent blockbusters on a big outdoor screen
- **Environmental Film Festival**, March, 202-342-2564, www.dc environmentalfilmfest.org; science and nature documentaries at dozens of venues
- **Filmfest D.C.**, April, 202-628-3456, www.filmfestdc.org; the best in international cinema
- **Reel Affirmations**, October, 202-986-1119, www.reelaffirmations. org; films exploring GLBT themes
- **Screen on the Green**, July-August, 877-262-5866, www.screenon thegreen.com; classic films shown outdoors on the Mall for free
- **Silverdocs**, June, 301.495.6738, www.silverdocs.com; documentary film festival cosponsored by the American Film Institute and Discovery Channel
- **Washington Jewish Film Festival**, December, 202-518-9400, www.dcjcc.org

LITERARY LIFE

In a city of words—speeches, laws, memos, even the words that declared the nation's independence—it's no surprise that the Washington area is one of the most literate places in the world. And Washingtonians' literary appetites are served by dozens of special interest libraries and hundreds of bookstores, from familiar national chains to an interesting array of independent and specialty bookstores, and plenty of used book dealers as well.

Washington is a stop on every author's book tour. Large and small bookstores alike host book signings several nights a week, often drawing tightly packed crowds. The Book World section of Sunday's *Washington Post* features a calendar of author nights at area bookstores. Check here for announcements of used book sales, too.

Most public and private museums have bookstores reflecting the subject matter of their collections; the National Air & Space Museum, the National Museum of Natural History, the National Gallery of Art and the National Building Museum have particularly good selections. So do the National Cathedral, the National Shrine, and the Washington Islamic Center, as well as college and university bookstores.

BOOKSTORES

All of the big chains—Borders, Barnes & Noble, Tower Books, and Books-A-Million—have locations in D.C. and the suburbs. Check the Yellow Pages. These stores have huge selections and most of the larger stores have cafés and host readings, concerts, and other events. But the Washington area also supports independent booksellers; some of these shops have devoted followings and their own stash of unusual gems. Check out:

- **Bridge Street Books**, 2814 Pennsylvania Ave. NW, 202-965-5200; location, location, location, between George Washington University and the gateway to Georgetown.
- **Chapters Literary Bookstore**, 445 11th St. NW, 202-737-5553, www.chaptersliterary.com; an in-your-face retort to the decline of the written word.
- **Cleveland Park Bookshop**, 3416 Wisconsin Ave. NW, 202-363-1112; offers a good selection of books, cards, and stationery.
- **Kramerbooks & Afterwords**, 1517 Connecticut Ave. NW, 202-387-1400; http://kramers.com; was Washington's first bookstore/café and is still a hip nightspot; open late every night and 24 hours on weekends.
- **Olsson's Books & Music**, six locations, www.olssons.com; a local chain known for its superior customer service and a thoughtful, if not huge, selection of books and CDs.
- **Politics & Prose**, 5015 Connecticut Ave. NW, 202-364-1919; www.politics-prose.com; often packed with crowds anxious to meet visiting authors, especially Washington luminaries from Sunday morning talk shows.
- **Trover Shop**, 221 Pennsylvania Ave. SE, 202-547-2665, www.trover.com; extensive selection of political books and magazines.
- **Vertigo Books**, 7346 Baltimore Ave., College Park, 301-779-9300; good selection on politics, African-American topics, and local authors as well as general fare.

NEWCOMER'S HANDBOOK FOR MOVING TO AND LIVING IN WASHINGTON D.C.

260

SPECIAL INTEREST

- **A Likely Story**, 1555 King St., Alexandria, 703-836-2498, www. alikelystorybooks.com; children's books
- **Blue Nile Books**, 2828 Georgia Ave. NW, 202-232-2583, www.nile valleyassn.org; specializes in health, metaphysical, and Afrocentric titles, and gifts.
- **Busboys & Poets Books**, 14th & V streets NW, 202-387-7638, http://busboysandpoets.com/books.htm; progressive political bookstore, café, and stage.
- **Dale Music**, 8240 Georgia Ave., Silver Spring, 301-589-1459, www. dalemusic.com; sheet music collections, symphony and opera scores, and music instruction books.
- **Franz Bader Bookstore**, 1911 I St. NW, 202-337-5440, specializes in art, architecture, and photography.
- **Lambda Rising**, 1625 Connecticut Ave. NW, 202-462-6969; one of the country's oldest and largest bookstores catering to the GLBT community.
- **Luna Books**, 1633 P St. NW, third floor, 202-332-2543, www.skewers-cafeluna.com; tucked into the upstairs dining room shared by Skewers restaurant and Café Luna, sells a small assortment of hard-to-find titles on politics and citizen activism, and it doubles as a meeting space for community organizations.
- **Maryland Book Exchange**, 4500 College Ave., College Park, 301-927-2510; www.marylandbook.com, is a huge retailer of new and used scholarly books and textbooks as well as general-interest titles
- **Brian McKenzie Infoshop**, 1426 9th St. NW, 202-986-0681, www.dcinfoshop.org; progressive political books and event space.
- **The Newsroom & International Learning Centre**, 1803 Connecticut Ave. NW, 202-332-2894, www.foreignmedia.com; carries hundreds of magazines and newspapers from all over the world.
- **Reiter's Scientific & Professional Books**, 2021 K St. NW, 202-223-3327; www.reiters.com, carries more than 60,000 titles in math, science, engineering, medicine, and philosophy.
- **U.S. Government Bookstore**, 710 North Capitol St. NW, 202-512-0132, http://bookstore.gpo.gov; the retail outlet for the Government Printing Office, which prints all federal publications and documents. If you want your very own copy of the North American Free Trade Agreement, this is the place.
- **Washington Law & Professional Books**, 1900 G St. NW, 202-223-5543, www.washingtonlawbooks.com; caters to lawyers, students, policy wonks, and accountants.

- **World Bank InfoShop**, 701 18th St. NW, 202-458-4500, www.world bank.org/infoshop; books and reports on international development.
- **The Writer's Center**, 4508 Walsh St., Bethesda, 301-654-8664, www. writer.org; local poetry, small-press titles, and resources for local authors.

The Washington area also supports dozens of **used book stores**— the **Washington Antiquarian Booksellers Association** keeps a fairly complete list at www.wababooks.com, and many used book dealers advertise in the Book World section of the *Post*. In addition, most public libraries have a book shop or an annual book sale, and don't overlook the thrift stores listed in **Shopping for the Home**.

LIBRARIES

Shhh! In public libraries and specialized private collections, from modest neighborhood museums to the Library of Congress and the National Archives, you'll find Washington piled high with historic, rare, and scholarly tomes.

PUBLIC LIBRARIES

Check the listings in the Neighborhood Profiles for a branch library near you. Or visit one of the flagship libraries listed here.

- **District of Columbia**, 202-727-0321, http://dclibrary.org; **Martin Luther King Jr. Memorial Library**, the District's main library, is located at 901 G St. NW. Dr. King is commemorated in a mural overlooking the lobby. The library has three floors of open stacks, special collections for the visually impaired, and the best single source of information about D.C. history: the **Washingtoniana Division**, which includes a reading room with reference and local history books, old and current city directories, local government archives, real estate plats, old newspapers on microfilm, and thousands of files of photos.
- **Montgomery County**, 240-777-0002, www.montgomerylibrary. org, has three regional libraries instead of a single flagship, and there are separate facilities for special format collections and the county archives. Regional libraries: Gaithersburg, 18330 Montgomery Village Ave., 301-840-2515; Rockville, 99 Maryland Ave., 240-777-0140; Wheaton, 11701 Georgia Ave., 301-929-5520. **Special Needs Library**, 6400 Democracy Blvd., Bethesda, 301-897-2212; TTY, 301-897-2217; **Montgomery County Archives**, 29 Courthouse Square, Room G09, Rockville, 301-279-1218; www.montgomeryarchives.org
- **Prince George's County**, 301-699-3500, www.prge.lib.md.us; the Hyattsville branch library at 6532 Adelphi Road, 301-985-4690, shares a building with the Prince George's County library system's offices. The

NEWCOMER'S HANDBOOK FOR MOVING TO AND LIVING IN WASHINGTON D.C.

262

branch includes the **Maryland Room** collection of state and county records and historical volumes, the Audio-Visual Division of the library system, and a bookstore. The county **Public Documents Library** is at 14741 Governor Oden Bowie Drive, Upper Marlboro, 301-952-3904.

- **Arlington County**, 703-823-5295, www.co.arlington.va.us; **Arlington County Central Library** at 1015 North Quincy Street, 703-228-5990, includes the **Virginia Room** collection of Northern Virginia historical information, oral histories, and the county archives.
- **Fairfax County**, 703-324-3100, www.co.fairfax.va.us/library; **Fairfax City Regional Library** at 3915 Chain Bridge Road, 703-246-2281, includes the **Virginia Room** collection of historical materials and the county archives.
- **Alexandria**, 703-519-5900, www.alexandria.lib.va.us; The **Charles E. Beatley Jr. Central Library** at 5005 Duke Street, 703-519-5900, is the flagship library with the largest collections. Special collections devoted to local history and records, genealogy, the Civil War, and rare books dating from the original Alexandria Library Company collection of the 1790s are located at the **Kate Waller Barrett Branch**, 717 Queen St., 703-838-4577 ext. 213.

LIBRARY OF CONGRESS

It's all here, including one of the first books ever printed on a press, a Gutenberg Bible. Under U.S. copyright law, two copies of every work copyrighted in the United States must be given to the Library of Congress—which doesn't quite keep everything, but is by far the largest library in the world. The historic Main Reading Room will look familiar if you remember Robert Redford and Dustin Hoffman squinting over library records in *All the President's Men;* but if you're here to do research, you'll probably spend more time in several of the 19 special reading rooms, from the Law Library or Manuscript Reading Room to the collections of film, audio recordings dating back to wax cylinders cut by Thomas Edison, or the library's 5 million maps and 14 million photos and prints. Only members of Congress have borrowing privileges here, but adults with photo ID may use materials in the reading rooms and make photocopies for scholarly purposes permitted by copyright law. The Jefferson Building is the main section, with special reading rooms in the Adams and Madison buildings next door: 101 Independence Avenue SE. Call 202-707-5000 or visit www.loc.gov.

NATIONAL ARCHIVES

Always keep the owner's manual in a safe place. The National Archives is the permanent home of the Constitution and the Declaration of

Independence, and you can visit them in their bombproof glass cases. Temporary exhibits might show the Louisiana Purchase, or the letter from General Cornwallis to General Washington surrendering King George's colonies, or the Emancipation Proclamation. There is also a reading room for genealogical research, where you can retrieve an ancestor's military records or immigration papers. A growing collection of historic recordings is open by appointment, and you can listen to President Nixon's secret tapes without the expletives deleted. The entrance to the genealogy and federal records offices is at 700 Pennsylvania Avenue NW; the Charters of Freedom exhibit hall is on the Constitution Avenue side, facing the Mall at 7th Street NW. Call 202-501-5000 or 800-234-8861, or visit www. archives.gov.

SPECIAL LIBRARIES

Students, researchers, policy wonks, and inquisitive citizens have access to dozens of special-interest libraries in Washington. The Business & Professional Women's Foundation, the Environmental Law Institute, the National Association of Broadcasters, the Population Reference Bureau, and the Urban Institute are just a few of the national organizations that have reference and lending libraries in the area. So do the colleges and universities listed in the **Higher Education** chapter, and most museums. Cabinet departments and many "alphabet soup" agencies—EPA, FBI, GSA, and dozens more—have libraries or information centers; for links, visit http://lcweb.loc.gov/flicc.

The libraries listed here, which are only some of the most significant collections, are open to the public, but may require an appointment or registration for a library card, and some charge a small fee. Call for policies and hours.

- **Arthur R. Ashe Jr. Foreign Policy Library**, 1774 R St. NW, 202-797-2304, www.transafricaforum.org; focusing on Africa and the Caribbean
- **American Institute of Architects Information Center**, 1735 New York Ave. NW, www.aia.org/library
- **Daughters of the American Revolution Library**, 1776 D St. NW, 202-628-1776, www.dar.org/library; books on U.S. history and genealogy, and many genealogical records dating from colonial times
- **Federal Election Commission**, 999 E St. NW, 202-694-1120, www.fec.gov; official records on campaign contributions and political action committees
- **Folger Shakespeare Library**, 201 East Capitol St. SE, 202-544-4600, www.folger.edu; Renaissance English collection including some original Shakespeare folios

NEWCOMER'S HANDBOOK FOR MOVING TO AND LIVING IN WASHINGTON D.C.

264

- **The Foundation Center**, 1627 K St. NW, 202-331-1400, www.fdn center.org/washington; reference materials on philanthropy and fundraising, including tax records and annual reports of many foundations and charities
- **Historical Society of Washington, D.C.**, at the City Museum, 202-383-1850, www.citymuseumdc.org; local history books, archives, correspondence, photos, prints, and slides
- **Middle East Institute**, 1761 N St. NW, 202-785-0183, www.mideasti.org; largest U.S. collection of materials on the Middle East except the Library of Congress
- **National Agricultural Library**, 10301 Baltimore Ave., Beltsville, 301-504-5755, www.nal.usda.gov; more than 3 million works related to farming, food, nutrition, biotechnology, biology, animal welfare, international trade, and other topics of interest to the USDA
- **National Library of Education**, 400 Maryland Ave. SW, 202-205-5015, www.ed.gov/NLE; books, journals, and microfilms on education theory, policy, and statistics
- **National Library of Medicine**, 8600 Rockville Pike, Bethesda, 301-594-5983, www.nlm.nih.gov; more than 5 million books, journals, technical papers, and other materials on health and medicine, including rare and antiquarian medical texts
- **National Genealogical Society**, 4527 N. 17th St., Arlington, 703-525-0050, www.ngsgenealogy.org; reference books and files to assist amateur and professional genealogy researchers
- **National Geographic Society**, 1145 17th St. NW, 202-857-7783, www.nationalgeographic.com/resources/ngs/library; books and journals on geography, cartography, natural history, travel, art, science, photography, and more
- **National Press Club**, 529 14th St. NW, 202-662-7523, http://npc.press.org/library; journalism, politics, and public affairs
- **Writer's Center**, 4508 Walsh St., Bethesda, 301-654-8664, www.writer.org; literary journals, books about writing, and works by local authors

ERE IN ONE OF THE MOST HIGHLY EDUCATED CITIES IN THE world, you'll find it is quite common for grown and working adults to be studying for an advanced degree or a second bachelor's degree, either at night or full time. It's no surprise that every institution listed here has grown in enrollment since 2000 and many have opened satellite campuses to accommodate busy mid-career students.

Even if you're not signing up for classes, the area's colleges and universities offer extensive libraries (see **Libraries** in the **Cultural Life** chapter) and a calendar crammed with distinguished lecturers, concerts, plays, sporting events, art exhibits, and more—often at bargain prices.

High schools maintain extensive collections of college and university literature: course catalogs, admissions information, scholarship bulletins, and more. Most high schools also employ guidance counselors with expertise in the complex process of choosing a college or university, getting admitted, and paying the bill. For adults returning to school, most of the same information is available in the reference section of the public library. For all prospective students, the **Greater Washington College Information Center** provides a wealth of free information at 202-393-1100 or www.collegeinfo.org.

TUITION ASSISTANCE

Students graduating from high school in D.C. get a consolation prize from Congress for not living in a state: they can, through the federal **D.C. Tuition Assistance Grant** program, attend any state university in the country at the residential tuition rate (up to $10,000 per year). The program also provides up to $2,500 toward tuition at private institutions in the greater Washington area and at designated "Historically Black Colleges and Universities." To be eligible, students must: have lived in D.C. for at

NEWCOMER'S HANDBOOK FOR MOVING TO AND LIVING IN WASHINGTON D.C.

266

least a year; be admitted to a four-year degree or certificate program at an eligible college or university; be enrolled at least half time; and begin undergraduate studies within three years after graduating from high school. One bachelor's degree to a customer—no discount for students seeking a second degree. For more information, call the program office at 202-727-2824 or visit http://seo.dc.gov (click on Financial Aid).

Maryland residents should check out the latest state financial aid programs offered through the **Maryland Higher Education Commission** at 800-974-0203 or www.mhec.state.md.us; Virginia residents, contact the **State Council of Higher Education for Virginia** at 804-225-2600 or www.schev.edu. For information about prepaid tuition plans and college savings accounts, visit www.collegesavingsmd.org or www.virginia 529.com.

COLLEGES & UNIVERSITIES

Schools marked (C) are commuter schools with no student housing.

DISTRICT OF COLUMBIA

- **The American University**, 4400 Massachusetts Ave. NW, 202-885-1000, www.american.edu; private university known for international student body and WAMU public radio station. Kogod School of Business offers the MBA degree. 12,000 students.
- **Catholic University of America**, 620 Michigan Ave. NE, 202-319-5000, www.cua.edu; owned and operated by the Catholic Church. Campus features impressive medieval and Renaissance styled architecture. 6,000 students.
- **Gallaudet University**, 800 Florida Ave. NE, 202-651-5000 (TTY/voice), www.gallaudet.edu; academically prestigious school catering to deaf and hearing-impaired students. Chartered by President Lincoln. See **Services for People with Disabilities** in the **Helpful Services** chapter. 2,000 students.
- **George Washington University**, 2121 I St. NW, 202-994-1000, www.gwu.edu; private university, teaching hospital, and law school whose campus is interspersed with the Foggy Bottom neighborhood. Top international studies programs. 20,000 students.
- **Georgetown University**, 37th and O streets NW, 202-687-4328, www.georgetown.edu; Jesuit school founded in 1789. Georgetown's law school (on Capitol Hill) and political science programs have produced many lawmakers, cabinet secretaries, and diplomats—and several presidents. 13,000 students.

- **Howard University**, 2400 6th St. NW, 202-806-2250, www. howard.edu; historically black university with teaching hospital, business school, and law school. 11,000 students.
- **Strayer University**, 1133 15th St. NW, 202-408-2400 or 888-378-7293, www.strayer.edu; private business and technical school, popular with mid-career adults looking to expand or update skills. Campuses in 15 metropolitan areas, with D.C. locations in Alexandria, Arlington, Germantown, Suitland, and Takoma Park as well as downtown. 23,000 students nationwide. (C)
- **Trinity College**, 125 Michigan Ave. NE, 202-884-9050, www.trinity dc.edu; Catholic women's college. Satellite campus on Capitol Hill offers evening classes for working adults. 2,000 students.
- **University of the District of Columbia**, 4200 Connecticut Ave. NW, www.udc.edu; public land-grant university. The David A. Clarke School of Law is a pioneering school emphasizing public-interest law and requiring every student to provide legal aid, under faculty supervision, to low-income clients. 5,000 students. (C)
- **USDA Graduate School**, 600 Maryland Ave. SW, 202-314-3320, www.grad.usda.gov; affordable evening and weekend continuing education courses. Ideal for working adults who need to expand their skills but don't need another degree. 150,000 part-time students. (C)

MARYLAND

- **Bowie State University**, 14000 Jericho Park Rd., Bowie, 301-464-3000, www.bowiestate.edu; part of the Maryland state university system. 5,000 students.
- **Columbia Union College,** 7600 Flower Ave., Takoma Park, 301-891-4000, www.cuc.edu; small Seventh-Day Adventist four-year college and MBA program. 1,000 students.
- **Montgomery College**, 900 Hungerford Dr., Rockville, 301-279-5310, www.mc.cc.md.us; public two-year college with satellite campuses in Germantown and Takoma Park. Many students complete basic courses here and transfer to a four-year school for more specialized study. 22,000 students. (C)
- **Prince George's Community College**, 301 Largo Rd., Largo, 301-336-6000, http://pgweb.pg.cc.md.us; public two-year college similar to Montgomery County's, with satellite campuses in Hyattsville, Laurel, and Camp Springs (Andrews Air Force Base). 12,000 students. (C)
- **University of Maryland**, University Blvd. & Campus Dr., College Park, 301-405-1000, www.umd.edu; major state university with strong engineering, physics, and journalism programs. Birthplace of Kermit

NEWCOMER'S HANDBOOK FOR MOVING TO AND LIVING IN WASHINGTON D.C.

268

the Frog; today, a scholarship endowed by alumnus Jim Henson promotes the study of puppetry. 33,000 students.

VIRGINIA

- **George Mason University**, 4400 University Dr., Fairfax, 703-993-1000, www.gmu.edu; known especially for information technology programs and conservative scholars such as Robert Bork and Stephen Fuller. Many big-name entertainers perform at the Patriot Center on campus. Satellite campuses (commuter only) in Arlington, Manassas, and Sterling. 29,000 students.
- **Marymount University**, 2807 North Glebe Rd., Arlington, 703-284-1500, www.marymount.edu; Catholic school with strong business and nursing departments. Satellite campuses in Sterling and Ballston. Formerly a women's institution, coed since 1986. 3,800 students.
- **Northern Virginia Center (VT/UVA)**, 7054 Haycock Rd., Falls Church, 703-358-1100; www.scps.virginia.edu or www.nvgc.vt.edu; continuing education campus shared by Virginia Tech and the University of Virginia. Emphasis on certificate programs in information technology. 17,000 students. (C)
- **Northern Virginia Community College**, 4001 Wakefield Chapel Rd., Annandale, 703-323-3000, www.nv.cc.va.us; public two-year college with additional campuses in Alexandria, Manassas, Sterling, and Woodbridge. 62,000 students. (C)

I N A CITY FULL OF PEOPLE ACCUSTOMED TO TAKING SIDES ON political issues, it's only natural that the home team draws fiercely loyal fans—from, as Washingtonians say, "both sides of the aisle." To long-time residents who remember the Washington Senators, 2005 was the end of the Dark Ages: the year major-league baseball returned to D.C., and you could tell a Republican from a Democrat by the choice of a Nationals cap— available in red or blue. Meanwhile, the Redskins hold the NFL record for consecutive sold-out home games, and the Wizards games at the Verizon Center have surpassed clubby steakhouses like The Palm as a place to spot the VIPs. (At press time, the name change from MCI Center to Verizon Center was expected to become official in early 2006.)

Of course, watching isn't everything. On summer weekends every public soccer field and tennis court in town is in use, and inline skaters play street hockey in front of the White House. To accommodate cyclists, skaters, and scooters, Beach Drive in Rock Creek Park and Sligo Creek Parkway in Silver Spring are closed to motor traffic on Sundays. During the winter, high schools, condo associations, and church groups organize ski trips to Appalachian resorts. And runners have to register months in advance to get a slot in the crowded annual Marine Corps Marathon.

Check the Sports sections of the *Washington Post* or *Washington Times* for thorough coverage of competitive sports—professional, collegiate, and even high school. Radio station WTEM-AM 980 specializes in sports coverage. Every local TV station carries sports talk shows, featuring interviews with coaches and players. And in the *Post*, Tony Kornheiser and Tom Boswell are the latest in a long line of great sports commentators.

In the Weekend section of Friday's *Post*, the "On the Move" pages list dozens of athletic clubs, classes, and events, covering opportunities to get involved in badminton, climbing, cycling, diving, equestrian, fencing, gymnastics, hiking, martial arts, rugby, running, skiing, volleyball, and

NEWCOMER'S HANDBOOK FOR MOVING TO AND LIVING IN WASHINGTON D.C.

270

more. And check the Yellow Pages for sporting goods stores—most have knowledgeable and enthusiastic salespeople who will be happy to refer you to opportunities to practice your favorite sports.

PROFESSIONAL & VARSITY SPORTS

For all professional games and venues in the Washington area, **Ticketmaster** is the standard ticket vendor: in D.C., 202-397-7328; Maryland, 410-547-7328; Virginia, 703-573-7328; from other area codes, 800-551-7328; or www.ticketmaster.com. Other ticket agencies buy cancellations and may have seats after the box offices and Ticketmaster are sold out. Check the classified ads in the *Post* for ads from ticket agents or check the *City Paper* and Craigslist for individual ticket sales—but, for major events such as Redskins games, watch out for counterfeit tickets.

PROFESSIONAL SPORTS

BASEBALL

During the Depression (1971–2004), most Washingtonians adopted the Baltimore Orioles as their home team. Now that we have a real home team again, it's a little awkward, but still exciting. The Nationals and the Orioles aren't direct rivals, and even in the Nats' first year at RFK Stadium, Oriole Park at Camden Yards remained crowded. RFK is a temporary home for the Nationals, with plans for a new stadium near the Washington Navy Yard; Camden Yards is a beautiful tribute to old-style ballparks, and there are no bad seats there. However, with tickets, refreshments, and souvenirs, either team's home game can add up to an expensive outing for a family; some choose instead to watch the Bowie Baysox, Frederick Keys, or Potomac Nationals—minor-league teams you can see up close and cheap.
- **Washington Nationals**, http://washington.nationals.mlb.com; tickets, 202-675-6287
- **RFK Stadium**, 22nd & East Capitol streets, 202-547-9077; Metro: Stadium-Armory (Blue and Orange lines)
- **Baltimore Orioles**, www.theorioles.com; Washington ticket office, 1666 K St. NW, 202-296-2473
- **Oriole Park at Camden Yards**, Pratt & Eutaw streets, Baltimore, 410-685-9800; MARC: Camden Station, Camden Line
- **Bowie Baysox**, 301-805-6000, www.baysox.com
- **Frederick Keys**, 301-662-0088, www.frederickkeys.com
- **Potomac Nationals**, 703-590-2311, www.potomacnationals.com
     For diehard Orioles fans who just can't get into the Nationals, there are special MARC commuter trains on weekends, and the last train back on

weeknights leaves 20 minutes after the end of the game. (See **Transportation** for details.) By car or train, Oriole Park is about an hour from the District.

BASKETBALL

Washington has been a basketball town ever since a local gym teacher named Red Auerbach agreed to coach Washington's first NBA team. The old Capitols faced the Minneapolis Lakers in the 1949 championship series; three years later, Auerbach moved to Boston and became the most successful NBA coach in history. A more recent legend, Michael Jordan, arrived in D.C. in 2000 to take the reins of the Washington Wizards. Attendance doesn't seem to vary with the team's fortunes, and the Metro is consistently crowded on game nights. The devotion of Washington fans is even more evident with the Wizards' sister team, the Women's NBA Washington Mystics, who always have the WNBA's best attendance record even when they have the worst playing record.

- **Washington Wizards**, 202-661-5050, www.nba.com/wizards
- **Washington Mystics**, 202-661-5050, www.wnba.com/mystics
- **Verizon Center**, 7th & F streets NW, www.mcicenter.com; Metro: Gallery Place-Chinatown (Red, Green, and Yellow lines)

FOOTBALL

The waiting list for tickets to a Washington Redskins home game is several years long, and every regular season game has been sold out since 1966. You can buy tickets from a scalper or from one of the ticket agents that advertise in the *Washington Post* classifieds; you can win tickets in a call-in contest on a local radio station; you can get friendly with someone who has season tickets or with a business associate whose firm has a stadium box to entertain clients; but you cannot just go buy a ticket to a Redskins game. (Well, maybe a pre-season exhibition.) The Redskins summer training camp is at Redskins Park in Ashburn in late July through late August. During football season, city streets are quiet during game time, as hundreds of thousands of residents settle in front of the TV. Diehard fans mute the sound on the TV and watch the screen while they listen to Sonny Jurgensen and Sam Huff call the game on WJFK-FM 106.7.

Off the field, there is ongoing controversy about the team's name. The first NFL team to win the Super Bowl under the leadership of an African-American quarterback (Doug Williams, 1988) faces perennial claims from Native American groups objecting to the name as a racial slur, and in 1999, the U.S. Patent & Trademark Office agreed, revoking trademark protection of the team's name and logo. A tradition dating to 1937 is hard to aban-

NEWCOMER'S HANDBOOK FOR MOVING TO AND LIVING IN WASHINGTON D.C.

272

don—the "Skins" were the first NFL team to have a marching band, and "Hail to the Redskins" is the oldest pro sports fight song in the nation—but, as the 1997 renaming of the Washington Bullets basketball team showed, loyal fans can adapt to change. Some sportscasters now refer to the team only as "Washington," avoiding the name.

Betcha didn't know: The Redskins aren't the only pro football team in town. The D.C. Divas—women's professional football—made their debut in 2001. The National Women's Football Association franchise plays at Prince George's Sports & Learning Complex, across the street from FedEx Field, from April through late June. Tickets are cheap and readily available, but it's real football. (The Divas' Donna Wilkinson became, in 2003, the first woman to ever rush for over a thousand yards in a season.)

If you do manage to get Redskins tickets, you can join the traffic jams on Route 202 or take a shuttle bus from the Metro to FedEx Field.

- **Washington Redskins** ticket office, 202-546-2222, www.redskins.com
- **D.C. Divas** ticket office, 202-656-5090, www.dcdivas.com
- **FedEx Field**, directions, 301-276-6248, www.redskins.com/fedexfield; Metro: shuttles from Landover (Orange Line) or Morgan Blvd. (Blue Line)
- **Redskins Park**, Route 28 & Waxpool Rd., Ashburn; see www.redskins.com for details.
- **Prince George's Sports & Learning Complex**, 8001 Sheriff Rd., Landover, 202-583-2400, www.pgsportsandlearn.com

HOCKEY

During the winter and spring, the NHL **Washington Capitals** share the Verizon Center with the men's and women's NBA teams, and you can readily spot the crowds of devoted "Caps" fans—a typical fan at a Capitals game is more likely to be wearing full team regalia than a Wizards or Mystics fan. Their team is more successful, too, usually making the division playoffs—but no Stanley Cup title yet. Contact the Washington Capitals at 202-661-5050 or www.washingtoncaps.com for more information.

SOCCER

The former home of the Redskins and Senators, and the temporary home of the Nationals, is mainly a soccer venue these days. RFK Stadium hosted World Cup matches in 1994 and first-round matches in the 1996 Summer Olympics; since then, it's been the home field of **D.C. United**, the first-ever Major League Soccer champions. Several United players have done tours of duty on the U.S. Olympic team. Among Washington's international population and suburban "soccer mom" households, the team has a small but passionate following. For tickets, call 202-587-5000 or visit www.dcunited.com.

No overview of Washington sports would be complete without mentioning the Washington Freedom, championship franchise of the short-lived Women's United Soccer Association. The Freedom roster included Olympic gold medalist Mia Hamm, who has been featured in ads calling her "the best football player in the world." This was already her home turf—she grew up in Fairfax County.

HORSE RACING

Pimlico Race Course, home of the Preakness Stakes and the Breeders' Cup, is an hour's drive from Washington in the northwest outskirts of Baltimore. Closer to home, catch thoroughbred racing at Laurel Park and harness racing at Rosecroft Raceway.

- **Pimlico Race Course**, Northern Pkwy. and Pimlico Rd., Baltimore, 410-542-9400, www.pimlico.com
- **Laurel Park**, Route 198 and Race Track Rd., Laurel, 301-725-0400, www.pimlico.com; MARC: Laurel Racetrack, Camden Line
- **Rosecroft Raceway**, Rosecroft Dr. off Brinkey Rd., Oxon Hill, Md., 301-567-4000, www.rosecroft.com

OTHER PROFESSIONAL SPORTS

- The **Booz-Allen Classic** golf tournament (formerly the Kemper Open) is held in June at the Tournament Players Club at Avenel in Potomac; visit www.pgatour.com or www.boozallenclassic.com.
- The **Legg Mason Tennis Classic** is held in August at William H.G. Fitzgerald Tennis Stadium in Rock Creek Park; see www.leggmason tennisclassic.com.
- **Figure skating** and **gymnastics** meets and exhibitions are held occasionally at the Verizon Center; check the arena's calendar at www.mcicenter.com.

COLLEGIATE SPORTS

Washington-area colleges and universities offer plenty of exciting NCAA action. Some big names—including Patrick Ewing and Boomer Esiason—have been made in college games inside the Beltway. Several collegiate basketball and football teams in the area have attracted a following beyond the campus, and fill prominent regional venues; others draw less attention, but may be exciting and affordable alternatives to the pros. For an overview of the NCAA Capital Athletic Conference, visit www.cacsports.com.

NEWCOMER'S HANDBOOK FOR MOVING TO AND LIVING IN WASHINGTON D.C.

274

Some of the most promising college baseball players in the country spend the summer in Maryland, playing serious ball (with wooden bats) in the Cal Ripken Sr. Collegiate Baseball League, giving their all for the big-league scouts. (Cal Sr., the legendary shortstop's father, was a longtime Orioles coach.) There are teams in Bethesda, College Park, Rockville, and Silver Spring; tickets are cheaper than a movie matinee, and you can sit just a few feet from the plate. For information, call 410-588-9900 or visit www.ripkensrcollegebaseball.org.

- **Catholic University of America**: the Cardinals have been to the Orange Bowl and other bowl games, but not in recent decades; Catholic U's athletic strength lately is in swimming and track. Tickets and information, 202-319-5286 or http://athletics.cua.edu
- **George Mason University**: the Patriots play basketball at the **Patriot Center**, also a major concert venue. Tickets, 202-397-7328 (Ticketmaster); information, www.gmusports.com
- **George Washington University**: Colonials basketball packs the Smith Center in Foggy Bottom. Tickets, 202-994-6650; information, www.gwsports.com
- **Georgetown University**: the Hoyas are best known for men's basketball, though the legendary Coach John Thompson retired in the late 1990s. The Hoyas often play the best hoops in Washington, and their home games are at the Verizon Center. Tickets, 202-687-4692; information, 202-687-7159, www.guhoyas.com
- **Howard University**: the Bison have a decent following in men's basketball and football, and consistently strong results in women's track. Tickets, 202-806-7198; information, www.howard-bison.com
- **Marymount University**: the Saints won the first seven consecutive women's basketball titles in the Capital Athletic Conference, founded in 1990, and remain consistently strong. Information, 703-284-1619 or www.marymount.edu/athletics
- **University of Maryland**: the Terrapins ("Terps") basketball and football teams draw loyal crowds to the Comcast Center and Byrd Stadium, respectively. Tickets, 301-314-8587 or http://umterps.collegesports.com; information, www.umd.edu/athletics
- **U.S. Naval Academy**: the Midshipmen take their college football seriously: when they score, especially in the annual Army-Navy game, cannons roar and plebes hit the deck for push-ups. Tickets, 800-874-6289; information, http://navysports.collegesports.com.

HIGH SCHOOL SPORTS

For in-depth coverage of high school sports, pick up a copy of *SchoolSports* magazine, free in newspaper boxes at Metro stations. If you can't find it, call 877-776-7894 or visit http://schoolsports.com. Also, any high school newspaper or web site will include plenty of coverage of the home team, and community newspapers usually cover the local high school football and basketball teams. Soccer, baseball/softball, volleyball, lacrosse, wrestling, swimming, and other varsity sports usually make the box scores in Sunday's *Washington Post*.

PARTICIPANT SPORTS

The single best resource for participant sports activities, from charity 10K races to weekly 30-and-over flag football games, is the Weekend section of the *Washington Post*; also, *Metro Sports Washington* is a free monthly tabloid with articles about participant sports and lists of classes, sporting venues, ski resorts, and more. Pick it up at any sporting goods store or in newspaper boxes around town, call 301-907-7474, or visit www.metro sportsdc.com.

Local recreation departments maintain parks, trails, beaches, tennis and basketball courts, baseball diamonds, soccer fields, pools, and other public amenities, and most offer lessons in a variety of sports.

- **D.C. Department of Parks & Recreation**, 202-673-7647, http:// dpr.dc.gov
- **Montgomery County Department of Recreation**, 240-777-6961, www.montgomerycountymd.gov
- **Prince George's County Department of Parks & Recreation**, 301-918-8100, www.pgparks.com
- **Arlington County Department of Parks, Recreation & Community Resources**, 703-228-3323, www.co.arlington.va. us/prcr
- **Fairfax County Park Authority**, 703-324-8702, www.co. fairfax.va.us/parks
- **Alexandria Department of Recreation, Parks & Cultural Activities**, 703-838-4343, www.ci.alexandria.va.us/recreation

BICYCLING

Whether you're in training for a triathlon or just enjoying the scenery and exercise, Washington offers plenty of first-rate cycling. The C&O Canal towpath, the Washington & Old Dominion Trail, the Rock Creek Park bike path, and others are detailed in the **Greenspace** chapter. In addition, the Capital Crescent Trail from Bethesda to Georgetown and the Metropolitan Branch Trail, under construction, from Silver Spring to Capitol Hill, are intended to serve bicycle commuters.

NEWCOMER'S HANDBOOK FOR MOVING TO AND LIVING IN WASHINGTON D.C.

276

Note: in most jurisdictions, children under 16 are required by law to wear approved helmets while riding; also, there are occasional outbreaks of muggings on various bike trails, and cyclists should not ride alone at night on area trails.

You can rent bicycles at:

- **Big Wheel Bikes**, 1034 33rd St. NW, 202-337-0254; 6917 Arlington Rd., Bethesda, 301-652-0192; 2 Prince St., Alexandria, 703-739-2300; 3119 Lee Hwy., Arlington, 703-522-1110; www.bigwheelbikes.com
- **CityBikes**, 2501 Champlain St. NW, 202-265-1564, http://city bikes.com
- **Fletcher's Boat House**, 4940 Canal Rd. NW, 202-244-0461, www. fletchersboathouse.com
- **REI**, 1701 Rockville Pike, Rockville; 9801 Rhode Island Ave., College Park; 11950 Grand Commons Ave., Fairfax; 3509 Carlin Springs Rd., Baileys Crossroads; 800-426-4840, www.rei.com
- **Washington Sailing Marina**, George Washington Pkwy., Alexandria, 703-548-9027, www.washingtonsailingmarina.com

For organized rides and touring, contact:

- **Bike the Sites**, 202-842-2453, www.bikethesites.com; leads guided tours promising "history, lore and scandal," covering "55 sites in three hours." Bikes and helmets provided, and the entire route is on bike paths.
- **Potomac Pedalers Touring Club**, 202-363-8687, www. bikepptc.org; leads local and getaway tours, including overnight trips. Web site features dozens of touring cue sheets.
- **Washington Area Bicyclist Association**, 202-518-0524, www.waba.org; leads trips and offers commuter advice, education, and advocacy—sort of the AAA for cyclists.

See **Transportation** for more information about local bike amenities, including the rules for carrying your bike on the Metro. For a calendar of races and cross-country tours, see the Weekend section of the *Post* or *Spokes* magazine, available free at bike shops.

BOATING

If you look out the window as you cross the Potomac during morning rush hour, you'll see local crew teams practicing in their shells. At Washington Harbour in Georgetown, motor yachts put in for dockside partying on summer evenings. And south of Hains Point, at the mouth of the Anacostia, the Potomac becomes a wide estuary where sizeable sailboats can catch the wind. Several marinas rent wet and dry slips, and Potomac River boathouses rent canoes, kayaks, and rowboats; the paddleboats on the Tidal Basin, in the shadow of the Jefferson Memorial, are a favorite with kids.

Within a two-hour drive from the Beltway, you can raft, canoe, or kayak some of the finest whitewater on the East Coast, or go tubing on the calmer stretches. The upper Potomac, the New River, the Youghiogheny (pronounced "yuckaHAYnee"), Antietam Creek, the Shenandoah, and the Savage make a paddlers' paradise of Western Maryland and the Harper's Ferry area of West Virginia. Closer to home, the lower 22 miles of the C&O Canal, between Georgetown and Swain's Lock, are ideal for flatwater canoeing.

The **Washington Boat Show** is held every February at the Convention Center—call 703-823-7960 or visit www.washingtonboat show.com. And if you want to haul the sheets without renting a boat, you can sign on with the **Sailing Club of Washington** (SCOW) at www. scow.org.

BOATHOUSES

- **Fletcher's Boat House**, 4940 Canal Rd. NW, 202-244-0461, www. fletchersboathouse.com
- **Jack's Boats**, 3500 K St. NW, 202-337-9642
- **Lake Needwood Boathouse**, off Muncaster Mill Rd., Rockville, 301-762-9500, www.mc-mncppc.org
- **Swain's Lock**, Swain's Lock Rd. off River Rd., Potomac, 301-299-9006
- **Thompson Boat Center**, Rock Creek Pkwy. & Virginia Ave. NW, 202-333-9543, www.thompsonboatcenter.com
- **Tidal Basin Boathouse**, 1501 Maine Ave. SW, 202-479-2426, www.tidalbasinpeddleboats.com

MARINAS & YACHT CLUBS

- **Belle Haven Marina/Mariner Sailing School**, Alexandria, 703-768-0018, www.saildc.com
- **Buzzard Point Marina**, Anacostia River, 202-488-8400
- **Capital Yacht Club**, Washington Channel, 202-488-8110, www.capital yachtclub.net
- **City Marina**, Alexandria, 703-868-4265, ci.alexandria.va.us/recreation
- **Columbia Island Marina**, Arlington, 202-347-0173, www.columbia island.com
- **Gangplank Marina**, Washington Channel, 202-554-5000, www. gangplank.com
- **James Creek Marina**, Anacostia River, 202-544-8844, www.james creek.com
- **Washington Marina**, Washington Channel, 202-554-0222, www. washingtonmarina.com

NEWCOMER'S HANDBOOK FOR MOVING TO AND LIVING IN WASHINGTON D.C.

278

- **Washington Sailing Marina**, Alexandria, 703-548-9027, www. washingtonsailingmarina.com

RIVER OUTFITTERS

These adventure travel centers offer guided trips, dropoff/pickup trips, and rentals on prime whitewater within a day trip of Washington:
- **Precision Rafting**, 800-477-3723, www.precisionrafting.com
- **River & Trail Outfitters**, 888-446-7529, www.rivertrail.com
- **River Riders**, 800-326-7238, www.riverriders.com
- **USA Raft**, 800-872-7238, www.usaraft.com

The **Anacostia Watershed Society**, 301-699-6204, www.anacostia ws.org, offers guided tours of the upper Anacostia River by canoe or pontoon boat.

BOWLING

Okay, Washington is different from the rest of the country: there are no public bowling alleys in the District of Columbia. None. There are a handful of bowling alleys in the suburbs; in D.C., guests of students can bowl at American University or GWU, and guests of the president can bowl at the White House.
- **Bowl America**, 1101 Clopper Rd., Gaithersburg; 6450 Edsall Rd., Alexandria; 9699 Lee Hwy., Fairfax; 140 S. Maple St., Falls Church; 5615 Guinea Rd., Burke; 4525 Stonecroft Blvd., Chantilly; 703-941-6300, www.bowl-america.com
- **Rinaldi Lanes**, 6322 Kenilworth Ave., Riverdale Park, 301-864-5940; 2945 S. Glebe Rd., Arlington, 703-684-5800
- **Strike Bethesda**, 5353 Westbard Ave., Bethesda, 301-652-0955, www.strikebethesda.com

EQUESTRIAN SPORTS

Northern Virginia is horse country, and most horse farms offer riding lessons. Visit www.virginiahorse.com for links to stables, farms, and equestrian organizations. In Maryland, for training in equestrian events, visit the **Prince George's Equestrian Center** at the Show Place Arena in Upper Marlboro, 301-952-7999, www.showplacearena.com. Closer to home, there are several public riding stables:
- **Meadowbrook Stables**, 8200 Meadowbrook Ln., Chevy Chase, 301-589-9026, www.meadowbrookstables.com
- **Rock Creek Park Horse Center**, 5100 Glover Rd. NW, 202-362-0117, www.rockcreekhorsecenter.com

- **Wheaton Regional Park Stables**, 1101 Glenallen Ave., Wheaton, 301-622-2424, www.wheatonparkstables.com

    The **Potomac Polo Club** can refer you to opportunities to get involved with the "sport of kings," and there are occasional polo matches on the Mall near the Lincoln Memorial on Sundays during the summer. Call 301-972-7288 or visit www.gopolo.com.

FISHING

In season, the Weekend section of the *Washington Post* runs a weekly fishing report listing water levels, temperatures, and what's biting in area streams and impoundments. The Chesapeake Bay gave Maryland its state tourism slogan, "Maryland is for Crabs," and the blue crab makes its way well into the tidal Potomac River. Check with local wildlife authorities for details about fishing licenses and limits on certain protected species—especially striped bass, also known as rockfish, the state fish of Maryland. Also ask about environmental advisories—shellfish in certain areas have elevated levels of mercury, and many Chesapeake Bay fish are infected with *Pfiesteria*. For fishing, boating, or hunting licenses, contact:

- **Maryland Department of Natural Resources**, 800-918-2870, www.dnr.state.md.us; for fish health advisories, call the Chesapeake Bay environmental hotline, 877-224-7229 or visit www.mde.state.md.us.
- **Virginia Department of Game & Inland Fisheries**, 800-986-2628, www.dgif.virginia.gov

GOLF COURSES

In addition to elite country clubs such as Congressional and Burning Tree, the Washington area has dozens of public golf courses, both commercial and community. Most area golf courses accept reservations online through www.teetimes.com.

DISTRICT OF COLUMBIA

For tee times or more information, call 202-554-7660 or visit www.golf dc.com.

- East Potomac Park, 202-554-7660
- Langston, 28th St. & Benning Rd. NE, 202-397-8638
- Rock Creek Park, 16th & Rittenhouse streets NW, 202-882-7332

NEWCOMER'S HANDBOOK FOR MOVING TO AND LIVING IN WASHINGTON D.C.

280

MARYLAND

- **Montgomery County Golf public courses**: Falls Rd., Potomac, 301-299-5156; Poolesville, 301-428-8143; Laytonsville, 301-948-5288; Rattlewood, Mt. Airy, 301-664-9000; Hampshire Greens, Silver Spring, 301-476-7999; www.montgomerycountygolf.com
- **Prince George's County Parks courses**: Bowie, 301-262-8141; Enterprise, Mitchellville, 301-249-2040; Henson Creek, Fort Washington, 301-567-4646; Paint Branch, College Park, 301-935-0330; Prince George's County Youth Golf Training Center, Landover, 301-772-2527; www.pgparks.com
- **Maryland-National Capital Park & Planning Commission courses**: Needwood, Rockville, 301-948-1075; Little Bennett, Clarksburg, 301-601-9209; Northwest Park, Wheaton, 301-598-6100; Sligo Creek, Silver Spring, 301-585-6006; www.mc-mncppc.org
- **Country clubs open to paying guests**: Glenn Dale, Bowie, 301-262-1166, www.glenndalegolfclub.com; Lake Arbor, Bowie, 301-336-7771

VIRGINIA

- **Fairfax County golf courses**: Burke Lake, Burke; Greendale, Alexandria; Pinecrest, Alexandria; Jefferson District, Falls Church; Laurel Hill, Lorton; Oak Marr, Oakton; Pleasant Valley, Chantilly; Twin Lakes, Clifton; 877-776-3272, www.co.fairfax.va.us/parks (click on Golf Courses).

HIKING

There are miles of hiking trails in Rock Creek Park, and in the section of the park north of Military Road you may forget you're in a city. The C&O Canal towpath offers easy walking all the way to the mountains of Western Maryland through the Potomac River valley, and both sides of the Potomac at Great Falls are prized by weekend hikers. See the **Greenspace** chapter for more detail on these nearby parks. Within a two-hour drive from the Beltway, you can reach some of the most popular hiking and backpacking areas in the eastern United States.

For trail atlases and hiking guides to areas within a day trip of Washington, visit the books department at:

- **Appalachian Trail Conservancy**, 888-287-8673, www.atctrail store.org
- **REI** (see Bicycling above)

- **Hudson Trail Outfitters**, 4530 Wisconsin Ave. NW; 12085 Rockville Pike, Rockville; 401 N. Frederick Ave., Gaithersburg; 9488 Fairfax Blvd., Fairfax; Springfield Mall; 1101 S. Joyce St., Arlington; 800-211-9753, www.hudsontrail.com
- **Patagonia**, 1048 Wisconsin Ave. NW, 202-333-1776, www.patagonia. com

  Check the Weekend section of the *Post* for notices of organized group hiking and backpacking trips. Or just explore:

- **Shenandoah National Park**: this 107-mile-long ridge 80 miles west of Washington is a favorite weekend getaway and, in the fall, parts of the park are actually overcrowded. Old Rag Mountain draws rock scramblers to its low timberline and massive cliffs, and the parking area at the trailhead is usually full on weekends in the summer. If you avoid the most crowded areas and times, you can immerse yourself in the woods of two dozen mountainsides, teeming with wildlife, waterfalls, and vistas. Call 540-999-3500 or visit www.nps.gov/shen.
- **The Appalachian Trail**: the "A.T." passes through Maryland about 60 miles north of Washington, crossing the Potomac near Harper's Ferry, where Maryland, Virginia, and West Virginia meet at the mouth of the Shenandoah River. Turn right and walk to Mt. Katahdin in Maine, 1,200 miles north; turn left and walk to Springer Mountain in Georgia, 900 miles south. Guidebooks are available at most bookstores and outfitters; for more information, contact the Appalachian Trail Conservancy at 304-535-6331 or www.appalachiantrail.org.
- **Prince William Forest Park**: less than 20 miles south of the Beltway, just off Interstate 95, this woodland park in the headwaters of Quantico Creek is one of the area's best-kept secrets. You can spend hours on the park's 35 miles of trail and see plenty of deer, and few, if any, people. Call 703-221-7181 or visit www.nps.gov/prwi.
- **Cunningham Falls State Park/Catoctin Mountain Park**: these two Maryland parks, less than two hours' drive north of Washington, offer easy day hikes and attract a lot of families. In Catoctin Mountain Park, you might glimpse a high chain link fence deep in the woods—it marks the perimeter of Camp David, the secluded weekend retreat of every president since Eisenhower. Call 888-432-2267 or visit www. dnr.state.md.us/publiclands.
- **Manassas National Battlefield Park**: you can retrace the steps of Stonewall Jackson and Robert E. Lee through the swamps, meadows, and woods of Bull Run, on scrupulously preserved hallowed ground barely 15 miles west of the Beltway. Call 703-361-1339 or visit www. nps.gov/mana.

NEWCOMER'S HANDBOOK FOR MOVING TO AND LIVING IN WASHINGTON D.C.

282

ICE SKATING

The Washington equivalent of going skating at Rockefeller Center is skating in the fountain in the **National Gallery Sculpture Garden** on the National Mall. For information, call 202-289-3360 or visit www. nga.gov/ginfo (click on Sculpture Garden).

   The Gardens Ice House in Laurel is a year-round skating facility with one ice rink in the summer and three in the winter. During the summer, two rinks are used for inline and roller skating. Call 301-953-0100 or visit www.thegardensicehouse.com.

   Most ice rinks are open from October through March and have certain hours set aside for hockey or figure skating; all provide skate rentals and lockers.

- **Cabin John**, 10610 Westlake Dr., Rockville, 301-365-2246, www. mc-mncppc.org
- **Fairfax**, 3779 Pickett Rd., 703-323-1132, www.fairfaxicearena.com
- **Ft. Dupont**, 3779 Ely Place SE, 202-584-3040, www.nps.gov/nace
- **Herbert Wells**, 5211 Paint Branch Pkwy., College Park, 301-277-3717, www.pgparks.com
- **Mt. Vernon RECenter**, 2017 Belle View Blvd., Alexandria, 703-768-3224, www.co.fairfax.va.us/parks
- **Pershing Park** (outdoors), 14th St. & Pennsylvania Ave. NW, 202-737-6938, www.pershingparkicerink.com
- **Tucker Road**, 1770 Tucker Rd., Ft. Washington, Md., 301-265-1525, www.pgparks.com
- **Wheaton**, Arcola & Orebaugh avenues, 301-649-3640, www. mc-mncppc.org

INLINE & ROLLER SKATING

Park rangers vigorously defend the grounds of national monuments from inline skaters, but there are many other places to go, including the paved bike trails along the Potomac River and Rock Creek. Washington Area Roadskaters, www.skatedc.org, can provide information about events and lessons. Their site includes links to thousands of local and general resources for inline and roller skaters and street hockey enthusiasts. CityBikes and REI rent inline skates—see Bicycling.

ROCK CLIMBING

There are 50-foot cliffs just five miles outside the Beltway, looming over the Mather Gorge below Great Falls of the Potomac. **Great Falls National Park** on the Virginia side and **C&O Canal National Historical Park** on the Maryland side are favorite spots for technical climbing and rock scrambling. See the **Greenspace** chapter for more information.

For serious climbers, the ideal weekend getaway is the **Spruce Knob–Seneca Rocks National Recreation Area** in West Virginia, about 200 miles away; the area is renowned for the grandest rock arches and pillars east of Utah. Call the visitors' center at 304-567-2827 or the ranger station at 304-257-4488, or visit the Monongahela National Forest web site at www.fs.fed.us/r9/mnf.

For indoor climbing or lessons, go to **Sportrock Climbing Center**, 1408 Southlawn Ln., Rockville; 5308 Eisenhower Ave., Alexandria; 45935 Maries Rd., Sterling; 703-212-7625, www.sportrock.com. **Wakefield Park RECenter** (see Health Clubs below) also has an indoor climbing wall.

RUNNING

For training or casual jogging, the Mall, the towpath, the banks of the Potomac, and the shaded, rolling hills of Rock Creek are as good as it gets; for more competitive running, the *Washington Post's* Weekend section lists 10Ks, 5-milers, and "fun runs" as well as formal and informal training groups. See the chapter on **A Washington Year** for information about the Marine Corps Marathon and the Army 10-Miler. For more ideas, check out the bimonthly ***Washington Running Report*** at www.runwashington.com or call 301-871-0005 to subscribe to the print edition.

SCUBA & SKIN DIVING

You won't get much field practice around town, but if you're planning a trip to Florida or Hawaii, you can get scuba and snorkeling lessons at these diving shops:

- **Adventure Scuba**, 13901 Metrotech Dr., Chantilly, 703-263-0427, www.scubava.com
- **American Watersports**, 6182 Arlington Blvd., Falls Church, 703-534-3636
- **Aquatic Adventures Scuba Academy**, 6300 Richmond Hwy., Alexandria, 703-765-3483
- **Atlantic Edge Scuba**, 213 Muddy Branch Rd., Gaithersburg, 301-990-0223, www.atlanticedge.com
- **Coral Edge Divers**, 11411 Sunset Hills Rd., Reston, 703-318-0170
- **The Dive Shop**, 3013 Nutley St., Fairfax, 703-698-7220, www.thediveshop-va.com
- **Divemasters Scuba Center**, 109 E. Diamond Ave., Gaithersburg, 301-670-0535
- **National Diving Center**, 4932 Wisconsin Ave. NW, 202-363-6123

NEWCOMER'S HANDBOOK FOR MOVING TO AND LIVING IN WASHINGTON D.C.

284

- **Sea Ventures**, 9444 Main St., Fairfax, 703-425-7676, www.seaventures-va.com
- **Splash Dive Center**, 25 S. Quaker Ln., Alexandria, 703-823-7680, www.splashdivecenter.com
- **Steve's Scuba School**, 6732 Montour Dr., McLean, 703-241-2222

SOCCER

Especially popular among children and teens, soccer is gaining a share of grownups' recreation time too. Contact one of the regional soccer associations for information about clubs and leagues:

- **Metro D.C./Virginia Soccer Association**, 703-492-5425, www.mdcvsa.org
- **Virginia Youth Soccer Association**, 703-551-4035, www.vysa.com
- **Maryland State Youth Soccer Association**, 410-987-7898, www.msysa.org

SWIMMING

Every summer, when temperatures pass 100° and the humidity is described by professional meteorologists as "oppressive," we see TV and newspaper images of people taking a desperate dip in the fountains of Dupont Circle or Freedom Plaza, or in the slimy and shallow Reflecting Pool on the Mall. Fortunately, there are plenty of public swimming pools and private swim clubs in the area, including heated indoor pools for winter training.

There are a few **public beaches** on the Chesapeake Bay (Sandy Point and Calvert Cliffs, 877-620-8367, www.dnr.state.md.us), and U.S. Route 50 is one long traffic jam every weekend during the summer as Washingtonians flock to Ocean City, Md., and Rehoboth Beach, Del. For a rustic alternative to the resort scene, visit Assateague Island National Seashore located just south of Ocean City—see **Quick Getaways** for more information.

Generally, outdoor pools are open from Memorial Day to Labor Day, or from the last day of school in June to the first weekday of September. Most public pools charge a nominal fee to residents and a slightly higher fee, typically around $5, to guests; ask about family discounts, season passes, and discounts for youth and seniors.

PUBLIC SWIMMING POOLS

- **D.C. Department of Parks & Recreation** operates 27 outdoor pools and 6 indoor pools. Call 202-673-7665 or visit http://dpr.dc.gov.

- **Montgomery County Department of Recreation** operates 7 outdoor pools and 4 indoor pools. Call the Aquatic Programs office at 240-777-6860 or visit www.montgomerycountymd.gov (click on Recreation under the Departments menu).
- **Prince George's County Department of Parks & Recreation** operates five outdoor pools; three indoor pools; and four "splash parks" with waterslides, fountains, and other fun features. Call 301-699-2400 or visit www.pgparks.com.
- **Arlington County Department of Parks, Recreation & Community Resources** operates indoor pools at Wakefield, Washington and Lee, and Yorktown high schools. Call 703-228-3323 or visit www.arlingtonva.us (click on Parks & Recreation).
- **Fairfax County** pools are located at county RECenters—see Health Clubs below.
- **Alexandria Department of Recreation, Parks & Cultural Activities** operates two full-sized pools for residents of all ages and four "neighborhood pools" for children 13 and under. Call 703-838-4843 or visit www.ci.alexandria.va.us/recreation.

See also Health Clubs below, as most gyms and YMCAs have indoor pools. Many colleges and high schools with swimming pools make their facilities available to the community during the summer and on weekends. Contact the college and university athletic offices listed under Collegiate Sports above or visit the **Potomac Valley Swimming** web site listing all regulation pools, public and private, in the Washington area: www.pvswim.org.

TENNIS

Public tennis courts abound in Rock Creek Park, along the Anacostia and Northwest Branch, and in countless neighborhood parks; in agreeable weather, all you need to do is grab a court and play. In the winter, you'll need reservations to play at an indoor tennis facility—there are only two inside the Beltway and a handful in the suburbs. Contact the **Maryland-National Capital Park & Planning Commission**, www.mc-mncppc.org, or call the specific venue:

- **Cabin John Regional Park**, 7801 Democracy Blvd., Bethesda, 301-469-7300,
- **Cosca Regional Park**, 11000 Thrift Rd., Clinton, 301-868-6462
- **East Potomac Park Tennis Center**, 1090 Ohio Dr. SW, 202-554-5962, www.eastpotomactennis.com
- **Fairland Sports & Aquatics Complex**, 13950 Old Gunpowder Rd., Laurel, 301-953-0030

NEWCOMER'S HANDBOOK FOR MOVING TO AND LIVING IN WASHINGTON D.C.

286

- **Rock Creek Park Tennis Center**, 16th & Kennedy streets NW, 202-722-5949, www.rockcreektennis.com
- **Wheaton Regional Park**, 11715 Orebaugh Ave., Wheaton, 301-649-4049

The indoor and outdoor courts of the **Southeast Tennis & Learning Center** in Congress Heights are open to the public when not in use by student and youth programs. Call 202-645-6242 or visit http://dpr.dc.gov. For information about tennis clubs and tournaments, contact the **U.S. Tennis Association**, Mid-Atlantic Section, at 703-556-6120 or www.midatlantic.usta.com.

ULTIMATE & DISC GOLF

You can usually find a pickup game of Ultimate on the Mall, the Ellipse, or any college campus. For information about leagues and tournaments, contact the Ultimate Players Association at 800-872-4384 or www.upa.org.

There is a public disc golf course on Paint Branch Parkway in College Park, near the Metro station. For information, call 301-445-4500 or visit www.pgparks.com/places and select "specialized sports facilities."

VOLLEYBALL

During the summer, there's always a pickup game somewhere on the Mall or in East Potomac Park. For a list of area leagues and tournaments, contact USA Volleyball, Chesapeake Region, at www.chrva.org or check the Weekend section of the *Post* for coming events.

HEALTH CLUBS

If you live in an apartment complex or work in a large office building, you might have access to a fitness center or weight room at little or no cost. If not, or if you prefer a health club with a wider range of amenities and services, you're never far from a full range of gyms and fitness centers. Most feature weight machines, stationary bikes, racquetball, swimming, aerobics, kickboxing, yoga, and all the latest trendy workouts; many clubs also offer personal trainers and "boot camp" regimens.

Generally, in the suburbs, you'll find "the Y" and the big three chains: Bally, Sport & Health, and Washington Sports Clubs. Downtown, you'll find more independent clubs, many of which double as social centers for urban singles.

- **Bally Total Fitness**, 12 locations, 800-515-2582, www.bally fitness.com
- **The Center Club**, 4300 King St., Alexandria, 703-820-8900

- **City Fitness**, 3525 Connecticut Ave. NW, 202-537-0539, www.fit physique.org
- **Club Fitness at Washington Center**, 1001 G St. NW, 202-637-4747
- **D.C. Jewish Community Center**, 1529 16th St. NW, 202-518-9400, www.dcjcc.org
- **Franklin Plaza Health Club**, 1200 K Street NW, 202-408-5645
- **Gold's Gym**, 20 locations, 202-554-4653 or 202-364-4653, www.goldsgym.com
- **One to One Fitness Center**, 1750 K St. NW, 202-452-1861; 555 13th St. NW, 202-383-8765; 3010 Williams Dr., Fairfax, 703-573-8083; Hyatt Regency Reston, 703-709-6100; 7929 Westpark Drive, Tysons Corner, VA, 703-848-0881; www.1to1fitness.com
- **Results - The Gym**, 1612 U St. NW, 202-518-0001; 315 G St. SE, 202-234-5678; www.resultsthegym.com
- **Sport & Health Clubs**, 24 locations, 703-556-6556, www.sportand health.com
- **Washington Sports Clubs**, 19 locations, 800-666-0808, www.my sportsclubs.com
- **YMCA of Metropolitan Washington**, 17 locations, 800-473-9622 or 202-232-6700, www.ymcawashdc.org

Fairfax County RECenters are comprehensive recreation and fitness centers featuring swimming pools, fitness rooms, spas, and racquetball courts. Other amenities, from volleyball courts to darkrooms and pottery studios, vary from one location to another. Fees are generally much lower than those of private health clubs. For more information, visit www.co.fair fax.va.us/parks (click on RECenters).

- **Alexandria**: George Washington RECenter, 8426 Old Mt. Vernon Rd., 703-780-8894; Mt. Vernon RECenter, 2017 Belle View Blvd., 703-768-3224
- **Annandale**: Wakefield RECenter, 8100 Braddock Rd., 703-321-7081
- **Chantilly**: Cub Run RECenter, 4630 Stonecroft Blvd., 703-817-9407
- **Falls Church**: Providence RECenter, 7525 Marc Dr., 703-698-1351
- **Franconia**: Lee District RECenter, 6601 Telegraph Rd., 703-922-9841
- **McLean**: Spring Hill RECenter, 1239 Spring Hill Rd., 703-827-0989
- **Oakton**: Oak Marr RECenter, Jermantown Rd. near Route 123, 703-281-6501
- **Springfield**: South Run RECenter, 7550 Reservation Dr., 703-866-0566

WASHINGTON D.C., WITH ITS HALF A MILLION PEOPLE, IS ALSO home to several wild bald eagles and hundreds of deer. The city's web of broad, tree-lined avenues and grand plazas, laid out by architect Pierre L'Enfant in 1790, supports abundant green spaces and a surprising array of wildlife. You'll find parks and open spaces, large and small, famous and obscure, dotting the landscape—parks with hiking and biking trails, parks with statues and benches, parks with playgrounds and ballfields, even parks for dogs. D.C. citizens and lawmakers are so proud of their green havens and sweeping boulevards they have kept L'Enfant's plan largely intact for more than two centuries. In 2001, philanthropist Betty Brown Casey established the **Casey Trees Endowment Fund** to make sure the District always remains a "city of trees"; for details or to volunteer, call 202-833-4010 or visit www.caseytrees.org.

D.C. is not alone in preserving green space. State and local governments in Maryland and Virginia protect tens of thousands of acres of woodland, riverside, marsh, and meadow for public enjoyment. Some private estates dating from colonial days invite visitors to formal gardens or secluded nature preserves. From Rock Creek Park, the 5,000-acre crown jewel of the region's natural areas, to the dozens of tiny wedge-shaped traffic medians crowned by statues honoring obscure frontiersmen, the region's parks are generally well-maintained, safe, and inviting.

Unless otherwise noted, the parks listed here are open daily from dawn to dusk and are free, although there may be fees for some events and attractions within. Many National Park Service sites charge a small admission fee for each vehicle; if you plan to visit more than a few times a year, it pays to get an annual pass from the National Parks Foundation at 888-467-2757 or www.nationalparks.org. Special lifetime passes are available for seniors and persons with disabilities.

NEWCOMER'S HANDBOOK FOR MOVING TO AND LIVING IN WASHINGTON D.C.

290

GENERAL INFORMATION

- **D.C. Department of Parks & Recreation** (playgrounds, ball fields, and recreation centers), 202-673-7660, http://dpr.dc.gov
- **Washington Parks & People** (urban greenspace), 202-462-7275, www.washingtonparks.net
- **Maryland Department of Natural Resources** (state parks and forests), 877-620-8367, www.dnr.state.md.us
- **Maryland-National Capital Park & Planning Commission** (local parks in the Maryland suburbs), 301-495-4600, www.mncppc.org
- **National Park Service**, National Capital Area, 202-690-5185, www.nps.gov
- **Northern Virginia Regional Park Authority** (local parks in the Virginia suburbs), 703-352-5900, www.nvrpa.org
- **Virginia Department of Conservation & Recreation** (state parks and forests), 800-933-7275, www.dcr.state.va.us
- **Potomac Riverkeeper**, www.potomacriverkeeper.org, and **Anacostia Riverkeeper,** www.anacostiariverkeeper.org (waterways and associated wetlands)

County and city park and recreation departments are listed under **Participant Sports** in the **Sports and Recreation** chapter.

MAJOR REGIONAL PARKS

These are huge greenspaces that span more than one jurisdiction.

ROCK CREEK PARK

Flowing almost 30 miles from Laytonsville, Md., to Georgetown, **Rock Creek** is filled with wooded parkland, sheltered trails, picnic groves, athletic fields, and several pockets of deep woods where you can quickly forget your proximity to the Beltway and the halls of government. A paved bike path follows the creek for much of its length, and on Sundays, Beach Drive—the park's main thoroughfare, and nowhere near a beach—is closed to motor vehicles and set aside for human-powered wheels.

Some of the park's major attractions warrant their own listings elsewhere in this book: Carter Barron Amphitheater, in **Cultural Life**; tennis and golf amenities, in **Sports and Recreation**; and the National Zoo, in this chapter. Near Gaithersburg, the creek is impounded to form Lake Needwood and Lake Frank, suburban family spots for fishing and boating. And in D.C., you can tour Pierce Mill, 202-426-6908, a grist mill whose waterwheel turned grindstones from the 1820s well into the 1990s.

Deer sometimes wander out of the park along Military Road NW in the District and throughout central Montgomery County; closer to the stream itself, the native trout have all but vanished, but frogs, snakes, salamanders, and turtles abound, and the woods are home to songbirds, owls, woodpeckers, raccoons, muskrats, and an occasional fox. A tributary stream in Cleveland Park is one of the few known habitats of the tiny Hays Spring amphipod—not exactly cute and furry, but the flea-like mud dweller is a uniquely Washingtonian creature.

Rock Creek Park is maintained by the National Park Service in D.C. and by the Maryland-National Capital Park & Planning Commission in Maryland. For more information, visit www.nps.gov/rocr.

C&O CANAL NATIONAL HISTORICAL PARK

If you were among the first to explore the internet, you may recall that the frontier of cyberspace in 1990 was navigated by "ftp" and "gopher" technology, and the World Wide Web was an eccentric fad. Likewise, in the early 19th century, innovators like Jefferson and John Quincy Adams were boosters of the barge canal, and little did they know that commercial railroads would connect the capital to the Ohio River before the Chesapeake & Ohio Canal could even be completed.

The artificial waterway along the eastern banks of the rocky Potomac did carry mule-drawn barges between Georgetown and the coal town of Cumberland, Md., until the early 20th century. In the 1970s, Supreme Court Justice William O. Douglas led the fight to preserve the ruins of the canal and restore the mules' towpath for hiking, biking, and jogging. Justice Douglas led hikes along the full length of the 185-mile towpath, a feat you can replicate today.

The southern 22 miles of the canal are fully restored; you can rent canoes at several places (see **Boating** in **Sports and Recreation**) or ride a sightseeing barge from the visitors' centers in Georgetown, 202-653-5190, or Great Falls, 301-767-3714. To the north, two major feats of early American engineering are preserved along the canal: the seven-arch stone aqueduct carrying the canal across the Monocacy River near Dickerson, and the 3/4-mile Paw Paw Tunnel through a mountain west of Hancock.

For more information, visit www.nps.gov/choh.

ANACOSTIA RIVER

Washington's "other" river is lined with federal and local parkland that links with Sligo Creek Park and Northeast Branch Park to preserve nearly uninterrupted ribbons of greenspace from Hains Point all the way to Wheaton and Beltsville. Bald eagles live here in growing numbers. The

NEWCOMER'S HANDBOOK FOR MOVING TO AND LIVING IN WASHINGTON D.C.

292

Anacostia's headwaters include Greenbelt Park, 301-344-3944, one of the largest stands of forest in the Washington area, and two of the region's outdoor gems: the National Arboretum and Kenilworth Park & Aquatic Gardens, both listed elsewhere in this chapter. Sligo Creek Park features a paved bike path connecting Northwest Branch Park in Hyattsville to Wheaton Regional Park (see the **Neighborhood Profiles**); on Sundays, Sligo Creek Parkway is closed to motor vehicles, providing a less crowded alternative to Rock Creek Park.

For more information, contact the Anacostia Watershed Society, 301-699-6204, www.anacostiaws.org.

DISTRICT OF COLUMBIA

- **The Mall and surrounding area**: America's front yard, the Mall stretches from the Ulysses S. Grant Memorial Pool, just west of the Capitol, to the Potomac River by the Lincoln Memorial. East of the Washington Monument, the Mall is crowded with people sunbathing or playing Frisbee or football—except when it's crowded instead with protesters, or with hordes of people celebrating the Fourth of July, Earth Day, or an inauguration. The east side of the Monument grounds is unofficially reserved for kite flying, and on any windy weekend, you can gawk at elaborate Chinese dragons and giant box kites, many purchased at the National Air & Space Museum nearby. Just west of the Monument is the World War II Memorial dedicated in 2004 with so many surviving veterans on hand that it was believed to be the largest gathering of senior citizens in history. To the west, along the Reflecting Pool, the Mall encompasses the Vietnam Veterans Memorial, the Korean War Memorial, the War Memorial Bandstand honoring veterans of World War I, and the Bicentennial Pond and Memorial, dedicated to the signers of the Declaration of Independence. These national shrines, like the Lincoln Memorial, need no introduction—they're always open and there's never a line or a fee. The only exception is the Washington Monument: to visit the observation deck, you need a free ticket assigning you an entry time. Tickets are available at the kiosk on the 15th St. side of the Monument grounds, or, for a small fee, you can order them in advance from Ticketmaster, 202-432-7328. For more information, call 202-426-6840 or visit www.nps.gov/wamo. Between the monument grounds and the White House is the Ellipse, a vast lawn that is home to the National Christmas Tree and the annual Pageant of Peace (see **A Washington Year**). Stroll around this area with your ADC Street Atlas, and you'll find obscure little monuments to, among others, the Boy Scouts; Albert Einstein; and Archie Butt, a White House aide who sacrificed his life for others aboard the *Titanic*.

- **East & West Potomac Park:** baseball diamonds, a golf course, bike paths, and plenty of fishing spots line the Potomac waterfront between the Lincoln Memorial and Hains Point, where the shallow Potomac swallows the Anacostia and becomes a big tidewater river. The east and west segments of the waterfront are divided by the inlet of the Tidal Basin. At the southern tip of East Potomac Park, Hains Point affords unique views of the Washington skyline and the river, and there's always a steady breeze. One of the most interesting pieces of statuary in this city of statues is here: Seward Johnson's sculpture "Awakening," where a buried giant yawns and stretches just before rising from the ground. Call 202-554-7660 for information about the golf course and other amenities.
- **Woodland parks:** from the air, D.C. looks as if a green octopus had picked the city up and squeezed. Throughout the city, especially near Rock Creek and the Anacostia River, long strips of woodland line tiny streams and valleys. Few residents live more than a 15-minute walk from some kind of nature preserve. Major parks between the Potomac and Rock Creek include Battery Kemble in Foxhall; Glover Archbold and Whitehaven off Wisconsin Ave. NW; and Soapstone Valley, Melvin C. Hazen, and Klingle Valley along Connecticut Ave. NW. Major parks east of the Anacostia River include Oxon Run off Wheeler Rd. SE, Ft. Stanton off W Street SE, Stanton along Pennsylvania and Alabama avenues SE, and the 400-acre Ft. Dupont off Minnesota Ave. NE. Throughout the city, your ADC Street Atlas will show dozens of smaller neighborhood parks—some no more than a city block. Many are the sites of old Civil War forts. A special gem is Theodore Roosevelt Island, 88 acres of woods and marsh in the middle of the Potomac, between the Kennedy Center and Rosslyn. If you can ignore the planes landing at Reagan National Airport nearby, and the Teddy Roosevelt Bridge carrying I-66 across the south end of the island, this is a fun little patch of wilderness. It's accessible only by a footbridge from the Virginia side, with its own parking area off the George Washington Parkway. The only man-made feature on the island—besides hiking trails—is a monument honoring the island's namesake.
- **Formal gardens:** one of the most spectacular and least visited spots in Washington is Dumbarton Oaks, the estate that hosted the founding summit of the United Nations. The Georgetown mansion is now a museum of Byzantine art, and the grounds encompass 16 acres of lovely old gardens. The estate is owned by Harvard University and is open to the public at no charge, 2 to 5 p.m. daily except holidays. The entrance is at 32nd and R streets NW. For more information, call 202-339-6401 or see www.doaks.org. The 57-acre grounds of the National Cathedral (see **Places of Worship**), including the Bishop's Garden,

NEWCOMER'S HANDBOOK FOR MOVING TO AND LIVING IN WASHINGTON D.C.

294

are open daily. Near the cathedral's sundial, look for the Glastonbury Tree—according to legend, it blooms only at Christmas and when royalty visits. With an appointment, you can visit the gardens and orchid greenhouse of the Hillwood Mansion in Van Ness, 202-686-5807, and the traditional gardens of the Japanese Embassy on Embassy Row, 202-238-6700. The Franciscan Monastery in Brookland welcomes visitors to its gardens and catacombs at 1400 Quincy St. NE. The grounds of the Capitol, and the park connecting the Capitol to Union Station, are a living museum of native and exotic trees, with many trees bearing plaques marking them as biological specimens planted by the architect of the Capitol or as memorials to great lawmakers. The Cherokee nation planted a sequoia here in 1970 to honor the bicentennial of Chief Sequoia.

- **Dog parks:** several neighborhood parks have gained a reputation as unofficial dog-walking parks—and meeting spots for dog-loving singles. See the **Pets** section in **Getting Settled** for more details.
- **National Zoological Park:** administratively part of the Smithsonian Institution and physically part of Rock Creek Park, the National Zoo was built in 1890 to house a herd of bison given to the Smithsonian. Today, the 175-acre zoo is a world leader in conservation biology as well as a tourist destination for three million people a year. This is not an old-fashioned zoo where animals are robbed of their dignity in austere cages; the Smithsonian has created artificial habitats that mimic the animals' native ecosystems. Visitors flock to see Sumatran tigers, komodo dragons, playful sea lions, and orangutans who commute from their home to their school by swinging from cables high above the human crowds. Two giant pandas, Tian Tian and Mei Xiang, arrived in 2000, and their son, Tai Shan, was born in 2005. The new century has also seen the births of tiger and cheetah cubs and an Asian elephant. Entrances are at 3001 Connecticut Ave. NW, on Harvard St. NW, and on Beach Drive in Rock Creek Park. There are free shuttle vans from the Woodley Park-Zoo/Adams Morgan Metro station on the Red Line. For more information, call 202-673-4800 or visit http://si.edu/natzoo.
- **Malcolm X Park:** still known by older residents as Meridian Hill Park, Malcolm X Park separates Adams Morgan from Columbia Heights, and uptown from downtown. High macadam walls with recessed fountains and stairwells enclose this oasis of gardens, fountains, and soccer fields. A statue of Joan of Arc gazes southward to a panoramic view of Washington—an insider's choice vantage for the Fourth of July fireworks. (Other evenings, the park is renowned as the gay red-light district; officially it is closed after dark.) In the 1980s, the park was effectively off limits to all but drug dealers and users; a civic organization now known as Washington Parks & People worked to make the

park a community gathering place again, and it is. During the summer, local bands play by the lower fountain and local painters peddle their works. Overlooking the northeast corner of the park, an old embassy building now houses the Josephine Butler Parks Center, where some two dozen community organizations share offices and meeting space. The old embassy ballrooms are a favorite venue for local fundraising dances and political receptions. Josephine Butler is remembered by longtime Washingtonians for her tireless efforts to improve D.C. communities, whether cleaning up neighborhood parks such as this one, promoting the performing arts, or working to make the residential parts of D.C. the 51st state. Washington Parks & People runs the center in her memory and continues to augment National Park Service stewardship of the park. For more information, call 202-387-9128.

- **National Arboretum:** The Arboretum is the USDA's tree preserve, a research facility in the form of a 450-acre park. On foot or bicycle, you can explore hundreds of species of labeled trees and shrubs, some nearly extinct in the wild; of the National Bonsai Collection housed in a pavilion here, naturalists Bill and Phyllis Thomas tell tourists that "this collection alone is worth a trip to Washington." Classes, workshops, and guided tours are available with reservations; call 202-399-5400 or visit www.usna.usda.gov. Entrance is on New York Ave. NE near Bladensburg Rd. On weekends and federal holidays, the Arboretum is served by Metrobus route X6 from Union Station.

- **Kenilworth Park & Aquatic Gardens:** In this wetlands park, private 19th-century gardens of water lilies have been allowed to spread naturally over the years, and the National Park Service has added cuttings from rare lotus plants and river grasses from all over the world. One Amazon lily here produces leaves six feet in diameter; another is a descendant of a millennium-old Chinese lotus. The entrance for walking visitors is on Douglas St. NW off Kenilworth Avenue, just inside the District; but purists insist that the best way to see the gardens is to paddle your kayak or canoe in from the Anacostia. For more information, call 202-426-6905 or visit www.nps.gov/kepa.

THE SUBURBS

In the counties neighboring D.C. there are more than 1,200 distinct parks, and even a brief overview would require a whole book; several such books are cited in the **Washington Reading List**. Here are some of the most interesting parks within a few miles of the Beltway:

- **Glen Echo Park:** easily mistaken for a storybook village, Glen Echo Park is a campus of pavilions and odd little buildings that once housed amusement park rides and attractions; a working antique carousel is

NEWCOMER'S HANDBOOK FOR MOVING TO AND LIVING IN WASHINGTON D.C.

296

the only overt relic of those days. Now the grounds, run by the National Park Service, are used mainly for craft studios, dance classes, children's theater, and art festivals. **Discovery Creek Children's Museum**, a nature center and wildlife clinic, is located here—202-364-3111 or www.discoverycreek.org; so is the historic home of American Red Cross founder Clara Barton. Entrance is on MacArthur Blvd. at Goldsboro Rd. west of Bethesda. For more information, call 301-492-6245 or see www.nps.gov/glec.

- **Great Falls:** cultural anthropologist Jack Weatherford studied Congress as a tribe, and wrote in *Tribes on the Hill* that Washington has been a significant crossroads of activity since prehistoric times—that it is no accident that the nation's capital is situated just below the geological "fall line" where a major river leaps off the Piedmont onto the coastal plain. Tribes of mastodon hunters settled here 20,000 years ago because the swamps between the Potomac and Anacostia were an intersection of the beasts' north-south and east-west migratory routes. Here at the fall line, the Potomac River roaring over 80-foot cliffs into the Mather Gorge is an arresting sight. Every year, a few people underestimate the river's power, ignore the posted warnings, venture too far onto the wet rocks, and vanish under the rapids. Expert kayakers can shoot the rapids in the gorge below the falls; above the falls, stick to the designated overlooks. The Virginia side is Great Falls National Park, off Old Dominion Dr. and Georgetown Pike; call 703-285-2965 or visit www.nps.gov/grfa. Admission is $4 per vehicle or $2 per person. Opens at 10 a.m. daily; closes at 4 p.m. in the winter, in the summer at 5 p.m. weekdays, and 6 p.m. weekends. The Maryland side is part of C&O Canal National Historical Park, listed above, and admission is free.
- **Seneca Creek State Park:** a forested link from Gaithersburg to the Potomac, Seneca Creek State Park protects some 4,500 acres along 12 miles of creek. In addition to the usual deer, foxes, raccoons, and other adaptive species, the more elusive bobcat and wild turkey have been seen here. You might also spot 300-year-old cypress trees, a seismic fault line, and evidence of the Native Americans who lived here 12,000 years ago. For more information, call 301-924-2127.
- **Patuxent River parks:** several detached sections of parkland line the Patuxent River, at the eastern boundaries of Montgomery and Prince George's counties. The tranquil river is ideal for canoeing and fishing. Some notable sections of the park include the **Triadelphia Reservoir**, north of Brighton Dam Rd. off New Hampshire Ave. in Brookeville; the **T. Howard Duckett Reservoir** off U.S. Route 29; **Patuxent Research Refuge**, off the Baltimore-Washington Parkway just beyond Beltsville; **Merkle Wildlife Management Area** in Croom; and **Jug Bay Wetlands Sanctuary** near Upper Marlboro. In

Montgomery County, call 301-489-4646 for information about fishing and boating on the reservoirs, or call the Washington Suburban Sanitary Commission at 301-699-4000. In Prince George's County, call 301-627-7074. Reservations are required for visits to certain ecologically sensitive areas.

- **Dyke Marsh:** south of Alexandria, Dyke Marsh is a 385-acre specimen of the pristine banks of the Potomac. Reached from the Belle Haven Marina access road from the George Washington Parkway, this wetlands preserve offers some of the best bird watching on the Potomac. For more information, call the superintendent of the George Washington Parkway at 703-289-2500, www.nps.gov/gwmp.

- **Mason Neck:** Telegraph Rd. south of Alexandria leads to some places not suited to casual exploration—Fort Belvoir Proving Ground, Davison U.S. Army Airfield, and the old D.C. prison at Lorton. Just south of these gray places, though, are some well-preserved greenspaces along the Potomac and the north shore of the Occoquan River: **Pohick Bay Regional Park**, taking its name from the Algonquin word for wetlands; **Mason Neck State Park**; and **Mason Neck National Wildlife Refuge**, 703-690-1297. These contiguous areas feature thriving marshes and hemlock forest, and nesting bald eagles as well as migratory birds. Along Gunston Rd. off U.S. Route 1.

- **Dranesville & Potomac Overlook Parks:** for the best views of the Potomac between Great Falls and Mt. Vernon, go for a walk in Dranesville District Park, 703-941-5008, in Fairfax County, off Georgetown Pike just outside the Beltway, or Potomac Overlook Regional Park, 703-278-8880, in Arlington County, on Marcey Rd. off Military Rd. Dranesville is secluded and largely undeveloped; Potomac Overlook features a nature center and archaeological sites exploring a Native American settlement.

- **National Colonial Farm:** this working demonstration farm is a model of environmentally advanced agriculture inspired by an era when all farming was organic. Crop varieties and edible wild plants harvested in colonial days are grown and studied here, as is the American chestnut tree—once the mighty Eastern counterpart to the California redwood, the chestnut was rendered nearly extinct by a blight in the mid-20th century. The chestnut grove here is part of an effort to cultivate a resistant variety. The farm site offers workshops and children's activities, and is open to visitors on weekends all year. The park is open daily, dawn to dusk. Located off Bryan Point Rd. in Accokeek, and accessible by ferry from Mt. Vernon across the Potomac. For information, call the Accokeek Foundation, 301-283-2113, or visit www.accokeek.org. (Other folklife demonstration farms include the **Claude Moore Colonial Farm** at Turkey Run Park, 6310 Georgetown

NEWCOMER'S HANDBOOK FOR MOVING TO AND LIVING IN WASHINGTON D.C.

298

Pike, McLean, 703-442-7557, www.1771.org, and **Oxon Hill Farm** in Oxon Hill, Md., 301-839-1177, www.nps.gov/nace/oxhi.)

- **Gravelly Point:** one of the most surprising natural areas in Washington is the parkland surrounding a lagoon between the Pentagon and National Airport. On the inland side of the lagoon, **Roaches Run Waterfowl Sanctuary** attracts migrating geese, ducks, herons, and egrets, despite the railroad tracks and I-395 just yards away. At the inlet of the lagoon, locals know the Gravelly Point picnic area as an offbeat place to bring a date—the great views of the Washington skyline are interrupted every few minutes as you get buzzed by jets landing on Reagan National Airport's main runway, just across the narrow inlet. For more information, call the superintendent of the George Washington Parkway at 703-557-8991.

HAZARDS

There are only two inherently dangerous wild animals in the Washington area: the poisonous copperhead snake and the deer tick. Several other creatures can ruin a camping trip, though, and warrant some precautions:

- **Copperheads** live in woods and meadows, and are not often seen; as the name suggests, their skin is the color of fallen leaves. If you do spot one, you can recognize it (if you want to get this close) by the diamond-shaped head and small pits below the eyes. Like all North American snakes, copperheads are shy and generally bite only if provoked.
- **Deer ticks** transmit Lyme disease, an aggressive form of arthritis that can become debilitating and even attack internal organs. After any outing in wooded areas, check yourself and your children and pets for ticks; the deer tick is about half the size of the more common, and less dangerous, dog tick. After a few days, deer tick bites begin to swell and take on a distinctive red bull's-eye appearance; get immediate medical attention, especially for small children. Precaution: wear insect repellent and keep your head and ankles covered.
- **Mosquitoes** can spread certain diseases, though they more commonly just leave the familiar itchy welts that go away after a few days. Summer outbreaks of the West Nile virus, carried by birds and then spread by mosquito bites, sometimes reach the mid-Atlantic region. In response, some communities spray pesticides to control mosquitoes. It's a losing battle. Washington is built on swamp land and ravenous mosquitoes abound in the summer. Precaution: get used to mosquito bites. Insect repellent helps, but we're outnumbered!
- **Gypsy moths** were introduced to North America by accident in the late 19th century and have been damaging forests ever since. The young caterpillars feed on leaves—almost any kind of leaves, but espe-

cially oak and other hardwoods—in the spring and early summer. If you have trees in your yard, you can protect them with inexpensive (or even homemade) caterpillar traps. Visit one of the home and garden stores listed in **Shopping for the Home**, or see www.gypsy-moth.com.

- **Bears** thrive in areas just 100 miles from the White House, especially in Shenandoah National Park and in the mountains of Western Maryland. Generally they want your food, not you, and they can and do break into unattended cars to get it. The American black bear seldom attacks people—just don't step between a mother and her cub. Precaution: if you're camping overnight—even in a cabin—keep your food in a drawstring bag hung from a tree.

- **Rabies carriers** include raccoons as well as mice and rats—which do not distinguish between "good" and "bad" neighborhoods. Some bats carry rabies, but the brown bats fluttering above D.C. at sunset eat insects and do not attack people. The city's ubiquitous gray squirrels (and the occasional black squirrel) do not carry rabies. Precaution: don't approach or feed raccoons. Keep trash covered in a pest-resistant trash can and rinse recyclable containers before putting them outside.

- **Giardia** are microbes that live in streams and spring water in the mountains near Washington; when ingested, they can cause nausea, diarrhea, and stomach pain, sometimes lasting for months. Precaution: no matter how pristine the water looks, run it through a filter rated for giardia. The microbe lives in a hard capsule and, unlike most bacteria, can survive boiling.

- **Poison ivy** flourishes near running water, and its oils can cause an itchy rash and blistering. Remember what young scouts say about wild plants with three leaves per stem: "Leaves of three, let it be." Precaution: for hiking, wear high-top shoes and tall socks; if you are exposed to poison ivy, be careful not to spread the oil to other parts of your body.

OTHER FLORA AND FAUNA

Inside the Beltway, you see squirrels and pigeons every day, and robins and other migratory birds in the spring and summer. Occasionally, you might see a garter snake, rabbit, hawk, eagle, or owl; and on summer evenings from twilight to midnight, you see the yellow flickers of the firefly beetle or "lightning bug." Around streams and ponds, look for frogs, turtles, and beavers; on larger ponds and rivers, especially along the Anacostia, you can see herons and cranes fishing in the shallows, along with plenty of ducks and geese.

You might be surprised to see seagulls circling above suburban parking lots—large paved spaces sometimes create air currents that remind the

NEWCOMER'S HANDBOOK FOR MOVING TO AND LIVING IN WASHINGTON D.C.

300

birds of the Chesapeake Bay, and they feed on litter. An occasional fox, opossum, or bobcat might show up in the outer suburbs or larger woodland parks, and coyotes have been spotted around the northern reaches of Rock Creek, but mostly these creatures are elusive. You see skunks occasionally and smell them fairly often, and in deep woods, you might glimpse a wild turkey.

The arrival of spring is marked by yellow forsythia and white dogwood blossoms; oak and gingko trees drop their distinctive seeds later in the summer. Tulip poplar, white pine, Virginia pine, magnolia, white birch, and dozens more broadleaf and evergreen trees thrive in Washington's temperate climate, and cultivated plants like azalea proliferate in many front yards. No patch of grass is immune to dandelions in the spring, and no cove of the lower Potomac (from Hains Point to the Bay) is immune to jellyfish in August; it's up to you whether those are nuisances or natural features of the place where you now live.

Visit www.audubonnaturalist.org for more information about non-human residents of the Washington area.

THERE ARE THREE SAFE GENERALIZATIONS THAT CAN BE MADE ABOUT Washington's weather: the summers are horrendously humid, the winters are slushy and icy, and the exceptions outnumber the rules. In March, temperatures can go from a freezing 30° to 80°, and back, within a few days. You can expect a week or two of 3-digit temperatures in August, and a week or two in January when you may need to take precautions against frozen pipes. Thunderstorms in February aren't unheard-of, nor light snow in April. Despite these rather dramatic exceptions, Washington has four predictable seasons—including a colorful, breezy fall and a delightful spring of dogwood and cherry blossoms.

August, on the other hand, is simply hell. It's hard to convey how humid it gets here—it's described as "oppressive" by weather forecasters, and you never quite get used to it. One longtime resident who grew up in Michigan says this is the only place where you need to take a shower after you get out of the shower. Many Washingtonians leave town every August, and central air conditioning is a big selling point in real estate listings. There is some cooling relief in the summer evenings, when you can almost set your watch by the 5 o'clock thunderstorms that ripple through. Several times a year these storms intensify and remind us that nature bats last: the news photo of a car crushed under a fallen tree limb, the banner across the bottom of the TV screen listing counties under a tornado watch, and the widespread power failures are all summertime rituals. A few tornadoes are spotted each year within 100 miles of Washington, and one actually hit suburban College Park in 2001.

The other weather-related ritual comes each winter with the evening news: a snowstorm is coming, and people wait in hour-long lines at the grocery store to stock up on milk and toilet paper. Travelers are stranded at the airport, and there's always someone from Buffalo or Minneapolis to

NEWCOMER'S HANDBOOK FOR MOVING TO AND LIVING IN WASHINGTON D.C.

302

explain that Washingtonians are all a bunch of wimps. And it's true—the Washington area does not cope well with snow. Schools close at the drop of a flake, and it takes only 12 inches to close all but the most essential elements of the federal government. But winter is only occasionally paralyzing—devotees of sledding and snowball fights will be satisfied only once or twice in a typical year. Most often the D.C. area experiences precipitation in the form of falling slush, called a "wintry mix" by local meteorologists. With temperatures often hovering just around freezing, winter storms drop ever-changing combinations of rain, snow, and sleet. When freezing rain leaves a sheet of ice on the city, watch out—the trees are beautiful, but the streets and ice-encrusted power lines can be deadly.

FLOODING

Once every five years or so, a hurricane makes its way up the Atlantic coast and grazes the Washington area. Flooding here is more often caused when a winter storm dumps a foot of snow on the Potomac watershed and it all melts within a week or two.

In Old Town Alexandria, authorities and neighbors scramble to protect the low-lying streets with sandbags. Most other homes and businesses along the Potomac are secure, except in the unusual 100-year floods, such as those after Hurricane Agnes visited in 1972. Hurricanes Gloria and Hugo, more recently, tore away chunks of the retaining wall of the C&O Canal, putting much of the beloved towpath out of commission for several years. This type of flooding happens roughly once a decade.

Flash flooding, which occurs after ordinary heavy thunderstorms, can push little suburban streams over their banks and into people's basements, and the occasional clogged storm drain can trap rainwater on city streets and paralyze traffic. If you live in a basement apartment or near a stream, you might want flood insurance.

LOCAL VARIATION

The counties bordering the District extend almost 40 miles from the White House. The northern part of Montgomery County, the western reaches of Fairfax, and southern Prince George's County have different climates, affected by their proximity to the mountains or the Chesapeake Bay and by their distance from the "heat island" created by a major city.

If you live in southern Montgomery County, you might wonder why county schools are closed when there are barely three inches of snow on the ground; well, it's because northern Montgomery County got eight inches of snow. Each county includes a certain number of snow days, usually five, in its calendar; once they're used up, the school year must be extended in June. (In the District, schools close when there's even a good chance of snow, because the city is notoriously inept at snow removal. A major snowstorm can make or break the political future of a mayor, so there are constant efforts to improve the snow emergency plan.)

Washington is right in the middle of the zone where winter precipitation changes from snow to rain; a common forecast is for "snow in the northern and western suburbs, rain to the south and east." That line coincides roughly with I-95, and in the summer, thunderstorms can wreak havoc west of I-95 and go unnoticed to the east.

The heat island effect means that temperatures are always a few degrees higher inside the Beltway than in the outer suburbs. Depending on where you lived before coming here, there might be a few other terms that are new to you: *wind chill,* an estimate of how much colder it feels on account of the wind; *heat index,* an estimate of how much hotter it feels on account of the humidity; and *heating degree days,* a measure of the severity of the winter and the cost in heating fuel. (Heating degree days measure the difference between the day's average temperature and 65° F. For example, to calculate the number of heating degree days in a given month, a meteorologist will add 5 for each day on which the average temperature was 60° F, 10 for each day on which the average temperature was 55° F, and so on.) The Washington area averages around 4,055 heating degree days per year, compared to 7,900 in Minneapolis or 150 in Miami. January here averages around 945 heating degree days; April averages 270. Utility companies use this information to estimate fuel costs.

SNOW EMERGENCIES

Major thoroughfares in the District and suburbs are marked with signs that say snow emergency route. When snow causes hazardous road conditions, local authorities may declare a "snow emergency," making it illegal to drive on snow emergency routes without snow tires or chains. If your vehicle gets stuck in the snow and you are not properly equipped, you may get a ticket. A snow emergency also allows taxi drivers to add a surcharge.

In icy conditions that don't quite force schools to close, local school districts will declare a late opening—schools will open one or two hours late in order to avoid mixing school buses with rush-hour traffic. Schools and some federal offices may close early if a snowstorm hits during the day.

Along with school closings, you will hear announcements on the radio saying the federal government has announced "liberal leave," which means government employees may take personal leave time without having scheduled it in advance. And many private employers follow the lead of the government—closing when the government closes, allowing employees to use leave time when the government does.

NEWCOMER'S HANDBOOK FOR MOVING TO AND LIVING IN WASHINGTON D.C.

304

The District and most neighboring jurisdictions have laws that require you to remove snow from the sidewalk in front of your house, and clear a path to your mailbox or front door, within 24 hours after the snow stops falling.

Finally, if you've moved here from a warm climate, learn how to prevent water pipes from breaking in cold weather. Few homes have insulated plumbing; if yours doesn't, whenever the temperature is expected to be in the 20s (Fahrenheit) for 24 hours or more, leave a little trickle of water dripping from the tap farthest from the point where the water pipe enters your house. Yes, it is wasteful—but much less wasteful than an avoidable broken pipe. (You can catch the water in a bucket and use it later.)

AIR POLLUTION

The Washington area has never been in compliance with the federal Clean Air Act, which limits the number of days per year a jurisdiction may exceed certain pollution levels. Here, the culprit is ozone—unlike the high-altitude ozone that protects us from the sun's ultraviolet radiation, ground-level ozone is an unwelcome byproduct of auto exhaust and industrial emissions. Ozone is a key ingredient in urban smog, and it's a respiratory irritant that can cause problems for people with asthma, seniors, and people doing strenuous exercise outdoors.

Air quality is monitored by the **Metropolitan Washington Council of Governments** (COG), a partnership of counties, municipalities, and state and federal agencies addressing regional issues such as transportation and suburban sprawl. The COG **air quality index** is included in most weather reports, along with pollen advisories for those with allergies, and ozone alerts are issued during the summer "ozone season," May–August. Under federal guidelines, COG declares "Code Yellow" days warning those who are susceptible to ozone-related problems to avoid any heavy exertion outdoors. "Code Orange" days warn susceptible persons to stay inside as much as possible; and everyone should avoid spending more than eight hours outside. On a "Code Red" day everyone is advised to stay inside and local buses waive their fares to help minimize car traffic. The region typically experiences half a dozen Code Red days per year.

For more information about regional air quality, visit www.mwcog.org/environment or call COG's **Air Quality Hotline** at 202-962-3299.

STATISTICS

Just for the record, here are the official average temperatures and precipitation totals for each month, compiled by the National Weather Service from every year on record at Reagan National Airport. The temperatures are rounded to the nearest degree, and the precipitation totals are rounded to the nearest inch. Remember, though, that these are averages; the "average" temperature in February may be in the high thirties, but there are plenty of evenings when temperatures in the low twenties make it a serious effort to wait for a bus. On a humid afternoon in July when it's 98° out, you don't care that the statistical average temperature is a mild 80°. And remember that three inches of precipitation in January is not the same as three inches in June—the same amount of water that falls as an inch of rain can fall as 5 to 15 inches of snow.

	Temperature (F)	Precipitation
January	33° to 36°	2" to 3"
February	36° to 39°	2" to 3"
March	46° to 48°	2.5" to 3.5"
April	55° to 57°	2" to 3"
May	65° to 67°	3" to 4"
June	74° to 76°	2" to 4"
July	79° to 80°	2.5" to 4"
August	77° to 81°	2.5" to 4.5"
September	70° to 72°	1.5" to 4"
October	58° to 61°	2" to 3.5"
November	48° to 51°	2" to 3.5"
December	38° to 41°	2" to 3.5"

WEATHER REPORTS & FORECASTS

Washington's favorite TV weather forecaster is Channel 4's Bob Ryan, whose team collects highly localized data from weather stations set up in elementary schools around the region. During a major snowstorm, or the occasional hurricane, Ryan and his colleagues just might be the most influential people in the nation's capital.

In addition to local broadcast news and The Weather Channel, you can call 936-1212 (in any area code) to get an hourly weather report sponsored by Verizon. For travel forecasts, marine advisories, sunrise/sunset, tides, and other details, see the weather page in the Metro section of the *Washington Post* or visit the weather page at www.nbc4.com. If you use e-mail, a cell phone, or a PDA, you can subscribe to services that send you customized weather alerts. A free service available from www.weather.com sends you a message announcing any weather advisories or warnings affecting your immediate area. You can also get detailed weather information, including a huge library of current satellite images, from the **National Weather Service** at www.nws.noaa.gov.

NEWCOMER'S HANDBOOK FOR MOVING TO AND LIVING IN WASHINGTON D.C.

306

THE NIGHT SKY

If you move here from a rural area or small town, you may complain that you can't see the stars; if you move here from New York City, you will be dazzled—especially on a clear winter night or after a heavy storm has rinsed the smog out of the air. In the inner suburbs and the outermost parts of the District, on residential side streets away from the orange glare of sodium-vapor streetlights, you can pick out constellations like Orion and the Big Dipper; in the outer suburbs, you can see much more—even meteors and passing satellites. Venus and Jupiter are easily mistaken for airplanes until you see that they're not moving. You'll have to take a road trip to see the glowing band of the Milky Way, but from most of the Washington area, you can see enough bright stars to get your bearings.

Aspiring astronomers can call 202-357-2000 for the Air & Space Museum's weekly recorded message explaining where and when to spot planets and first-magnitude stars; also, the museum's Albert Einstein Planetarium offers virtual tours of the night sky. So does **Arlington Planetarium**, 1426 N. Quincy St., Arlington, 703-358-6070, www.arlington.k12.va.us/instruct. For upcoming satellite passes visible from your exact location, visit www.heavens-above.com. And for a calendar of stargazing events, lectures, and "open telescope" nights at area observatories, visit **National Capital Astronomers** at www.capitalastronomers.org.

I F YOU CAME FROM A SMALL TOWN, YOU MAY HAVE GONE TO *THE* Methodist church, *the* Catholic church, or *the* synagogue. No problem. But in Washington, you will find dozens of each, plus Buddhist viharas, Muslim mosques, Ethiopian Orthodox churches, Korean Baptist churches, and a whole suburban town built by the Seventh-Day Adventist Church. Moravians, Mennonites, Swedenborgians, Antiochans, Armenian Apostolics, Byzantine Catholics, and Huguenots each have congregations here. The golden spires of the Washington Mormon Temple rise like Oz from the trees of Rock Creek Park. The Gothic towers and gargoyles of the Washington National Cathedral look like they belong in 16th-century Europe, as does the brightly painted dome of the Basilica of the National Shrine of the Immaculate Conception. And amid the constant buzz of downtown traffic, around the corner from a Staples office supply store, you can attend services at the New York Avenue Presbyterian Church, just as Abraham Lincoln did when he lived in Washington.

FINDING A PLACE OF WORSHIP

If you belong to a congregation in your old hometown, your religious leader might be able to refer you to a kindred congregation in Washington. On Saturdays, the Religion section in the *Washington Post* includes a page of classified ads which lists places of worship and their weekly and daily services; also, the Yellow Pages has extensive listings under "Churches" and "Synagogues." The phone book listings are arranged by denomination and include sections for nondenominational, interdenominational, and independent churches, as well as metaphysical and spiritual science centers.

These interfaith agencies, representing congregations working together to address hunger, homelessness, and other urban problems, might be able to refer you to a congregation that fulfills your spiritual needs:

NEWCOMER'S HANDBOOK FOR MOVING TO AND LIVING IN WASHINGTON D.C.

308

- **Council of Churches of Greater Washington**, 202-722-9240
- **InterFaith Conference of Metropolitan Washington**, 202-234-6300, www.ifcmw.org
- **Washington Interfaith Network**, 202-518-0815, http://wind c-iaf.org

The **National Council of Churches**, 212-870-2227, www.ncccusa.org, publishes the *Yearbook of American & Canadian Churches*, a directory listing of thousands of Christian churches. Order one for $35 at 888-870-3325 or browse the directory links at www.electronicchurch.org.

Other online directories of churches—generally limited to Christian denominations—include http://dcregistry.com/churches, http://netmin-istries.org, http://churches.net, and www.forministry.com.

Synagogues serving all branches of Judaism are listed at www.jew-ishdc.org (click on Religious Life). In addition, the **Jewish Information and Referral Service (JIRS)** is a comprehensive information and referral service for all things Jewish in the greater metropolitan area. JIRS' services include a searchable online database at www.jirs.org, childcare referral, information packets for people considering a move to the area, and more.

Of course, in all but the largest churches—those that draw congregations from miles around—the character of the neighborhood will give you a good idea of the character of services. Catholic services at Blessed Sacrament in Chevy Chase are very different from Catholic services at St. Augustine in Shaw; and a Baptist church in the outer suburbs might have a busy youth ministry and family counseling center, while a sister church in the inner city might devote its social ministries to a soup kitchen or home-less shelter. If you're attracted to a place of worship far from your home, remember to check weekend bus and Metro schedules, or allow time for heavy traffic near larger churches.

HISTORIC PLACES OF WORSHIP

These are grand places of worship that draw many visitors of all faiths—for worship, concerts, tours emphasizing art and architecture, special book-stores and gift shops, or just for curiosity.

- **Washington National Cathedral**, Wisconsin & Massachusetts avenues NW, 202-966-2171 (general information) or 202-537-6200 (services); www.cathedral.org/cathedral. The National Cathedral is a functioning Episcopal church—home of the Episcopal Diocese of Washington—and, at the same time, a universal house of worship honor-ing faith traditions from all over the world. If you look around carefully, or ask a tour guide, you will find embedded stones from Jerusalem, the Appian Way, and the Moon; and, yes, one of the thousands of different gargoyles and grotesques is carved in the image of Darth Vader. The

Bishop's Garden and the "close," or grounds, of the cathedral are inviting in their own right, and on a nice day, you will probably see lots of people with easels and charcoal or paint, trying to capture the grandeur of the Gothic buttresses and the boxwood hedges.

- **Basilica of the National Shrine of the Immaculate Conception**, 4th St. & Michigan Ave. NE, 202-526-8300, www.nationalshrine.com. The flagship Roman Catholic church in the United States, the National Shrine is one of the ten largest churches in the world, with dozens of chapels under its distinctive multicolored dome. The Pope confers the designation of "basilica" on churches of special historic or cultural significance, and rare peregrine falcons have designated this basilica a nesting place.

- **Washington Islamic Center**, 2551 Massachusetts Ave. NW, 202-332-8343, www.theislamiccenter.com. With Arabic minarets towering above the trees along Embassy Row and onion-shaped archways trimmed in turquoise and gold, "The Mosque" can make you do a double-take and believe, for a moment, you're in Riyadh or Istanbul. This is the oldest genuine mosque, built facing Mecca, in the United States. In 2001, after the terrorist attacks that destroyed the World Trade Center and damaged the Pentagon, President George W. Bush paid a historic visit here to promise the Muslim community that the nation's war against terrorism would not be a war against Islam.

- **Washington Mormon Temple**, Stoneybrook Dr. & Beach Dr., Kensington, 301-587-0144, www.ldschurchtemples.com. The towering, castle-like temple of the Church of Jesus Christ of Latter-Day Saints is a major landmark along the Beltway, inspiring a graffiti artist to caption the looming edifice by painting, on an overpass across the highway, "Surrender Dorothy." Only baptized Mormons are allowed inside the temple itself, but a visitor center on the grounds hosts concerts and lectures. In December, the wooded grounds are lit by thousands of tiny white Christmas lights in the trees, casting a halo on cloudy skies; choirs and a live nativity draw crowds to the visitor center.

- **National Presbyterian Church**, 4101 Nebraska Ave. NW, 202-537-0800, www.natpresch.org. The flagship Presbyterian church in the United States, the National Presbyterian Church and National Presbyterian Center occupy a sleek modern sanctuary just off Embassy Row.

- **St. Matthew's Cathedral**, 1725 Rhode Island Ave. NW, 202-347-3215, www.stmatthewscathedral.org. The Cathedral of St. Matthew the Apostle is the mother church of the Catholic Archdiocese of Washington, and under the distinctive green dome, Pope John Paul II celebrated mass here in 1979. The annual Red Mass in the fall seeks divine guidance for the legal profession, and is attended by members of the Supreme Court, the Cabinet, and Congress.

NEWCOMER'S HANDBOOK FOR MOVING TO AND LIVING IN WASHINGTON D.C.

310

- **St. John's Episcopal Church**, 16th & H streets NW, 202-347-8766; standing just across Lafayette Square from the White House, St. John's is known as the "Church of the Presidents"—for more than a century, every President has attended services here.

CHURCHES IN THE COMMUNITY

Most congregations have volunteer programs and community outreach services, but here are just a few of the larger churches whose charitable ministries play a big role in D.C. civic life:
- **All Souls Unitarian Church**, 16th & Harvard streets NW, 202-332-5266
- **First Congregational Church**, 945 G St. NW, 202-628-4317
- **Friends Meeting of Washington**, 2111 Florida Ave. NW, 202-483-3310
- **Scripture Cathedral**, 8th & O streets NW, 202-483-9400
- **Shiloh Baptist Church**, 1500 9th St. NW, 202-232-4000
- **St. Aloysius Parish**, 19 I St. NW, 202-336-7200
- **St. Augustine Catholic Church**, 15th & V streets NW, 202-265-1470
- **Union Temple Baptist Church**, 12th & W streets SE, 202-678-8822
- **United House of Prayer for All People**, 601 M St. NW, 202-289-1916

RESOURCES

These faith-based agencies are a good place to start as you look for your place of worship. There are thousands of possibilities here—large and small, grand and simple, conservative and liberal, famous and obscure— from major Baptist and Unitarian Universalist churches with a thousand members and roots dating to the Underground Railroad to little Pentecostal storefronts and service-oriented urban ministries, to Far Eastern meditation centers. This is by no means a complete list, and no substitute for the listings in the newspaper and phone book, but these religious denominations have regional or national directories online or major information centers in Washington:
- **African Methodist Episcopal:** www.amecnet.org or Second Episcopal District, 202-842-3788, www.amec2nd.org
- **Baptist: American Baptist Churches Mission Center**, 800-222-3872, www.abc-usa.org
- **Baha'i:** D.C. Baha'i Center, 800-228-6483 or 202-291-5532, www.dcbahai.org
- **Brethren:** Southeast Christian Fellowship, 202-581-3387
- **Buddhist, Theravadan:** Buddhist Vihara Society, 202-723-0773, www.buddhistvihara.com

- **Buddhist, Zen:** Zen Buddhist Society of Washington, 202-829-1966
- **Christian Methodist Episcopal:** Seventh Episcopal District, www.cmesonline.org, 202-829-8070
- **Christian Science:** 202-783-4325 (recorded information)
- **Episcopal/Anglican:** www.edow.org, 800-642-4427 or 202-537-6555
- **Friends (Quakers):** Baltimore Yearly Meeting, 800-962-4766 or 301-774-7663, www.bym-rsf.org; regional offices for D.C., Maryland, Virginia, and southern Pennsylvania
- **Hindu:** Gandhi Memorial Center & Golden Lotus Temple, 202-229-3871
- **Islamic (Muslim):** Idara Dawat-O-Irshad, 703-256-8622, www.irshad.org; Muslim Community Center, 301-384-3454, www.mccmd.org
- **Jewish, Conservative:** United Synagogue of Conservative Judaism, 301-230-0801, http://uscj.org
- **Jewish, Orthodox:** Orthodox Union, 212-807-7888, www.ou.org
- **Jewish, Reconstructionist:** Jewish Reconstructionist Federation, 301-206-2332, www.jrf.org
- **Jewish, Reform:** Union for Reform Judaism, http://urj.org, 888-842-8242 or 202-232-4242
- **Jehovah's Witnesses:** Washington, D.C. Central Unit, 202-832-9177
- **Latter-Day Saints (Mormons):** www.lds.org; Washington Mormon Temple, 301-587-0144
- **Lutheran, Evangelical:** Evangelical Lutheran Church in America, 800-638-3522, www.elca.org
- **Lutheran, Missouri Synod:** 888-843-5267, www.lcms.org
- **Mennonite:** Washington Community Fellowship, 202-543-1926
- **Methodist, United:** Washington Episcopal Area, 202-546-3110
- **Moravian:** Moravian Church in America, 800-732-0591, www.moravian.org
- **Orthodox:** Orthodox Church in America, www.oca.org; Orthodox Christian Foundation, www.ocf.org
- **Nazarene:** National Church of the Nazarene, 202-723-3252
- **Pentecostal, Assemblies of God:** General Council of the Assemblies of God, www.agfinder.org, 417-862-2781
- **Pentecostal, Church of God in Christ:** www.cogic.org
- **Pentecostal, International:** 405-787-7110, www.iphc.org
- **Presbyterian:** National Presbyterian Center, 202-537-0800, www.natpresch.org
- **Roman Catholic:** Catholic Information Center, 202-783-2062, www.catholic.net
- **Scientology:** Founding Church of Scientology, 202-667-6245, http://foundingchurch.scientology.org

NEWCOMER'S HANDBOOK FOR MOVING TO AND LIVING IN WASHINGTON D.C.

312

- **Seventh-Day Adventist:** Columbia Union Conference, 301-596-0800, www.columbiaunion.org
- **Unitarian Universalist:** Unitarian Universalist Association of Congregations, 617-742-2100, www.uua.org
- **United Church of Christ:** Office of General Ministries, 216-736-2100, www.ucc.org
- **Wesleyan:** Chesapeake Wesleyan District, 410-571-9235

GAY & LESBIAN SPIRITUAL GROUPS

The *Washington Blade* (see **Newspapers and Magazines** in **Getting Settled**) runs a calendar of religious services and congregations that welcome the gay and lesbian community, and there are plenty. Some additional resources for gay and lesbian people of faith are:

- **Bet Mishpachah Gay & Lesbian Synagogue**, 202-833-1638, www.betmishpachah.org
- **Dignity—Gay & Lesbian Catholics, Families, and Friends**, 703-912-1662, www.dignitywashington.org
- **Metropolitan Community Church**, 202-638-7373, www.mccdc.com

NEW AGE & SPIRITUALITY

For a comprehensive guide to New Age spiritual centers, ayurveda, meditation, mysticism, Pagan, shamanist, yoga, and Wiccan spiritual resources, pick up a copy of ***Pathways*** magazine at any health food store or bookstore. Also available online at www.pathwaysmag.com.

WASHINGTONIANS PERFORM ROUGHLY HALF A MILLION HOURS of volunteer service every year—tutoring, coaching youth sports, cleaning up neighborhood streams and parks, selling tickets to the local symphony, giving museum tours, staffing libraries and fire departments, supporting political campaigns, serving food to the needy, repairing inner-city homes and schools, and painting over graffiti. At some of the most prominent soup kitchens and shelters, if you want to volunteer on Thanksgiving or Christmas, you actually need to make reservations months in advance. The other 363 days of the year, there's no shortage of places that will welcome your contributions of physical labor, professional skills, or the time and the dedication to stuff envelopes and make phone calls.

The spirit and impact of volunteers is honored here by a series of bronze medallions along **The Extra Mile (Points of Light Volunteer Pathway)** on 15th Street NW between Pennsylvania Avenue and G Street. The first 20 medallions were dedicated in 2005 by former president George H.W. Bush, who first referred to the nation's volunteers as "a thousand points of light"; space is reserved for 50 more. Frederick Douglass, Helen Keller, Clara Barton, Cesar Chavez, and Harriet Tubman were among the first honorees. For more information, contact the Points of Light Foundation at 202-729-8165 or visit www.extramile.us.

Volunteering is a great way to meet people in your new community. Any national organization you've supported in the past undoubtedly has a chapter in Washington, and for any cause that captures your interest, there's probably a community organization here too. If you attended a big university or prominent small college, there's probably an alumni officer here—a volunteer opportunity in its own right as well as a source of ideas. If you join a religious congregation, ask about community service programs. If you don't know where to begin, check out *Finding Fun & Friends*

NEWCOMER'S HANDBOOK FOR MOVING TO AND LIVING IN WASHINGTON D.C.

314

in Washington: An Uncommon Guide to Common Interests by Roberta Gettesman. These resources can also help you find ways to volunteer:

- **Greater D.C. Cares** works with dozens of community organizations to arrange monthly or occasional volunteer opportunities for groups or families. Individual members may team up to participate in group projects, and many employers organize workplace volunteer projects through the service. Call 202-777-4440 or visit www.dc-cares.org.
- *Washingtonian* magazine lists volunteer opportunities at www.washingtonian.com/schools.
- **The *Washington Post*** on Thursdays, in the D.C. Extra and suburban Extra sections, lists volunteer opportunities and donations needed at a variety of local charities.
- **DoingSomething** organizes groups to be matched with local charities for a variety of service projects. Call 202-393-5051 or visit www.doingsomething.org.

VOLUNTEER BUREAUS

Volunteer bureaus are city or county agencies that keep track of current and permanent volunteer opportunities at area nursing homes, soup kitchens, libraries, animal shelters, museums and more:

- **D.C. Commission on National & Community Service**, 202-727-7925, www.cncs.dc.gov
- **Alexandria Volunteer Bureau**, 703-836-2176, www.alexandriavolunteers.com
- **Arlington County Volunteer Office**, 703-228-1760, www.arlingtonva.us (click on Volunteers)
- **Volunteer Fairfax**, 703-246-3460, www.volunteerfairfax.org
- **Montgomery County Volunteer Center**, 240-777-2600, www.montgomerycountymd.gov (click on Volunteers)
- **Prince George's Volunteer Center**, 301-699-2800, www.multimax.com/pg/volunteer

For information on volunteer agencies in outlying areas, agencies specializing in senior and retired volunteers, or links to state and national service programs, contact the **Governor's Office on Service & Volunteerism** (Maryland) at 410-767-4803 or www.gosv.state.md.us, or the **Virginia Office of Volunteerism** at 800-777-8293 or www.dss.state.va.us/community/volunteer.

AREA CAUSES

Here is just a sample of the kinds of organizations in constant need of volunteer help. Some have structured volunteer programs with training sessions and schedules; others are grateful when you walk in off the street and help sort donated books or clothing for an hour. In addition to the organizations listed in this chapter, keep in mind that many of the community institutions listed elsewhere in this book rely on volunteers:

- **Political organizations**—see **Getting Settled**
- **Food co-ops and farmers' markets**—see **Shopping for the Home**
- **Parks and trails**—see **Greenspace**
- **Children's programs**—see **Childcare and Education**
- **Animal shelters**—see **Getting Settled**
- **Thrift stores**—see **Shopping for the Home**
- **Services for people with disabilities**—see **Helpful Services**
- **Neighborhood festivals and special events**—see **Neighborhood Profiles** and **A Washington Year**
- Practically every institution listed in **Cultural Life** and **Sports and Recreation**

Note that you may be greeted with caution when you offer your services to an agency that deals directly with children. Don't take it personally; since you care enough about children to volunteer in an after-school program or summer camp, you understand the agency's duty to check your references and perhaps run a criminal background check.

If you have special skills—legal or medical training, web design, desktop publishing, writing and editing, or accounting, or if you have a license to drive large trucks and buses, experience facilitating meetings, or a background in catering and you know how to prepare meals for 400 people—be sure to mention them. Don't be shy. Any nonprofit organization will be happy to hear from you.

AIDS & HIV

- **ACT UP/DC**, 202-547-9404, www.actupdc.org
- **Braking the Cycle AIDS Ride**, 212-989-1111, www.brakingthe cycle.org
- **D.C. AIDS Information Hotline**, 202-332-2437, www.wwc.org
- **Food & Friends**, 202-488-8278, www.foodandfriends.org
- **Prevention Works! D.C.**, 202-588-5580, www.preventionworks dc.org

ALCOHOL ABUSE

- **Alcoholics Anonymous**, 202-966-9115, www.aa-dc.org
- **Alcolicos Anonimos de Habla Hispana**, 202-797-9738
- **Mothers Against Drunk Driving**, Greater Washington, 202-374-2487, www.madd.org

NEWCOMER'S HANDBOOK FOR MOVING TO AND LIVING IN WASHINGTON D.C.

316

CHILDREN/YOUTH SERVICES

- **Boys & Girls Clubs of Greater Washington**, 301-562-2001, www.bgcgw.org
- **Children's Defense Fund**, 202-628-8787, www.childrens defense.org
- **Court Appointed Special Advocates**, 202-328-2191, http://casa. volunteermatch.org
- **D.C. SCORES**, 202-234-4103, www.americascores.org/dc
- **For Love of Children**, 202-462-8686, www.flocdc.org
- **Higher Achievement Program**, 202-842-5116, www.higher achievement.org
- **KaBoom!** (playground construction), 202-659-0215, ext. 225, www. kaboom.org
- **Sasha Bruce Youthwork**, 202-675-9340, www.sashabruce.org

CRIME PREVENTION

- **Metropolitan Police Department Auxiliary**, 202-727-4314
- Contact your local police station listed in the Neighborhood Profiles for information about neighborhood-based Citizens On Patrol or "Orange Hats" programs.

SENIOR CARE & SERVICES

- **Geriatric Day Care Center, Downtown Cluster of Congregations**, 202-347-7527
- **IONA Senior Services**, 202-966-1055, www.iona.org
- **Meals On Wheels**, 202-966-8111 or call 800-677-1116 to find the nearest local program

ENVIRONMENTAL PROTECTION

- **Anacostia Watershed Society**, 301-699-6204, www.anacostia ws.org
- **Arlingtonians for a Clean Environment**, 703-228-6427, www. arlingtonenvironment.org
- **Audubon Naturalist Society**, 301-652-9188, www.audubon naturalist.org
- **Casey Trees Endowment Fund**, 202-833-4010, www.casey trees.org

- **Chesapeake Climate Action Network**, 301-891-6726, www.chesapeakeclimate.org
- **Clean Water Action**, 202-895-0420, www.cleanwateraction.org
- **Coalition for Smarter Growth**, 202-588-5570, www.smartergrowth.net
- **Earth Conservation Corps**, 202-554-1960, www.earthconcorps.org
- **Earthjustice Legal Defense Fund**, 202-667-4500, www.earthjustice.org
- **Friends of the Earth**, 202-783-7400, www.foe.org
- **Greenpeace**, 202-462-1177, www.greenpeaceusa.org
- **National Park Service**, National Capital Region, 202-619-7077, www.nps.gov/ncro
- **Sierra Club**, New Columbia Chapter, 202-488-0505, www.sierraclub.org
- **Washington Parks & People**, 202-462-7275, www.washingtonparks.net
- **Washington Regional Network for Livable Communities**, 202-244-1105, www.washingtonregion.net

GAY, LESBIAN, BISEXUAL & TRANSGENDER SERVICES

- **Gay & Lesbian Activists Alliance**, 202-667-5139, www.glaa.org
- **Gay & Lesbian Alliance Against Defamation**, 202-986-1360, www.glaad.org
- **Parents and Friends of Lesbians & Gays (P-FLAG)**, 202-638-3852, www.pflagdc.org
- **Pride at Work, Baltimore-Washington**, 202-434-1150 ext. 6, www.igc.org/prideatwork
- **Sexual Minorities Youth Assistance League**, 202-546-5940, www.smyal.org

HEALTH & HOSPITALS

Researchers at NIH and other institutions are always recruiting volunteers for clinical trials. If you meet the physical requirements for a particular study, you can make a contribution to medical science and often receive a stipend and free physical checkups during the study. Check the *Washington City Paper* classifieds.

- **American Cancer Society**, 202-483-2600, www.cancer.org
- **American Heart Association**, National Capital Area Council, 202-686-6888, www.americanheart.org/dc

NEWCOMER'S HANDBOOK FOR MOVING TO AND LIVING IN WASHINGTON D.C.

318

- **American Lung Association of D.C.**, 202-682-5864, www.aladc.org
- **Center for Science in the Public Interest**, 202-332-9110, www. cspinet.org
- **Children's National Medical Center**, 202-884-2063, www. cnmc.org
- **Hospice of Washington**, 202-966-3720, www.washington home.org
- **Hospital for Sick Children**, 202-832-4400 or 800-226-4444, www. hfscsite.org
- **National Rehabilitation Hospital**, 202-877-1000, www.nrh rehab.org
- **Whitman-Walker Clinic**, 202-797-3500, www.wwc.org

HUNGER & HOMELESSNESS

- **Bread for the City**, 202-265-2400, www.breadforthecity.org
- **Capital Area Food Bank**, 202-526-5344
- **Coalition for the Homeless**, 202-347-8870, www.dccfh.org
- **Community for Creative Nonviolence** (CCNV), 202-393-1909, http://users.erols.com/ccnv
- **D.C. Central Kitchen**, 202-234-0707, www.dccentralkitchen.org
- **D.C. Habitat for Humanity**, 202-610-2355, www.dchabitat.org
- **Homes Not Jails**, 202-297-4430, www.homesnotjails.org/dc
- **Martha's Table**, 202-328-6008, www.marthastable.org
- **So Others Might Eat**, 202-797-8806, www.some.org

INTERNATIONAL

- **Amnesty International**, Mid-Atlantic Region, 202-544-0200, http:// amnestyusa.org
- **Ayuda Inc.**, 202-387-0324
- **Calvary Bilingual Multicultural Education Center**, 202-332-4200, www.cbmlc.org
- **Casa del Pueblo**, 202-332-3422, www.faithumcmd.org
- **Central American Refugee Center**, 202-328-9799
- **Hostelling International**, 202-737-2333, www.hiwashington dc.org
- **Latin American Youth Center**, 202-319-2225, www.layc-dc.org
- **Meridian International Center**, 202-667-6800, www. meridian.org
- **Spanish Education Development Center**, 202-462-8848

- **Washington Inner-City Self Help** (WISH), 202-332-8800
- **Youth for Understanding Host Families**, 800-872-0200, www.youthforunderstanding.org

LEGAL AID

- **Bread for the City Legal Clinic**, 202-265-2400
- **D.C. Public Defender Service**, 202-628-1200, www.pdsdc.org
- **Legal Aid Society of D.C.**, 202-628-1161, www.legalaiddc.org
- **Legal Counsel for the Elderly**, 202-434-2170; www.aarp.org/ foundation
- **National Lawyers Guild**, 202-296-5600 or 212-627-2656, www. nlg.org
- **Neighborhood Legal Services Program**, 202-682-2720, www. nls.org
- **Washington Legal Clinic for the Homeless**, 202-872-1494, www.legalclinic.org

LITERACY

- **D.C. Reading Is Fundamental**, 202-638-6053 (Northwest office), 202-561-0800 (Southeast office), www.rif.org
- **Everybody Wins!**, 202-624-3957, www.everybodywinsdc.org
- **Junior League of Washington**, 202-337-2001, www.jlw.org
- **Literacy Volunteers of America**, 202-387-1772, www.lvanca.org
- **Washington Literacy Council**, 202-387-9029, www.washington literacycouncil.org

MEN'S SERVICES

- **Men Can Stop Rape**, 202-265-6530, www.mencanstoprape.org
- **The Men's Council of Greater Washington**, www.menswork.org

MENTORING & CAREER DEVELOPMENT

- **Byte Back**, 202-529-3395, www.byteback.org
- **City Vision**, 202-272-2448, www.nbm.org/Education/Design/ CityVision.html
- **Environmentors Project**, 202-347-5300, www.environmentors.org
- **Service Corps of Retired Executives** (SCORE), 202-205-6762, www.score.org
- **Suited for Change**, 202-293-0351, www.suitedforchange.org

NEWCOMER'S HANDBOOK FOR MOVING TO AND LIVING IN WASHINGTON D.C.

320

PEACE & SOCIAL JUSTICE

- **D.C. Peace & Economic Justice Program**, American Friends Service Committee, 202-265-7997, www.afsc.org
- **Gray Panthers of Metropolitan Washington**, 202-347-9541, www.graypanthers.org
- **Peace Action**, 202-862-9740, www.peace-action.org
- **Physicians for Social Responsibility**, 202-898-0150, www.psr.org
- **20/20 Vision**, 301-587-1782, www.2020vision.org
- **Washington Peace Center**, 202-234-2000, www.washington peacecenter.org

POLITICS & CITIZENSHIP

Contact your local board of elections, listed in **Getting Settled**, for information about serving as a precinct worker, election judge, or voter registrar.

- **Alliance for Democracy**, 888-466-8233, www.thealliancefor democracy.org
- **American Civil Liberties Union**, National Capital Area, 202-457-0800, www.aclu-nca.org
- **Common Cause**, 202-833-1200, www.commoncause.org
- **League of Women Voters**, 202-429-1965, www.lwv.org
- **Stand Up for Democracy**, 202-232-2500, www.standupfordemocracy. org
- **U.S. Public Interest Research Group**, 202-546-9707, www. uspirg.org

TRANSPORTATION

During big snowstorms, area hospitals need people who own vehicles with 4-wheel drive and all-weather tires to be on call to transport doctors and ambulatory patients. Local news broadcasts announce the appropriate hotlines during snow emergencies.

- **Metropolitan Washington Council of Governments Carpool Line**, 800-745-7433
- **Travelers Aid**, 202-546-1127, www.travelersaid.org
- **Washington Area Bicyclist Association**, 202-628-2500, www.waba.org

VETERANS

- **American Legion,** 202-861-2700, www.legion.org
- **Disabled American Veterans**, 202-554-3501, www.dav.org
- **National Gulf War Resource Center**, 301-585-4000, www. ngwrc.org
- **Veterans of Foreign Wars**, Washington Office, 202-543-2239, www. vfw.org
- **Veterans History Project**, 202-707-4916, www.loc.gov/vets

WOMEN'S SERVICES

- **Calvary Women's Services**, 202-783-6651, www.calvaryservices. org
- **D.C. Rape Crisis Center**, 202-232-0789, www.dcrcc.org
- **House of Ruth**, 202-667-7001, www.houseofruth.org
- **My Sister's Place**, 202-529-5261, www.mysistersplace.org
- **Planned Parenthood of Metropolitan Washington**, 202-347-8500, www.ppmw.org
- **Washington Area Clinic Defense Task Force**, 202-797-6577, www.wacdtf.org
- **The Women's Center**, 703-281-2657, www.thewomenscenter.org

VOLUNTEER WORK DAYS

- **Martin Luther King Day of Service** is a nationwide volunteer program observing the Martin Luther King Jr. holiday as "a day on, not a day off." Contact the Corporation for National Service at 202-606-5000 or www.mlkday.org.
- **Earth Day** activities in hundreds of communities are listed at www.earthday.net. April 22 or the nearest weekend.
- **Rebuilding Together** (formerly Christmas in April/Sukkot in April) organizes workdays to repair the homes of senior citizens and low-income families: 202-965-2824, www.christmasinaprildc.org.
- **Hands On D.C.** is an annual workathon in which thousands of people help renovate inner-city schools and collect pledges from sponsors to endow scholarship funds in those schools: 202-667-5808, www.hands ondc.org. Late April or early May.
- **Greater D.C. Cares Day** (formerly the Servathon): 202-777-4466, www.dc-cares.org

NEWCOMER'S HANDBOOK FOR MOVING TO AND LIVING IN WASHINGTON D.C.

322

- **Make a Difference Day** is a nationwide volunteer mobilization sponsored by *USA Weekend* magazine and the Points of Light Foundation: 800-416-3824, http://usaweekend.com/diffday. Late October.
- **December 25 Community Service Day** is a program of the D.C. Jewish Community Center: 202-518-9400, www.dcjcc.org

CHARITABLE GIVING

Residents of the District give more than half a billion dollars a year to charity. That figure includes the gifts of major philanthropists, but many small donations add up; thousands of Washingtonians give to charity through the **United Way** campaign (or, for federal workers, the **Combined Federal Campaign**). One easy way to give is to choose a credit card or long distance phone service that gives a percentage of its receipts to charity—many large charities have their own affinity cards issued in partnership with financial institutions, and **Working Assets** provides credit cards, long distance service, and investment services that pay annual dividends to nonprofits selected each year by account holders. For details, contact Working Assets at 800-537-3777 (for credit cards) or 800-788-0898 (for long distance), or visit www.workingforchange.com.

During the annual United Way/Combined Federal Campaign in the fall, you'll see posters at Metro stations and bus stops advertising the work of local charities and their CFC number, requesting that you set up a voluntary weekly payroll deduction, in any amount you specify. **TouchDC** is an online directory of local charities at www.touchdc.org; the site is sponsored by the Washington Regional Association of Grantmakers, the Foundation Center, the Nonprofit Roundtable, the United Way, CFC, and other leaders in Washington-area philanthropy.

Charitable Choices, www.charitablechoices.org, publishes an annual booklet profiling CFC charities meeting certain standards of fiscal responsibility and low ratio of overhead to program spending—but note: among the charities meeting those standards, only those paying a fee are listed in the guide. Other sources of information about specific charities include:

- **Council of Better Business Bureaus Philanthropic Advisory Service**, 703-276-0100, www.bbb.org
- **The Foundation Center**, 202-331-1400, www.foundationcenter.org
- **National Center for Charitable Statistics**, 202-261-5801, http://nccs.urban.org
- **National Committee for Responsive Philanthropy**, 202-387-9177, www.ncrp.org

Here are some general charities and federated funds that address a variety of social needs:

- **Catholic Charities**, 703-549-1390, www.catholiccharitiesusa.org
- **Combined Federal Campaign of the National Capital Area**, 202-628-2263, www.cfcnca.org
- **Greater Washington Urban League**, 202-265-8200, www.gwul.org
- **Jewish Federation of Greater Washington**, 301-230-7200, www.jewishfedwash.org
- **Salvation Army**, 202-783-9085, www.salvationarmyusa.org
- **United Black Fund**, 202-783-9300, www.ubfinc.org

I N SOME PARTS OF THE WASHINGTON AREA, YOU CAN'T DO ANYTHING without a car; in other neighborhoods, a car would be more of a hassle than benefit. Generally, within the District a car is a lifestyle choice, not a necessity; in 2005, the *Washington Post* estimated that 60% to 65% of D.C. households do not have cars. In the inner suburbs, a car is decidedly useful—especially for a household with kids—but dedicated singles or couples can manage without one. Outside the Beltway, most communities are designed on a scale negotiable only by cars—don't expect to be within walking distance of a grocery store or other basics.

It's easy to travel between D.C. and the suburbs, or within D.C., by public transportation, but the real challenge for a growing number of commuters is the issue of travel between suburbs. Suburbanites don't just commute to the District—millions work in the tech industry hotbeds of Northern Virginia and the I-270 corridor in Maryland. Commuting between Maryland and Virginia is an arduous grind no matter how you do it.

Washington's roads are more congested than any other in the nation except in Los Angeles, in terms of average commute times calculated by the Census Bureau. For roughly a quarter-million residents of the Washington area, the daily commute takes an hour or more in each direction; for more than a million residents, the commute is longer than half an hour.

How do you keep your commute from becoming a daily dose of stress? First, if you move here with a job lined up, keep the commute in mind as you look for a place to live. In heavy traffic, even a 15-minute commute can be frustrating. Likewise, if you find a home here and you're looking for a job, think twice about a long commute—if you feel stressed by the time you get to work, you'll not likely keep that job for long. (Note that a long commute and a long distance aren't the same thing. A 10-mile commute by mass transit might be faster and less aggravating than a 5-mile drive at peak times.) Try to avoid driving to work alone; if public trans-

NEWCOMER'S HANDBOOK FOR MOVING TO AND LIVING IN WASHINGTON D.C.

326

portation doesn't work for you, consider carpooling. Or, if the route is safe and short enough, try riding a bike or walking to work.

Finally, you may be able to cut back on daily commuting. Ask your employer about telecommuting—working at home—at least one or two days a week. Many employers, especially federal agencies, are discovering that workers who don't have to commute every day are happier and more productive, wherever they do their jobs.

GETTING AROUND

METRORAIL

True to its reputation, Metrorail rapid transit—"the Metro"—is clean, safe, and reliable. It's crowded at rush hour and after a game or concert at the Verizon Center, and fares can add up quickly, but taking the Metro downtown from the suburbs is almost always cheaper and easier than finding and paying for parking.

On the 25th anniversary of Metrorail service, in 2001, the *Washington Post* commented, "The Metro system has become—among many other things—a gathering place, a unifier, a matchmaker, a land developer, an economic power and a community planner." The *Post* reported that Metro trains carry 600,000 passengers a day and keep 270,000 cars off the area's congested roads, saving 12 million gallons of gasoline each year. In fact, the Metro is almost too popular—transit officials are worried that, by 2020, the system will be paralyzed by overcrowding.

Visitors often say the Metro system isn't user-friendly, but if you just read the instructions and maps, you'll soon be tired of hearing such complaints. All the information you need is posted just inside the entrance to any station: a big, easy-to-read map of the system; a detailed street map of the neighborhood surrounding the station; schedules for bus routes serving the station; a chart showing travel times and fares to every other station; and, most important if you're going out at night, a sign showing the departure times of the last train leaving the station in each direction. (Metrorail closes around 12:30 a.m. except on Friday and Saturday nights, when it closes around 2 a.m.)

The farecard vending machines need not be intimidating either. These magnetic cards can be encoded with any amount of money from $1.35 to $39.95. Look at the destination chart on the station manager's kiosk to see how much money you'll need to put on your card. Your farecard will let you through the station gates and will deduct the proper fare when you exit. If, at your destination, you discover that there's not enough value on the card to pay for your trip, you can add money at the "Exitfare" machine.

Fares range from $1.35 to $3.90 depending on the length of your trip and time of day—they're lower during off-peak times (rush hour is 5:30 to 9:30 a.m. and 3 to 7 p.m.). If you will be transferring from the Metro to a bus, get a bus transfer from the dispenser at the station where you board the Metro—the transfer shows the time and the station, and is proof to the bus driver that you paid a Metro fare. This will give you an 85-cent discount on the bus. There is no discount for transferring from the bus to the Metro.

Most suburban stations have parking lots, but many fill up early on weekdays. Also, at many stations, a SmarTrip card (see Passes & Discounts below) is the only accepted method of payment. Every station has also feeder bus routes and a "Kiss & Ride" loop for passengers getting dropped off or picked up.

A word about the names of Metro stations: the Metro board is always under pressure from some civic association, chamber of commerce, or university to add the name of a neighborhood or institution to the name of an existing station. Thus the Woodley Park stop is officially identified as "Woodley Park-Zoo/Adams Morgan," for example, and Vienna is now "Vienna-Fairfax/GMU." Those are an awkward mouthful, and nobody except Metrorail operators actually refers to stations by their unabridged official names. Both for easier reading and to acquaint you with the names by which these places are actually known in real conversation, this book refers to each Metro station by the simplest and most conventional form of its name.

For more information, call the **Washington Metropolitan Area Transit Authority** (Metro), visit www.wmata.com, or call 202-637-7000 and plan to spend a few minutes on hold. On the web site, click on "Commuter Tips" under "How to Travel" to find a savings calculator that will help you compare the cost of driving versus public transportation.

RIDER ETIQUETTE

It's illegal to eat or drink on the Metro, on buses, or in stations, and the law is enforced. (Tourists may get off with a warning, but your local ID will tell the authorities you should know better.) Seats facing sideways must be offered to elderly or disabled passengers.

On station escalators, the rule is: stand on the right, walk on the left. Posted and recorded announcements about escalator safety may seem like schoolmarmish fussing (watch out for loose clothing, untied shoelaces, etc.), but in fact people have been seriously injured on Metro station escalators, all in easily preventable accidents.

If there are no seats available on a crowded train, stand as far from the doors as you can so you don't block people getting on and off. If you're near a door and people are pushing to get off the train, you can help a lot by step-

NEWCOMER'S HANDBOOK FOR MOVING TO AND LIVING IN WASHINGTON D.C.

328

ping off the train and getting back on after the rush. You won't miss the train. On the other hand, there's always someone who sprints to get a foot or a briefcase in the door just after the loud electronic chimes and recorded voice announce "doors closing." Metrorail trains are not elevators—the doors don't reopen when you nudge them apart. They close. Trying to board a train after the closing chimes is dangerous as well as poor etiquette. During rush hour, the next train is usually just a minute or two behind.

You will spot the seasoned commuters the first time you ride a Metro train on a weekday: they've mastered the art of tuning out background noise so they can read the latest John Grisham novel, and they're wearing business suits and tennis shoes—at the office, they will change into office shoes. You might also notice them walking the length of the platform while waiting for the train—you know you're getting assimilated when you know just where to board the train in order to be near the escalator at your destination.

BUS

The **Metrobus** system is the main feeder bus line serving all Metrorail stations throughout D.C. and the Maryland and Virginia suburbs. With only three exceptions, the Metrobus fare is $1.25. Express routes making long trips into the outer suburbs (or BWI Airport) are $3; certain routes in Fairfax County are $1 and certain routes in Southeast D.C. are 75 cents. You are offered a free "transfer" (a time-stamped transfer pass) when you board any public bus in the area, and it's good for unlimited trips of equal or lesser value on any local bus system in the area for the next two hours. A regional all-day bus pass is $3. For more information, visit www.wmata.com or call 202-637-7000.

Downtown D.C. **Circulator** buses make a crosstown loop from Georgetown to Union Station via K Street NW and Massachusetts Avenue NW and a midtown loop from the Convention Center to Southwest waterfront via 7th Street. The two Circulator lines intersect at Mt. Vernon Square just south of the Convention Center. The fare is $1 (35 cents with a Metrorail transfer) and the buses run every 5–10 minutes from 7 a.m. to 9 p.m. daily. You can pay the fare on board or buy a ticket from a vending machine at most Circulator bus stops (where you don't need exact change and you can use a credit card). You board on the honor system; random inspections are held for proof of payment, with substantial fines for fare evasion. For more information, visit www.dccirculator.com or call 202-962-1423.

Metrobus routes also connect to these local bus systems in the suburbs:
- **Ride On** buses serve Montgomery County and connect to Metro stations on the Red Line; 240-777-7433, www.rideonbus.com.

- **The BUS** routes serve Prince George's County and connect to Metro stations on the Blue, Orange, and Green lines; 301-324-2877, www.goprincegeorgescounty.com (click on Transit Services).
- **ART** (Arlington Transit) buses serve Arlington County and connect to Metro stations on the Orange, Blue, and Yellow lines; 703-228-RIDE, www.commuterpage.com/ART.
- **DASH** buses serve Alexandria, including the Pentagon, and connect to Metro stations on the Blue and Yellow lines; 703-370-DASH, www.dashbus.com.
- **Fairfax Connector** buses serve Tysons Corner, Reston, and Herndon and connect to Metro stations on the Orange Line; 703-339-7200, www.fairfaxconnector.com.
- **GEORGE** buses serve Falls Church and connect to East and West Falls Church Metro stations on the Orange Line; www.ci.falls-church.va.us.
- **CUE** buses serve Fairfax City and connect to Metro stations on the Orange Line; 703-385-7859, www.fairfaxva.gov.
- **TAGS** buses serve Springfield and connect to the Franconia-Springfield Metro station; 703-971-7727, www.springfieldinterchange.com (click on Commuter Solutions).
- **Maryland MTA** commuter buses serve outlying areas such as Annapolis, Columbia, Frederick, Hagerstown, Waldorf, and even Kent Island in the Chesapeake Bay. Most fares are $5, with a discount for monthly passes; 866-743-3682, www.mtamaryland.com.
- Virginia commuter bus lines serving outlying areas include **FRED** buses to Fredericksburg; **Haymarket** and **Martz Franklin** buses to Warrenton; **Loudoun Commuter** buses to Leesburg; and **OmniRide** buses to Prince William County. For more information, visit www. commuterconnections.org (click on Transit).

Information about many smaller bus and commuter van lines serving the outer suburbs is available at www.commuterpage.com.

PASSES & DISCOUNTS

Weekly and monthly bus passes allow unlimited travel on Metrorail or Metrobus, and some are good on both bus and rail. Pick up a brochure at any station listing the various combination bus/rail passes and figure out your particular transit needs; generally, the passes save you money if you commute five days a week and make a few trips in addition to your daily commute. For many frequent riders, though, the main benefit is convenience.

- **SmarTrip** cards are permanent plastic farecards that can be encoded with up to $180 at a time. You can "register" your SmarTrip card and, in

NEWCOMER'S HANDBOOK FOR MOVING TO AND LIVING IN WASHINGTON D.C.

330

the event that it is lost or stolen, it will be replaced with a new card encoded with the value of your card at the time you reported it missing. If your card's remaining value is less than the fare for your trip, you can go into "overdraft" and leave the station, add money later, and the balance will be deducted from your next trip. You can also transfer the value of a regular farecard, up to $7, to your SmarTrip card. At most Metro station parking garages, you must pay with a SmarTrip card. The cards are also good on most local buses.

- **Metrochek** is a fare voucher issued by employers as a fringe benefit. Employers may pay for Metrocheks or provide them as part of pretax earnings (so your commuting expenses are tax-sheltered). The Metrochek, in denominations of $20, can be used as a farecard or redeemed at one of the service counters below for bus passes. Many employers offer free parking as an employee benefit; if you commute by bus or Metro, ask about the Metrochek program or consider asking for the cash equivalent of a parking space. If you need proof of commuting expenses in order to be reimbursed by an employer or client, you can buy passes at a retail outlet and get a receipt; also, some farecard vending machines accept credit cards and dispense receipts.
- **Metrobus tokens** are available in packs of 10 or 20 and are handy if you aren't in the habit of making sure you have exact change. They're sold in clear plastic bags, so you can inspect them before buying to make sure none of them is a Salvadoran 5-centavo coin, which is exactly the same size and color.

COMMUTER STORES

These retail outlets sell passes and tokens for Metro and area buses and provide a wealth of maps, schedules and advice.

- **Metro Sales Office**, inside the Metro Center station on the Red, Blue, and Orange Lines
- **WMATA** (Metro) Headquarters, 600 5th Street NW, 202-637-7000, www.wmata.com
- **Commuter Express**, 8401 Colesville Road, Suite 150, 301-565-5870
- **The Commuter Store**, Ballston Common Mall, 703-528-3541; Crystal City Shops North, 703-413-4287; Rosslyn Metro Center, 703-525-1995
- **The Connector Store**, Springfield Mall; Franconia-Springfield Metro station; Park & Ride, 1860 Wiehle Avenue, Reston; Park & Ride, 12530 Sunrise Valley Drive, Herndon
- **Old Town Transit Shop**, 1775-C Duke Street, Alexandria, 703-299-6227
- Online at **www.commuterpage.com** (information) and **www.commuterdirect.com** (purchases)

COMMUTER TRAIN

Maryland Rail Commute (MARC) and Virginia Rail Express (VRE) commuter trains from Union Station, just off Capitol Hill, serve Baltimore and its far suburbs; Brunswick, Md.; and Manassas and Fredericksburg, Va. Buses connect Frederick, Md., to the Brunswick line. Suburban sprawl is not quite so advanced that those places qualify as part of the Washington area, but these trains may be a good option for commuting from the outer sub-urbs, like Gaithersburg or Bowie. And a weekday MARC fare to Baltimore is $14 round trip, compared to $36 for an Amtrak ticket. MARC trains also serve Marshall BWI Airport, so ground transportation to BWI—at least on weekdays—is much cheaper than to busier Dulles Airport. Special MARC trains run at night when the Baltimore Orioles play home games at Camden Yards.

Single-trip tickets and monthly passes are sold at Union Station and during rush hour at other stations; for a few dollars extra, you can pay the fare aboard the train. Photo ID is required.

• **MARC**, 800-325-RAIL; www.mtamaryland.com
• **VRE**, 703-684-1001; www.vre.org

CAR

On major thoroughfares, rush hour can last from 6 to 9:30 a.m. and 4 to 7 p.m. Most local radio stations carry traffic reports every 10 minutes during rush hour; WTOP-FM (103.5) features "weather and traffic together on the eights" 24/7. Chronic traffic jams occur at several points on the Capital Beltway, including both Potomac River crossings, and along Interstates 95 and 270. The dreaded "Mixing Bowl"—the junction of I-95, I-395, and the Beltway in Springfield—is cited by AAA as one of the ten most congested interchanges in the country; with construction in progress to ease the pres-sure, it will get worse for several years before it gets better. (In fact, the Mixing Bowl has its own web site, www.springfieldinterchange.com, and a toll-free hotline, 877-959-5222, to keep commuters informed of progress, traffic disruptions, and alternatives.)

Heavy traffic isn't limited to highways. Most major streets carry more traffic at peak times than urban planners ever imagined, but at least it's moving traffic—unless there's an accident. Always have an alternative route in mind and pay attention to traffic reports.

The Capital Beltway is not as confusing as it may seem. Yes, part of it is marked I-95 and all of it is marked I-495, but most signs on approaching highways just say "Beltway." Traffic reporters and a few signs refer to the

NEWCOMER'S HANDBOOK FOR MOVING TO AND LIVING IN WASHINGTON D.C.

332

Inner Loop and the Outer Loop, which are simply the clockwise (inner) and counterclockwise (outer) sides of the divided highway.

There are only two toll highways in the Washington area, both connecting the Virginia suburbs with outlying Dulles International Airport: the Dulles Toll Road and the privately operated Dulles Greenway. Potomac and Anacostia River bridges in the area are toll-free. There is one toll crossing: White's Ferry, a quaint old working auto ferry on the Potomac River between Leesburg, Va., and Poolesville, Md.—but it's more of a scenic attraction than a commuter thoroughfare.

If you're driving in the city, especially near Embassy Row north of Dupont Circle, keep in mind: foreign diplomats have immunity from prosecution and are not bound by local laws requiring drivers to carry liability insurance. For cars with diplomatic license plates, traffic laws and parking restrictions are pretty much optional.

Newcomers from snowy climates are often quick to point out that Washingtonians don't know how to drive in snow, or how to remove it. Even though the whole city practically shuts down with a few inches of snow, accidents are common. If you get stuck on roads marked snow emergency route during a declared snow emergency (read: when it's snowing) and your vehicle isn't fitted with snow tires or chains, you may get a ticket.

On Thursdays, check out "Dr. Gridlock," a traffic advice column in the *Washington Post,* also available online at www.washingtonpost.com. For information about vehicle registrations, residential parking permits, insurance, and driver's licenses, see **Getting Settled**.

TRAFFIC REPORTS ON DEMAND

Most TV and radio news web sites now have a traffic page, often with live cameras showing the traffic at key interchanges. In Northern Virginia, you can call 511 for traffic information or visit www.511virginia.org.

CARPOOLS AND SLUG LINES

Carpooling saves you money and eases congestion on area roads, which in turn saves you time. If your workplace or a nearby coffee shop has a bulletin board, you might find a carpool partner posted. Otherwise, try calling the **Ride Finders Network**, 800-745-RIDE, or the **Metropolitan Washington Council of Governments Carpool Line**, 800-745-7433. In Northern Virginia, call **Fairfax County RideSources**, 703-324-1111. Several major commuter highways have lanes reserved for high-occupancy vehicles. HOV-2 lanes are open to vehicles with at least two occupants (including the driver); the real perk for carpools is HOV-3 lanes for vehicles with at least three occupants. HOV lane designations are in effect only during rush hour and only in the direction of peak travel—inbound in the morning and outbound in the evening. At other times, the lanes are open to all traffic.

In Virginia, there are HOV-2 lanes on I-66 and HOV-3 lanes on I-95 and I-395. In Maryland, there are HOV-2 lanes on I-270. Looking ahead to 2010 and beyond, Virginia is considering the use of HOT (high occupancy/toll) lanes, open to carpools or to single-occupant vehicles that pay a toll for the privilege of using the less-congested lanes. For details about HOV lanes, including hours, visit www.vdot.virginia.gov and www.sha.state.md.us.

The **slug line** is a unique Northern Virginia tradition that helps commuters take advantage of HOV lanes. Solo drivers in Northern Virginia visit a slug line (there are actually several) to pick up additional commuters headed downtown in the morning, to form an impromptu carpool, and visit a downtown slug line in the evening to pick up commuters bound for Virginia. It's a completely unofficial system and yet well organized and reliable, complete with a web site showing the locations of morning and evening slug lines: www.slug-lines.com.

The **Guaranteed Ride Home** program is a project of Commuter Connections. Register with Commuter Connections at www.commuter connections.org or call 800-745-7433. If you take a carpool or mass transit to work and an emergency or unscheduled overtime prevents you from getting home the same way, you'll be given a ride home or be reimbursed for taxi fare.

CAR SHARING

If you need a car occasionally but not often enough to own one, consider joining a car-sharing network: **Flexcar**, 202-296-1359, www.flexcar.com or **Zipcar**, 866-494-7227, www.zipcar.com. Members share a fleet of cars kept at designated Metro stations and other central locations such as major apartment complexes. Whenever you need a car, for an hour or a week, just make reservations by phone and you'll be billed for the time and mileage. Plans vary, but expect to pay around $30/year for membership and $9/hour or $60/day. The fees include gas, insurance, and the cost of maintenance. Flexcar and Zipcar membership nearly doubled in 2004, according to the *Washington Post*, to some 14,000 users sharing more than 200 cars.

TAXIS

In D.C., taxis don't have meters. Instead, the city is divided into zones and sub-zones, and the fare is based on the number of zones between pickup and drop-off. The zone system was intended to standardize fares and prevent drivers from taking advantage of out-of-town passengers; instead, despite the zone maps prominently displayed in every D.C. cab, passengers complain that the system is confusing. Indeed, the maps don't show

NEWCOMER'S HANDBOOK FOR MOVING TO AND LIVING IN WASHINGTON D.C.

334

any landmarks—just the streets that mark zone boundaries—so you need to be familiar with the city's major roads in order to find your current location on the zone map.

There is perennial talk of returning to a meter system, but drivers object to the cost of new equipment; plus, the zone system works to the advantage of passengers riding through heavy traffic, when meters would charge for idle time as well as distance. There are flat surcharges for rush hour, for extra passengers, and during declared snow emergencies. Temporary surcharges are sometimes authorized when gas prices rise faster than taxi fares.

Cab drivers are required to display their license at all times, and to use air conditioning at the passenger's request from May 15 to October 15 and heat from October 16 to May 14. Smoking is prohibited. Drivers may stop and pick up additional passengers while you're in the vehicle.

Every cab displays the passenger's bill of rights, which affirms that any paying customer has a right to be taken to any location within the District. Still, many taxi drivers refuse to drive to addresses in rough neighborhoods, and some refuse to pick up passengers whom they deem suspicious; though illegal, such practices are fairly common.

Unless you look "suspicious," you should have no problem hailing a cab on a major thoroughfare in the District. Except at Metro stations, don't count on hailing a cab in the suburbs. Call:

- **Action Taxi**, 301-840-1000
- **Arlington Yellow Cab**, 703-522-2222
- **Barwood**, 301-984-1900
- **Bowie**, 301-430-7200
- **Capitol**, 202-546-2400
- **Dial**, 202-829-4222
- **Diamond**, 202-387-6200
- **Fairfax Yellow Cab**, 703-534-1111
- **Red Top**, 202-328-3333
- **Regency**, 301-990-9000
- **Silver**, 301-270-6000
- **Yellow Cab of D.C.**, 202-544-1212

In the suburbs, taxis use meters that charge for distance, idle time, and extra passengers. If you take a Maryland or Virginia cab into the District, you'll pay the metered rates within the District; if you take a District cab into the suburbs, your fare will be based on mileage—and most drivers will quote a fare at the beginning of the trip.

Allow at least half an hour if you're calling a cab at rush hour or in bad weather. Most cab companies will accept credit cards, if you give your number to the dispatcher when you call, and all will provide receipts on request.

CAR RENTALS

These national chains rent cars, minivans, and pickup trucks on a daily or weekly basis, and most have pickup and drop-off points throughout the Washington area—though selection is better at airports and Union Station. Of these, only Alamo and National will rent cars to drivers under 25 years old. If you don't have a major credit card, forget it.

- **Alamo**, 800-327-9633, www.alamo.com
- **Avis**, 800-831-2847, www.avis.com
- **Budget**, 800-527-0700, www.budgetdc.com
- **Dollar**, 800-800-4000, www.dollar.com
- **Enterprise**, 800-736-8222, www.enterprise.com
- **Hertz**, 800-654-3131, www.hertz.com
- **National**, 800-227-7368, www.nationalcar.com
- **Thrifty**, 800-847-4389, www.thrifty.com

BIKE

Many Washingtonians commute by bike, sometimes in a business suit and bike helmet. Bicycles are vehicles, according to law—unless there's a sign expressly prohibiting bikes, cyclists are entitled to use the road and are required to obey the same traffic signs, signals, and rules as motor vehicles. In D.C. and Maryland, children under 16 are required to wear helmets, and in downtown traffic, everyone should.

Except during rush hour and on the Fourth of July, bikes are allowed on the Metro, with some restrictions:

- Bikes are allowed only at the ends of the subway car—on weekdays, only one bike at a time at each end of the car, and on weekends and holidays, no more than two at a time.
- You must dismount and walk your bike through the station and hold onto it at all times (no kickstands).
- If the train is evacuated due to an emergency, you must place your bike on a seat, out of the way, and leave it behind.
- Cyclists under 16 must be accompanied by an adult.

Most stations have bike racks outside, and some have bike lockers, which can be leased for $70/year or $45/six months, plus a $10 key deposit. For locker rentals, call 202-962-1116 or visit www.wmata.com. There's a waiting list at most stations.

Some, but not all, local buses are equipped with bike racks.

Bicycle shops are listed under **Bicycling** in **Sports and Recreation**, and sporting goods stores are listed in **Shopping for the Home**.

NEWCOMER'S HANDBOOK FOR MOVING TO AND LIVING IN WASHINGTON D.C.

336

SEGWAY

Segway Human Transport gyroscopic scooters are still new on the scene, but are an increasingly familiar sight in downtown D.C. After some initial confusion, Metro adopted a policy that treats Segways like bicycles—they're allowed on the trains during off-peak hours only; only at the ends of each car; and no more than one at a time (two on weekends and holidays) at each end. They cannot be carried on buses. And unlike bicycles, they're expected to be ridden on the sidewalk, not in the street.

Little herds of Segways make the rounds of the tourist sites, led by **City Segway Tours**, 877-734-8687, www.citysegwaytours.com/washington. If you're interested in buying one, the area's first dealership is **Capital Segway**, with locations at Georgetown Park mall and 1350 I Street NW, 202-333-2586, http://capitalsegway.com.

ON FOOT

If you live in a downtown neighborhood like Dupont Circle or Adams Morgan, many errands might take longer by car than on foot, once you take traffic and parking into account. You'll see city dwellers with their own folding carts for grocery shopping, and lawyers dragging thick files on a luggage cart. In the downtown business district, you even see buttoned-down executives on folding scooters borrowed from their kids.

On many street corners in D.C., and on busy streets in the suburbs, you have to press a button to activate the pedestrian crossing signal. Look for a little gray or yellow box with a button in the middle, on a pole about waist high.

Walk D.C. is a clearinghouse promoting pedestrian safety and amenities in the Washington area. For more information call 202-744-0595 or visit www.walkdc.org.

TELECOMMUTING

Telecommuting, or telework, is gaining currency as an alternative to commuting. Some employers allow, even encourage, employees to work at home one or two days a week if their jobs make it feasible. A large company or government agency with some employees telecommuting each day can ultimately save money on expensive office space as well as parking or transit benefits. In the outlying suburbs, there are a few "telework centers" where you can rent office space by the day or the hour, so you can use a well-equipped workstation without trekking inside the Beltway to do it. Ask whether your employer has a telework policy, or contact the

Metropolitan Washington Council of Governments at 202-962-3200 or www.mwcog.org for information about setting up a telework arrangement. The web site also lists telework centers.

A variation on the concept of telework is **flextime**, a policy that allows office workers to select a schedule other than the standard 9-to-5 workday; they still work 40 hours a week (or whatever they otherwise would), but they aren't adding to—or suffering—rush-hour traffic. As with telework, ask your employer or consult the Council of Governments for more information.

ON THE DRAWING BOARD

The Metrorail system opened in stages from 1976 to 2005 and is now complete as originally envisioned. Planners' eyes look toward Dulles Airport and to an east-west Purple Line for the northern suburbs. Meanwhile, the public and private sectors are looking at plans for commuter boats along the Potomac and Anacostia rivers, light rail along several city thoroughfares, and a Metrorail or light rail connection to Marshall (BWI) Airport. For updates on these new amenities, talk to a real estate agent or visit one of the commuter stores or web sites listed under **Passes & Discounts** above.

REGIONAL/NATIONAL TRAVEL

AMTRAK

Amtrak passenger trains stop at Union Station and Marshall BWI Airport, and some also stop in New Carrollton, Md., or Silver Spring. Union Station is a major stop on the rail line from Atlanta to Boston, and long-haul trains stop here to switch from a diesel locomotive for points south to an electric locomotive for the Northeast.

The express Metroliner to New York is frequent and expensive (usually around $120 each way), and the high-speed Acela to Boston reaches speeds of 150 mph where track conditions permit.

Go to www.amtrak.com or call 800-872-7245 for more information. Be sure to check for promotions and discounts. You need to show photo ID to buy tickets; if you buy tickets at one of the automated kiosks at Union Station, you will be asked to show ID on the train.

BUSES

Greyhound and **Peter Pan Trailways** buses serve the Greyhound bus terminal at 1st and L streets NE, a few blocks from Union Station (but an unsavory walk at night). This is the cheapest way to get to other East Coast

NEWCOMER'S HANDBOOK FOR MOVING TO AND LIVING IN WASHINGTON D.C.

338

cities without driving—if you buy tickets at least a week in advance, New York is $35 one way, Atlanta $50, and Boston $40. Some Greyhound routes also stop in Silver Spring, Arlington, or Springfield. Photo ID required.

- **Greyhound**, 800-231-2222; www.greyhound.com
- **Peter Pan Trailways**, 800-343-9999; www.peterpanbus.com

Several smaller bus companies run express routes from Chinatown in D.C. to Chinatown in Manhattan, and some of these lines also serve Philadelphia, Atlanta, and other East Coast cities. These buses, advertised mainly by word of mouth, get you to New York for less than $40 round trip—about the same price as a one-way Greyhound fare. These cheap, reliable buses are an open secret among budget-savvy travelers and are collectively known as "the Chinatown bus."

- **Apex Bus**, www.apexbus.com, 202-408-8200
- **Today's Bus**, www.today-bus.com, 888-688-0898
- **New Century Travel**, www.2000coach.com, 215-627-2666
- **Dragon Coach**, www.ebusticket.com, 800-475-1160
- **Washington Deluxe**, www.washny.com, 866-287-69 32
- **Vamoose**, www.vamoosebus.com, 877.393.282

AIRPORTS

It may never again be possible to use one of the Washington area's three major airports without remembering September 11 and the plane that struck the Pentagon, just a few hundred yards from Reagan National Airport. New security measures make air travel to and from Washington safer and, of course, less convenient.

Call your airline to find out how much carry-on baggage you may bring—for many domestic flights it's just one bag—and for the latest policies on curbside check-in. Call ahead for the latest carry-on restrictions—the list of prohibited items has changed several times since 2001. Random searches and interviews may remain common practice for years to come, so arrive well before your flight; airlines recommend at least two hours. If you're being dropped off or picked up, the farewells or reunions will have to take place in the main lobby of the terminal—only ticketed passengers are allowed past the security checkpoints.

Ronald Reagan Washington National Airport is still called "National" by everyone who lived here prior to the second Bush administration. (When Congress renamed Washington National Airport in 1998, liberals and conservatives alike pointed out that it was already named after a former president, George Washington.) Its short runway limits the size of aircraft it can handle, but a new terminal and tower handle the crowds. The busy airport, just a few minutes from downtown by cab or Metro, has shuttles every half hour to New York and Boston.

Dulles International Airport is dominated by the renowned and beautiful glass-sided terminal designed by I.M. Pei. Long runways make Dulles the heavy-duty international airport in the region. For most domestic flights, you'll board a unique "mobile lounge"—a giant bus whose height adjusts to connect to aircraft gates—and ride across the tarmac to a midfield terminal. Outlying Dulles is an expensive cab ride west of the city, but Metrobus route 5A serves the airport from L'Enfant Plaza and Rosslyn Metro stations for $3. For more ground transportation options, contact **Washington Flyer**, 703-661-6655 or 888-927-4359, www.washfly.com, or **SuperShuttle**, 800-258-3826, www.supershuttle.com.

Thurgood Marshall International Airport (still better known as Baltimore-Washington International or BWI) is closer to Baltimore than to Washington and, unlike Dulles, is just beginning to grow its own business district. Its remote location generally means cheaper flights, though, especially on no-frills AirTran and Southwest Airlines. Metrobus route B30 makes $3 express trips from the Greenbelt Metro station. The airport is also accessible by rail: MARC and Amtrak trains stop nearby, and frequent shuttle buses run between the airport and the BWI Rail Station. For more ground transportation options, contact **SuperShuttle** at 800-258-3826, www.supershuttle.com.

Each airport's web site includes a list of the airlines it currently supports and their toll-free numbers, as well as information about airport parking, security, and flight delays:

- **Reagan National Airport**, 703-417-8000, www.metwash airports.com/National
- **Dulles International Airport**, 703-661-2700, www.metwash airports.com/Dulles
- **Thurgood Marshall International Airport**, 301-261-1000, www.bwiairport.com

I N A CITY WHOSE BIGGEST PRIVATE INDUSTRY IS TOURISM, HOTEL space is diverse and plentiful, from no-frills motels along I-95 to historic grand hotels like the Willard and the Hay-Adams. The most exclusive crash pad in the nation is Blair House at 16th and Pennsylvania, across the street from the White House. To stay there, you must be an official guest of the President—a visiting king or prime minister, for example, or a President-elect preparing to move in.

For the rest of us, there are options at every level of price, luxury, convenience, and service. When tourists and conventions crowd the downtown hotels, consider staying at a bed & breakfast, a hostel, or a hotel in the suburbs—most hotels offer shuttle service to the nearest Metro station.

Room rates here are among the highest in the nation, but the fluctuations are the same as elsewhere: rooms are cheapest in the winter and when you make reservations well in advance. Always ask about discount offers—many aren't advertised and may change from day to day—and discounts for seniors, veterans, military personnel, and AAA members are common. However, no combination of discounts or good timing will be likely to get you into a big hotel in the District for less than $100 a night; a room in a first-class hotel can easily command $350 or more. Prices aren't quite as high in the suburbs, or in quirky little downtown hotels such as the Tabard Inn or the Brickskeller. Also, in the suburbs, you escape the 14.5% hotel room tax assessed by the District, which pays for the new convention center.

Just for kicks, note: the historic Jenny Lind Suite in the corner dome of the Willard InterContinental, with a round window framing the view of the Washington Monument, goes for a little over $3,000 a night. For most of the 19th century, this hotel did the job of Blair House today—it was the accommodation for heads of state and the incoming President-elect. In the

NEWCOMER'S HANDBOOK FOR MOVING TO AND LIVING IN WASHINGTON D.C.

342

days before civil service, when the President personally appointed every federal clerk and bureaucrat, job-seekers would loiter in the Willard's lobby hoping to bend the new President's ear for a moment. (Yes, this is where *lobbying* was invented.)

Top-of-the-line hotels will pamper you, anticipating your every need—for a price, of course. Big convention hotels, either downtown or in the Crystal City section of Arlington, offer the most amenities—including restaurants and shops, health clubs, short-term newspaper subscriptions, and a "business center" with internet stations, fax machines, and copiers.

Cheaper than luxury hotels and nicer than convention hotels, bed & breakfast guesthouses aren't just for country getaways. Many historic mansions downtown, especially between Georgetown and Logan Circle, have been turned into B&Bs where $100 will buy better accommodations and hospitality than at many hotels.

If you need temporary lodgings for more than a few weeks, an extended-stay hotel or even a sublet might suit you better. Few hotel rooms have kitchens, and few hotels have self-service laundry rooms, which are offered at an extended-stay facility. If your timing is good, you might be able to rent a condo or house for a few months—or even line up a house-sitting deal, taking care of pets and plants and doing housekeeping chores in exchange for free housing. Check **Craigslist,** www.craigslist.net, or the *Washington City Paper* for leads on rentals and house-sitting.

The listings in this chapter are just a sample of the types of accommodations available in a city where 25,000 hotel rooms collectively see more than 20 million visitors each year. For more complete listings, check the Yellow Pages or the District's tourism web site, www.washington.org, where you can search by price range and location. If you're a member of AAA, don't forget you can get a AAA travel guide—with updated hotel and motel listings—for free.

RESERVATIONS & DISCOUNTS

If you do end up in a traditional hotel, there are several ways to save money. Ask a travel agent about promotions—most Washington residents have never heard of "Holiday Homecoming," a tourist-oriented series of shopping and entertainment packages between Thanksgiving and Valentine's Day, as it's marketed only outside the Washington area and on www.washington.org. Internet-based airline ticket agencies, such as **Expedia.com** and **Orbitz.com**, also offer hotel reservations. Also try these reservation services, which offer their own discounts:

- **Central Reservation Service**, 800-894-0680, www.centralhotel reservations.com
- **Quikbook,** 800-789-9887, www.quikbook.com

- **Washington D.C. Accommodations,** 800-503-3330, www.wdca hotels.com
- **Washington, D.C. Convention & Tourism Corp.,** 800-422-8644, www.washington.org

Note that some reservation services charge cancellation fees or require advance payment, and their discounts usually cannot be combined with promotions offered by hotels, credit card affinities, or other organizations.

LODGINGS

At any hotel, room rates vary based on the time of year; rates are highest between Memorial Day and Labor Day, lowest from January (in inauguration years, February) through mid-March. Rates can be higher on weekends than on weekdays, and some hotels offer lower rates for longer stays. Of course, the rate per person is higher in single-occupancy rooms than in doubles or triples, and the savings on rooms booked several months in advance can be significant.

The letter "U" after a listing denotes union hotels whose workers are represented by Hotel & Restaurant Employees Local 25; for the latest list, visit www.hotellaboradvisor.info.

LUXURY HOTELS

Expect to pay at least $250 per night at these landmark hotels—and more, sometimes hundreds more, for a view or a suite. But also expect impeccable service, elegant surroundings, and maybe even a sense of history.

- **Fairmont Washington, D.C.** (formerly the Washington Monarch), 2401 M St. NW, 800-257-7544 or 202-429-2400, www.fairmont.com; some suites have bigger living and dining rooms than you'll find in some apartments, making the Fairmont a favorite of Hollywood film crews on location in Washington.
- **Four Seasons,** 2800 Pennsylvania Ave. NW, 800-332-3442 or 202-342-0444, www.fourseasons.com; in a city where elegance is often synonymous with historic vintage, this modern Georgetown hotel is as elegant as postwar properties get. Consistently among the top-ranked hotels in the nation for service, luxury, and dining.
- **Hay-Adams,** 16th & H streets NW, 800-424-5054 or 202-638-6600, www.hayadams.com; these exclusive rooms—individually decorated with antiques, silk, and molded plaster, and some offering views of the White House—have attracted visiting luminaries since Amelia Earhart, Charles Lindbergh, and Ethel Barrymore stayed here in the 1920s. Among locals, the Hay-Adams is known for afternoon tea and as a studied specimen of architecture in the Italian Renaissance style. (U)

NEWCOMER'S HANDBOOK FOR MOVING TO AND LIVING IN WASHINGTON D.C.

344

- **Henley Park Hotel,** 926 Massachusetts Ave. NW, 202-638-5200, www.henleypark.com; a beautiful little hotel in an elegant historic building near the new convention center offers a pleasant alternative to standard convention hotels.
- **Hotel Washington,** 15th St. & Pennsylvania Ave. NW, 877-512-6314 or 202-638-5900, www.hotelwashington.com; the stately hotel a block from the White House promises "a front row seat for the parade of history," and often delivers. (U)
- **Jefferson Hotel,** 1200 16th St. NW, 866-270-8118 or 202-347-2200, www.thejeffersonwashingtondc.com; this historic and pricey hotel features antique furniture, canopy beds, fireplaces, and a discreet register of famous guests who need to be close to the White House. (U)
- **L'Enfant Plaza Hotel,** 480 L'Enfant Plaza SW, 800-635-5065 or 202-484-1000, www.lenfantplazahotel.com; this modern high-rise offers spacious suites, first-class service, and a location on the working side of the federal district—near the headquarters of three cabinet departments, plus NASA, the GSA, and the FAA. (U)
- **Renaissance Mayflower,** 1127 Connecticut Ave. NW, 800-228-7697 or 202-347-3000, www.renaissancehotels.com; two weeks after this Beaux-Arts hotel opened, President Coolidge held his inaugural ball here; later, FDR wrote his "nothing to fear but fear itself" speech here. Other names that have appeared on the guest register include Churchill, Truman, and Eisenhower. (U)
- **Ritz-Carlton,** 1150 22nd St. NW, 800-241-3333 or 202-835-0500, www.ritz-carlton.com; renovated for the 21st century, this four-star hotel still has featherbeds in every room, but also high-speed internet lines.
- **The Watergate Hotel,** 2650 Virginia Ave. NW, 800-289-1555 or 202-965-2300, www.watergatehotel.com; it's not just the scene of Washington's most famous burglary—the Watergate is a complex of luxury apartments, shops, a four-star French restaurant, and this four-star hotel to match. (U)
- **Willard InterContinental,** 14th St. and Pennsylvania Ave. NW, 800-442-7375 or 202-628-9100, http://washington.intercontinental.com; even in Washington, it's hard to pack more history—or more elegance—into one commercial building.

LARGE HOTELS

Most of these are chain hotels and will be familiar, but a few stand out: the Marriott Wardman Park (the old Sheraton, if the locals look puzzled when you use its proper name) is the city's largest hotel, a vast uptown citadel with 1,345 rooms; nearby, overlooking Rock Creek Park, the elegant Omni

Shoreham is a favorite venue for high school proms; the J.W. Marriott, a block from the White House and across the street from the Treasury Department, offers luxury, prestige, and a coveted view of parades and fireworks; and the Hilton Washington's sleek 1960s contours are instantly recognizable to those who remember the evening news footage of President Reagan and three aides surviving John Hinckley's ambush there in 1981.

As a Washington resident, you're likely to visit the Hilton, the Wardman Park, the Shoreham, and a few Hyatts and Doubletrees sooner or later for conferences, luncheons, dances, and meetings. Even with competition from the convention center, these hotels are always hosting some national conference or trade show.

Expect to pay $100 to $250 a night.

- **Best Western,** 800-780-7234, www.bestwestern.com; two locations in D.C., nine in the suburbs
- **Crowne Plaza - The Hamilton,** 14th & K streets NW, 877-424-4225 or 202-682-0111, www.ichotelsgroup.com
- **Doubletree Hotels & Guest Suites,** 800-222-8733, www.double treehotels.com; two locations in D.C., three in the suburbs
- **Embassy Suites,** 800-362-2779, www.embassy-suites.com; three locations in D.C., five in the suburbs
- **Hilton Hotels,** 800-445-8667, www.hilton.com; three locations in D.C., nine in the suburbs; some (U)
- **Holiday Inn,** 888-465-4329, www.holiday-inn.com; five locations in D.C., 18 in the suburbs; some (U)
- **Hyatt Hotels & Resorts,** 800-591-1234, www.hyatt.com; three locations in D.C., six in the suburbs; Hyatt Regency (U)
- **Marriott Hotels,** 800-228-9290, www.marriott.com; 13 locations in D.C., 11 in the suburbs, including Courtyard by Marriott suites and Residence Inn extended-stay hotels; Marriott Wardman Park (U)
- **Omni Shoreham,** 2500 Calvert St. NW, 800-444-6664 or 202-234-0700, www.omnihotels.com (U)
- **Quality Inn & Suites,** 877-424-6423, www.qualityinn.com; 10 locations in the suburbs
- **Radisson,** 800-333-3333 or www.radisson.com; three locations in the suburbs
- **Washington Plaza Hotel,** 10 Thomas Circle NW, 800-424-1140 or 202-842-1300, www.washingtonplazahotel.com
- **Wyndham Hotels,** 877-999-3223 or www.wyndham.com; Wyndham City Center, 1143 New Hampshire Avenue NW, 202-775-0800; Wyndham Washington D.C., 1400 M St. NW, 202-429-1700

NEWCOMER'S HANDBOOK FOR MOVING TO AND LIVING IN WASHINGTON D.C.

346

SMALL HOTELS

These are smaller hotels that attract tourists and couples rather than the business travelers who stay in the big chain hotels. If you book ahead and ask about promotions, you might get into one of these establishments for as little as $70 a night, and even the premium rooms are less expensive than those at luxury hotels—though the service and atmosphere can be just as charming.

- **Brickskeller Inn,** 1523 22nd St. NW, 202-293-1885, www.the brickskeller.com; a bargain if you don't mind sharing a bathroom with a neighboring room, this Continental-style guesthouse is also home of The Brickskeller saloon, serving more than 700 kinds of beer from around the world—some imported exclusively to "The Brick"
- **Capital Hotels** offer the style and amenities of a luxury hotel at (slightly) lower rates: St. Gregory, 2033 M St. NW, 800-829-5034 or 202-530-3600; Beacon Hotel, 1615 Rhode Island Ave. NW, 800-821-4367 or 202-296-2100; www.capitalhotelswdc.com (U)
- **Capitol Hill Suites,** 200 C St. SE, 202-543-6000, www.capitolhill suites.com; modern suites with kitchenettes on the Hill for the price of single rooms in the business district
- **Carlyle Suites,** 1771 New Hampshire Ave. NW, 866-468-3532 or 202-234-3200, www.carlylesuites.com; named the city's "Official Art Deco Hotel" by the Art Deco Society of America; spacious suites at rates competitive with double rooms
- **Channel Inn,** 650 Water St. SW, 800-368-5668 or 202-554-2400, www.channelinn.com; "Washington's Only Waterfront Hotel" overlooks Washington Channel and Hains Point
- **The Churchill,** 1914 Connecticut Ave. NW, 800-424-2464 or 202-797-2000, www.thechurchillhotel.com; this elegant high-rise features big rooms and an attractive location between Dupont Circle and Embassy Row
- **Georgetown Inn & The Latham,** 3000 M St. NW, 888-876-0001 or 202-333-8900, www.georgetowncollection.com; upscale rooms and suites in the heart of Georgetown
- **Hotel Harrington,** 12th & E streets NW, 800-424-8532 or 202-628-8140, www.hotel-harrington.com (U); popular tourist hotel downtown with student discounts; with low rates and established reputation, it fills up quickly in the summer
- **Hotel Lombardy,** 2019 I St. NW, 800-424-5486 or 202-828-2600, www.hotellombardy.com; suites with kitchens at rates comparable to plain rooms in larger hotels

- **Hotel Madera,** 1310 New Hampshire Ave. NW, 800-430-1202 or 202-296-7600, www.hotelmadera.com; bargain rates, convenient to Georgetown and Dupont Circle, and guests have privileges at neighborhood health clubs
- **Jurys Washington Hotel,** 1500 New Hampshire Ave. NW, www.jurysdoyle.com; a modern hotel right on Dupont Circle
- **Morrison-Clark Inn,** 1015 L St. NW, 800-222-8474 or 202-898-1200, www.morrisonclark.com; the city's only inn listed on the National Register of Historic Places, this elegant hotel, with antique furnishings and a highly rated restaurant, is one of the most luxurious hotels in its price range
- **Normandy Inn,** 2118 Wyoming Ave. NW, 202-483-1350, www.jurys doyle.com; elegant Kalorama location convenient to Dupont Circle and Adams Morgan
- **Phoenix Park Hotel,** 520 North Capitol St. NW, 800-824-5419 or 202-638-6900, www.phoenixparkhotel.com; decorated in the style of an Irish manor, this Capitol Hill hotel has two popular Irish pubs in its storefront (U)
- **The River Inn,** 924 25th St. NW, 800-874-0100 or 202-337-7600, www.theriverinn.com; convenient to George Washington University and the State Department
- **Savoy Suites,** 2505 Wisconsin Ave. NW, 800-944-5377 or 202-337-9700, www.savoysuites.com; Georgetown cousin of Dupont Circle's Carlyle Suites
- **Tabard Inn,** 1739 N St. NW, 202-785-1277, www.tabardinn.com; country-style inn whose courtyard restaurant is always crowded for its famous Sunday brunch. Some rooms have shared baths, but may be the best bargains in downtown D.C.
- **Topaz Hotel,** 1733 N St. NW, 800-775-1202 or 202-393-3000, www.topazhotel.com; upscale suites at bargain rates on a nice residential street near Dupont Circle
- **Travelodge,** 800-578-7878, www.travelodge.com; one location in D.C., three in the suburbs
- **Washington Court Hotel,** 525 New Jersey Ave. NW, 800-321-3010 or 202-628-2100, www.washingtoncourthotel.com; steps from Union Station, many rooms here offer views of the Capitol five blocks away

BUDGET HOTELS & MOTELS

At these no-frills establishments, you can almost always get a room for less than $100, and sometimes as little as $30 or $40. Naturally, the locations aren't the most convenient, but the savings will cover a lot more than your bus fare.

NEWCOMER'S HANDBOOK FOR MOVING TO AND LIVING IN WASHINGTON D.C.

348

- **Adams Inn,** 1744 Lanier Place NW, 800-578-6807 or 202-745-3600, www.adamsinn.com
- **The Braxton Hotel,** 1440 Rhode Island Ave. NW, 800-350-5759 or 202-232-7800, www.braxtonhotel.com
- **Days Inn,** 800-329-7466, www.daysinn.com; one location in D.C., nine in the suburbs
- **Econo Lodge,** 877-424-6423, www.econolodge.com; nine locations in the suburbs
- **Howard Johnson Hotels & Lodges,** 800-446-4656, www. hojo.com; one location in D.C., two in the suburbs
- **Ramada,** 800-272-6232, www.ramada.com; eight locations in the suburbs
- **Red Roof Inns,** 800-733-7663, www.redroof.com; one location in D.C., seven in the suburbs
- **Super 8,** 800-800-8000, www.super8.com; one location in D.C., two in the suburbs

EXTENDED-STAY HOTELS

It could take a few months to find the perfect home. Perhaps the most convenient arrangement while you're searching is an extended-stay hotel. These facilities, also called corporate apartments, offer furnished suites by the day, week, or month. **BridgeStreet Accommodations**, 800-278-7338 or www.bridgestreet.com, and **Oakwood**, 800-902-0832 or www.oakwood.com, have dozens of locations in the area. Other extended-stay hotels, and apartment buildings that rent furnished units on a short-term basis, include:

- **The Barton House,** 2525 North 10th St., Arlington, 703-525-2600, www.bartonhouse.com
- **Bragg Towers,** 99 South Bragg St., Alexandria, 703-354-6300
- **The Chastleton,** 1701 16th St. NW, 888-739-5615 or 202-387-8101, www.apartments.com/chastleton
- **The Remington,** 661 24th St. NW, 800-225-3847 or 202-223-4512, www.remington-dc.com
- **Residence Inn by Marriott,** 888-236-2427, www.residenceinn. com; three locations in D.C., 13 in the suburbs
- **The Virginian,** 1500 Arlington Boulevard, Arlington, 703-522-9600, www.virginiansuites.com

HOTELS AND THE AMERICANS WITH DISABILITIES ACT

According to **Wheels Up! Wheelchair Travel Specialists**, www. wheelsup.com, "Disabled access to our capital city rates high marks in just about every respect. Hotels (though pricey) offer many ADA standard accommodations—including a few with roll-in showers instead of the more-common bathtub with handrails. And budget-minded visitors can find accessible rooms not far outside the District (Arlington, Alexandria, the Maryland suburbs) at much more reasonable prices."

All large hotels, and most smaller hotels downtown, meet or exceed Americans with Disabilities Act standards for wheelchair access, Braille signage, audible elevator signals, audiovisual fire alarms, and trained support staff. Top-tier luxury hotels emphasize personal service and will expertly accommodate any guest's needs; smaller hotels—especially in historic buildings—may or may not be fully equipped for special needs. Ask when you make reservations—almost all hotels in the Washington area have at least a few wheelchair-friendly rooms, and most rooms in the Hilton, Hyatt, and Marriott chains are fully accessible.

The **ENDependence Center of Northern Virginia** maintains a list of ADA-compliant hotels at www.ecnv.org (click on FAQs). **Travelocity**, www.travelocity.com, and **Travelweb**, www.travelweb.com, let you search for wheelchair-accessible hotels.

B&Bs

Bed & breakfast guesthouses, or "B&Bs," can be great bargains on luxurious accommodations and great service—or they can be disappointing rip-offs. Most B&Bs are "quaint" or "eccentric," but there's good quaint and bad quaint. The 21 properties affiliated with **Bed & Breakfast Accommodations** are a good bet, and they're almost all well-appointed quarters in postcard-ready mansions. Call 877-893-3233 or visit www.bnbaccom.com. Other reputable B&Bs include:

- **The Dupont at The Circle,** 1604 19th St. NW, 888-412-0100 or 202-332-5251, www.dupontatthecircle.com
- **Embassy Inn,** 1627 16th St. NW, 800-234-9111 or 202-234-7800
- **Hereford House,** 604 South Carolina Ave. SE, 202-543-0102
- **Kalorama Guest House at Kalorama Park,** 1854 Mintwood Place NW, 202-667-6369
- **Kalorama Guest House at Woodley Park,** 2700 Cathedral Ave. NW, 202-328-0860
- **Windsor Inn,** 1842 16th St. NW, 800-423-9111 or 202-667-0300

HOSTELS & GUESTHOUSES

There's only one official youth hostel in D.C. displaying the **Hostelling International/American Youth Hostels** medallion, at 1009 11th Street NW, 202-737-2333 or www.hiwashingtondc.org. You can stay there

NEWCOMER'S HANDBOOK FOR MOVING TO AND LIVING IN WASHINGTON D.C.

350

for $20 a night if you have a current membership card ($28/year). In peak season, however, official youth hostels reserve the right to bump domestic travelers in favor of international guests.

If you belong to a church or faith-based organization, check to see if there are any affiliated **guesthouses** in Washington—most welcome respectful visitors of all faiths, but do not advertise except in denominational magazines or newsletters. Quiet, inexpensive semi-private lodgings are available in two Quaker guesthouses: the William Penn House on Capitol Hill, 202-543-5560, www.quaker.org/penn-house, and Davis House off Dupont Circle, 202-232-3197. Dorm rooms are sometimes available at Wesley Theological Seminary at American University, 202-885-8600, www.wesleysem.edu, and women between the ages of 18 and 34 can rent rooms at the Young Women's Christian Home on Capitol Hill, 202-546-3255.

In addition to these nonprofit youth hostels, several **commercial hostels** offer communal or semi-private lodgings at the lowest prices available. Some have curfews or other limitations; on the other hand, some provide breakfast.

- **Allen Lee Hotel,** 2224 F St. NW, 202-331-1224, www.allenlee hotel.com; inexpensive lodgings near George Washington University; some rooms with shared bath; 2-week minimum.
- **Columbia Guest House,** 2005 Columbia Rd. NW, 202-265-4006; probably the cheapest rooms within a few blocks of Adams Morgan and Dupont Circle
- **International Guest House,** 1441 Kennedy St. NW, 202-726-5808, www.bedandbreakfast.com; European-style hostel with dorms, curfews, communal bathrooms, and a 20-minute bus ride from downtown, but for $25/night or $160/week you get breakfast and afternoon tea. One-week limit for U.S. citizens, two weeks for international guests.

COLLEGE DORMS

During the summer, if space is available, most area colleges and universities rent rooms in student housing. Dorm rooms for paying tenants are no different from those for students: you share a bathroom with the rest of the hall, you get a small room with basic furnishings, and you might not be allowed to have alcoholic beverages on the premises. Rates are slightly higher than at hostels and lower than anywhere else. Of course, priority goes to enrolled students and participants in summer programs or conferences on campus, but some space is generally available between late May and mid-August. Contact:

- **American University Residential Life & Housing Services** (4-week minimum), 202-885-3370, www.american.edu/other.depts/reslife
- **Catholic University of America Summer Housing & Conferences,** 202-319-5277, http://summer.cua.edu
- **Gallaudet University Visitors Center,** 202-651-5000 (voice & TTY), www.gallaudet.edu
- **George Washington University Community Living & Learning Center,** Summer Housing Services, 202-994-9193, http://gwired.gwu.edu/cllc
- **Georgetown University Conference & Guest Services,** 202-687-4560, www.georgetown.edu/housing/summer
- **Howard University Office of Residence Life,** 202-806-6131, www.howard.edu/residence
- **University of Maryland—College Park Conference & Visitor Services,** 301-314-7884, www.resnet.umd.edu/summer·

NOW THAT YOU LIVE IN ONE OF THE WORLD'S MOST POPULAR tourist destinations, where will you go on vacation? In the winter or when you have out-of-town guests, you can visit the Smithsonian museums, the monuments, and the touristy side of Washington, but when the summer hordes of tourists clog the Smithsonian Metro station, you might want to head for the mountains or the beach.

Classified ads in *Washingtonian* magazine and the *Washington City Paper* list beach houses and mountain cabins for rent, and *Washingtonian* and the *Washington Post* Sunday magazine run seasonal issues focusing on weekend getaways, which carry extra advertising from bed-and-breakfast lodgings, resorts, and destination towns.

For travelers on a budget, the bulletin boards or student newspaper classifieds at area colleges and universities are replete with people seeking rideshares to New York, Richmond, and other day-trip destinations. The advertiser might be offering gas money to share a ride or offering a ride to share expenses.

BLUE RIDGE MOUNTAINS

Just 80 miles west of the Lincoln Memorial, a much larger stone figure looms 4,000 feet above the Shenandoah Valley: Stony Man Mountain, one of the high points (in more than one sense) of **Shenandoah National Park**. It resembles the face of a sleeping giant when viewed from scenic Skyline Drive along the park's 107-mile ridge. An easy nature trail leads to the cliffs, with great views across the Shenandoah Valley to the west and, on a clear day, the next few ridges of the Appalachians.

Bookstores and hiking outfitters in the Washington area offer a selection of hiking guides to Shenandoah's waterfalls and granite peaks. In the fall, you might find the parking lot at the head of a popular trail overcrowded with D.C. license plates as city dwellers clamor for a dose of

NEWCOMER'S HANDBOOK FOR MOVING TO AND LIVING IN WASHINGTON D.C.

354

autumn leaves. Look especially for *Circuit Hikes in Shenandoah National Park,* published by the Potomac Appalachian Trail Club, and *The New Appalachian Trail* by Edward B. Garvey.

South of the park, the **Blue Ridge Parkway** makes a 469-mile scenic link between Shenandoah and **Great Smoky Mountains National Park** on the Tennessee/North Carolina border. Looking west from Shenandoah, you can see Massanutten Mountain, the near edge of the vast **George Washington National Forest**; the south end of the long, narrow mountain features the closest ski slopes to Washington. To the north, where the Blue Ridge meets the Allegheny range, Western Maryland offers some of the finest whitewater paddling in the mid-Atlantic—the Youghioheny River, Antietam Creek, and the lower Shenandoah (which flows south to north).

Throughout the Blue Ridge Mountains, the valleys and foothills are teeming with quaint little towns famous for antique shopping. **New Market** and **Sperryville**, along U.S, Route 211 in Virginia, are the most fertile antiquing grounds. The Shenandoah Valley is also renowned for its caverns, vast limestone chambers in the porous rock of the ancient riverbed. Of the cave systems open to tourists, **Luray Caverns** are the most famous, perhaps because of the unique Stalacpipe Organ, where natural rock formations are played like the tines of a music box.

For more information on these and other attractions, contact:

- **Shenandoah National Park**, 540-999-3500, www.nps.gov/shen; National Park Service camping reservations, 800-365-2267 or http://reservations.nps.gov
- **George Washington National Forest**, 540-740-8310 or www. southernregion.fs.fed.us/gwj; National Forest Service camping reservations, 877-444-6777, www.reserveusa.com
- **Shenandoah Valley Travel Association**, 877-847-4878, www. svta.org
- **Blue Ridge Parkway**, 828-298-0398, www.nps.gov/blri

See the **Greenspace** and **Sports & Recreation** chapters for more information about parks, camping, hiking, and paddling.

BEACHES

From Memorial Day to Labor Day, U.S. Route 50 east of Washington becomes one long traffic jam as Washingtonians flock to the shore—mostly to the boardwalk resorts of **Ocean City**, Md. and **Rehoboth Beach**, Del. Generally speaking, Ocean City attracts a college crowd and Rehoboth is popular with gay men. Both offer boardwalk culture exactly as you would expect: saltwater taffy, skee-ball arcades, fries and funnel cakes, R-rated t-shirts, and plenty of volleyball.

If you prefer a rustic beach, head south from Ocean City to **Assateague Island**, a protected National Seashore and home to the famous wild horses who have flourished here since a long-forgotten wreck of a Spanish galleon. The island is also home to the endangered piping plover and other rare shorebirds. North of Rehoboth Beach, **Cape Henlopen**, Del., and **Cape May**, N.J., connected by ferries across the mouth of the Delaware Bay, also offer shorebirds a carefully preserved dune habitat.

About four hours northeast of the Beltway is **Atlantic City**, N.J., the Las Vegas of the East, where there is also a traditional boardwalk, but that's not why people go. It's all about slot machines, blackjack, roulette, keno, and other opportunities to donate some of your money to Donald Trump; and, in the evening, you can catch the same acts you associate with Vegas—Don Rickles, Tom Jones, and others trying to fill the Sinatra gap. You already know all the street names here, by the way—this is where Monopoly was invented, and the only square on the Monopoly board you won't find in real-life Atlantic City is "Go."

- **Ocean City Visitor Office**, 800-466-2326, www.ocean-city.com
- **Rehoboth Beach**, 800-441-1329, www.rehoboth.com
- **Assateague Island National Seashore**, 410-641-1441, www.nps.gov/asis
- **Cape May**, 609-884-5508, www.covesoft.com/capemay
- **Cape Henlopen State Park**, 301-645-8983, www.destateparks.com
- **Atlantic City**, 888-228-4748, www.atlantic-city-online.com

AMUSEMENT PARKS

You don't have to drive far to ride classic roller coasters and splash in a giant wave pool. There are world-class thrill rides and amusements right in the suburbs, at **Six Flags America** in Largo, Md., on Central Avenue east of Route 193. Locals might still refer to the place by one of its former names, "Wild World" or "Adventure World," as it has had a few facelifts. Roller-coaster enthusiasts may want to take a few longer trips, though, after checking out the ride reviews at www.ultimaterollercoaster.com. Nearby parks include:

- **Busch Gardens—The Old Country & Water Country USA**, Williamsburg, Va., 757-253-3350, www.buschgardens.com
- **DelGrosso's Amusement Park**, near Pittsburgh, 866-684-3538, www.delgrossos.com
- **Hersheypark**, Hershey, Pa., 800-437-7439, www.hersheypa.com
- **Paramount Kings Dominion**, near Richmond, 804-876-5561, www.kingsdominion.com

NEWCOMER'S HANDBOOK FOR MOVING TO AND LIVING IN WASHINGTON D.C.

356

- **Six Flags America**, Largo, 301-249-1500, www.sixflags.com/america
- **Six Flags Great Adventure & Hurricane Harbor**, Jackson, N.J., 732-928-1821, www.sixflags.com/greatadventure

A day at an amusement park can be a very expensive proposition for a family, but there's never any reason to pay full price to go to Six Flags America or Kings Dominion. There's always a grocery store or drugstore giving out coupons, or get some friends together for a group rate.

Children who aren't quite old enough to appreciate visceral thrill rides might enjoy the tamer attractions at **Sesame Place**, near Philadelphia, 215-752-7070, www.sesameplace.com—a Sesame Street theme park—or **Dutch Wonderland** in Lancaster, Pa., 717-291-1888, www.dutch wonderland.com.

Preservationists are working to restore The Enchanted Forest, a defunct theme park in Ellicott City, Md., that once delighted younger kids with boat rides, giant slides and playhouses inspired by nursery rhymes and fairytales.

SOUTHEASTERN PENNSYLVANIA

Drive an hour north of Baltimore and you'll need to keep an eye out for horse-drawn buggies. These days, the low-tech Amish sects grudgingly stick reflective orange triangles on their black carriages, but they adhere to a religious order that forbids them from having telephones in their homes, putting rubber tires on their tractors, or fighting. They did introduce pretzels to this side of the Atlantic, and name-brand snack foods such as Snyder and Utz hail from Amish country and bear Amish family names.

Lancaster County is the heart of "Pennsylvania Dutch" country (a name based on a mistake in translation—the Amish are of German descent, or Deutsch), and there is an influence of Amish culture in York, Reading, and Hanover. Moravians and Quakers, both descendants of the same pacifist Anabaptist movement as the Amish, also settled here; in addition to Amish shoofly pie and snickerdoodles, you'll find spiky Moravian stars adorning front porches, and Moravian sugar cakes at old-fashioned general stores. Historic markers identify many farms and old buildings as sites on the Underground Railroad, the 19th-century network of "safe houses" where Quaker abolitionists helped slaves run to freedom.

This is also outlet shopping country, where day trippers from Baltimore and Philadelphia scour outlet malls in search of designer dresses and coats at a fraction of the retail price.

- **Lancaster County**, 800-723-8824, www.padutchcountry.com
- **York**, 888-858-9675, www.yorkpa.org
- **Reading/Berks County**, 800-443-6610, www.readingberkspa.com

COLONIAL SITES

D.C. residents are fond of pointing out that the District is legally a colony today, but "colonial heritage" generally doesn't refer to the four corner-stones of the District. Within three hours' drive, you can visit:

- **Williamsburg**, Va., 800-447-8679, www.history.org; this restored 17th-century settlement is a living museum, where music students from William & Mary don colonial dress to play the same hornpipes and reels that entertained the Redcoats back in the day. Here, on May 15, 1776, the colonial Virginia assembly met and decided to send a resolution to the Continental Congress proposing that the 13 colonies declare their independence from England. They took down the British flag and replaced it with the flag of the Grand Union—which today flies over Williamsburg every year from May 15 to July 4.
- **St. Mary's City**, Md., 800-762-1634, www.stmaryscity.org; older than Williamsburg and less touristy, this partially restored settlement is where the colony of Maryland was founded in 1634. An ancestor of the First Amendment was born here—the first religious tolerance law made by Europeans in North America. Ongoing archaeological work here makes headlines every few years, and in the early 1990s a metal coffin from colonial times was found to contain scientific pay-dirt: pristine samples of the 17th-century atmosphere, never touched by car exhaust or factory smoke. The bluffs above the St. Mary's River, and the rocky beaches of nearby **Point Lookout State Park**, offer some of the most spectacular sunsets within a day's drive of Washington.
- **Jamestown**, Va., 888-593-4682, www.historyisfun.org; the first recorded European settlement in North America. Almost 200 years later, in nearby **Yorktown**, Gen. Cornwallis surrendered King George's colonies to Gen. Washington.
- **Monticello**, Va., 804-984-9822, www.monticello.org; the mansion on the back of the nickel, designed by and for architect Thomas Jefferson in his spare time.

CIVIL WAR SITES

A diner on the northern outskirts of Frederick, Md., is known as Barbara Fritchie's, and patrons are reminded that she was the Maryland woman who defied Jackson's Confederate troops on the march, as recalled by poet John Greenleaf Whittier. "Shoot, if you must, this old gray head, but spare your country's flag," she said. Moved by her gallantry, General Stonewall Jackson turned to his rebels, stating "Who touches a hair of yon gray head dies like a dog; march on." Whether that story is embellished or not, the Civil War raged through Northern Virginia, Western Maryland, and well

NEWCOMER'S HANDBOOK FOR MOVING TO AND LIVING IN WASHINGTON D.C.

358

into Pennsylvania for four years before the destruction of supply lines from Atlanta led to General Lee's surrender at Appomattox. The flash point that started it all is just a 90-minute drive or a short train ride north of the Beltway. Where the Shenandoah meets the Potomac, and Maryland, Virginia, and West Virginia come together is **Harper's Ferry**, site of John Brown's raid in preparation for, Brown believed, an epic conflagration.

- **Antietam**, Md., 301-432-5124, www.nps.gov/anti; this tranquil river-side field, looking much as it did in 1862, was the scene of a pivotal battle that slowed Gen. Lee's army, deterred the British from recognizing the Confederate nation, and opened the door for the Emancipation Proclamation.
- **Fredericksburg**, Va., 800-678-4748, www.fredericksburgva.com; this is where Clara Barton and Walt Whitman tended casualties of the Spotsylvania and Chancellorsville battles; the city itself preserves a walkable old town section near the Rappahannock River.
- **Gettysburg**, Pa., 717-334-6274, www.gettysburg.com; **Gettysburg National Military Park**, 717-334-1124, www.nps.gov/gett; the bloodiest battle ever fought on American soil drew President Lincoln here to dedicate the cemetery with the words now chiseled in stone at the Lincoln Memorial. The battlefield itself is well preserved, and the town offers many interpretive attractions—including a wax museum, a 360-degree panoramic painting, an observation tower, and a narration of the battle over a giant map illuminating troop movements.
- **Harper's Ferry**, W.Va., 304-535-6298, www.nps.gov/hafe; the town, nestled between two rivers, was declared by maverick abolitionist John Brown to be the provisional capital of the United States after he seized the federal armory there to equip his posse of freed slaves for the battle he envisioned. Before touring the well-preserved historic town, stop on the Maryland side of the Potomac at the Maryland Heights trailhead on Route 340 and take a leisurely walk up the hill; the postcards in town are no substitute for seeing that view for yourself.
- **Manassas National Battlefield Park**, 703-361-1339, www.nps.gov/mana; Bull Run is a quiet little creek with a cute little stone bridge that was twice the object of bloodshed. It was during the first battle here that Gen. Thomas Jackson stonewalled the Union troops and earned his nickname. Except for the highway across it, the battle-field is well preserved. This is a day trip, not a weekend getaway—indeed, the city of Manassas is practically a suburb of Washington.

NEW YORK

With a Greyhound bus almost every hour, several airlines offering hourly shuttles during the day, and new high-speed train service via Amtrak, you can easily go see a Broadway show in the evening and still go to work in Washington the next morning—or, check out www.nycvisit.com for a guide to accommodations in the Big Apple. It's a nice place to visit, but it's not the nation's capital. In New York, you actually have to *pay* to get into the museums!

BEACH & MOUNTAIN HOUSES

Check the classified ads in *Washingtonian* magazine, the *City Paper*, and the *Post* Sunday magazine for opportunities to rent, sublet, share, or even buy a vacation home. A cabin in the mountains can be quite inexpensive, if you plan to use it enough to get your money's worth; buying a beachfront house or condo may pay for itself through rentals.

In beach communities, you should have no trouble finding a rental agent or broker to help you lease or buy property. If you're looking outside the major beach resorts listed in this chapter, search http://official citysites.org for the appropriate community web site—if you're buying a place of your own or buying into a timeshare arrangement, you'll want to look at web sites created by and for residents, not visitors.

TRAVEL BARGAINS

With the emergence of online ticket agents such as www.expedia.com and www.orbitz.com, it's easy to shop around for the lowest scheduled fares; but if you're headed to a common destination, start with the *City Paper* classifieds—there's always someone selling unwanted airline tickets to Chicago or Atlanta, train tickets to New York, or bus tickets to Atlantic City. Also visit www.craigslist.org and browse the "housing swap," "vacation rentals" and "tickets" sections. Airfares are generally lower from Marshall BWI than from Dulles and Reagan National airports, and lower to busy destinations than to smaller cities. "Coming & Going" is a column in the Travel section of the Sunday *Post* that keeps track of travel bargains and promotions.

Most colleges and universities have at least an unofficial "ride board," where travelers in need of a ride, or vice versa, can post their needs and browse for potential matches. Ride-sharing ads appear in the *City Paper* and www.craigslist.com too.

For a list of small, independent accommodations, pick up a directory of bed-and-breakfast inns at any major bookstore or visit www.travel assist.com/reg. Rates are often much lower than at hotels and motels, and you get much nicer rooms and hospitality than the same money would buy at a hotel.

STA Travel, 800-781-4040 or www.statravel.com, is a full-service travel agency specializing in budget travel for students as well as young-at-heart

NEWCOMER'S HANDBOOK FOR MOVING TO AND LIVING IN WASHINGTON D.C.

360

travelers who are more interested in adventure than tightly scripted tour packages. Visit the STA Travel store at 800 21st Street NW or 3301 M Street NW.

Finally, please be assured that you're never too old for a youth hostel. The 4,500 friendly, inexpensive, no-frills lodgings around the world that display the Hostelling International symbol are open to anyone with a friendly attitude and a current membership card, available for $28/year. Join at www.hiayh.org or call 301-495-1240.

ADD UP THE EVENTS HOSTED BY THE MUSEUMS, LIBRARIES, theaters, parks and monuments, neighborhood associations, congregations, charities and civic groups, not to mention athletic venues; multiply them by all the cities and counties in the D.C. area; and you'll understand why residents here complain that there's not enough time.

Check the newspapers for features and listings of upcoming events. The *Washington City Paper* and the Weekend section of the *Washington Post* (Fridays) are the best places to look for upcoming concerts, gallery and museum openings, plays, readings, lectures, tours, craft fairs, and other special events; for book signings and discussions, check the Book World section of the *Post* on Sundays. On the first Sunday of the month, the Style section of the *Post* lists charity galas. The *Common Denominator* is good for civic events in the District. The *Washington Business Journal* covers conventions, trade shows, and networking events. Also check the **Neighborhood Profiles** for additional listings of community festivals—street fairs, town birthdays, and other folksy events that are popular with local residents and make for fun, inexpensive outings. The neighborhood events listed here are those that draw big crowds.

If a location is not listed below, it's because the location changes from year to year. For more information about these festivities, check the *Post* or the *City Paper* a week or two before the event.

JANUARY

- **Martin Luther King Jr. Day** observance, Lincoln Memorial, 202-619-7222; the annual ceremony culminates with a broadcast of Dr. King's "I Have a Dream" speech. See **Volunteering** for information about related community service activities.

NEWCOMER'S HANDBOOK FOR MOVING TO AND LIVING IN WASHINGTON D.C.

362

- **Wammie Awards**, www.wamadc.com, 202-338-1134; nominees and past honorees perform at the Washington Area Music Association's annual awards ceremony.

FEBRUARY

- **Chinese New Year** celebration, Chinatown, 202-328-4748; D.C.'s Chinatown hosts a week-long ethnic festival culminating in a parade under the Friendship Arch at 7th & H streets NW. Metro: Gallery Place-Chinatown
- **Frederick Douglass' birthday** observance, Frederick Douglass House, 202-426-5961, www.nps.gov/frdo; Black History Month is commemorated with a tribute to the abolitionist leader at his historic home in Anacostia. Metro: Bus W6/W8 from Anacostia
- **Lincoln's Birthday** observance, Lincoln Memorial, 202-426-6841, www.nps.gov/linc; with fanfare from military bands, the President lays a wreath at the memorial and a prominent speaker delivers the Gettysburg Address.
- **Washington Boat Show**, Convention Center, 703-823-7960, www.washingtonboatshow.com; if you're looking for a new yacht, this is the place. Metro: Mt. Vernon Square.
- **Washington's Birthday** observances, Mt. Vernon, 703-780-2000, www.mountvernon.org; Old Town Alexandria, 703-838-4200; Washington Monument grounds, 202-426-6841, www.nps.gov/wamo; festivities include a parade and ceremony at George Washington's estate, with a performance by the U.S. Army Fife & Drum Corps; a parade in Alexandria in the shadow of the Masonic memorial to Washington (Metro: King Street); and a musical tribute at the Sylvan Theatre at the Washington Monument (Metro: Smithsonian).

MARCH

- **Environmental Film Festival** (see **Cultural Life**)
- **Helen Hayes Awards**, 202-337-4572, www.helenhayes.org; Washington's theater community—called the nation's second-largest by Variety magazine—honors its best performances at this Washington Theatre Awards Society gala named after the venerated District native.
- **Smithsonian Kite Festival**, Washington Monument grounds, 202-357-3030, www.kitefestival.org (sometimes in early April); kite enthusiasts show off their most elaborate kites and stunt skills. Metro: Smithsonian
- **St. Patrick's Day Parade**, along Constitution Ave. NW, 202-637-2474, www.dcstpatsparade.com; all the pubs are overcrowded on

March 17, but there's plenty of room to celebrate along the parade route. Metro: Archives-Navy Memorial or Federal Triangle

APRIL

- **African-American Family Celebration**, National Zoo, 202-673-4717, www.nationalzoo.si.edu; the Easter Monday festival at the Zoo features music, dance, and interactive activities for all ages. Metro: Woodley Park-Zoo
- **Cherry Blossom Festival**, Tidal Basin, 202-661-7584, www.national cherryblossomfestival.org; crowning a week of entertainment, games, and a 10K under the blooming cherry trees, the city's largest annual parade marches down Constitution Avenue. Metro: Federal Triangle
- **Christmas in April/Sukkot in April**, various locations, 202-965-2824, www.christmasinaprildc.org; volunteers make repairs to the homes of senior citizens and low-income families, and in community centers, shelters, and inner-city schools.
- **Earth Day** celebration, The Mall and various locations, 202-518-0044, www.earthday.net (global directory of Earth Day events); the big-tent environmental exposition, with its big-name entertainment, is held every five years, but many communities hold smaller Earth Day fairs where you can find out more about local environmental groups and how to lend a hand.
- **Emancipation Day** parade, Pennsylvania Ave. NW, 202-661-7581, www.culturaltourismdc.org; April 16, the anniversary of the 1862 law ending slavery in D.C., was celebrated with a parade from 1886 to 1901, and the tradition was revived in 2002.
- **Hands On D.C.**, various locations, 202-667-5808, www.handson dc.org; teams of volunteers give a day's work to neighborhood schools—and raise money for scholarships from sponsors supporting their efforts.
- **Smithsonian Craft Show**, 888-832-9554, www.smithsoniancraft show.com; artisans from all over the country compete to be selected for this exhibition and sale.
- **Take Back the Night** march and rally, Dupont Circle, 877-739-3895, www.nsvrc.org; this annual protest against domestic violence is the signature event of Sexual Assault Awareness Month. Metro: Dupont Circle
- **Washington International Film Festival** (see **Cultural Life**)
- **White House Easter Egg Roll**, 202-456-7041, www.nps.gov/whho; an Easter Monday tradition on the South Lawn of the White House. Open to children ages three to six, accompanied by an adult. Free, but advance tickets are required—visit the information kiosk on the Ellipse south of the White House. Metro: McPherson Square

NEWCOMER'S HANDBOOK FOR MOVING TO AND LIVING IN WASHINGTON D.C.

364

MAY

- **Andrews Air Force Base Air Show**, 301-981-4600, public.andrews. amc.af.mil/jsoh; this flying parade includes the Thunderbirds fighter aerobatics team, the B-2 stealth bomber, and vintage and modern military aircraft.
- **Cathedral Flower Mart**, Washington National Cathedral, 202-537-6200, www.cathedral.org/cathedral; this flower show and sale features cuttings from the Bishop's Garden. Metro: 30 series bus from Tenleytown or N series from Dupont Circle
- **Greater D.C. Cares Day**, various locations, 202-777-4466, www.dc-cares.org; thousands of volunteers spend the day helping to improve neighborhood schools, parks, and low-income housing. To support the ongoing work of Greater D.C. Cares, each participant collects pledges from sponsors, as in a walkathon.
- **Memorial Day** observances, Arlington National Cemetery, 703-607-8000, www.arlingtoncemetery.org; Vietnam Veterans Memorial, 202-393-0090; The Mall, 202-426-6841, www.nps.gov/vive; the President lays a wreath at the Tomb of the Unknowns (Metro: Arlington Cemetery). Similar ceremonies are held at the Vietnam Veterans Memorial. The National Symphony Orchestra plays a free concert at the Capitol end of The Mall, and the Rolling Thunder motorcycle parade along Constitution Avenue honors POW and MIA soldiers.
- **WHFStival**, M&T Stadium in Baltimore, 410-481-1057, www. live1057.com; WHFS-FM hosts an all-day lineup of alternative rock bands—sort of a one-day Lollapalooza.

JUNE

- **Alexandria Red Cross Waterfront Festival**, 703-549-8300, www.waterfrontfestival.org; in the nation's largest outdoor event to benefit the American Red Cross, Alexandria's nautical heritage is celebrated with a weekend of arts and entertainment to welcome vintage tall ships. Metro: bus 28A/28B from King Street
- **Booz-Allen Classic** golf tournament, www.boozallenclassic.com; the annual PGA Tour event formerly known as the Kemper Open is held at Avenel in Potomac.
- **Capital Jazz Fest**, Merriweather Post Pavilion, 301-218-0404, www. capitaljazz.com; big-name jazz artists gather for three days of celebration.
- **Capital Pride**, 13th St. & Pennsylvania Ave. NW, 202-797-3510, www.capitalpride.org; a parade honoring the GLBT community (and

friends) culminates at a street festival with big-name entertainment. Metro: Federal Triangle

- **Dupont-Kalorama Museum Walk**, various locations between Dupont Circle and Calvert St. NW, 202-387-4062, www.dk museums.com; a weekend of free admission and special activities at a dozen private museums.

- **Festival of American Folklife**, The Mall, 202-357-2700, www.folk life.si.edu (continues through the Fourth of July); interactive exhibits, craft demonstrations, music, and storytelling in a tent city celebrate the history and cultural diversity of the United States. Metro: Smithsonian

- **Juneteenth**, various locations, www.juneteenth.com; a traditional celebration of the Emancipation, Juneteenth is observed on June 19 with vigils, parades, and festivals at Freedom Plaza, the Capitol, and the Frederick Douglass House. An emerging new holiday—specific events and sponsors vary each year.

- **Louisiana Swamp Romp**, Wolf Trap, 703-255-1860, www.wolf trap.org; hoo-wee, the Washington area has its own annual festival of zydeco music and dance.

- **National Capital Barbecue Battle**, 12th St. & Pennsylvania Ave. NW, 202-828-3099, www.barbecuebattle.com; sample the entries by restaurants and amateurs in the regional barbecue contest. Metro: Federal Triangle

- **Potomac Celtic Festival**, Morven Park, Leesburg, 703-938-9779, www.potomaccelticfest.org; traditional and modern music, dance and crafts celebrate the Celtic cultures of Ireland, Scotland, Cape Breton, and even Celtic France, Spain, and North Africa.

- **Shakespeare Free for All**, Carter Barron Amphitheater, 202-547-1122, www.shakespearetheatre.org; the Shakespeare Theatre Company gives free performances of a different Shakespeare play each year, often featuring screen stars such as Kelly McGillis or Sabrina LeBeauf. Advance tickets are required and go quickly, four to a customer. Metro: bus S2/S4 from Silver Spring

- **Takoma Park Jazz Festival**, 301-589-4433, www.tpjazzfest.org; dozens of local jazz artists fill six stages all day, and it's free. Metro: shuttle bus from Takoma

- **Unifest**, Martin Luther King Jr. Avenue SE, 202-678-8822, www.union temple.com; a two-day street festival celebrates Anacostia. Metro: Anacostia

- **Wolf Trap Jazz & Blues Festival**, Wolf Trap, 703-255-1860, www.wolftrap.org; famous and up-and-coming artists fill several stages for four days of concerts.

NEWCOMER'S HANDBOOK FOR MOVING TO AND LIVING IN WASHINGTON D.C.

366

JULY

- **A Capital Fourth**, The Mall, www.pbs.org/capitolfourth; the fireworks at the Washington Monument are accompanied by a free National Symphony Orchestra concert on the west lawn of the Capitol, ending a full day of pop, jazz, country, and patriotic concerts on the Mall. Metro: Smithsonian
- **Bastille Day** celebration, along Pennsylvania Ave. NW, 202-296-7200; waiters and waitresses with full trays race from Les Halles restaurant at 12th and Pennsylvania to the Capitol and back. Metro: Archives-Navy Memorial
- **Screen on the Green**, Monday evenings on the Mall, www.screen onthegreen.com; see classic American films on a giant outdoor screen. Metro: Smithsonian
- **Latino Festival**, along Pennsylvania Ave. NW, 202-671-2825, http://ola.dc.gov; a parade and a weekend of festivities showcase the large and diverse Latino community in Washington. Metro: Archives-Navy Memorial or Federal Triangle
- **Legg Mason Tennis Classic** (see **Sports & Recreation**)
- **Minnesota Avenue Day**, Minnesota Ave. & Benning Rd. NE, 202-396-1200, www.mhcdo.org; this summertime street festival is second only to Unifest as the largest neighborhood celebration "east of the river." Metro: Minnesota Avenue
- **Virginia Scottish Games**, Alexandria, 703-912-1943, www.va scottishgames.org; a festival of Scottish heritage featuring traditional music, dancing, and food—including real haggis.
- **Washington Theater Festival**, Source Theatre, 202-462-1073, www.sourcetheatre.com (through August); rising stars in the local theater community present dozens of new plays and staged readings. The series culminates in the 10-Minute Play Competition, with a different set of short plays every night for a week. Metro: bus 52/54 from McPherson Square

AUGUST

- **Governor's Cup**, from Annapolis to St. Mary's City, Md., 240-895-4484, www.smcm.edu/govcup; the most prestigious yacht race on the Chesapeake is also one of the biggest overnight regattas on the East Coast.
- **Maryland Renaissance Festival**, Crownsville, Md., 800-296-7304, www.rennfest.com (through October); one of the nation's largest

Renaissance fairs, "RennFest" celebrates the Tudor era with games, pageantry, food, mead and jousting—the official state sport of Maryland.

- **Montgomery County Agricultural Fair**, Gaithersburg Fairgrounds, 301-926-3100, www.mcagfair.com; a classic county fair, right out of *Charlotte's Web*, with animal and harvest shows, carnival games, rides, cotton candy, and funnel cakes. Ride-On bus: 55/59 from Rockville
- **Stone Soul Picnic**, RFK Stadium, 202-306-1111, www.majic1023. com; the all-day free festival is the biggest annual soul concert in the mid-Atlantic region.

SEPTEMBER

- **Adams Morgan Day**, 202-328-9451, www.adamsmorganday.org; only Mt. Pleasant Day rivals the size of this annual street festival, organized by neighborhood businesses. Watch the *InTowner* or the *City Paper* for details. Metro: Bus 42 from Dupont Circle
- **Arts On Foot**, locations throughout Penn Quarter, www.arts onfoot.org; in the downtown gallery district dozens of public and private galleries and studios hold open houses. Also look for street performances, a "Cooking as Art" demonstration, the Shakespeare Theatre's annual sale of used props, and sidewalk sales by local artists. Metro: Gallery Place-Chinatown or Metro Center
- **Black Family Reunion**, The Mall, 202-737-0120, www.ncnw. org/blackfamily.htm; this huge two-day festival celebrates African-American culture with entertainment, food, games, and exhibits. Metro: Smithsonian
- **Capital Soulfest**, 202-332-8100; older and younger generations of big-name soul and R&B artists perform at an all-day concert and party.
- **D.C. Blues Festival**, Carter Barron Amphitheater, 202-962-0112, www.dcblues.org; D.C. Blues Society artists offer a day and evening of free concerts. Metro: bus S2/S4 from Silver Spring
- **Elderfest**, Freedom Plaza, 13th St. and Pennsylvania Ave. NW, 202-724-5622, http://dcoa.dc.gov; this celebration and expo for the senior community features entertainment, exhibits, and free health screenings. Metro: Federal Triangle
- **International Children's Festival**, Wolf Trap, 703-255-1860, www.wolftrap.org; young performing artists from the Washington area and around the world present a weekend of family entertainment.
- **Kennedy Center Open House**, 202-467-4600, www.kennedy-center.org; the nation's living museum of the arts and memorial to President Kennedy offers a full day of free performances on its seven stages. Metro: Foggy Bottom-GWU

NEWCOMER'S HANDBOOK FOR MOVING TO AND LIVING IN WASHINGTON D.C.

368

- **Prince George's County Fair**, Prince George's Equestrian Center, 301-579-2598, www.countyfair.org; half an hour's drive from the Capitol, Pennsylvania Avenue becomes a country road through rolling fields and horse farms. This land is among the first places where Native Americans cultivated tobacco. A traditional agricultural fair honors the agrarian history of Prince George's County.
- **Takoma Park Folk Festival**, 301-589-0202, www.tpff.org; local folk musicians and dancers representing traditions from all over the world gather for a day of free performances on six stages. Metro: shuttle bus from Takoma

OCTOBER

- **Army 10-Miler**, 202-685-3361, www.armytenmiler.com; *Runner's World* magazine calls it one of the top 100 races in the nation: a flat course through the monumental city, which attracts some 16,000 runners each year. Register early.
- **Art-o-Matic**, www.artomatic.org, 202-661-7589 (sometimes in November); hundreds of local visual and performing artists and filmmakers show and sell their work in this grassroots, all-volunteer exhibition.
- **Halloween Drag Races**, 17th & Q streets NW, www.dlp.org/alpha; Washington's gay community and friends celebrate Halloween off Dupont Circle with contests for drag queens in high heels. Metro: Dupont Circle
- **Marine Corps Marathon**, 800-786-8762, www.marinemarathon.com; you don't have to be a Marine, but you do have to register early and be able to run a 26.2 mile loop, from the Marine Corps Memorial (the "Iwo Jima Memorial") in Rosslyn to Capitol Hill and back.
- **Reel Affirmations** GLBT film festival (see **Cultural Life**)
- **Takoma Park Street Fair**, www.takomafestival.com; Old Town Takoma Park merchants, artisans, community organizations, and musicians celebrate the community. Metro: Takoma
- **WAMA Crosstown Jam**, various locations, 202-338-1134, www.wamadc.com; a weekend of concerts by hundreds of local musicians at dozens of clubs and coffeehouses around town raises money for the Washington Area Music Association.
- **Washington International Horse Show**, Verizon Center, 301-987-9400, www.wihs.org; a week of indoor equestrian competition brings competitors from all over the world into downtown Washington. Metro: Gallery Place-Chinatown

NOVEMBER

- **Veterans Day**; memorial events at Arlington National Cemetery, 703-607-8000, www.arlingtoncemetery.org, and throughout D.C.

DECEMBER

- **A Christmas Carol at Ford's Theatre**, 202-347-4833, www.fords theatre.org; the classic tale is staged every year at the historic venue. Metro: Metro Center
- **The Christmas Revels**, Lisner Theatre, 202-723-7528, www.revels dc.org; Old World carols, dances, and mummers' plays are performed by a lively chorus in period garb. Metro: Foggy Bottom
- **Festival of Lights**, Washington Mormon Temple grounds, 301-587-0144, www.ldschurchtemples.com; the Washington area's biggest display of lights, along with free choral concerts in the visitor's center.
- **First Night Alexandria**, 703-836-1526, www.firstnightalexandria. org; **First Night Montgomery**, Silver Spring, 240-777-6821, www.montgomerycountymd.gov; these family-oriented public New Year's Eve celebrations include music, games, dances, and no alcohol.
- **Kennedy Center Holiday Festival**, 202-467-4600, www.kennedy-center.org; the Kennedy Center itself is wrapped in a giant red ribbon, and the gift inside is a month of free holiday performances, including a Christmas Eve "Messiah" sing-along. Metro: Foggy Bottom-GWU
- **Pageant of Peace**, The Ellipse, 202-208-1631, www.nps.gov/ whho/pageant; music and family activities celebrate the lighting of the National Christmas Tree and the smaller trees representing each state and territory.
- **Wildlife Arts Festival**, Woodend, Chevy Chase, 301-652-9188, www.audubonnaturalist.org; the Audubon Naturalist Society kicks off the holiday season with a sale of works by local artists to benefit regional conservation efforts.

WASHINGTON AREA GUIDES

T HIS IS A MAJOR TOURISM CITY AND THERE ARE COUNTLESS GUIDES to the museums and attractions. This is a handpicked list of the best or most distinctive. Check with booksellers for the latest editions.

- **Arcadia**, www.arcadiapublishing.com, publishes a series of guidebooks for neighborhood walking tours, written by local historians and providing detailed and informative notes.
- *The Everything Guide to Washington, D.C.* by Lori Perkins, Adams Media Corp.; you'll want a tourist guide for detailed information about the museums and monuments that can fill as many weekends as you can spare, and to help you host visiting friends and family; there are dozens of guidebooks, and this is one of the most knowledgeable.
- *Greater Washington Area Bicycle Atlas*, Jim McCarthy & Sharon Gang, Washington Area Bicyclist Association & Hostelling International; WABA knows bike routes, and these ride notes are expertly tested in detail.
- *Natural Washington* by Richard L. Berman & Deborah McBride, EPM Publications; parks and natural areas from Manassas to the Bay are profiled in detail in this knowledgeable pocket guide.
- *StationMasters*, Bowring Cartographic, 2003; this little book contains maps of the immediate areas surrounding each Metro station, identifying key buildings and points of interest.

D.C. HISTORY

- *Above Washington* by Robert W. Cameron, Cameron & Co., 1981; there are lots of coffee-table picture books of Washington, but this one stands out. Though it's a bit dated, it emphasizes aerial photos of living

NEWCOMER'S HANDBOOK FOR MOVING TO AND LIVING IN WASHINGTON D.C.

372

neighborhoods as well as national landmarks, and includes a section of "then and now" photos of historic neighborhoods.

- **Civil War to Civil Rights: Washington D.C.'s Downtown Heritage Trail** by Richard T. Busch and Kathryn Schneider Smith, Howell Press, 2001; these self-guided walking tours visit famous and offbeat sites in downtown D.C. that have played important roles in the history of the city and the nation. Available free at historic sites around town.
- **A Literary Map of Metropolitan Washington, D.C.** by Martha Hopkins and Sheila Harrington, Women's National Book Association, www.wnba-books.org/wash, 2001; a folding map created in partnership with the Library of Congress shows important sites in the city's literary history, including the homes and graves of famous authors who lived here.
- **On This Spot: Pinpointing the Past in Washington, D.C.** by Douglas Evelyn & Paul Dickson, National Geographic Society, 1999; every neighborhood, if not every block, in D.C. has a story, but not every historic place has a marker or a brochure to explain its significance. This book fills you in on a lot of arcane history.
- **Washington Album: A Pictorial History of the Nation's Capital** by Bob Levey and Jane Freundel Levey, Washington Post Books, 2000; like Bob Levey's column in the *Post*, this book reflects a city of real people and real neighborhoods, not just monuments and tourist attractions.

BIOGRAPHIES & MEMOIRS

Some of these people grew up in Washington and made their mark on the world; others came here and made their mark on the city. But they all walked the streets of your new hometown.

- **Let Me Tell You a Story: A Lifetime in the Game** by Red Auerbach with John Feinstein, Back Bay Books, 2005; the legendary Boston Celtics coach grew up in Washington and coached high school and pro basketball here.
- **Clara Barton: Professional Angel** by Elizabeth Brown Pryor, University of Pennsylvania Press, 1998; **Woman of Valor** by Stephen B. Oates, Free Press, 1995
- **Ben Bradlee: A Good Life** (autobiography), Simon & Schuster, 1995; the Watergate-era *Washington Post* editor has been one of the most prominent figures in social and political Washington since he was JFK's friend and neighbor in Georgetown in the 1950s.
- **William O. Douglas: My Wilderness: East to Katahdin** (memoir), Doubleday, 1961; in this collection of essays, the Supreme Court Justice and accomplished hiker recounts, among other adventures, his travels

along the C&O Canal—one of the most eloquent narratives ever written about natural areas in greater Washington.

- *Frederick Douglass: Narrative of the Life, My Bondage and My Freedom* (autobiography), 1845
- *Daniel Drayton: Personal Memoir,* Negro University Press, 1969; in 1848, this local merchant—along with Paul Jennings, a former slave employed by Sen. Daniel Webster—led a sensational attempt to smuggle 77 slaves to freedom. Originally published in 1855 under the title *Personal Memoir of Daniel Dreyton, For Four Years And Four Months A Prisoner, For Charity's Sake, In Washington Jail*
- *Duke Ellington: Music Is My Mistress* (autobiography), Da Capo Press, 1976; *Beyond Category: The Life and Genius of Duke Ellington* by John Edward Hasse, Da Capo Press, 1995
- *Katharine Graham: Personal History* (autobiography), Vintage Books, 1998; *Power, Privilege, and the Post: The Katharine Graham Story* by Carol Felsenthal, Seven Stories Press, 1999; *Katharine the Great: Katharine Graham and Her Washington Post Empire* by Deborah Davis, Institute for Media Analysis, June 1991
- *Helen Hayes: My Life in Three Acts* (autobiography with Katherine Hatch), Harcourt, 1990; the "first lady" of Washington theater is the namesake of the most prestigious theater awards off Broadway.
- *The Life of Pierre Charles L'Enfant* by Hans Paul Caemmerer, Da Capo Press, 1970
- *Frederick Law Olmsted: A Clearing in the Distance* by Witold Rybezynski, Scribner, 1999
- *Robert Gould Shaw: Blue-Eyed Child of Fortune* (letters collected by Russell Duncan), University of Georgia Press, 1999; a friend of Lincoln's son, Col. Shaw commanded the first African-American regiment in the U.S. Army, and the heart of D.C. now bears his name.
- *John Philip Sousa, Marching Along: Recollections of Men, Women and Music* (memoir) 1928; reissued by Integrity Press, 1994; the Washingtonian composer is one of the few individuals in history who is widely credited with introducing an entire genre of music—the march written for brass band.
- *Doug Williams: Quarterblack: Shattering the NFL Myth* (memoir with Bruce Hunter), Bonus Books, 1990; the Washington Redskins quarterback was the first African-American to lead a team to victory in the Super Bowl.

Of course, political biographies and memoirs also offer unique perspectives on the city and its culture. Perhaps the most fascinating—and certainly the most revealing—glimpses of "inside the Beltway" society are

NEWCOMER'S HANDBOOK FOR MOVING TO AND LIVING IN WASHINGTON D.C.

374

those in the memoirs of Watergate figures such as H.R. Haldeman, John Dean, Jeb Magruder, and the *Washington Post* duo of Bob Woodward and local native Carl Bernstein. Their secret source, Mark Felt, better known as Deep Throat, also published his memoirs in 2005.

Finally, there's one person who had a profound impact on Washington without ever even visiting the city: James Smithson, the British chemist who left his money to the United States "to endow a facility in Washington for the increase and diffusion of knowledge." Since 1846, the Smithsonian Institution has grown into one of the most revered scholarly organizations in the world, and it includes several of the world's most popular museums. The Smithsonian released an official biography, *James Smithson and His Bequest*, in 1879; a more contemporary portrait is offered in *James Smithson and the Smithsonian Story* by Leonard J. Carmichael and J.C. Long, Putnam, 1965.

CHILDREN

- *Independent School Guide for Washington, D.C. and Surrounding Area*, published by Lift Hill Press, is the most comprehensive directory of private and parochial schools.
- *Underground Train* by Mary Quattlebaum, illustrated by Cat Bowman Smith, Yearling Books, 1997; this delightful children's book teaches toddlers what to expect from their first ride on the Metro.
- *Dreamland: A Lullaby* and *Halley Came to Jackson* (both HarperCollins) are children's books by Mary Chapin Carpenter, the native Washingtonian country music star, who still lives in Georgetown.

FICTION

Washington shows up in many classic and contemporary novels—especially in works by Tom Clancy, Gore Vidal, and Allen Drury. In the 1959 Pulitzer Prize novel *Advise and Consent,* Drury wrote of Washington:

It is a city of temporaries, a city of just-arriveds and only-visitings, built on the shifting sands of politics, filled with people passing through. They may stay fifty years, they may love, marry, settle down, build homes, raise families, and die beside the Potomac, but they usually feel, and frequently they will tell you, that they are just here for a little while. Someday soon they will be going home. They do go home, but it is only for visits, or for a brief span of staying-away; and once the visits or the brief spans are over ('It's so nice to get away from Washington, it's so inbred; so nice to get out in the country and find out what people are really thinking') they hurry back to their lodestone and their star, their self-hypnotized, self-mes-

*merized, self-enamored, self-propelling, wonderful city they cannot
live away from or, once it has claimed them, live without.*

Drury also knew his way around the streets of D.C., and the halls of power.
But not all novels set in Washington revolve around politics. Check out
these thrillers:

- **Dark** (2001) and **Seeking Salamanca Mitchell** (2004), both by Kenji
  Jasper, and his memoir, **The House on Childress Street** (2006). These
  are set in neighborhoods that don't usually show up in novels.
- **Dupont Circle** by Paul Kafka-Gibbons, Houghton Mifflin, 2001; of the
  novel and the neighborhood, Kafka-Gibbons writes: "In Dupont Circle
  poor meets rich, old meets young, gay meets straight, native meets
  new arrival, and the peoples, styles, and languages all squish together
  to form America."
- **The Exorcist** by William Peter Blatty, 1971; the classic horror novel, reissued by HarperCollins in 1993, is loosely based on actual events that took
  place in the quiet Maryland suburbs along the upper Anacostia River.
- **Who's Afraid of Virginia Ham?** by Phyllis Richman, HarperCollins,
  2001; the third whodunit by the longtime *Washington Post* food critic is
  a sequel to **Murder on the Gravy Train** (2000) and **The Butter Did It**
  (1998).

DIRECTORIES & REFERENCE BOOKS

- **ADC**, www.adcmap.com, publishes a series of excellent detailed street
  atlases of the District and neighboring counties, showing zip codes,
  Metro lines, post offices, and other useful details. The index includes
  special sections for parks, schools, police and fire stations, and other
  points of interest. The regional atlas covering the entire area discussed
  in this book is a substantial investment, but worth it.
- **Opportunities in Public Affairs** from Brubach Publishing is a must if
  you're looking for work on the Hill, on K Street (lobbying), or in the
  nonprofit sector; for more specialized listings, subscribe to
  **Environmental Career Opportunities, International Career
  Opportunities, or Opportunities in Arts & Media**. These are not classified ads—many of the listings are based on insider knowledge not
  published anywhere else. The subscription rates may seem pricey, but
  this is the next best thing to having a personal "mole" in hundreds of
  agencies and companies. (Don't buy these papers at newsstands—subscribers will have a week's head start on you. Call 800-315-9777 or visit
  www.brubach.com.)
- **Leadership Directories**, www.leadershipdirectories.com, is the
  publisher of the *Congressional Yellow Book, Corporate Yellow Book, Law
  Firms Yellow Book,* and other definitive directories of key players in gov-

NEWCOMER'S HANDBOOK FOR MOVING TO AND LIVING IN WASHINGTON D.C.

376

ernment, business, and nonprofits. They're expensive, and you probably don't need to own a set unless you're a journalist or politico, but it's good to be familiar with your public library's copies.

- **Washington Business Journal Book of Lists** is an annual compilation of the Top 25 lists that appear in the *Washington Business Journal*, www.bizjournals.com/washington, every week—collectively, a "who's who" (and "who's doing what") guide to the area's leading companies in every field from aerospace to interior design.
- **Zagat Survey Washington D.C. & Baltimore Restaurants** is an annual summary of reader evaluations of hundreds of area restaurants. Thorough cross-indexing—not just by cuisine, neighborhood, and price range, but also outdoor seating, fireplaces, late hours, and dress codes—make up for the lack of detail. Other titles from Zagat, www.zagat.com, rate hotels, attractions, and other amenities.
- **Newcomer's Handbook for the USA** by Mike Livingston (First Books, www.firstbooks.com, 2005) is a comprehensive cultural overview of everyday life in the United States to help new immigrants or long-term visitors get their bearings.

Finally, don't forget the Yellow Pages and the White Pages—both have front sections full of useful consumer information about local services; recorded information by phone about everything from auto repairs to heart surgery to news headlines to soap opera updates; stadium and theater seating charts; and everything you need to know about your local phone service, including troubleshooting and do-it-yourself repairs.

AGING & ELDER CARE

- **D.C. Office on Aging**, 202-724-5622, http://dcoa.dc.gov
- **Maryland Department of Aging**, 800-243-3425, www.mdoa. state.md.us
- **Virginia Department for the Aging**, 800-552-3402, www.aging.state.va.us
- **American Association of Retired Persons**, 202-434-7700, www.aarp.org; AARP Legal Services Network, 888-687-2277, www. aarp.org/families
- **Elder Care Locator**, U.S. Administration on Aging, 800-677-1116, www.aoa.gov
- **National Council on the Aging**, 202-479-1200, www.ncoa.org
- **Social Security Administration**, 800-772-1213, www.ssa.gov
- **Medicare** (Center for Medicare & Medicaid Services), 800-633-4227, www.medicare.gov

ANIMALS

LICENSING & ANIMAL CONTROL

- **D.C. Animal Control Shelter**, 202-576-6664
- **Montgomery County Police**, Division of Animal Control & Humane Treatment, 301-279-1249, www.co.mo.md.us/services/police
- **Prince George's County Animal Control Commission**, 301-883-6009
- **Arlington County Office of the Treasurer**, 703-228-3255, www.co.arlington.va.us/treas
- **Fairfax County Department of Tax Administration**, 703-222-8234, www.co.fairfax.va.us/dta
- **Alexandria Police**, Animal Control/Protection Service, 703-838-4774

NEWCOMER'S HANDBOOK FOR MOVING TO AND LIVING IN WASHINGTON D.C.

378

SHELTERS

- **Washington Humane Society**, 202-234-8626, www.washhumane. org
- **Washington Animal Rescue League**, 202-726-2556, www.warl.org
- **Montgomery County Humane Society**, 240-773-5960, www. mchumane.org
- **Animal Welfare League of Arlington**, 703-931-9241, www. awla.org
- **Fairfax County Animal Shelter**, 703-830-1100, www.co. fairfax.va.us/police/animalservices
- **Animal Welfare League of Alexandria**, 703-838-4774, www. alexandriaanimals.org

AUTOMOBILES

STATE LICENSING & REGISTRATION

- **D.C. Department of Motor Vehicles,** 202-727-5000, http:// dmv.washingtondc.gov
- **Maryland Motor Vehicle Administration**, 800-950-1682, www.mva.state.md.us
- **Virginia Department of Motor Vehicles**, 866-368-5463, www. dmv.state.va.us

LOCAL REGISTRATION & PARKING PERMITS

- **Arlington County**, 703-228-3135, http://payment.arlingtonva.us
- **Fairfax County**, 703-222-8234, www.co.fairfax.va.us/dta
- **Alexandria**, 703-838-4560, http://alexandriava.gov

TOWED AUTOMOBILES

- **D.C. Impound Lot**, 202-727-5000
- **Montgomery County Police**, 301-840-2454 or 301-279-8000
- **Prince George's County Police**, 301-772-4740
- **Arlington County Police**, 703-228-4040
- **Fairfax County Police Traffic Division**, 703-280-0587
- **Alexandria Code Enforcement Bureau**, 703-838-4360

BIRTH & DEATH CERTIFICATES

- **District of Columbia**, 202-671-5000, http://doh.dc.gov
- **Maryland**, 800-832-3277, mdpublichealth.org/vsa
- **Virginia**, 804-662-6200, www.vdh.state.va.us/vitalrec

CONSUMER PROTECTION

- **D.C. Department of Consumer & Regulatory Affairs**, 202-442-4400, http://dcra.dc.gov
- **D.C. Corporation Counsel**, Office of the Attorney General, 202-727-3400, http://occ.dc.gov
- **Maryland Office of the Attorney General**, Consumer Protection Division, 410-528-8662, www.oag.state.md.us
- **Virginia Department of Agriculture and Consumer Services**, Office of Consumer Affairs, 800-552-9963, www.vdacs.virginia.gov
- **Better Business Bureau**, 202-393-8000, www.dc.bbb.org
- **Consumer Product Safety Commission**, 800-638-2772, www.cpsc.gov; product recall listing, www.recalls.gov
- **Federal Communications Commission**, 888-225-5322, www.fcc.gov
- **Federal Trade Commission**, 202-382-4357, www.ftc.gov
- **FirstGov for Consumers** (federal resources), www.consumer.gov
- **Federal Consumer Information Center**, 888-878-3256, www.pueblo.gsa.gov
- **Scambusters**, www.scambusters.org

See **Getting Settled** for regulatory agencies that oversee cable TV companies; see **Helpful Services** for small claims courts.

CRISIS HOTLINES & EMERGENCY SOCIAL SERVICES

It is always appropriate to call 911 and request police and/or emergency medical services if any person is in immediate danger of physical harm. These hotlines are additional resources to call in a dangerous or worrisome situation that is not an immediate emergency; when in doubt, call 911 instead. The main number for the **D.C. Department of Human Services**, www.dhs.dc.gov, is **211**; call 211 for general intake and referrals in nonemergency situations in D.C. involving homeless persons, welfare, underage runaways, and other vulnerable residents.

ALCOHOL & DRUG ABUSE

- **Alcoholics Anonymous**, 202-966-9115, www.aa-dc.org

NEWCOMER'S HANDBOOK FOR MOVING TO AND LIVING IN WASHINGTON D.C.

380

- **D.C. Addiction Prevention & Recovery Administration**, 888-793-4357, http://app.doh.dc.gov
- **D.C. Central Intake Division, Department of Health**, 202-727-0668, http://dchealth.dc.gov
- **Tobacco Control Program**, D.C. Preventive Health Services Administration, 202-442-5433, http://doh.dc.gov
- **Second Genesis**, 866-563-6527 or 301-563-6527, www.second genesis.org
- **Montgomery County Department of Health & Human Services**, 301-279-1332, www.montgomerycountymd.gov
- **Prince George's County Department of Health**, 301-583-5920 or 301-856-9400, www.goprincegeorgescounty.com
- **Arlington County Department of Human Services**, 703-228-4900, www.arlingtonva.us
- **Fairfax-Falls Church Community Services Board**, 703-573-5679 (emergency), www.co.fairfax.va.us/csb
- **Alexandria Health Department**, 703-838-4400, www.alexandria va.gov/city/health

BATTERED WOMEN SHELTERS & HOTLINES

- **My Sister's Place**, 202-529-5991, www.mysistersplacedc.org
- **House of Ruth**, 202-347-2777, www.houseofruth.org

CHILD ABUSE HOTLINES

- **District of Columbia**, 202-671-7233
- **Montgomery County**, 240-777-4417
- **Prince George's County**, 301 731-1203 or 866-382-7474
- **Arlington County**, 703-228-4848
- **Fairfax County**, 703-324-7400
- **Other Northern Virginia jurisdictions**, 800-552-7096
- **Childhelp USA**, 800-422-4453, www.childhelpusa.org
- **National Center for Missing & Exploited Children**, 800-843-5678, www.missingkids.com

HUMAN SERVICES

- **D.C. Child & Family Services Agency**, 202-442-6000, http://www.cfsa.dc.gov
- **Focus Adolescent Services** (referrals), 877-362-8727 or 410-341-4216, www.focusas.com

RAPE CRISIS

- **D.C. Rape Crisis Center**, 202-333-7273, www.dcrcc.org
- **Sexual Assault Follow-up Program**, D.C. Preventive Health Services Administration, 202-442-5893, http://doh.dc.gov
- **Montgomery County Sexual Assault Crisis Line**, 240-777-4357
- **Arlington Violence Intervention Program**, 703-228-4848
- **Fairfax County Rape Crisis Hotline**, 703-360-7273
- **Alexandria Sexual Assault Response & Awareness**, 703-683-7273

SUICIDE PREVENTION

- **D.C. Hotline**, 202-223-2255 or 888-793-4357
- **National Hopeline Network**, 800-784-2433
- **National Suicide Prevention Lifeline**, 800-273-8255

YOUTH CRISIS & RUNAWAYS

- **Covenant House Nineline**, 800-999-9999, www.covenant house.org
- **Girls & Boys Town Hotline**, 800-448-3000, www.girlsandboys town.org
- **National Runaway Switchboard**, 800-786-2929
- **National Youth Crisis Hotline**, 800-448-4663
- **Sasha Bruce Youthwork Crisis Hotline**, 202-547-7777, www.sashabruce.org

HUMAN RIGHTS & DISCRIMINATION

- **D.C. Office on Human Rights**, 202-727-4559, http://ohr.dc.gov
- **Maryland Commission on Human Relations**, 800-637-6247, www.mchr.state.md.us
- **Virginia Council on Human Rights**, 804-225-2292, www.chr.state.va.us
- **Montgomery County Human Relations Commission**, 202-777-8450, www.montgomerycountmd.gov
- **Prince George's County Human Relations Commission**, 301-883-6170, www.goprincegeorgescounty.com
- **Arlington County Human Rights Commission**, 703-358-3929
- **Fairfax County Human Rights Commission**, 703-324-2953
- **Alexandria Office of Human Rights**, 703-883-6170

NEWCOMER'S HANDBOOK FOR MOVING TO AND LIVING IN WASHINGTON D.C.

382

- **U.S. Department of Justice, Civil Rights Division**, 202-514-2000; 800-514-0301 (disability matters); 800-896-7743 (housing), www.usdoj.gov/crt

ELECTED OFFICIALS & GOVERNMENT SWITCHBOARDS

ELECTED OFFICIALS

- **Mayor of the District of Columbia**, 202-727-1000, http://dc.gov
- **D.C. Council**, 202-724-8000, www.dccouncil.washington.dc.us
- **D.C. Advisory Neighborhood Commissions**, 202-727-9945, http://anc.washingtondc.gov
- **Governor of Maryland**, 800-811-8336, www.governor. maryland.gov
- **Governor of Virginia**, 804-786-2211, www.governor.virginia.gov
- **Maryland General Assembly**, 301-970-5400 or 800-492-7122, http://mlis.state.md.us
- **Virginia General Assembly**, 888-892-6948 (Senate), 877-391-3228 (House), http://legis.state.va.us
- **Montgomery County Executive**, 240-777-2500, www.montgomery countymd.gov
- **Montgomery County Council**, 240-777-7900, www.montgomery countymd.gov
- **Prince George's County Executive**, 301-952-4131, www.goprince georgescounty.com
- **Prince George's County Council**, 301- 952-3794, www.goprince georgescounty.com/council
- **Arlington County Board**, 703-228-3130, www.arlingtonva.us
- **Fairfax County Board of Supervisors**, 703-324-3151, www.co.fairfax. va.us
- **Alexandria City Council**, 703-838-4000, www.alexandriava.gov
- **U.S. House of Representatives**, 202-224-3121, www.house.gov
- **U.S. Senate**, 202-224-3121, www.senate.gov
- **White House**, 202-456-1111 (comment line); 202-456-1414 (general information), www.whitehouse.gov

AREA MUNICIPALITIES

- **Alexandria**, 703-838-4500, www.ci.alexandria.va.us
- **Berwyn Heights**, 301-474-5000, http://berwyn-heights.com
- **Bladensburg**, 301-927-7048, www.bladensburg.com
- **Bowie**, 301-262-6200, www.cityofbowie.org
- **Brentwood**, 301-927-3344

- **Cheverly**, 301-773-8360, www.cheverly.com
- **Chevy Chase**, 301-654-7144, www.townofchevychase.org,
- **Chevy Chase View**, 301-949-9274, www.chevychaseview.org
- **Chevy Chase Village**, 301-654-7300, www.ccvillage.org
- **College Park**, 301-864-8666, www.ci.college-park.md.us
- **Colmar Manor**, 301-277-4920
- **Cottage City**, 301-779-2161
- **District of Columbia**, 202-727-1000, http://dc.gov
- **Edmonston**, 301-699-8806
- **Fairfax**, 703-385-7855, www.fairfaxva.gov
- **Falls Church**, 703-248-5014, www.ci.falls-church.va.us
- **Gaithersburg**, 301-258-6300, www.gaithersburgmd.gov
- **Garrett Park**, 301-933-7488, www.garrettpark.org
- **Greenbelt**, 301-474-8000, www.ci.greenbelt.md.us
- **Herndon**, 703-435-6800, www.town.herndon.va.us
- **Hyattsville**, 301-985-5000, www.hyattsville.org
- **Kensington**, 301-949-2424, www.tok.org
- **Laurel**, 301-725-5300, www.laurel.md.us
- **Mt. Rainier**, 301-985-6585, www.mountrainiermd.org
- **North Brentwood**, 4507 Church St., 301-699-9699
- **Reston**, 703-437-9580, http://reston.org
- **Riverdale Park**, 301-927-6381, www.ci.riverdale-park.md.us
- **Rockville**, 301-309-3000, www.rockvillemd.gov
- **Somerset**, 301-657-3211, www.townofsomerset.com
- **Takoma Park**, 301-270-1700, www.takomaparkmd.gov
- **University Park**, 301-927-2997, www.upmd.org
- **Vienna**, 703-255-6300 www.ci.vienna.va.us
- **Washington Grove**, 301-926-2256, www.washingtongrovemd.org

AREA COUNTIES

- **Montgomery County**, 240-777-1000, www.montgomerycounty md.gov
- **Prince George's County**, 301-350-9700, www.goprincegeorges county.com
- **Arlington County**, 703-228-3000, www.co.arlington.va.us
- **Fairfax County**, 703-324-7329, www.co.fairfax.va.us

OFFICIAL GUIDES

- **District of Columbia**, www.rrc.dc.gov
- **Maryland**, www.sailor.lib.md.us
- **Virginia**, www.vipnet.org

NEWCOMER'S HANDBOOK FOR MOVING TO AND LIVING IN WASHINGTON D.C.

384

EMERGENCY

- **Fire, Police, Medical**, 911
- **Poison Control Center**, 800-222-1222
- **Federal Emergency Management Agency**, Disaster Assistance Information, 800-621-3362 www.fema.gov
- **Gas Leaks**, 703-750-1000
- **Downed Power Lines**, 202-872-2000
- **Power Failures**, 877-737-2662; life-threatening emergency, 202-872-3432
- **Water & Sewer Leaks**, D.C., 202-612-3400
- **Toxic Spills**, 800-262-8200

   See **Police** listings below for local and federal law enforcement non-emergency numbers.

ENTERTAINMENT

- **Fandango**, 800-326-3264, www.fandango.com
- **TicketMaster**, 202-397-7328 or 800-551-7328, www.ticket master.com
- **Tickets.com**, www.tickets.com
- **Ticketplace**, www.ticketplace.org
- **Washington Performing Arts Society**, 202-785-9727, www.wpas.org

GARBAGE & RECYCLING

- **D.C. Department of Public Works**, 202-727-1000, http://dpw.dc.gov
- **Montgomery County Solid Waste Services Division**, 240-777-6400, www.montgomerycountymd.gov/solidwaste
- **Prince George's County Department of Environmental Resources**, 301-883-5810, www.goprincegeorgescounty.com
- **Arlington County Department of Environmental Services**, 703-228-4488, www.arlingtonva.us
- **Fairfax County Department of Public Works & Environmental Services**, 703-802-3322, www.co.fairfax.va.us/dpwes
- **Alexandria Department of Transportation & Environmental Services**, 703-751-5130, http://ci.alexandria.va.us/tes

HEALTH & MEDICAL CARE

CHILDHOOD LEAD POISONING PREVENTION

- **D.C. Childhood Lead Poisoning, Screening and Education Program**, 202-671-5000, http://doh.dc.gov
- **Maryland Lead Hotline**, 800-776-2706, www.mde.state.md.us
- **Lead-Safe Virginia**, 877-668-7987, www.vahealth.org/leadsafe

DEPARTMENTS OF HEALTH, HOTLINES

- **D.C. AIDS Information Hotline**, 202-332-2437, www.wwc.org
- **D.C. Department of Health**, 202-671-5000, http://doh.dc.gov; Division of Cancer Control, 202-442-5905; Bureau of Diabetes Control, 202-442-9157; Immunization Information, 202-576-7130; Sexually Transmitted Diseases Clinic, 202-698-4050; Medicaid, 202-442-5988
- **Maryland Department of Health & Mental Hygien**e, 877-463-3464, www.dhmh.state.md.us
- **Virginia Department of Health**, Alexandria, 703-519-5979; Arlington, 703-228-4992; Fairfax, 703-246-2411; www.vdh.state.va.us
- **U.S. Department of Health & Human Services**, 877-696-6775, www.hhs.gov
- **Montgomery County Department of Health & Human Services**, 240-777-1245, www.montgomerycountymd.gov
- **Prince George's County Department of Health**, 301-883-7834, www.goprincegeorgescounty.com
- **Arlington County Department of Human Services**, 703-228-1300, www.co.arlington.va.us/dhs
- **Fairfax County Department of Health**, 703-246-2411, www.co.fairfax.va.us/hd
- **Alexandria Health Department**, 703-838-4400, alexandria va.gov/city/health

MEDICAL & DENTAL REFERRALS

- **General Practitioners**, 800-362-8677, www.1800doctors.com
- **Specialists**, 866-275-2267, www.abms.org
- **Alternative Practitioners**, www.pathwaysmag.com
- **Dentists**, 202-547-7613, www.dcdental.org; outside D.C., www.ada.org

NEWCOMER'S HANDBOOK FOR MOVING TO AND LIVING IN WASHINGTON D.C.

386

MENTAL HEALTH

- **D.C. Department of Mental Health**, 202-673-7440 or 888-793-4357, http://dmh.dc.gov
- **Maryland Department of Health & Mental Hygiene**, 800-888-1965, www.dhmh.state.md.us/mha
- **Virginia Department of Mental Health, Mental Retardation & Substance Abuse Services**, 800-451-5544, www.dmhmrsas.virginia.gov

WORKERS' COMPENSATION

- **D.C.**, 202-671-1000, http://does.dc.gov
- **Maryland**, 800-492-0479, www.wcc.state.md.us
- **Virginia**, 877-664-2566, www.vwc.state.va.us

HOUSING

- **D.C. Department of Consumer & Regulatory Affairs**, 202-442-4400, http://dcra.dc.gov
- **D.C. Historic Preservation Review Board**, 202-442-7600, www.planning.dc.gov
- **D.C. Tenants Advocacy Coalition**, 202-628-3688, www.tenac.org
- **Montgomery County Department of Housing & Community Affairs**, 240-777-3600, www.montgomerycountymd.org
- **Prince George's County Department of Housing**, 301-883-4663, www.goprincegeorgescounty.com
- **Arlington County Housing Information Center**, 703-228-3765, www.co.arlington.va.us
- **Fairfax County Tenant-Landlord Commission**, 703-222-8435, www.co.fairfax.va.us/consumer
- **Alexandria Office of Housing**, 703-838-4545, www.alexandriava.gov/city/housing
- **Fair Housing Information Clearinghouse**, 800-343-3442, www.hud.gov/offices/fheo
- **Home Fire Inspections**, D.C. Fire & EMS Department, 202-673-3331, http://fems.dc.gov

INTERNET SERVICE PROVIDERS

- **America Online**, 800-827-6364, www.aol.com
- **AT&T WorldNet**, 800-967-5363, www.att.net

- **Cox Communications**, 703-378-8422, www.cox.net
- **Earthlink**, 800-327-8454, www.earthlink.net
- **Microsoft Network**, 800-426-9400, www.msn.com
- **NetZero**, 877-665-9995, www.netzero.net
- **Verizon Internet**, 800-638-2026, www.verizon.net

LABOR

- **U.S. Department of Labor, Wage & Hour Division**, 888-487-9243, www.wagehour.dol.gov
- **Equal Employment Opportunities Commission**, 202-663-4900, www.eeoc.gov
- **Occupational Safety & Health Administration**, 800-321-6742, www.osha.gov

LEGAL REFERRAL

- **D.C. Bar Legal Service Sourcebook**, 202-737-4700, www.dcbar.org
- **Montgomery County Bar Association**, 301-279-9100, www.montbar.org
- **Prince George's County Bar Association**, 301-952-1440, www.pgcba.com
- **Virginia State Bar Lawyers Referral**, 800-552-7977, www.vsb.org
- **Legal Aid Society of D.C.**, 202-628-1161, www.legalaiddc.org
- **Neighborhood Legal Services Program**, 202-682-2720, www.nlsp.org/DC

LIBRARIES

- **District of Columbia**, 202-727-0321, http://dclibrary.org
- **Montgomery County**, 240-777-0002, www.montgomerylibrary.org
- **Prince George's County**, 301-699-3500, www.prge.lib.md.us
- **Arlington County**, 703-823-5295, www.co.arlington.va.us
- **Fairfax County**, 703-324-3100, www.co.fairfax.va.us/library
- **Alexandria**, 703-519-5900, www.alexandria.lib.va.us

LOTTERY

- **D.C. Lottery**, 202-645-8000, www.dclottery.com
- **Maryland Lottery**, 410-230-8730, www.msla.sailorsite.net
- **Virginia Lottery**, 703-494-1501, www.valottery.com

NEWCOMER'S HANDBOOK FOR MOVING TO AND LIVING IN WASHINGTON D.C.

388

MARRIAGE LICENSES

- **District of Columbia**, 202-879-4840; domestic partnership certificates, 202-442-9303
- **Montgomery County**, 240-777-9460
- **Prince George's County**, 301-952-3288
- **Arlington County**, 703-228-4510
- **Fairfax County**, 703-691-7320
- **Alexandria**, 703-838-4400

PARKS & RECREATION

- **D.C. Department of Parks & Recreation**, 202-673-7660, http://dpr.dc.gov
- **Washington Parks & People**, 202-462-7275, www.washingtonparks.net
- **Maryland Department of Natural Resources**, 877-620-8367, www.dnr.state.md.us
- **Maryland-National Capital Park & Planning Commission**, 301-495-4600, www.mncppc.org
- **Virginia Department of Conservation & Recreation**, 800-933-7275, www.dcr.state.va.us
- **Montgomery County Department of Recreation**, 240-777-6961, www.montgomerycountymd.gov
- **Prince George's County Department of Parks & Recreation**, 301-918-8100, www.pgparks.com
- **Northern Virginia Regional Park Authority**, 703-352-5900, www.nvrpa.org
- **Arlington County Department of Parks, Recreation & Community Resources**, 703-228-3323, www.co.arlington.va.us/prcr
- **Fairfax County Park Authority**, 703-324-8702, www.co.fairfax.va.us/parks
- **Alexandria Department of Recreation, Parks & Cultural Activities**, 703-838-4343, www.ci.alexandria.va.us/recreation
- **National Park Service**, 202-690-5185, www.nps.gov

POLICE & HOMELAND SECURITY

- **Emergency**, 911
- **Crime Solvers** (anonymous tip line), 800-673-2777
- **D.C. Metropolitan Police Department**, 311, http://mpdc.dc.gov; corruption hotline, 800-298-4006; hate crimes hotline, 202-727-0500

- **Montgomery County Police Department**, 301-279-8000, www.montgomerycountymd.gov
- **Prince George's County Police Department**, 301-333-4000, www.goprincegeorgescounty.com
- **Arlington County Police Department**, 703-228-4040, www.arlingtonva.us
- **Fairfax County Police Department**, 703-691-2131, www.co.fairfax. va.us/police
- **Alexandria Police Department**, 703-838-4444, www.ci.alexandria. va.us/police
- **Maryland State Police**, 800-525-5555, www.mdsp.org
- **Virginia State Police**, Northern Virginia Division, 703-323-4500, www.vsp.state.va.us
- **Bureau of Alcohol, Tobacco, Firearms & Explosives**, 202-927-8810 or 888-283-8477; arson hotline, 888-283-3473; bomb hotline, 888-283-2662; firearms hotline, 800-283-4867
- **Federal Bureau of Investigation**, 202-324-3000, www.fbi.gov
- **Transportation Security Administration**, 866-289-9673, www.tsa.gov
- **U.S. Capitol Police**, 202-228-2800
- **U.S. Coast Guard**, 202-366-4000; Atlantic search & rescue, 757-398-6390; www.uscg.mil
- **U.S. Customs & Border Protection**, 202-354-1000, www.customs.gov
- **U.S. Department of Homeland Security**, 800-237-3239, www.dhs.gov or www.ready.gov
- **U.S. Marshals Service**, 202-353-0600, D.C. evictions, 202-616-8633, www.usdoj.gov/marshals
- **U.S. Park Police**, 202-619-7105, www.nps.gov/uspp
- **U.S. Secret Service,** 202-406-8000, www.secretservice.gov

POST OFFICE

- **U.S. Postal Service**, 800-275-8777, www.usps.com

ROAD CONDITIONS & TRAFFIC INFORMATION

- **Federal Highway Administration** traffic information, 511, www.fhwa.dot.gov/trafficinfo
- **Maryland Coordinated Highways Action Response Team**, 410-582-5605, www.chart.state.md.us
- **Virginia Department of Transportation Hotline**, 800-367-7623, www.virginiadot.org
- **Reach the Beach**, 800-541-9595

NEWCOMER'S HANDBOOK FOR MOVING TO AND LIVING IN WASHINGTON D.C.

390

SCHOOL DISTRICTS

- **D.C. Public Schools**, 202-724-4222, www.k12.dc.us
- **D.C. Public Charter Schools**, 202-328-2660, www.dcpublic charter.com
- **Montgomery County**, 301-309-6277, www.mcps.k12.md.us
- **Prince George's County**, 301-952-6001, www.pgcps.pg.k12.md.us
- **Arlington County**, 703-228-6000, www.arlington.k12.va.us
- **Fairfax County**, 703-246-2991, www.fcps.k12.va.us
- **Alexandria**, 703-824-6600, www.acps.k12.va.us
- **Falls Church**, 703-248-5600; www.fccps.k12.va.us

SHIPPING SERVICES

- **DHL**, 800-225-5345, www.dhl-usa.com
- **FedEx**, 800-463-3339, www.fedex.com/us
- **UPS**, 800-742-5877, www.ups.com
- **U.S. Postal Service Express Mail**, 800-275-8777, www.usps.com

SPORTS

PROFESSIONAL

- **Baltimore Orioles** (AL) 202-296-2473, www.theorioles.com
- **Bowie Baysox** (AA baseball) 301-805-6000, www.baysox.com
- **D.C. Divas** (WNFA), 202-656-5090, www.dcdivas.com
- **D.C. United** (MLS), 202-587-5000 or visit www.dcunited.com
- **Potomac Nationals** (Class A baseball), 703-590-2311, www.potomacnationals.com
- **Washington Capitals** (NHL), 202-661-5050, www.washingtoncaps.com
- **Washington Mystics** (WNBA), 202-661-5050, www.wnba.com/mystics
- **Washington Nationals** (NL), 202-675-6287, http://washington.nationals.mlb.com
- **Washington Redskins** (NFL), 202-546-2222, www.redskins.com
- **Washington Wizards** (NBA), 202-661-5050, www.nba.com/wizards

COLLEGIATE

- **Cal Ripken Sr. Collegiate Baseball League**, 410-588-9900, www.ripkensrcollegebaseball.org

- **Catholic University Cardinals**, 202-319-5286, http://athletics. cua.edu
- **George Mason Patriots**, 202-397-7328, www.gmusports.com
- **GW Colonials**, 202-994-6650, www.gwsports.com
- **Georgetown Hoyas**, 202-687-4692, 202-687-7159, www. guhoyas.com
- **Howard Bison**, 202-806-7198, www.howard-bison.com
- **Maryland Terrapins**, 301-314-8587, www.umd.edu/athletics
- **Marymount Saints**, 703-284-1619, www.marymount.edu/athletics
- **Navy Midshipmen**, 800-874-6289; information, http://navy sports.collegesports.com

TAXES

- **Internal Revenue Service**, 800-829-1040 (help) or 800-829-4477 (recorded information), www.irs.gov
- **D.C. Chief Financial Officer**, 202-727-2476, www.cfo.washington dc.gov
- **Maryland Comptroller of the Treasury**, 800-MD-TAXES, http://individuals.marylandtaxes.com
- **Virginia Department of Taxation,** 804-367-8031 (information), 888-268-2829 (forms), www.tax.state.va.us
- **D.C. Board of Real Property Assessments & Appeals**, 202-727-6860
- **Maryland Department of Assessments & Taxation**, Montgomery County office, 301-279-1355; Prince George's County office, 301-952-2955; www.dat.state.md.us
- **Arlington County Department of Real Estate Assessments,** 703-228-3920, www.co.arlington.va.us/dmf
- **Fairfax County Tax Information**, 703-222-8234, www.co. fairfax.va.us/dta
- **Alexandria Department of Real Estate Assessments**, 703-838-4646, www.ci.alexandria.va.us/city/reasearch

TELEPHONE SERVICE

LOCAL

- **Verizon**, D.C., 202-954-6263; Maryland, 301-954-6260; Virginia, 703-954-6222; www.verizon.com
- See **Public Service Commissions,** under **Utilities** below, for the current list of authorized local phone companies

NEWCOMER'S HANDBOOK FOR MOVING TO AND LIVING IN WASHINGTON D.C.

392

LONG DISTANCE

- **AT&T**, 800-222-0300, www.att.com (see also Verizon)
- **MCI WorldCom**, 800-950-5555, www.mci.com
- **SBC**, 877-430-7228, www.sbctelecom.com
- **Sprint**, 800-877-7746, www.sprint.com
- **Starpower**, 877-782-7769, www.starpower.net
- **Verizon**, 800-343-2092, www.verizon.net
- **Working Assets**, 800-788-0898, www.workingforchange.com

WIRELESS

- **Cingular**, 866-246-4852, www.cingular.com
- **Sprint/Nextel**, 800-777-4681, www.sprintpcs.com.
- **T-Mobile**, 800-866-2453, www.t-mobile.com
- **USA Mobility**, 800-333-4722, www.usamobility.com
- **Verizon Wireless**, 800-922-0204, www.verizon.com

DIRECTORY ASSISTANCE

- **Local and long-distance numbers**, 411
- **Toll-free numbers**, 800-555-1212
- **http://people.yahoo.com**
- **www.anywho.com**
- **www.bigbook.com**
- **www.switchboard.com**
- **www.whowhere.lycos.com**
- **www.worldpages.com**

TELEVISION—CABLE AND SATELLITE

- **Comcast**, 800-266-2278, www.comcast.com
- **Cox Communications** (Northern Virginia), 703-378-8422, www.cox.com
- **RCN** (formerly Starpower), 800-746-4726, www.rcn.com
- **DirecTV**, 800-237-5988, www.directv.com
- **Dish Network**, 800-732-6401, www.dishnetwork.com

TIME

- **Time of Day**, 844-2525 (any area code)
- **U.S. Naval Observatory Atomic Clock**, 202-762-1401

TOURISM & TRAVEL

- **International Association for Medical Assistance to Travelers**, 716-754-4883, www.iamat.org
- **Travelers Aid**, 202-546-1127; www.travelersaid.org
- **Washington, D.C. Convention & Visitors Association**, 202-789-7000, www.washington.org
- **Washington D.C. Visitor Information Center**, 202-328-4748, www.dcvisit.com
- **Maryland Office of Tourism Development**, 866-639-3526, www.mdisfun.org
- **Virginia Tourism Corporation**, 800-847-4882, www.virginia.org

TRANSPORTATION

AIRPORTS

- **Reagan National Airport**, 703-417-8000, www.metwash airports.com/National
- **Dulles International Airport**, 703-661-2700, www.metwash airports.com/Dulles
- **Marshall BWI International Airport**, 301-261-1000, www.bwi airport.com

COMMUTER RESOURCES

- **www.commuterpage.com**
- **Metropolitan Washington Council of Governments**, 800-745-7433 (carpooling), 202-962-3200 (telework), www.mwcog.org
- **Fairfax County RideSources**, 703-324-1111, www.fairfax county.gov/fcdot
- **Guaranteed Ride Home**, 800-745-7433, www.commuter connections.org
- **Slug Line** information, www.slug-lines.com
- **Flexcar** (shared cars), 202-296-1359, www.flexcar.com
- **Zipcar** (shared cars), 866-494-7227, www.zipcar.com
- **Washington Area Bicyclist Association**, 202-518-0524, www.waba.org
- **Walk D.C.**, 202-744-0595, visit www.walkdc.org

NEWCOMER'S HANDBOOK FOR MOVING TO AND LIVING IN WASHINGTON D.C.

394

COMMUTER TRAINS

- **MARC**, 800-325-7245, www.mtamaryland.com
- **VRE**, 703-684-1001, www.vre.org

COUNTY BUSES

- **ART** (Arlington), 703-228-7433, www.commuterpage.com/ART
- **The BUS** (Prince George's County), 301-324-2877, www.goprince georgescounty.com
- **CUE** (Fairfax City), 703-385-7859, www.fairfaxva.gov.
- **DASH** (Alexandria), 703-370-3274, www.dashbus.com.
- **Fairfax Connector**, 703-339-7200, www.fairfaxconnector.com.
- **GEORGE** (Falls Church), www.ci.falls-church.va.us
- **Ride On** (Montgomery County), 240-777-7433, www.rideonbus.com
- **TAGS** (Springfield), 703-971-7727, www.springfieldinterchange.com

METRORAIL & METROBUS

- **Washington Metropolitan Area Transit Authority (Metro)**, 202-637-7000, www.wmata.com; student fares (D.C. public schools), 202-671-0537; senior & disabled fares, 202-962-1245
- **Weekly & Monthly Passes**, www.commuterdirect.com

NATIONAL TRAIN & BUS SERVICE

- **Greyhound**, 800-231-2222, www.greyhound.com
- **Peter Pan Trailways**, 800-343-9999, www.peterpanbus.com
- **Amtrak**, 800-872-7245, www.amtrak.com

TAXIS

- **Action Taxi**, 301-840-1000
- **Barwood**, 301-984-1900
- **Bowie**, 301-430-7200
- **Capitol**, 202-546-2400
- **Dial**, 202-829-4222
- **Diamond**, 202-387-6200
- **Red Top**, 202-328-3333
- **Regency**, 301-990-9000
- **Silver**, 301-270-6000

- **Yellow**, D.C., 202-544-1212; Arlington, 703-522-2222; Fairfax, 703-534-1111

UTILITIES

See the **Emergency** listings above for emergency numbers to report gas leaks, downed power lines, and other utility hazards that do not pose an immediate danger to life or property. When in doubt, call 911.

ENERGY

- **Potomac Electric Power Company** (Pepco), 202-833-7500, www.pepco.com
- **Dominion Virginia Power**, 888-667-3000, www.dom.com
- **Washington Gas**, www.washgas.com. Call 703-750-1000
- **Miss Utility Hotline** (buried gas lines), 800-257-7777, www.miss utility.net
- **Utility choice information**, D.C.: 202-895-0950, www.dciselectric. com; Maryland: 800-800-4491, www.md-electric-info.com/ questions; Virginia: 877-937-2004, www.yesvachoice.com

WATER

- **D.C. Water & Sewer Authority**, 202-354-3600, www.dcwasa.com
- **Washington Suburban Sanitary Commission** (Maryland), 301-206-4001 or 800-634-8400, www.wssc.dst.md.us
- **Arlington County Department of Public Works**, 703-228-3636, www.co.arlington.va.us/dpw
- **Fairfax County Water Authority**, 703-698-5800, www.fcwa.org
- **Virginia-American Water Co.** (Alexandria), 703-549-7080; www.vawc.com/alex
- **Falls Church Public Utilities Division**, 703-248-5071, www.ci. falls-church.va.us
- **EPA Safe Drinking Water Hotline**, 800-426-4791, www. epa.gov/safewater

PUBLIC SERVICE COMMISSIONS

- **D.C. Public Service Commission**, 202-626-5100, www.dcpsc.org
- **Maryland Public Service Commission**, 410-767-8028 or 800-492-0474, www.psc.state.md.us
- **Virginia State Corporations Commission**, 804-371-9967 or 800-552-7945, www.state.va.us/scc

NEWCOMER'S HANDBOOK FOR MOVING TO AND LIVING IN WASHINGTON D.C.

396

VOTER REGISTRATION

- **D.C. Board of Elections & Ethics**, 202-727-2525, www.dcboee.org
- **Maryland State Board of Elections**, 800-222-8683, www.elections.state.md.us
- **Montgomery County Board of Elections**, 240-777-8500, www.montgomerycountymd.gov
- **Prince George's County Board of Elections**, 301-952-3270, www.co.pg.md.us
- **Virginia State Board of Elections**, 800-552-9745, www.sbe.state.va.us
- **Alexandria Office of Voter Registration**, 703-838-4050, www.alexandriavoter.org
- **Arlington County Registrar of Voters**, 703-228-3456, www.arlingtonva.us
- **Fairfax County Electoral Board & General Registrar**, 703-222-0776, www.co.fairfax.va.us/eb

WEATHER

- **Verizon Weather Recording**, 936-1212 (any local area code)
- **Air Quality Hotline**, 202-962-3299
- **National Weather Service** online, www.nws.noaa.gov

WOMEN

- **Maryland Commission for Women**, 877-868-2196, www.marylandwomen.org
- **Montgomery County Commission for Women**, 240-777-8300, www.montgomerycountymd.gov
- **Prince George's County Commission for Women**, 301-265-8420, www.goprincegeorgescounty.com
- **Arlington County Commission on the Status of Women**, 703-228-3314, www.co.arlington.va.us
- **Fairfax County Office for Women**, 703-324-5730, www.co.fairfax.va.us/ofw
- **Alexandria Office on Women**, 703-838-5030, www.ci.alexandria.va.us/oow

MIKE LIVINGSTON is a D.C. native and lifelong resident of the Washington area. He wrote the *Newcomer's Handbook for the USA* (First Books, 2005) and is a freelance writer and editor whose clients include the Citizen Policies Institute, Conservation International, *Legal Times,* Nonprofit Watch, the Points of Light Foundation, *Roll Call*, and the *Washington Business Journal.* Mike was the Green Party candidate for D.C.'s "shadow" congressional seat in 1998 and remains active in Green politics. He is also an emergency medical technician and CPR instructor with the Takoma Park Volunteer Fire Department and a media liaison for Safe Kids Worldwide. He graduated from Guilford College in 1993 with a B.A. in political science and peace studies, and now resides in Takoma Park.

The author gratefully acknowledges the insights and contributions of Susan Doran, Linda Weinerman, Jeremy Solomon, and everyone who worked on past editions of this book: Bernadette Duperron, Lorin Kleinman, Leslie & Jeremy Milk, and especially Ricia Chansky.

NEWCOMER'S HANDBOOK FOR MOVING TO AND LIVING IN WASHINGTON D.C.

400

NEWCOMER'S HANDBOOK FOR MOVING TO AND LIVING IN WASHINGTON D.C.

402

NEWCOMER'S HANDBOOK FOR MOVING TO AND LIVING IN WASHINGTON D.C.

404

NEWCOMER'S HANDBOOK FOR MOVING TO AND LIVING IN WASHINGTON D.C.

406

NEWCOMER'S HANDBOOK FOR MOVING TO AND LIVING IN WASHINGTON D.C.

408

NEWCOMER'S HANDBOOK FOR MOVING TO AND LIVING IN WASHINGTON D.C.

410

NEWCOMER'S HANDBOOK FOR MOVING TO AND LIVING IN WASHINGTON D.C.

412

NEWCOMER'S HANDBOOK FOR MOVING TO AND LIVING IN WASHINGTON D.C.

414

NEWCOMER'S HANDBOOK FOR MOVING TO AND LIVING IN WASHINGTON D.C.

416

NEWCOMER'S HANDBOOK FOR MOVING TO AND LIVING IN WASHINGTON D.C.

418

Reprinted with permission of the Washington Metropolitan Area Transit Authority